Utopian Communism and Political Thought in Early Modern England

UTOPIAN COMMUNISM AND POLITICAL THOUGHT IN EARLY MODERN ENGLAND

Timothy Kenyon
University of Liverpool

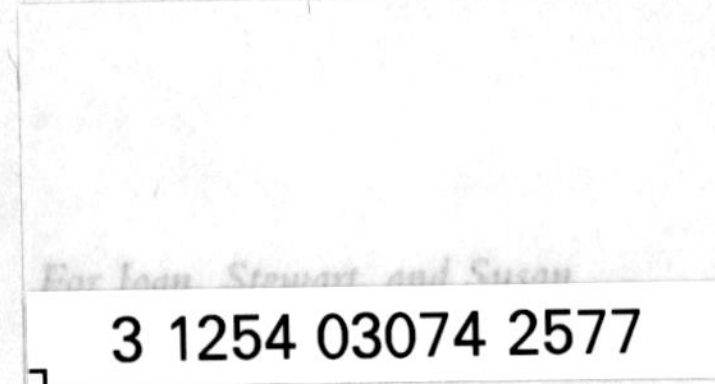

First published in Great Britain in 1989 by
Pinter Publishers Limited
25 Floral Street, London WC2E 9DS

British Library Cataloguing in Publication Data

A CIP catalogue record for this book is available from the British Library
ISBN 0 86187 772 1

Library of Congress Cataloging-in-Publication Data

Kenyon, Timothy, 1955–
Utopian communism and political thought in early/modern England/
Timothy Kenyon.
p. cm.
ISBN 0-86187-772-1
1. More, Thomas, Sir, Saint, 1478–1535. Utopia. 2. Winstanley, Gerrard, b. 1609—Contributions in political science. 3. Utopian socialism—England—History. I. Title.
HX810.5.Z6K46 1989
335′ : 02—dc20 89-22781
CIP

Typeset by Florencetype, Kewstoke, Avon
Printed and bound in Great Britain by Biddles Ltd

Contents

Preface vii
Abbreviations ix

PART I

1. Introductory: philosophical bearings 3
Methodology: contexts and concepts 4
Utopianism, millenarianism and political philosophy 17
The Fall of Man and the status of property 25

PART II

2. Thomas More's conception of the human condition 39
Philosophical traditions and the conundrum in More's thought 39
More's theology 48
The Fall and the human predicament 63
Tudor England as the fallen condition and More's analysis of private property 67

3. The Utopia of moral conduct 74
Communism and the Utopian economy 74
The state and the Utopian polity 83
The family and the community 87
The education of the virtuous citizen 93
The ends of life 95
The Utopian worldview 108
Freedom and moral behaviour in *Utopia* 110

PART III

4. Gerrard Winstanley's conception of the human condition 121
Winstanley's theology 121
The Fall of Man and the Myth of the Norman Yoke 131
Stuart England as the fallen condition 145
The prospect of a restoration on earth 151

5. The development of Gerrard Winstanley's thought 153
Premises and propositions 153
The Digger experiment 168
The interim phase of re-evaluation 186
The resort to utopian communism 191

6. Winstanley's utopian institutionalism: the ideal commonwealth 193
The communist system of *The Law of Freedom* 194
The moral regeneration of the individual 203
The coherence of Winstanley's utopian institutionalism 216

PART IV

7. Conclusion 227
Property theory and utopian communism 227
Changing intellectual perspectives 234

Notes 242
Index 278

Preface

Of the recent contributions to knowledge effected by the community of scholars interested in political philosophy the development of our understanding of the political thought of the early modern period and of our awareness of the significance of that thought has been considerable. This book, which deals with a number of aspects of early modern thought, is intended as a further contribution to that trend. In it, I attempt to address a range of issues germane to the political philosophy of the period via a detailed analysis of the work of two thinkers, Thomas More and Gerrard Winstanley, who might be regarded as radical political theorists. The book is therefore concerned with ideas and opinions that were often not of the 'mainstream'. However, whereas it examines the nature of the utopian genre rather than that of the more conventional political treatise, this study does so by suggesting that the utopian communism of the period is understandable only by reference to more conventional outlooks. For this reason, the analysis is wide-ranging. It exhibits, therefore, the shortcomings of a work which should, but because of limited space cannot, address its arguments more thoroughly.

I have tried to develop the analysis in such a way that the sections on More and Winstanley may be read discreetly by readers merely interested in either of these thinkers. Even so, I would obviously hope that more is to be gained by considering the book as a whole. I am conscious of intruding upon existing debates on the interpretation of the writings of More and Winstanley. The secondary literature on More is vast; that on Winstanley less considerable. I have tried to restrict my consideration of this scholarship to that which is of immediate concern to the subject matter of this book—thus I am conscious of neglecting a great deal. The same is true of my consideration of, in particular, medieval political philosophy and theology, certain aspects of property theory, and the social context of the period. I have attempted to use the annotation to indicate not only sources, but also where particular points of interest might be followed up. For this reason I have refrained from including a bibliography, even though the annotation cannot represent the extent of either the available primary or secondary literature. My apologies are therefore extended to any authors who may feel that I have not adequately acknowledged their work.

I am grateful to the editors of *History of European Ideas*, *History of Political Thought* and the *Journal of the History of Philosophy* for permission to develop ideas previously made public in those journals.

Our times are such that no first book can see the light of day unless its author has enjoyed considerable and varied support. The following persons, often in ways known to themselves alone, have sustained me. It is a pleasure to acknowledge the help of Keith Aldermen, Lincoln Allison, Ian Anderson, David Andrews, Gerald Aylmer, Diane Baker, Cyril Barrett, John Bone, Jim Bulpitt, Humphrey Butters, Bernard Capp, Robin Clifton, Vanessa Couchman, John Cunliffe, Alistair Edwards, Joe Femia, Jack Lively, David Mervin, Pete Morriss, Kenneth Muir, Geraint Parry, Alan Porter, Andrew Reeve, John Rimmer, J.J. Scarisbrick, Robert Skidelsky, Hillel Steiner, Alan Strogen, T.J.A. Thomas, Wendy Tracey, Albert Weale, and Ursula Vogel. The ultimate debt is to the people to whom this book is dedicated.

Abbreviations

Aquinas, *ST*	Thomas Aquinas, *Summa Theologiae*, ed. Fathers of the English Dominican Province (London, 1964–)
Aristotle, *Ethics*	*The Nicomachean Ethics*, trans. J.A.K. Thomson, (Harmondsworth, 1976)
Augustine, *City*	Augustine, *City of God* (Harmondsworth, 1984)
Bacon, *Works*	Francis Bacon, *Works*, ed. J. Spedding, R.L. Ellis and D.D. Heath (London, 1868–1901)
CSPD	Calendar of State Papers, Domestic Series
Econ. HR	*Economic History Review*
EETS	*Early English Text Society*
HJ	*The Historical Journal*
H & T	*History and Theory*
Hobbes, *EW*	Thomas Hobbes, *The English Works of Thomas Hobbes*, ed. Sir William Molesworth (London, 1839–45, 1966 edn)
JHI	*Journal of the History of Ideas*
JMH	*Journal of Modern History*
Locke, *Works*	John Locke, *The Works of John Locke* (11th edn, London, 1812)
Marx and Engels, *Works*	Karl Marx and Freidrich Engels, *Collected Works of Karl Marx and Freidrich Engels* (London, in progress)
Milton, *Prose Works*	John Milton, *The Complete Prose Works of John Milton, ed. D.M. Wolfe (New Haven, CT, 1953–)*
More, CW	Thomas More, *The Yale Edition of the Complete Works of Sir Thomas More* (New Haven, CT, in progress)
Utopia	*Utopia*, ed. E.L. Surtz and J.H. Hexter (New Haven, CT, 1965)
CW5	*Responsio ad Lutherum*, ed. J.M. Headley (New Haven, CT, 1969)
CW6	*Dialogue Concerning Heresies*, ed. T.M.C. Lawler,

	R. Marius and G. Marc'hadour (New Haven, CT, 1981)
CW8	*The Confutation of Tyndale's Answer*, ed. L.A. Schuster, R.C. Marius, J.P. Lusardi and R.J. Schoeck (New Haven, CT, 1973)
CW9	*The Apology*, ed. J.B. Trapp (New Haven, CT, 1979)
CW12	*A Dialogue of Comfort Against Tribulation*, ed. L.L. Martz and F.E. Manley (New Haven, CT, 1976)
CW13	*A Treatise on the Passion, A Treatise to Receive the Blessed Body, Instructions and Prayers*, ed. G.E. Haupt (New Haven, CT, 1976)
CW14	*De Tristia Christi*, ed. C.M. Miller (New Haven, CT, 1976)
More, *EW*	Thomas More, *The English Works of Sir Thomas More*, ed. W.E. Campbell (London, 1931)
P & P	*Past and Present*
Phil.	*Philosophy*
P. Qtyly	*Philosophical Quarterly*
PR	*The Philosophical Review*
PS	*Political Studies*
PT	Political Theory
Winstanley, *Works*	Gerrard Winstanley, *The Works of Gerrard Winstanley*, ed. G.H. Sabine (Ithaca, NY, 1941, repr. New York, 1965) and cross-referenced to *The Law of Freedom and Other Writings*, ed. C. Hill (Harmondsworth, 1973; Cambridge, 1983)
Winstanley, *Several Pieces*	*Several Pieces Gathered into One Volume* (Manchester Public Library)

Part I

1
Introductory: philosophical bearings

One characteristic of intellectual activities is that the element of self-awareness entailed in such pursuits inevitably sponsors concern as to whether the said activity is being conducted correctly. To put this another way, an intellectual discipline is in part identifiable as such because to engage in that discipline is to be aware of the methodological problems occasioned by that very engagement. Political philosophy is an intellectual discipline of this sort. What exactly occurs when an individual 'does political philosophy' is often a matter for dispute. Yet arguments of this kind constitute one aspect of 'doing political philosophy'. Analysis of the nature of the subject itself and of methodologies appropriate to its conduct thus becomes internalized within the subject. In the case of political philosophy this has, particularly in recent years, given rise to a series of profoundly complex debates. Political philosophy has been written about for over two thousand years. In the late twentieth century the activity can legitimately be seen as embracing a variety of related subsidiary activities; the history of political thought, ideological debate, contemporary political theory, conceptual analysis, methodology, and so on.

In terms of the methodological demands imposed, it would be difficult to imagine a more exacting subject matter than that of this book. The aim of this book is to analyse the thought of two writers. Thomas More and Gerrard Winstanley, who are distinguished by, among other things, a critical evaluation of what they regarded as conventional understandings of the appropriate role and form of property and ownership affecting the social, political and moral facets of the human condition. An analysis of this sort begs a series of questions. Why did More and Winstanley respectively offer an alternative perspective on ownership and its implications? What existing body of opinion is being appraised; to what degree is it being criticized, to what degree sustained? Why did these two thinkers each adopt the utopian genre as the mode in which to write a treatise proposing communal ownership? In terms of their own concerns and objectives, to what extent can More and Winstanley respectively be regarded as advancing theoretically convincing proposals? In what significant respects did these two thinkers differ and why? These are difficult issues. They are worth addressing not least because within the recent upsurge of interest in early modern theories of property, although considerable progress has been made in developing our understanding of the writings of thinkers who by and large supported the concept of private ownership, little detailed analysis of this aspect of the thought of early modern critics of private ownership currently exists.

There is one certain way for a piece of scholarship quickly to become dated and that is for its author to announce himself or herself an adherent of the latest 'method'. The same result is equally readily achieved by fervently espousing a critique or revision of the latest method. Recent political philosophy has been much preoccupied with methodology and there is some temptation to minimize one's consideration of this issue in the interests of brevity and in the hope that one's work might thereby become more readable. The danger here is that the well-atuned reader is likely to attempt to discern the method surreptitiously being supported. Honesty would therefore appear to be the best policy. Thus, I have no compunction in commencing with what passes as a statement detailing the approach I regard as appropriate to the subject in question. This approach is discursive and analytical. The demands of the subject matter are such that an initial consideration of four main issues is required. They are: the conduct of enquiry into the history of thought, conceptual analysis; a consideration of the concept of utopianism; and an introduction to pertinent aspects of the intellectual background.

Methodology: contexts and concepts

1

In a way the issue upon which all else turns when it comes to examining the appropriate method for investigating the history of political ideas is that of whether political philosophy through the ages has been addressing a series of universal or general considerations. Recent declamations should serve to instruct as to the error of assuming that such is the universality of concern within the history of political ideas that contemporary problems can be elucidated in terms of issues addressed and arguments advanced in the 'classical texts'. Even so, to become unduly reticent in this respect is to regard the history of political ideas as an essentially alien body of work. I approach, therefore, the writings of the early modern era with at least one conviction in mind, and this is that if there is any universal aspect within the history of political thought, it is the apprehension that the human condition had best be perceived as a *predicament*. Celebration of the human condition is not endemic to the history of ideas. Recommendation for the amelioration of the human condition is as intrinsic to social theory as the very perception of the human condition as some form of predicament. This allows, of course, for the possibility that 'the predicament' can be described in various ways.

If political thought is to be understood in terms of the human condition conceived as a predicament, at least two very difficult issues arise: one is the question of what actually constitutes the human condition; the other is that of how the human condition prevails upon political thought. These problems are implicitly addressed in Hannah Arendt's claim that 'whatever touches or enters into a sustained relationship with human life immediately assumes the character of a condition of human existence. This is why men, no matter what they do, are always conditioned beings'.[1] Michael Oakeshott, for example, sustains a similarly pervasive account in maintaining that political philosophy is a process of reflection involving 'the relation of political life, and the values and purposes pertaining to it, to the entire conception of the world that belongs to a civilization'.[2] For Oakeshott 'the human predicament is a universal appearing everywhere as a particular'.[3] The questions arises, then, as to what relation a text embodying political thought bears to the context of the human condition. In Oakeshott's view 'the meaning lies, as it always must lie, in a unity in which the separate existence of the text and the context is resolved'.[4] This statement will serve to set the terms of debate. How is this resolution, wherein lies the understanding of meaning, to be brought about?

One constituent of the human condition is the body of thought and expression actually addressed to the analysis of that situation. If, to whatever degree, the circumstances of the human condition are causally determining, then thought, and the language which itself determines the perimeters of thought, are factors in the broader context constituting the human condition. Our understanding of this context turns upon the differentiation of 'meaning', a quest embracing the analysis of writings which have addressed the human condition or some aspect of it. The reader will appreciate that this assumption leaves many weighty philosophical problems unexamined. Even so, it is evident that the method employed for interpreting texts in the history of thought will bear at least some relation to the reasons for pursuing such enquiry. For example, in the early 1960s J.B. Plamenatz insisted that 'its purpose is to help us to decide what to do and how to go about doing it',[5] a stance which has since been much criticized in certain quarters for leading the discipline astray by countenancing an essentially superficial and insensitive appreciation of texts. Talk of this kind recalls the work of A.O. Lovejoy, who is similarly condemned for conceiving of the history of thought as being composed of a series of 'unit ideas' recurring in successive ages and spheres.[6] The question of what should constitute an appropriate attitude to the subject was taken up, again in the early 1960s, by Isaiah Berlin, who contested that the history of political thought must entail the adoption of discarded states of mind and investigation into 'the models, paradigms, and conceptual structures that govern various outlooks whether consciously or not'.[7] At the hypothetical extremes, therefore, the options facing the would-be historian of political thought are depicted in stark relief. Either all-out extrapolation and the plundering of logical argument is envisaged, or enquiry is to be confined to the identification of factors determining the meaning of a text which, thereafter, is to be regarded as sacrosanct. The space between these extremes is vast; within it lies the methodological approach adopted in this book, an attitude explicable only in terms of recent consideration of methodology and the history of ideas.

2

The nature of the relationship between a text and the context in which it is formulated remains an unsettled consideration. Few historians of political thought would be inclined to disagree with John Dunn's view that the risk of distortion is always likely to attend the abstraction of any argument advanced in a historical text from its 'context of truth criteria'.[8] 'The problem of interpretation', according to Dunn, 'is always the problem of closing the context.'[9] The exact manner in which a context, however construed, informs a text is an issue of considerable importance and two particular questions come to mind when the issue is addressed. One concerns the problem of how exact a form of determinism is postulated by the notion of a contextual approach to textual interpretation. The other involves the problem of whether just one version of contextual interpretation is generally applicable.[10] Both these problems entail concern as to how narrow an appreciation of 'the context' it is appropriate to sustain.

Should it be the case that evidence is revealed to support the view that identifiable 'contexts' have determined thought to the extent that the ideas of the past are discernible via an appreciation of those contexts, then a significant insight into the conduct of enquiry into the history of ideas would be revealed. Yet such a breakthrough would not dispel every obstacle to the achievement of the emulative creativity required of the student of the history of ideas. Quite basic questions would remain as to why the enquiry is being undertaken at all and as to whether there is room for the kind of analysis which in effect amounts to engaging dead men in debate.

Two related approaches sustain contextual interpretation as it is now understood: one conceives of contexts as paradigms; the other regards language as the fundamental constituent of the context. Certain critics proceed by construing the context as a linguistic paradigm.

3

The idea that political discourse is in some sense contextually orientated has prompted the view that the history of political thought can be appreciated in terms of a series of intellectual paradigms. Understanding a context as a paradigm would explain why the preoccupations of certain epochs seem alien to the modern reader because paradigm theory suggests not only that a body of thought can remain dominant for many years but also that opinion may change and move on. The work of T.S. Kuhn on social explanation and the history of science has been vastly influential in this respect.

Critical of the view that scientific discovery is incremental or cumulative, Kuhn sees scientific 'progress' as differentiated by a series of paradigms, defined as 'universally recognized scientific achievements that for a time provide model problems and solutions for a community of practitioners'.[11] According to this appreciation of an intellectual activity such as science, each paradigm is sanctioned by institutional and sociological conventions to the effect that periods of normality are characterized by puzzle-solving within a basic framework. As, in the normal course of events, such activity is disrupted by the discovery of anomalies ultimately inexplicable within the conventions of the existing paradigm, that approach is discredited and, often via an apparently revolutionary breakthrough, a new paradigm is instituted.[12] This theory of intellectual history has been appropriated with some enthusiasm by scholars who see parallels between the history of science and that of political thought. Sheldon Wolin, for example, is especially assertive in this respect in that he believes the great political thought to have been accomplished by thinkers keen to amend society, especially at times of revolutionary turmoil.[13]

Paradigm theory has undoubtedly a number of attributes to recommend it, but it needs to be applied advisedly. The obvious affinity between the notion of paradigms and the idea that the history of thought is explicable in terms of a succession of 'worldviews' should defer also to the difficulties attending this latter way of looking at things. Paradigms might well, in certain spheres of human activity, serve to explain both the conventional and the unconventional, but concern is nevertheless aroused by the suspicion that the theory maintains an overly deterministic appreciation of 'normality'. It is also evident that, with respect to the history of political thought, it is not clear how the theory is to be applied, unless, that is, we are to think in terms of a series of overlapping paradigms, an appreciation that does some damage to the explanatory force of the theory. Even so, in proceeding to examine the idea of the Fall of Man, its hold over the imagination of generations, and its ultimate demise, we shall be looking at a body of thought that demonstrates *some* characteristics of a 'paradigm'. The idea of the paradigm is not, however, confined to the actual content of thought. Some scholars, of whom the most eminent is J.G.A. Pocock, see paradigms within the history of political thought as embracing a unity between thought and the mode of its expression. If the essential characteristic of the paradigm is conventionality then the *modus operandi* of the paradigm is language.

4

In the *Philosophical Investigations* Wittgenstein propounded a contextual view of meaning: ' For a *large* class of cases—though not for all—in which we employ the word "meaning" it can be defined thus: the meaning of a word is its use in language.'[14] The influence, either acknowledged or implicit, of pronouncements of this kind has been considerable and few historians of thought in the late twentieth century would deny being affected by the methodologies informed by this conception of meaning, although the route via which Wittgenstein's message has travelled has often been circuitous. The work, for example, of J.L. Austin on speech acts has exercised tremendous influence. Austin's view is that 'to say something *is* to do something, . . . *in* saying something we do something, . . . even *by* saying something we do something'.[15] The key to this position is that statements are construed as actions the *illocutionary force* and *intention* of which may impart more information than that suggested by the formal or apparent meaning.[16] The successful performance of an illocutionary act thus turns upon the securing of a respondent *uptake* on the part of the recipient of the statement, a result informed by the existence of linguistic *conventions.*[17]

The appeal of this conception of language to scholars concerned to distinguish the meaning of the written statements of times past does not need to be laboured. Thus the suggestions of philosophers who have sought to refine Austin's positions have also been brought to bear upon intepretation in the history of thought. P.F. Strawson's view that the conventional facet of illocutionary acts may not be quite so general as Austin assumed[18] has led many historians of political thought to agree that the *absence of conventionality* might provide the illocutionary force of certain texts, a consideration of some significance, for instance, when it comes to evaluating utopian works. For Strawson, Austin's apprehension of intention requires refinement; it is not so much the case that intentions invoke responses but that a response must turn upon the recognition of the very intention to provoke. For Strawson, 'an essential feature of the intentions which make up the illocutionary complex is their overtness. They have, one might say, essential avowability.'[19]

In many respects the work of Austin and Strawson is complemented by that of H.P. Grice on 'meaning'. Here again the emphasis is upon the idea that meaning entails the recognition of the intention to produce a response, a process governed by a convention termed by Grice the 'inference element'.[20] This whole emphasis upon the meaning of linguistic statements being intentions which must to some significant degree be circumscribed by convention has prompted a number of scholars to infer a good deal from Kuhn's contention that his understanding of paradigms is in certain respects similar to Wittgenstein's theory of language.[21]

5

Pocock's belief that political thought effectively constitutes 'the exploration and sophistication of political language'[22] is sustained by the supposition that, rather than there being a 'history of political philosophy' awaiting investigation, the political thought of the past is constituted by a series of conventional languages. In regarding matters in terms of 'conceptual languages of political discussion found in particular societies at particular times',[23] Pocock insists, even in the tempered terms of recent retrospective appraisals of his work, that interpretative method should take into account the consideration that language exists *prior* to the use to which it is put by particular thinkers. The clue to the meaning of texts lies, therefore, in identifying the context. For Pocock, the languages of political discourse construed as 'structures of givens' effectively define meaning.[24] This apparently determinist view of language might explain Pocock's propensity to think in terms of *linguistic paradigms*. Of what probably amount to hundreds of explications of this position the following is fairly representative:

> The historian's first problem, . . . is to identify the 'language' or 'vocabulary' with and within which the author operated, and to show how it functioned paradigmatically to prescribe what he might say and how he might say it.[25]

A method, which appears to some as unconstrained historicism, recommending the 'empirical' study of languages rather than the analysis of the theory expressed by language[26] has done little to recommend Pocock's work to scholars who regard themselves still as *philosophers* of political thought. Pocock simply questions the enterprise supported by the 'analytic tradition'.[27]

Pocock's methodological stance, at least in its earlier and robust form, raises a very real difficulty in respect of the ideas considered in this book because it is argued below that the social philosophies of More and Winstanley are substantially informed by their respective perceptions of the concept of the Fall of Man. There is every reason to suppose that this idea fulfils the criteria of a paradigmatic language in much the same way as the subjects associated with Pocock's own enquiries—classical republicanism, *virtu*, the 'ancient constitution', eschatological concepts such as the 'elect nation', and so on. The problem, however, is that in working within the framework of the idea of the Fall neither More nor Winstanley developed their social philosophy to the exclusion of other 'languages', nor did they always adhere to a conventional body of thought to the preclusion of conceptual exploration and, especially in Winstanley's case, quite substantial innovation. Recently, however, Pocock has argued as follows:

> the language determines what can be said in it; there is a history formed by the interactions of *parole* and *language*. We do not say that the language context is the only context which gives the speech act meaning and history, though we shall infallibly be accused having said that; we say only that it is a promising context with which to begin.[28]

It is tempting but impossible here to digress into whether this reflection represents a reformulation of his earlier position. It is not, I think, unfair to regard the problem of linguistic determinism as one which, in the early days of the development of this broad methodology, troubled Quentin Skinner rather more than it did Pocock.

6

Such is the volume of Skinner's contribution on methodology and the history of political thought[29] that an adequate distillation of what he envisages is wellnigh impossible. Even so, such has been the influence of this body of work that no serious enquiry into the political thought of the early modern period can proceed without clarifying the manner in which its methodological approach stands in relation to Skinner's.

Sceptical of unmitigated textualism, particularly that seeming to support the notion of certain universal ideas enjoying self-sufficiency by recurring in 'classical texts', and worried by unrefined contextualism, Skinner insists that the historian of political thought must become sensitive to the use and meaning of the language employed in such discourse. Of essence to this technique is the requirement that that *intentions* of authors must be reclaimed, a process achievable only by becoming conversant with 'the appropriate context of conventions and assumptions from which [their] intentions can be decoded'[30]—in effect, language. Thus Skinner draws upon the appreciation of language and meaning discussed above.[31]

For Skinner, it is the *status*, or *point* or *use*, rather than the immediate or superficial meaning of language that is likely to yield genuine understanding of written statements. To write is to perform an action, the interpretation of that action turns upon the conventions relating action to meaning to understanding, and these conventions are constituted by language.[32] Intention is thus integral, but not necessarily prior, to meaning.[33]

Such is the validity to Skinner of the conception of meaning in terms of 'speech acts' that he views interpretation in the history of ideas as an exercise involving the recovery, redescription, and explanation of statements-as-actions.[34] The following encapsulates this requirement:

> To identify . . . the illocutionary force co-ordinate on a given occasion with the ordinary meaning of the given utterance is equivalent to understanding the nature of the [linguistic] action performed by the speaker in uttering his given utterance.[35]

For the modern-day analyst as for the original author and audience, understanding depends upon securing uptake.[36] The argument is summarized thus:

> to understand the illocutionary force of an utterance is to recover what the agent saw himself as doing in issuing it, since this process is clearly equivalent to recovering the primary intentions with which the given utterance was issued . . . to understand what the agent saw himself as doing, and so to grasp the intended illocutionary force of his utterance, is equivalent to understanding what he must have meant by what he said.[37]

The accurate uptake or perception of intentions, upon which meaning turns, presupposes then the existence of mutually recognized communicable conventions informing that meaning.[38] It is important to be aware that although Skinner thinks in terms of the conventionality of discourse, he does so in such a way as to recognize the possibility that creative and innovatory styles of discussion might emerge, albeit in critical relation to established modes of discourse.[39]

The question of whether a language affords room for manoeuvre raises the issue of whether a language might be so pervasive as to be paradigmatic.

While Skinner is to be discovered talking in terms of the 'context of conventions', he sustains a deliberate reticence as to the notion of linguistic paradigms. Instead, and this is particularly borne out in Skinner's most thoroughgoing application of his approach,[40] he sees the thought of the past as the 'history of ideologies'. What this may or may not involve in terms both of the constraints and influences upon authors and the requirements made of modern scholarships is further discussed below. At this stage, however, we might anticipate our argument by suggesting that to characterize political discourse as ideological may entail a particular apprehension of the *conceptual* nature of the language of politics.

7

The broad range of approaches emphasizing linguistic contextualism and intentionalism has generated a series of quite commonly expressed reservations. A recent study of this entire methodological positions suggests that rather than constituting a 'school', the attribution of affinity between Pocock and Skinner in particular, needs to be moderated.[41] As has been suggested above, much turns upon the issue of 'narrowing the context': Pocock is seen as preferring broad but susceptibly closed paradigms; Skinner as promoting the quest for somewhat more precise linguistic intentions. Even so, questions have arisen as to how such approaches are to be implemented and precisely what the purpose of studying the history of ideas in these ways actually is.

While a fairly substantial body of opinion has emerged to criticize paradigmatic and intentionalist approaches, this has not in the main been to the total detriment of such revisionism. Scholars have remarked upon the utility of these methods, especially in providing a facility to *exclude* rather than to *identify positively* particular interpretations.[42] However, what appears most worrying to many minds is the prospect of the revisionist method itself assuming a paradigmatic hold over the study of the history of political thought.[43] Against the applicability of just one theory, the case has been advanced for the claims of a variety of contextual appraisals;[44] in particular, one group of scholars argues for the diligent consideration of wider social contexts.[45]

A major point of contention arises from consideration of the presupposition that seems to be most under attack from the revisionist methods—the view that the history of political thought is in some sense a cumulative tradition related to perennial problems of the human condition. Several scholars wonder whether this perhaps long-cherished assumption is quite so misguided,[46] and similar doubt has been expressed as to whether the thought of ages past should be treated as that of 'alien cultures'.[47] In general, concern appears to persist over the suspicion that revisionist methods take as their starting point the assumption that the 'endemic problem' approaching is invalid, rather than actually demonstrating that shortcoming. Doubts of this kind are often expressed in conjunction with misgivings over whether paradigmatic or linguistic-intentionalist interpretations detract from the operation of the *creative process* within the history of thought. The danger, in the view of one commentator, is that of the revisionist methods imputing too great a degree of *determinism* to the history of thought.[48] These various critical insights ultimately call to mind the crucial issue of what enquiry into aspects of the history of political thought should actually be attempting to achieve. Clearly, the objectives of a discipline are going to be informed by the methods and techniques available for its pursuit, but what worries J.V. Femia is that proponents of the revisionist method 'come perilously close to mistaking the origins of a statement for its logical status'.[49] In essence, what is in question here is whether, even supposing the facility for accurately recovering intentions by various means advocated, that exercise in itself fulfils the objectives of the discipline. The issue is whether the meaning of a text once recovered should then be subjected to the type of logical analysis associated with what could loosely be termed the analytical tradition.

The methodology informing the forthcoming chapters is elaborated below. At this stage it is appropriate to make it clear, and this will become manifestly evident, that the assumption of a reserved approach to the revisionist methods does not entail an attempt to remain immune from their influence. My main concern is not so much with the absolute validity of these approaches but with how, shortcomings accepted, they are best developed and operationalized. In one sense, therefore, this book is an exercise in methodological pluralism, an attitude which calls into debate another recent body of opinion on political discourse—that which addresses the form and status of the concepts employed in the language of politics.

8

So far we have been examining appraisals of political discourse which stress the conventionality of language. We now turn to views which take it as axiomatic that the concepts employed in political discourse are unlikely to be characterized by consensus as to their meaning.

One common manner of introducing this problem is to suggest that, whereas the terms employed in the natural sciences are descriptive and thus amenable to resolute definition, the vocabulary of moral and political discourse is evaluative and thereby indeterminate.[50] There remains, however, a question as to precisely how normative concepts should be understood. In the view of W.B. Gallie, for example, such concepts may be subsumed under a 'single explanatory hypothesis'.[51]

If it is the case that the meaning of normative concepts such as justice, freedom, the good life, and so on, are likely to be the subject of dispute, then it is important to be clear as to the nature of that disagreement. On this matter harmony of opinion is far from evident. Most scholars would confirm Gallie's claim that this facet of moral and political discourse involves 'concepts the proper use of which inevitably involves endless disputes about their proper use on the part of their users'[52]—concepts which are incapable of yielding general or standard or correct definitions.[53]

However, a problem arises over precisely how the inevitability of dispute over use should be regarded.

A substantial body of opinion follows Gallie in characterizing such terms as 'essentially contested concepts' by assuming that users of such concepts must advance in a *competitive* but 'rational' manner rival definitions.[54] It is along these lines that W.E. Connolly stipulates that

> the internal complexity of the concept, combined with the relative openness of each of its unit criteria, provides the space within which these disputes take place, and because of these very features, operational tests and formal modes of analysis do not provide sufficient leverage to settle such disputes.[55]

9

Argumentation occasioned by dispute over the appropriate arrangement of unit criteria to support various definitions of a concept prompts the question of how the dual elements of consensus and competition are maintained within such debate. Concern of this kind inspires Gallie to attempt to differentiate 'essentially contested concepts' from disputes which are merely 'radically confused'.[56] Radical confusion, apparently, occurs when supporters of differing views are, in fact, arguing not over the meaning of one concept but over two quite distinct concepts. However, whereas it may well be the case that the parties to such a debate eventually realize their mistake by, for example, arriving at distinct determinate definitions, there is no guaranteeing that *during the course of their argument* they are aware that theirs is a 'radically confused' rather than an 'essential contest'. Radical confusion is therefore a retrospective judgement recognizing the absence of consensus over common ground, namely that the argument has been about the meaning of one concept; essential contestability presupposes that argument is about the meaning of one term. This is important because the manner in which the balance between consensus and contest within conceptual debate is conceived has a considerable bearing upon the ultimate understanding of political discourse.

In illuminating his appreciation of essential contestedness Gallie advances a series of conditions[57] one of which exemplifies what he sees as the competitive nature of political discourse:

> to use an essentially contested concept means to use it against other uses and to recognize that one's own use of it has to be maintained against these other uses . . . to use an essentially contested concept means to use it both aggressively and defensively.[58]

In accounting for the disposition to contest meaning, Gallie is aware of the need to explain the manner in which the actual perimeters of debate are defined. To this end he introduces the notion that concepts, the meaning of which are contested, derive 'from an original exemplar whose authority is acknowledged by all the contestant users of the concept'.[59] Clearly, the purpose of the exemplar is to afford that element of consensus within and according to which dispute takes place. This is an intriguing suggestion not least because from the point of view of forthcoming chapters More's *Utopia* might be viewed as the exemplar for the concept of utopianism. However, matters are not quite so straightforward. In referring to 'the internally complex, and variously describable, and peculiarly "open" character of the exemplar's achievement',[60] Gallie indicates an awareness that consensus attending the exemplar might operate to frustrate subsequent conceptual debate. Even so, it is far from evident that conceptual debate might not encompass argument as to the identification of *the exemplar*. Yet without some basic adherence to the idea that the meaning of just one concept is being disputed the attribute of contest so emphasized by Gallie and other adherents to the notion of 'essential contestedness' stands in danger of getting out of hand.

It is not surprising that supporters of the idea of essentially contested concepts are more at ease in describing the nature of conceptual dispute than in accounting for a balance of conflict and consensus. The competitive character of essentially contested concepts is particularly stressed by John Gray, who talks of 'the presence of intractable definitional disputes' informed by 'patterns of thought associated with rival forms of social life'.[61] The *ideological* confrontation extolled by Gray is attended by the intimation that participants in conceptual debates are sustained by the belief that such disputes might be resolved if only rival opinion can be converted to the view to which they adhere. The intellectual tensions occasioned by engaging in this type of debate are presumably quite profound. A stream of commentators has argued that users of political concepts must at once adhere to and defend a particular preferred understanding yet remain aware that others feel the same way about their respective positions.[62] The requisite state of mind, therefore, would appear to involve a concern to promote a particular view in the belief that conceptual dispute is resolvable in one's favour while at the same time recognizing, first, that others share this ambition for their views, and second, that all are engaging in a debate that is likely to endure indefinitely.

10

The theory of essentially contested concepts has done much to sharpen our understanding of this aspect of the language of politics. Even so, the approach entails a number of residual difficulties. Among these the problem of striking an appropriate balance between contest and consensus, the question of whether such debates are in principle resolvable, and the issue of whether all such debates may be characterized as 'ideological', all suggest that the notion of essential contestedness, however, refined does not fulfil Gallie's original ambition of providing a single method of conceptual analysis. In essence, it is simply not apparent that contestation is an *a priori* facet of conceptual analysis.

One of the more useful contributions to emerge from recent debate on the nature of conceptual analysis is the understanding developed of the internal structure of concepts. For example, in suggesting that 'we cannot specify an invarient set of necessary and sufficient conditions for the proper applications of the concept', Connolly advances an appreciation of the '*cluster concept* to which a broad range of criteria apply'.[63] If concepts are composites of various complex criteria, the definition and use of such concepts will entail the choice and ordering of such criteria. The issue of how concepts are operationalized will relate in turn to that of the intellectual disposition favoured by respective users of concepts. There is in effect a world of difference between on the one hand, promoting one particular understanding of a concept as the proper use of that idea in all circumstances and, on the other, regarding a particular definition as one of many that could be culled from the range of truth criteria informing a concept and as operationally satisfactory only in certain circumstances. The adoption of this latter propensity presupposes the limits of operationalism. Rather than thinking in terms of developing a plausible operational definition into a full-blown claim to have ascertained the meaning of the concept, deluded ambitions concerning the prospects for resolution and determinancy are eschewed.[64] Given that it is in the nature of conceptual analysis that consensus is unlikely to obtain as to what could, in any situation, constitute *the operational test*, the indeterminacy of a concept should extend to indeterminacy as to its operational validity. So, in essence, within normative discourse, operationalism or the use of stipulative definitions can entail determinacy only in association with the specification of the particular circumstances attending the use of such definitions.

The intellectual disposition appropriate to the advancement of stipulative operational definitions of this kind, that which brings to mind ideas of methodological and value pluralism, goes some considerable way towards ameliorating the problem thrown up by the notion of essential contestedness. The requirement that the ambivalent users of concepts are at once contestants while at the same time remaining conscious of the indeterminacy of the concepts the meaning of which they contest, is dispelled once the limits of operationalism are recognized. It is important to be aware that the assertion of conceptual indeterminacy does not preclude the possibility that concepts may be used ideologically or even subjectively, but that what is in question is whether the use of a concept in moral or political discourse is necessarily so.[65]

11

It is quite remarkable that recent methodological reappraisals of two facets of political philosophy—the history of political thought and conceptual analysis—have proceeded more or less in isolation from one another. A rather more eclectic approach not surprisingly verifies the claims of methodological pluralism.

Revisionist techniques for the study of the history of political thought turn upon the basic claim that the language of politics is to some marked degree conventional. Appraisals of contemporary political discourse view that medium as conceptually indeterminate. It is interesting to observe that, whereas Skinner used the term 'ideology' to denote languages that emerge as conventional, for adherents of the notion of essential contestedness 'ideology' implies disagreement.[66] It is, of course, possible that the ideologies identified by Skinner ('liberty', 'the state') as emerging in the early modern period succeeded in the manner envisaged by analysts who believe that concepts are ideologically contestable. However, even if this were the case, it seems unlikely that the use of the terms and concepts that are the essence of political discourse would ever go conventionally unchallenged, a consideration of which Skinner is undoubtedly aware.

The admission of conceptual ambiguity accords with the proviso, highlighted by Strawson, that meaning may turn as much upon the unconventional as upon the conventional. The crucial point here is that not only should the indeterminate nature of the concepts employed in political language tell against the pervasion of linguistic paradigms but, even where a conventional understanding is recovered, the very form of political concepts allows for the possibility of that convention being operationally inappropriate. In effect, what this means is that there is room within the history of political thought for an approach that is analytical. To take an illustrative example, in a subsequent chapter of this book it is argued that the conception of citizenship proposed in More's *Utopia* is seriously at odds with the theological understanding of human freedom to which More adhered. Our approach identifies the 'Fall of Man' as a convention, or language, or indeed paradigm, which profoundly influenced More's thinking. But we also go on to analyse the logical status of More's response to the problems presented by this tradition of thought. If the 'Fall of Man' was a language it was, by More's time, one which afforded sufficient internal and logical disputation as to be susceptible to considerable indeterminacy.

The purpose of this book is certainly to recover the 'intentions' of More and Winstanley, and a range of contextual approaches are employed in so doing. For example, it is argued that although both thinkers employed the medium of a utopia through which to advance political recommendations, the meaning of both *Utopia* and *The Law of Freedom* is to a considerable extent informed by concerns expressed therein that are identifiably *conventional*. But utopianism also affords scope for theoretical innovation. It is thus appropriate to enquire whether proposals of this kind actually constitute cogent recommendations *in terms of the intentions of their authors*.

We turn now to an analysis of the concept of utopianism. The objective here is to identify an operational definition of utopianism appropriate to the subject matter of this book. This exercise is undertaken in accordance with the understanding of conceptual operationalism outlined above. It is not, therefore, intended to offer a definition of utopianism *per se*.

Utopianism, millenarianism, and political philosophy

1

The plethora of arguments generated by contention as to what may be entailed by the term 'utopia'[67] suggests that utopianism is an ambiguous concept. It is incumbent upon those who utilize the concept, therefore, to be clear as to what understanding they are working with. Such clarity is encouraged through the provision of an operational definition. The basic premise informing the conception of utopianism developed below is that those utopias produced by thinkers such as More and Winstanley are far closer to what may be regarded as the mainstream of political thought than is often supposed. In particular, utopian political philosophy implicitly defers to the circumstances and constraints apprehended by contemporary conceptions of the human condition. To this extent, such works should not be addressed as if they are markedly conventional. A work such as More's *Utopia* is, therefore, susceptible to the type of linguistic-contextual analysis developed by the methodological revisionism discussed above.[68]

The analysis of utopianism is often compounded by the fact that two avenues of approach are employed simultaneously: on the one hand, a conceptual enquiry, involving the attempt to identify the generic features of the idiom; on the other, a contextual approach relating utopianism to wider developments in the history of ideas, such as changing appreciations of mankind's facility to 'progress'. The paradox here is, of course, that attempts to embrace the historical perspective may ultimately frustrate the endeavour to isolate a coherent understanding of the concept. Over time, the various works now subsumed under the heading 'utopian' have differed in form, content and intent quite substantially. The analysis of utopias is also often characterized by a propensity to view such works pejoratively. This outlook, as is suggested below, may often arise from the inclination to read utopias literally and with the gift of hindsight. The view advanced in this section seeks to develop an understanding of what the concept of utopianism entails with the object in mind of providing an operational definition appropriate to the understanding of the work of More and Winstanley.

2

In recent years considered analysis of utopianism has increasingly tended to the view that the meaning of the concept is indeterminate.[69] Even so, this trend has not entirely discouraged the attempt to discern a determinate definition, or as de Jouvenal has it, 'a substantive meaning, such that the extension of the term is the same for all participants'.[70] Appraisal of the nature of utopianism has in the main been dominated by two lines of approach. The first, emphasizing the historical perspective, entails the association of utopianism with successive systems of thought within the history of ideas. Thus, from the perspective of an assumed initiation into the resolution of these ideas, the utility of the concept is assessed in the light of the ideals it has purportedly recommended. The second mode of investigation, the attempt to produce a 'grand theory', looks at the criteria and attributes of utopianism with the object in mind of providing a determinate definition, however unwieldy. By briefly looking at examples of these two approaches it is possible to isolate several of the more contentious issues that attend the debate over the meaning of utopianism. In this way, the operational definition offered at the end of this section will hopefully enjoy greater credence.

At various times social theorists have employed various brands of utopianism as the medium appropriate to the articulation of their proposals. As time has gone on such works are often subjected to intense criticism. They may be regarded as 'pre-Enlightenment' or, under the dystopian influence of Huxley and Orwell, as anachronistically aliberal and authoritarian. A problem arises as to whether valid conceptual insights are to be ascertained by assuming a *historial perspective* because the conceptual nuances of utopianism are such as to leave certain critics ambivalent as to their reaction to utopianism. Marxism, for example, is often regarded both as an anti-utopian position and as the apparent successor to a distinct strand of utopian thought.

The analysis of utopianism provided by Marx and Engels emerged in conjunction with their appreciation of historicism and determinism. Despite an initial interest the empirical study of socialism, American utopian communities being regarded as proof of the practicability of communism,[71] Marx and Engles developed a disparaging understanding of the utopianism of Fourier, Owen and Saint-Simon. The essence of this uncompromising critique is that utopian communism, as distinct from scientific socialism, had failed to perceive and to accommodate for the workings of the forces of history. Thus the utility of utopianism as a method of social enquiry is brought into question. German socialism, argues Marx, opposes all utopianism because that latter is devoid of any capacity to distinguish the historically inevitable.[72] Contemplating social reform without considering the implications of the capitalist mode of production is both 'reactionary and utopian'.[73] In *The Manifesto of the Communist Party* Marx and Engels claim that the utopian socialists wrote at a time when the nature of the class struggle remained undeveloped. Thus, because the necessary material conditions for the emancipation of the proletariat were not then evident, the utopian socialists were obliged to resort to a 'fanatical and superstitious belief in the miraculous effects of their social science'.[74] Such writers are accused of failing to respond appropriately to the revolutionary activism of a proletariat at last beginning to organize itself to effect the reconstruction of society.[75] In essence, Marx and Engels deemed it 'utopian' to envisage social harmony at precisely the time when class antagonism was emerging as an instrument of social change. Thus they contend that 'as the modern class struggle develops and takes definite shape, this fantastic standing apart from the contest, these fantastic attacks on it, lose all practical value and all theoretical justification'.[76]

By regarding utopianism as a historically specific and ultimately redundant mode of analysis, Marx and Engels undoubtedly contributed to the development of a pejorative view of the activity, one which emphasizes the divorce of utopian thought from the workings of history, from mankind's immediate condition, and effectively from 'reality'. The obvious counter to the claim that utopianism contradicts 'reality' construed as historical materialism is that it is incumbent upon proponents of this view to provide a valid alternative account. Whether Marx and Engels were successful in this respect, and indeed whether their own social analysis is strictly delineated from utopianism remains open to question. What is perhaps of more immediate concern stems from Marx's and Engel's failure to distinguish the categories of *means* and *ends* within utopianism. This is not an uncommon shortcoming, but it is particularly pronounced in their case and is therefore worth investigating.

Marx and Engels contend that the end advocated by the utopian socialists is the reconstruction of society and that the (mistaken) means advanced to achieve this end is a brand of 'social science'. The argument from historical materialism, however, sees the emancipation of the proletariat, for example, as an element within the alternative (and actual) means of achieving social reorganization.[77] Thus, by assigning the emancipation of the proletariat and the entire purview of social reconstruction to the category of desired ends (from the attributed utopian socialist perspective), and by asserting that, contrary to this view, the emancipation of the proletariat is a facet of the only possible means of attaining this ideal, Marx and Engels attempt to emphasize the futility of institutional planning as a method of securing desired ends.

The contention that the development of new modes of production will inevitably and exclusively result in social reorganization challenges the validity of utopianism by questioning its realism, in this case its historicism. At the very least, however, the persistence of doubt concerning the materialist interpretation of history suggests that the continued consideration of utopianism from a conceptual rather than from an exclusively historical point of view is justified. The case for regarding utopianism pejoratively as a misguided anachronism is not proven. Nor is the assumption that utopianism will always be estranged from the 'realities' of the human condition and hence from serious social theorizing.

An alternative historical appreciation of utopianism is sponsored in the work of Karl Mannheim. Here the suggestion is that utopianism constitutes an intellectual orientation towards social change; a 'state of mind is utopian when it is incongruous with the state of reality within which it occurs.[78] By confronting what Mannheim conceives as 'ideologies', utopias possess a tendency to undermine the existing social order, at least from the point of view of existing ideologies. Therefore, 'utopian' thought will always appear 'in principle unrealizable'.[79]

A fundamental difference between the Marxist response to utopianism and that developed by Mannheim and his disciples is that, whereas the former celebrates the expiry of utopianism and the dawning of scientific socialism, the latter regards utopianism as an essentially dynamic phenomenon. The key point to be grasped is that for Mannheim utopianism is not by definition unrealistic, although from the point of view of a dominant ideology it may be deemed so.[80] Hence, despite a rather ubiquitous catalogue of movements that may at one time or another have appeared 'utopian', and an emphasis upon somewhat unrestrained idealism, Mannheim's approach does take into consideration the facility of utopianism to analyse existing social circumstances and to prescribe methods for their amelioration. Even so, in the hands of some scholars[81] an approach broadly similar to Mannheim's leads to an appreciation of utopianism which so extends the scope of the concept that any identifiably radical stance might be subsumed under this heading.[82] The danger here is that utopianism will appear unrealistic because it is overtly idealistic.

There are, then, drawbacks to regarding utopian thought as a phenomenon assignable to specific periods, shortcomings which are illustrated by considering Judith Shklar's work in this area. Following Mannheim's distinctions, Shklar suggests that utopia was replaced by ideology at the watershed of the French Revolution.[83] According to this view, classical utopianism was a historically specific movement which reached its zenith with the *social optimism* of the Enlightenment, an outlook which Shklar believes to have been dissipated by Romanticism and Catholic fatalism.[84] Shklar sees this faith in progress as being largely restricted to Enlightenment social philosophy because such an outlook would have been incongruous with the earlier and prolonged adherence to the doctine of original sin.[85] Thus, on this account, much pre-Enlightenment social philosophy falls outside the scope of utopianism precisely because it embraces disparaging appreciations of human potential.

The equation with utopianism of optimism concerning the prospects of an improvement in Man's moral and social circumstances, extending even to the aspiration to human perfectibility, is dubious. Social harmony rendered possible by the total moral renewal of mankind does not appear to be a necessary criterion of utopianism. During the early modern period a number of works which are identifiably utopian were written by thinkers who retained an essentially pessimistic assessment of human perfectibility and of 'progress' in general. As J.C. Davis suggests, ideal societies within which social arrangements are harmonized by means of the moral improvement of mankind might appropriately be termed 'Perfect Moral Commonwealths'.[86] In cases where it is envisaged that social reform may not be contingent upon any moral transformation, it is reasonable to anticipate that the emphasis will lie with reconstruction brought about by institutional means.

A number of works in the secondary literature on utopianism are characterized by the conviction that an adequate definition of the concept must embrace as comprehensive a catalogue as possible of its unit criteria. Quite often, some of the definitional difficulties encountered in 'historical' analyses appear in an acute form in approaches which might be labelled *grand theory*. What is offered below is but a brief and illustrative set of examples.

A propensity appears to have developed in the mid-twentieth century for exploring the implications of utopian idealism and what might be meant by 'perfection'.[87] Often, this approach was accompanied by exhaustive surveys of the range of texts that might appropriately be regarded as 'utopian'. Not surprisingly, the very indeterminacy of the concept inevitably prompted disagreement as to which texts deserved consideration.

By concentrating upon the variety of possible ends that might be postulated by utopias, work of this kind served better to illustrate the complexity of utopianism than to actually produce coherent analyses. This contrasts markedly with some more recent scholarship which, in deferring to the ambiguity of the notion, has sought to provide a more disciplined analysis of the tradition.[88] In general, recent scholarship has sought to dispel pejorative understandings of utopianism by demonstrating that very often utopias will bear a substantial resemblance to the society of the author. Thus, the analysis of utopias and utopianism has moved towards an appreciation which stresses that the meaning of utopian social philosophy is often to be discovered by analysing the situation addressed by the author. Scholars are, therefore, concerned rather more than was once the case to identify the precise characteristics of the socio-political utopia. These criteria may now be considered.

3

Our discussion to date indicates that the analysis of utopianism has often been confused and formless. Such is the nature of the concept that it is impossible to lay down a set of defining criteria which might enjoy universal adherence. However, several fundamental issues or *contested criteria* emerge as central to the question of how utopianism and social theory are related. The first of these involves the status of utopian social philosophy as a literary form.

The view that utopianism cannot embrace serious social theorizing has often been supported by the belief that the genre is an essentially fictional device. Thus it is argued that because the utopian impulse involves the endeavour to escape the constraints of time and place, utopias assume the form of literary fiction. However, this outlook has not contributed to any consistency of approach in dealing with works such as Plato's *Republic* or Harrington's *Oceana*.[89] The differentiation of 'social theory' and 'literary utopia' has often been quite arbitrary. The crucial point at issue is that if a particular work is regarded as being 'utopian' when that term is taken as denoting a fictional vehicle for escapism, then the possibility of utopianism and social theory coalescing to provide a means of seriously analysing the human condition is precluded. This impression is, to say the least, contentious.

The status of utopianism as a genre extends to a second central issue, namely that of whether utopias can embrace the 'realistic'. Responses to this question vary. Some scholars see utopianism as a kind of *jeu d'esprit*; others appraise the concept as a medium for the articulation of often unpalatable conceptions of mankind's predicament. One obvious implication of the understanding that utopianism might be in some way prescriptive is that the author of a utopia might use the medium to recommend the reform of social institutions. Quite clearly, if such proposals are intended seriously to be considered they must tangibly relate to acknowledged apprehensions of mankind's predicament. This places an obvious constraint upon the degree of speculation or fantasy in which the author might indulge should he intend to advance a social statement which is to be recognized as such. All this suggests that utopian social philosophy must, to a considerable degree, defer to conventional understandings of what might be regarded as 'realistic' proposals. In particular, the utopian theorist's appreciation of human nature and of mankind's potential is likely to carry considerable weight if the work is to enjoy a reputation as a coherent social theory. The admission that men's moral faculties are impaired and are likely to remain so would certainly preclude the anticipation of a 'Perfect Moral Commonwealth' but might favour the production of a utopia identifiable as a work of social philosophy.

The third issue with which I am here concerned follows on from what has gone before. This is the relationship between realism, the scope of utopian idealism, and proposed methods for the achievement of ideals—a range of difficulties constituting the most intriguing and intransigent aspect of utopianism. As has been indicated, it is often the case that, with regard to utopian 'means and ends', overt idealism is seen as a necessary condition of utopianism, and that such idealism is informed by such a range of understandings of 'perfection' that a comprehensive list of ideals and ends must be incorporated into the definition of the concept. Somewhat predictably, the citation of various ideals as independent criteria of the concept has resulted in profound disagreement as to what is denoted by the term 'utopia'. More promising is the avenue of approach which concentrates attention upon the methods proposed by utopian social theorists for the attainment of their respective ends and ideals. Thus, the statement of such ends can be left to the discretion of the author and need not be included in a definition of the concept. At the very least, restricting the discussion of the nature of utopian idealism to the abstract by regarding utopian ends as variables has the virtue of keeping operational definitions within manageable proportions.

A good deal obviously hinges upon the manner in which utopian thought, and in particular its idealism, is deemed 'realistic'. In this respect it is opportune to cite a position traceable to Spinoza, which regards ideals as by nature relative.[90] Thus an ideal cannot be distinguished as such unless it bears some conceivable relation to an existing reality, condition, or state of affairs. The whole issue of whether, and in what respect, utopianism and social theory correspond, turns upon the relativism of utopian idealism. This question is compounded by the time factor. It is pertinent to enquire whether a 'realistic' ideal is one which is ultimately realized (if so, is it still an ideal?) or whether a utopian ideal appeared realizable in principle at the time of writing. The latter possibility seems to convey more of the atmosphere of utopian social philosophy but it still leaves unresolved the difficulty of how the apparently realizable is conceived. The answer to this question must ultimately be contextual; the extent to which an ideal is perceived as realistic will be informed by considerations such as contemporary evaluations of human nature and potential, of the prospects for the amelioration of environmental constraints, of the climate of institutional reform, and so on. It is for reasons such as these that the intellectual history of utopianism has often coincided with that of 'progress', optimism and human perfectibility. Properly conducted, the conceptual analysis of utopianism will always have cause to resort to considerations of historical contextualism. By the same token, as a tool of philosophical enquiry the conceptual analysis of utopianism should seek only to render operational definitions for use in the analysis of specific instances of the genre. Before providing a working definition according to which the utopianism of More and Winstanley is to be understood in subsequent chapters, it is necessary to seek additional clarification by examining the relationship between utopianism and a further notion with which it is associated, namely millenarianism.

4

Particularly with respect to the social radicalism of the seventeenth century, scholars are inclined to use the terms 'utopian' and 'millenarian' interchangeably.[91] With regard to the writings of many radicals this correlation is of no great consequence; the terms in question are so all-embracing that either might serve to describe the position of a particular writer at a particular time. However, with regard to the work of Gerrard Winstanley this is not the case. For reasons that are elaborated below it is necessary to delineate within Winstanley's thought a period in which he was identifiably a millenarian thinker and a subsequent phase in which his thought is distinctly utopian. Elsewhere, and in considerable detail, I have suggested that the millenarianism of the mid-seventeenth century might be analysed in terms of an 'eschatological continuum' differentiating forms of expectation in terms of nature and intensity.[92] The major consideration in determining where along this continuum a writer might be broadly located is the issue of how the millenium is conceived in terms of the social reformation proposed and what element of human discretion this affords. Very literal interpretations of the Second Coming might preclude any element of utopianism on the grounds that the new order is not to be determined by mankind. At the other extreme, more general eschatological beliefs might coincide with utopianism, especially if millenarian expectation is confined to the assumption that the reform of society is to be accomplished via human agency. In briefly elaborating upon these distinctions the scholarship of B.S. Capp and J.C. Davis is acknowledged.

In distinguishing the utopian social philosophy with which this book is concerned from the main body of millenarian thought, two important considerations emerge. The first is the means by which the ideal society is to be established. From the millenarian point of view this work must be left to God, who may intervene either directly or though His agents, the saints. From the utopian point of view, the ideal society can be established only by Man, working unaided, often with limited resources, and in conditions of adversity. The second is the issue of the moral regeneration of mankind. Some millenarians were liable to postulate as an ideal the perfection of human nature. Utopians, on the other hand, were more liable to formulate their idealism in mundane terms. In contrast, for example, to the millenarianism of the Fifth Monarchists,[93] the utopian social theorists with which we are concerned conceived of man as an artificer.

The tendency in the secondary literature to refer to the milennium as a utopian condition emanates from the ambiguity of both terms. However, scholars such as Capp and Davis have had reason to distinguish these terms rather more precisely by effecting operational definitions of each. Davis, for instance, is categorical in asserting that 'the distinctions between the millenarian and utopian are clear and necessary. The millenarian scarcely concerns himself with the details of a society which is coming. Since it is inevitable such a concern would be irrelevant'.[94] Similarly, Capp defines millenarianism as the 'belief in a perfect society to be established through divine intervention,[95] and distinguishes this specific form of millenarianism from that utopianism which envisages 'a perfect society to be created by man's unaided efforts'.[96] By implication, Capp alludes to the institutional facet of utopianism, a criterion emphasized by Davis who argues that 'institutional perfection is to be won by men's efforts and decisions and not by the actions of a *deus ex machina*'.[97]

The foregoing categorization does not preclude the possibility of utopian social theory correlating to some degree with apocalyptic ideas or millenarianism of a more ubiquitous and spiritual form. However, in this sense 'millenarianism' is one among a number of factors influencing the system of thought informing a utopia. Should millenarianism be the predominant influence, utopianism as a means of expressing prescriptive social theory is no longer reconcilable to such a system of thought. It is, therefore, incorrect to assume that millenarians are prone to utopianism of whatever form. Only by advancing stipulative operational definitions can the necessary clarity be attained for analysing the social theory of the early modern period.

5

As is intimated above, the ambiguity of a concept does not preclude the possibility of a particular definition being stipulated in order that the term be operationalized. The range of unit criteria discernible within the concept of utopianism and the array of possible permutations and orderings that these criteria might yield suggests that the analysis of particular utopian works requires and is facilitated by an adherence to an operational definition. Quite obviously, therefore, definitions will differ according to various circumstances. We are now in a position to provide a definition of utopianism appropriate to the analysis of the social theory of writers such as More and Winstanley.

In this study I take utopianism to be (i) a literary but non-fictional medium which (ii) defers to 'reality' in the sense of the prevailing worldview and circumstances of the human condition, and which (iii) proposes to amend these conditions by institutional means so far as that is feasibly possible in order to (iv) attain an ideal.

In positing the first of these criteria, that utopianism is a literary device, the implication is not that the concept represents an inappropriate medium for the articulation of social ideas. Instead, the emphasis is upon the institutional malleability afforded by the utopian genre rather than upon any inclination to fictional fantasy. While social utopias may depict the 'perfection' of a new order, it is reasonable to anticipate that such idealism will be constrained by an appreciation of the limitations of human potential, which is in turn likely to be contextually informed. Thus utopian social theory affords scope for the critique of existing society and for proposing what may often be a quite radical programme of reform.

The understanding that utopianism is a literary device employed within the context of one society for the contemplation of an as yet imaginary society, has encouraged pejorative impressions of the concept's utility. Such assumptions can only be confounded if an operational definition incorporates the contention that utopian social theory must not significantly diminish the pervasiveness of existing circumstances. Ironically, such 'realistic' utopianism is often rejected as insufficiently 'utopian'.[98] However, such realism affords the differentiation of this strand of utopianism, which might often be characterized by its detailed institutional analysis, from the indiscriminate use of the term 'utopian' to denote schemes which are the product of imaginary fancy or those which envisage social harmony or the resolution of scarcity as being effected by means of the transformation of human nature. The most pertinent aspect of this operational definition is, then, the emphasis placed upon organizational and institutional reform.

According to our operational definition, utopianism is a literary device, respecting contemporary appreciations of reality, and is primarily concerned in the first instance with institutional as opposed to moral reformation. On this account a utopia, although predicating an ideal society, need not be conceived as an end in itself. In this sense, utopianism is as much instrumental and prescriptive as it is descriptive. Hence the stipulation that utopianism may aspire to the attainment of an end or ends, but that these objectives are contingent. Utopias may be devised with specific ends in mind but, with respect to the definition of the concept, those ends assume the status of variables. Whereas it is impractical and unnecessary to specify the precise form of the ends postulated by a social utopia, it is possible to assert that such a work must propose the institutional means of realizing its particular ends.

The Fall of Man and the status of property

1

In what remains an important contribution to the understanding of the thought of the era, W.H. Greenleaf claims that 'during the early-modern period it was of course axiomatic that humanity had been corrupted by the Fall'.[99] As a theme of theological doctrine, philosophical enquiry, and basic relief, the idea of the 'Fall of Man' was indeed pervasive; but the notion afforded scope for considerable variation. Not only did the early modern period witness a shift of attitude according to which consideration of the Fall was significantly amended, but the appraisal of specific issues, such as the evaluation of political obligation or property theory, also underwent change. While, therefore, it is possible to identify certain general considerations extending from the idea of the Fall, it would be a mistake to assume that thinking on these matters remained consistent throughout the period. Theorists such as More and Winstanley, who proposed via the medium of a utopia the reform of social institutions, could hardly be anything but profoundly influenced by the notion of the Fall. An appreciation, however, of the manner in which the perception of the Fall changed through the early modern period affords a crucial insight into why and how the social thought of thinkers so set apart in time as More and Winstanley should exhibit shared presuppositions yet should differ in terms of proposals for the amelioration of the human condition.

The early modern period is one in which a particularly abject apprehension of the doctrine of the Fall gradually ceased to exercise its hold on the contemporary mentality. Prior to this, as biblical accounts were successively reinforced by St Paul, St Augustine, and latterly Calvin, the doctrine of original sin was sharpened. Medieval appreciations of the Fall represent an apogee in that the prevalent social formations of the time and the doctrine itself were undoubtedly mutually reinforcing. The *casual nexuses* informing the breakdown of this worldview are far from easy to differentiate, but what is evident is that during the early modern period movement of opinion among contemporary commentators concerning how the institutional manifestations of the Fall were to apply and be justified was rapid. Given the quite remarkable explanatory facility of the idea of the Fall, so fundamental an amendment of opinion must be seen as constituting one of the great realignments of the Western intellectual outlook.

The explanatory force of the idea of the Fall was substantial. Even in the hands of relatively unsophisticated thinkers the notion could be used not merely to account for existing circumstances but also to posit the continuation of such a state of affairs to the extent that the idea of the 'Fall of Man' satisfies certain criteria of the intellectual paradigm. Thus, either explicitly or implicitly, much of the literature and social thought of the period defers to the idea of the Fall. This needs to be explained.

Essentially, the story of the Fall was capable of providing a rationale for the far from perfect condition of everyday life and (under elaboration with regard to science, ethics, and the dicussion of material circumstances) of sustaining a prognosis for the future consistent with the appraisal of the present. Thus, the perceived shortcomings of the human predicament could not be dismissed as an aberration. Fundamental to the explanatory power of the doctrine was the facility of particularly the Augustinian conception of the Fall to come to terms with the problem of evil. The notion of the congenital corruption of Man was devastatingly influential. According to this view, Man is not only responsible for the introduction of evil into the world and for the ruination of his own character, but that very defect is taken as indicating that evil must and will continue. It is this tight circle that much of the thought of the Enlightenment period attempted to penetrate. In conjunction with the interpretation of Christ's Passion, the idea of the Fall could be exercised to reconcile men to the limitations of their predicament without thereby suggesting that human existence is purposeless. Furthermore, under elaboration, the theory could be developed to afford an analysis of the institutional fabric intricate enough to sustain an ambivalent appreciation of the state, the family, private property, and so on—one which viewed these arrangements as necessary but unpleasant constraints upon human freedom. These are issues that any utopian theorist was obliged to address.

It is worth noting in passing, although this is not the main purpose of this section, that viewed philosophically the doctrine of the Fall was not without its shortcomings. These pertain especially to the question of causation and to the problem of identifying the nature and intentions of the God-as-Creator who presumably anticipated Man's potential to commit the original sin. It will suffice at this stage to point out that, on occasions when the doctrine proved philosophically troublesome, its explanatory force was not necessarily diminished. Doctrinal elaboration upon the themes of faith and divine grace invariably proved more than sufficient to sustain the overall coherence of the idea of the Fall.

2

Historians of thought are often appropriately wary of speculating upon the intellectual disposition of past eras, the so-called 'spirit of the age'. With respect, however, to the early modern period there is undoubted justification in taking a lead from contemporaries who alluded to their situation with reference to the Fall, thereby proffering a pessimistic assessment. In the words of one scholar, Charles Webster, 'meditation on the Fall and the corruption of human nature had come to preclude any thought of regeneration, which seemed too distant to bear thinking about'.[100] Similarly, Christopher Hill believes that the idea of the Fall 'not only testifies to the existence of a happier condition before the introduction of private property and the state, but also shows that man is too sinful to maintain such a condition on earth'.[101] Such, indeed was the success of the theory in reconciling men to their predicament that it undoubtedly contributed to the helplessness and despair that were commonplace.[102] So, belief that the consequences of the Fall were ineradicable encouraged the conviction that any significant improvement in mankind's earthly condition was unlikely. As long as such assumptions endured, self-confidence remained understandably restrained.

3

An important aspect of the theory of the Fall is the considerable time and effort expended in speculation on the form of the original condition and on the consequences of its passing.[103] The attendent mythologies of Paradise, the Golden Age and Arcadia need not detain us here. Of greater importance, particularly in analysing social theory informed by the idea of the Fall, is the concern to differentiate between the 'natural' and the 'conventional'. Patristic thought identified the pre-lapsarian condition with the state of nature,[104] but as the demand for theoretical sophistication grew a distinction between the unfallen and thereby natural original condition and the fallen and thereby conventional societal arrangements became less tenable. In part, such amivalence was inspired by the consideration that, although the loss of the original condition was to be bemoaned, Christ's Passion implied the possibility of a form of recovery.[105]

With the reception of Aristotelianism medieval thought assumed what was often an ambiguous attitude to the identity of the natural and the conventional. This is particularly true of medieval assessments of private ownership,[106] and of the developing concern to locate the origins and to stipulate conditions for the legitimacy of government. In time, although the tendency remained to regard those conditions obtaining before the Fall as 'natural', it was not necessarily the case that that situation was equated with the state of nature. This was evident once contract theory had emerged as an advanced medium for the analysis of political ideas, especially if such contractarianism drew upon the natural law tradition. Further complication was occasioned by the consideration that the state of nature could assume a historical and/or deductionist form.[107] The contractarianism of Thomas Hobbes may be read in either of these ways, although it is interesting to note that Hobbes attributes the insecurity of the state of nature, upon which a good deal turns, to mortality occasioned by the original sin.[108]

Developments within the natural law tradition, especially those influenced by the recovery of Aristotle, led to an increased questioning of the belief that the institutional arrangements of the fallen condition must be entirely conventional. Thus, even given the constraints imposed upon the human condition by the fact of the Fall, social philosophy began to turn to the idea that elements of the natural and the good might be incorporated into institutional arrangements. The emergence of political ideas which drew upon the notion of 'natural rights' set in motion a trend which eventually contributed to the questioning of the very notion that the Fall represented a constraint upon what might be achieved politically. Part of the significance of the utopian political thought examined below is that both More and Winstanley addressed the issue of social reform in a manner which reflects a concern not only to distinguish the natural and the recoverable from the sphere of the conventional, but also to examine the question of whether criteria exist in the light of which conventional institutions (both actual and proposed) might be assessed.

4

A powerful motif regularly discussed in association with the theory and imagery of the Fall is the notion of the 'dominion over nature'. This complex theme brings together the suppositions that as a consequence of the Fall the natural realm had become less amenable to Man's will, and that a desire to understand the workings of nature would bode ill because such enquiry reproduced the curiosity about knowledge of a specifically prohibited kind that originally occasioned the Fall. Thus, in a mutually reinforcing manner, the belief that enquiry into the workings of the environment should not be strenuously pursued sustained the conviction that the natural world represented a hostile domain which could not be understood and thereby brought under Man's control. Basil Willey's definition of 'forbidden knowledge' as 'that which presents itself as a distraction or seducement from what is . . . considered the main purpose of life' captures not only the spirit of the fear that 'to study nature was to repeat the original sin of Adam',[109] but also the inference that to demonstrate concern with the natural realm was to neglect the proper purpose of life by tampering with the satanic. The significance of overcoming this appreciation of Man's lowly place in the universe, by postulating that discovering the secrets of nature might promote the alleviation of the human condition, which in turn encouraged a more confident estimation of human potential and the advancement of science, is examined below.[110]

Consideration of the general issue of knowledge, power, and the natural, often led to curiously ambivalent attitudes. For example, it was assumed that, as a corollary of the loss of dominion at the Fall, Man had thenceforth to labour for subsistence. Thus labour came to be regarded as a necessary burden mitigated only by the fact that it could bring some albeit limited relief. It has not gone unnoticed[111] that during the early modern period the spirit of scientific enquiry, which was inspired in part by the desire to improve mankind's earthly circumstances, developed in conjunction with the understanding that a more assertive attitude to work could yield economic benefits.

A similar form of ambivalence is discernible in the widespread assumption that such was the capriciousness of nature that Mankind's earthly circumstances must be susceptible to quite arbitrary turns of fortune. Thus, beliefs and practices of a 'magical' kind are conceivable as an attempt to understand and even to appease the forces of the universe.[112] In effect, although intellectual and popular attitudes influenced by the notion of the Fall often encouraged a climate of pessimism and impotence, they did so without entirely precluding the possibility of a more assertive and confident attitude to knowledge and nature emerging. That a shift in attitude of this kind did indeed occur in the early modern period has an important bearing upon how the respective utopias of More and Winstanley should be read and understood. In the words of Keith Thomas, whose work on these matters is authoritative, 'from the mid-seventeenth century there was an increasing disposition to play down the Fall and to stress, not the decay of nature, but its benevolent design'.[113]

5

During the course of this book we shall have occasion to examine the views of a number of thinkers concerning the relationship between the Fall and the nature and purpose of social institutions. In, at this stage, simply preparing the way, it is necessary to establish that although thinkers such as St Augustine contended that the 'natural' arrangements of the 'pre-lapsarian' situation had been replaced by social institutions maintained by convention, the supposition that 'post-lapsarian' social institutions were necessarily conventional did not go uncontested. By the thirteenth century it was being argued in certain circles that social institutions might well be in some sense 'natural' and thereby sustain aspects of 'the good'. It is also important to establish that the rationale supporting this view introduced into the analysis of the relationship between the Fall and social institutions the possibility of a critique one manifestation of which is utopianism of the kind developed by More and Winstanley.

The notion that Man's sinfulness has introduced a substantial element of chaos into the cosmos inspired the belief that whatever order still pervaded the universe must be at best fragile and continually susceptible to dissolution. The ideal affording perspective to this apprehension was that of an ordered universe regulated by the 'great chain of being',[114] in which various elements, both spiritual and temporal, existed in balanced correspondence within an hierarchical ordering. Hence the understanding that human sinfulness had disrupted the orderly functioning of this system.[115] Social and political unrest was perceived as the most dreaded evidence of the disarray thus precipitated. For this reason the attempt to constrain sin was regarded as prerequisite to the upholding of social order. As Greenleaf suggests, the conviction that paradise could be regained only in heaven meant that contemporaries often subscribed to a view according to which 'a premium was put on the maintenance of the existing social order and . . . any attempt to change it, in the name, for instance, of individual rights and equality, was false, unnatural and sinful'.[116] For this reason, institutions such as the state and private property were often cited as fundamental to the effort to restrain sinfulness.

As we shall subsequently discover, this assumption generated a number of ancillary issues not least of which were, first, that turning upon enquiry as to whether the institutions associated with the restraint of fallen Man enjoyed a natural or a conventional status, and second, the question of whether, as corollaries of 'the curse', such institutions should be regarded as punitive and/or potentially ameliorative. Undoubtedly, contemporaries derived considerable consolation from the supposition that, despite his degeneracy, Man had nevertheless developed a series of social institutions capable of mitigating, if not of eradicating, the situation initiated at the Fall. This appreciation often posited the correlation of political authority and private property; the one sustaining the other in the endeavour to discipline fallen Man.[117]

6

The analysis developed in this book centres upon the contention that the shared concern of More and Winstanley was to propose, through their respective utopian writings, the institutional means of effecting an improvement in men's actions. To understand what this involves requires a grasp of the notion that the interpretation of the 'Fall of Man' and of its implications informed the social philosophies of both More and Winstanley. For both thinkers, the fact of the Fall provided not only a reason for believing that human behaviour required amendation but also the clue to how that objective might be effected. The tradition of associating the idea of the Fall to theories of property provides an insight as to why both More and Winstanley can appropriately be regarded as, in one sense or another, 'utopian communists'.

It is necessary to do some groundwork in establishing the significant role played by the idea of the 'Fall of Man' within the history of property theory.[118] This is a potentially vast topic ripe for scholarly reconsideration. Our own analysis is, however, necessarily fleeting.

The idea of the Fall and its association with social theory has been treated in a number of ways. A.J. Carlyle, for example, stressed the doctrinal links between the Fall and private property:

> The institution of property . . . represents both the fall of man from his primitive innocence, the greed and avarice which refused to recognize the common ownership of things, and also the method by which the blind greed of human nature may be controlled and regulated.[119]

In the view of the Richard Schlatter, however, this doctrinal position also served something of an ideological function:

> The Fall of Man provided the social and political theorists of Christendom with a conservative argument more persuasive and subtle than Aristotle's theory of natural inequality and natural slavery.[120]

In tracing the theoretical origins of the association of the Fall with, in particular, private property and labour, it is evident that no one consistent appreciation prevailed until the early modern period. Indeed, the consideration of the interrelationship of both natural law and convention in attempting to discern a theory capable of legitimizing private property often led to substantial ambivalence of outlook.

Such uncertainty emerged as a function of the complexity of what was at issue. For example, in order to argue that private property *originated* at the Fall it was necessary to offer some appreciation of the system of ownership existing prior to that event and of the form and purpose of the private property introduced at that point. Simply to identify private property as a facet of the curse begged the question of how the curse itself should be interpreted because the restraints imposed upon human conduct by the institutions associated with the curse were liable to be regarded as either necessary burdens or, according to circumstance, potential benefits.

Ambivalence along these lines in turn sustained debate on whether communism had been the natural form of ownership, on whether private property was entirely conventional or might accord with the natural law, and on what the constituents of the argument legitimizing private property might be.

A major concern of Greek political philosophy, one to which we shall return, is the attempt to establish that form of ownership most conducive to developing the virtue of the citizen. As is well understood, the processes by which medieval opinion was influenced by Platonic and Aristotelian thought on these matters often served to confound an already complicated situation. In essence, the recovery of Aristotle enabled a challenge to be mounted to the view that the natural and original condition sustained communism while the corruption of human nature both introduced and required private property. The manner in which this theory of private property was developed and refined, the contribution of Stoic philosophy, the process of embodiment in Roman Law, the role of patristic opinion, and the treatment by Canon lawyers such as Gratian in the *Decretum* of the earlier synthesis effected by St Isidore of Seville, are considered at length elsewhere and cannot be elaborated upon here.[121] The point that needs to be made, however, is that, whereas this line of development established the view that private property was conventional and could be justified in terms of the corruption of human nature, a question remained as to whether all this meant that private property was actually contrary to the *ius naturale*. The contention that the original condition had been characterized by communism seemed to suggest that the *ius naturale* posited usufructory rights rather than anything approximating a fully-fledged right of private ownership. To minds anxious to defend such rights of possession or to curtail the emphasis upon human corruption in providing a rationale for private property, the evident need was to provide an account capable of justifying private ownership in conjunction with a wider concern to establish the case for natural *dominium*.[122] The case for proceeding with caution in moving from the concerns and language of late medieval natural law theorists to seventeenth-century natural rights thinkers is becoming increasingly apparent. However, it remains fair to suggest that the endeavour, instigated in the thirteenth century, to defend as natural and just a conception of private ownership[123] introduced a form of argument, the language of natural rights, that was implicitly to be utilized by Winstanley to attack prevailing conceptions of private ownership.

A key factor in providing for the justification of private property on the grounds that such a form of ownership was at least not contrary to the *ius naturale* was the recovery and utilization of Aristotle's views on the naturalness of private property. Although the extent to which this understanding replaced arguments developed from convention should not be overstated, it is evident that, in the hands particularly of Aquinas, the view gained credence that what had originally been owned in common could, subject to limitation, be owned privately. Thus private property was advocated as natural and, in a sense, 'good'. Even so, the view also persisted that, this notwithstanding, the most perfect state would sustain common ownership. In that the monastic ideal was defended along these lines, the association of private property with at least some understanding of moral degeneracy continued to prevail. Furthermore, and Aquinas was not unaware of this, a position which developed a theory of private ownership from a basis in common use was required to say something of the situation of the needy individual whose plight might be regarded as having in some part been occasioned by the existence of rights of private ownership designed to preclude, at least to some degree, common use. What emerged, as conventionalists such as Duns Scotus were quick to demand, was a notion of private ownership restrained in its extent by the duty of charity to the needy.

At this juncture it is worth making two points in order to relate the foregoing summary to the more immediate concerns of this book. The first is that Aquinas's attempt to provide an account of the natural basis of private ownership did little to reduce the ambivalence pervading consideration of ownership in the light of the Fall. This is because, taken to its conclusion, Aquinas's position appeared capable of being used to justify the state's defence of private property and/or its intervention in support of charitable redistribution to the needy. Thus confusion as to what was natural and what conventional in sustaining property rights remained. It is the absence of any hard differentiation in this respect that enabled More to argue, as circumstances required, both that private property might be sustained by positive law and that, given the neutrality of the *ius naturale*, communism might be advocated as a preferred system of ownership. Second, the attempt to derive a 'natural' theory of private ownership via arguments extended from the initial proposition of common use opened the way to the understanding that the very concept of private ownership required considerable elaboration for that concept to be consistently justified. However, the attempt by seventeenth-century natural rights theorists to provide such conceptual refinement unintentionally opened the way for Winstanley and subsequent radicals to highlight the shortcomings of attempting to justify the exclusive ownership of land in terms of arguments based upon first appropriation.

Such arguments, in the hands of Locke for example, were often based upon an attenuated notion of labour entitlement.[124] This is of significance because, again in association with understandings of the Fall and the curse, labour might be perceived as at once obligatory[125] and remedial. We shall investigate below the manner in which More and Winstanley treated the issue of labour in association with their respective interpretations of the Fall and conceptions of ownership. Beforehand, we conclude this analysis of the impact of the Fall upon early modern political thought by considering the manner in which opinion during the period changed.

7

During the early modern period many writers paid considerable attention to the problem of the Fall and its consequences. However, as time proceeded, thought on these matters did not remain static. Indeed, the estimation in particular of the facility of mankind to achieve an improvement in the circumstances of an earthly existence came in for quite marked revision. This development can be traced by considering the views of three of the most eminent and prolific writers of the period: Richard Hooker (1554–1600), John Milton (1608–74) and John Locke (1632–1704).

Hooker's appraisal typifies a view which enjoyed considerable endorsement at the time—the abject acceptance that Man's ambition and pride had not only contributed to his fall but, as an innate and ineradicable characteristic of human nature, had also perpetuated the woeful consequences of that demise. In a lengthy sermon devoted to this subject, Hooker describes pride as:

> a vice which cleaveth so fast unto the hearts of men, that if we were to strip ourselves of all our faults one by one, we should undoubtedly find it the very last and hardest to put off.[126]

Pride is so maligned for a variety of reasons. The trait is regarded as the ultimate repository of all sinfulness. Through pride Lucifer had fallen, and through it he had induced Man to fall. Manifestations of pride are characteristic of Man's reluctance to reconcile himself to his rightful position in an ordered universe. While humility is constantly counselled, pride remains basic to the human constitution; political ambition and social chaos are its consequences. Hooker here echoes the disposition of the preceding centuries; but, even as he wrote, attitudes in certain circles were changing in a manner that was to become increasingly commonplace as the seventeenth century proceeded.[127]

Few minds were more profoundly stimulated by the imagery of the Fall than Milton's. Clearly, much of Milton's epic poetry deals with the themes of Man's fall and redemption, but concern with the cosmic drama is also a recurrent feature of his social thought. The course of human history, the immediate impact of the civil disorders, and his own traumatic personal life, are all regarded by Milton as typical of the predicament he describes as 'the misery that hath bin since Adam'.[128] Milton argues that God bestowed both reason and the free will with which to exercise it upon Adam.[129] God then confronted Adam with temptation. So long as Adam exercised reason and controlled the will by subduing passion, he derived great merit from his virtuous and abstemious conduct. However, in using these same faculties to commit freely the original sin all such merit was lost. Consequently, contends Milton, it is obvious that Man has only himself to blame for the condition in which, since the time of Adam, he has found himself.

Milton discusses the Fall in terms typical of the assumptions of the age. He insists, for instance, that having been born with the impediments and innate consequences of original sin, all men inevitably lived out their time commiting sin.[130] Given the impossibility of escape from this situation, Man must reconcile himself to it. Milton's assessment of knowledge is similarly circumspect; he describes knowledge as 'that doom which Adam fell into of knowing good and evill, that is to say of knowing good by evill'.[131] Significantly, however, in his evaluation of contract theory, Milton argues that men must subject themselves to the authority of government because they recognize that in their fallen condition the restraints provided by such arrangements are the only viable means of averting chaos.[132] Although Milton's appreciation of the human condition is sobering, he nevertheless counters despair with an expression of hope: 'all which, being lost in Adam, was recover'd with gain by the merits of Christ'.[133]

Locke's evaluation of the 'Fall of Man' accords with changes in the wider worldview, to which his writings were contributory.[134] In particulary, by exploring the implications of the sensationalist epistemology, Locke brings into question an assumption that had conventionally sustained an attitude of self-depreciation—the notion that *responsibility* for the original sin was innately transmitted to all men.[135] Locke accepts that Adam had fallen from a pristine condition of considerable advantage, and by his actions had, on behalf of all men, forfeited earthly bliss and immortality. Yet Locke does not accept that the guilt for Adam's original sin is to be borne by all subsequent generations. Locke's is an essentially just and good God whose righteousness is not commensurate with the view that men are necessarily sinful. Thus Locke is able to postulate that 'though all die in Adam, yet non are truly punished, but for their own deeds'.[136] Furthermore, Locke refrains from assuming that, this being the case, men are nevertheless profuse sinners. Quite obviously, opinion of this kind contributed to a growing optimism concerning the circumstances of human life, an appreciation some distance from the abject image proferred by Hooker.

8

The period of time separating More and Winstanley witnessed an albeit gradual revision of the worldview and of the manner in which Man's predicament was apprehended. The early modern period fostered a remission of the feelings of helplessness generated in part by the prevailing and essentially pessimistic appreciation of the doctrine of the Fall. In assessing this situation E.M.W. Tillyard concludes of the perceptions of the age that 'the Fall . . . was primarily responsible for the tyranny of fortune, and, this being so, man could not shift the blame but must bear his punishment as he can'.[137] At the dawning of the early modern period, in the early sixteenth century, the spirit of the age still very much promoted the passive acceptance of the predicament. The impact, however, of a variety of complex and often related factors, the Reformation, the emergence of a new cosmology. 'Baconianism', 'Cartesianism', empiricism and the sensationalist epistemology, all contributed to and illustrated substantial changes in mental attitudes and the wider perspective on the prospects of human achievement. For Thomas More, such an understanding of the human condition would have been quite incomprehensible; for Winstanley, however, in the reinterpretation of the meaning of the 'Fall of Man' lay the possibility of envisioning an altogether different prognosis for Man.

Part II

2

Thomas More's conception of the human condition

Thomas More's social thought cannot be appreciated other than in the light of his theological and philosophical opinions. One reason for this being the case is that the social and political ideas advanced in *Utopia* reflect the complexities and tensions evident within More's other writings. It is to this body of work, therefore, that we must initially turn. In so doing we commence with a consideration of various intellectual currents which influenced More's thinking. This also provides an opportunity to develop some of the themes introduced in the last section.

Philosophical traditions and the conundrum in More's thought

1

In that it represents More's major contribution to the evaluation of secular institutions, it is appropriate to approach the analysis of *Utopia* by addressing two questions: whether and to what extent More believed that human action would be directed towards the good; and what he understood of the role of social institutions in affecting action. The intellectual tradition or traditions to which More adhered had such a bearing upon *Utopia* that the work is likely to appear complex almost to the point of incoherence to the modern reader versed in the analytic tradition and accustomed to perceiving moral and political philosophy as the repository of 'competing traditions'.[1]

The circumstances informing the composition of his various works provide sufficient evidence to suggest that More was not a systematic thinker in the sense of being a philosopher engaged upon a discernible 'project'. However, More clearly understood himself to be writing within and by recourse to a systematic tradition—one of considerable complexity, yet broadly comprising the synthesis within Christian philosophy of Augustinianism and Aristotelianism. This system was inherently fragile and subject to periodic redefinition. Indeed, the Lutheran schism of More's own time marked an attempt to attain greater coherence at the cost of narrowing the scope of enquiry. Had More himself been a more thoroughgoing Augustinian, *Utopia* would read somewhat more systematically than it does. That this is not the case is largely explicable in terms of More's adherence to a body of thought drawn together from two broad intellectual traditions which, particularly with regard to their respective treatments of human potential, proved ultimately irreconcilable. That More adhered to such a synthesis explains both his resort to utopianism and the analytical shortcomings of that project.

What follows in this section should be read only as a consideration of those aspects of the medieval and early Renaissance engagement in philosophy pertinent to an understanding of More's purposes in writing *Utopia*. Broader issues, recently and currently the subject of scholarly enquiry,[2] are largely neglected.

2

The political problem with which More grappled in *Utopia*, the issue of whether secular affairs might be so ordered as to enhance the possibility of the individual attaining the ultimate good of reconciliation with God, is an aspect of the legacy bestowed by the endeavours of the medieval mind to assimilate Aristotelian philosophy and politics into an understanding of the human condition informed by a psychology traceable to Augustine. More is a fairly typical representative of the tendency to revere classical opinion on ethical matters while remaining wary of the threat posed to established theological doctrine by so philosophizing about ethics. Thus, aspects of classical and particularly of Aristotelian thought were deemed acceptable, whereas others were not.

Essential to the Aristotelian view is a teleology specifying as the purpose of human existence the pursuit, as the good, of happiness in this life. This understanding is itself informed by a neo-Platonic psychology supporting the view that the good is intellectually discernible. Such an identification of knowledge with virtue accords with the belief that to lead the good life is to apprehend the universe by rational means. What is more, such insight is to be attained via universal precepts, of which those of natural justice are a fundamental aspect. This is the background to Aristotle's causal theory of human action,[3] according to which choosing the good turns upon deliberating rationally. On this view, however, behaving badly is to act out of character by failing to deliberate adequately.

Aristotle's theory of free choice presupposes that the attainment of understanding is synonymous with becoming virtuous. Thus, for Aristotle, education and the acquisition of good habits could generate moral rectitude. Engaging in the good life is to be participant in an appropriate context; the family and the *polis* are obvious examples. It is clear, therefore, that Aristotle's view of natural justice readily lends itself to the belief that the institutional sphere is that in which the good is to be attained.

What is of paramount significance here is the consideration that whereas the formal structure of Aristotle's account of moral responsibility, which stresses the 'where it is in our power to act, it is also in our power not to act, and where we can refuse we can also comply'[4] appears to align with Christian conceptions of free choice, the two views are markedly at odds once attention turns to the issue of whether men actually have the *capacity* to fulfil such a requirement. As has been noted, Aristotle's belief that men may attain the good in this life is comparatively modest when set against the Christian conception of the ultimate good.[5] Yet, by the same token, from the Christian point of view the consequences of immorality are far more calamitous than the temporal unhappiness evident to Aristotle. So, even though Aristotle's philosophy contains much that appealed to the medieval mind it was seen then as being crucially at odds with the accepted understanding of Man's ultimate end, and of the prospects for earthly felicity. This, of course, is because medieval pyschology was galvanized by the twin doctrines of the 'Fall of Man' and redemption through the grace of God, and more especially by Augustine's version of these theories.

3

Augustine's account of the Fall is unmitigatingly candid.[6] Man is created good, is spoiled by sin, and may be restored only by the good grace of his Creator. The vexed question of Man's potential to transgress is treated by Augustine as an exemplification of divine providence, and the consequences of transgression are discernible in the resolution of history:

> from the misuse of free will there started a chain of disasters: mankind is led from that original perversion, a kind of corruption at the root, right up to the disaster of the second death, which has no end.[7]

The pride motivating the original transgression also led Adam to compound his offence by failing to seek recompense of God. Evil, construed by Augustine as the absence of goodness, could only thereafter be restored by divine intervention. Man in this respect is impotent; he is subject to divine retribution in a situation recoverable only through grace. This understanding of human potential and psychology, informed as it is by Augustine's belief in the congenital nature of sinfulness and the ineradicable conflict of the flesh and the spirit, did much to sustain an abject appraisal of the human condition which was to persist for centuries to come. On this account, as Man turns to himself and adheres less firmly to the Supreme Being, he becomes estranged from the good, less real and less happy.

Leaving to one side the debates generated within medieval philosophy on, for example, divine illumination and the potential intellect, it is still possible to discern that Augustine bequeathed to the medieval mind an impression of human potential profoundly circumscribed by Man's pride and self-centredness, his distance from God, and his immiseration in an earthly existence flawed by materialism and the quest for power. Thus,

Augustine's solution to the problem of evil is based upon his understanding of the *perversion of the will.*

However diverse the reception of Augustine's thought,[8] the pervasive influence of his indictment of Man is undeniable.[9] It is this outlook that, on the recovery of Aristotelianism, generated a diversity of opinion which extended through More's *Utopia* and beyond. In essence, the point of contention is that whereas Aristotle sees humans as possessing a facility not only to perceive universal values but also to apply these in a social context, the Augustinian view regards Man as so incapacitated as to be incapable of achieving this good without divine grace.[10] While for Plato and Aristotle reason is independently motivating, for Augustine the intellect is moved by the will and the will is defective.[11]

4

As a consequence of the recovery of Aristotelian philosophy in the schools of Western Europe there arose the need to provide an understanding of human action capable of reconciling the view of the philosopher with those supported by established Christian doctrine. At issue was the relationship between reason, the will, and divine grace, a question eventually addressed at some length by, among other thinkers concerned with the social implications of these problems, Thomas More. It is conventionally accepted that the philosophy of Thomas Aquinas represents the epitome of the attempt to construct a synthesis from the Aristotelian pyschology of reason and the medieval conception of the *liberum arbitrium* sustained by the Augustinian psychology of the will. Just how widely the Thomist synthesis was accepted is still a matter for debate, but it is abundantly clear that opinion differed on the question of how action is determined. The tendency among Dominican philosophers was to link freedom with a differentiated conception of reason whereby 'superior reason' is deemed correct, 'inferior reason' is regarded as fallible in the sense of being susceptible to making choices leading to sin, and 'practical reason' is advanced as a basis for a theory of law. Often opposed to this line of thought stood Franciscan opinion, most notably in the work of Scotus and Ockham. Less impressed by Aristotelian theories of action, this tradition links reason with the will, via complex theories of voluntarism, so as to propound an essentially positivist account of law. Asserting the frailty of reason in restraining the will implies not only an overwhelming reliance upon intercessionary grace, but also indicates that the prospects for attaining a moral life in a political context are limited.[12]

Aristotelian accounts of rational action did not simply replace established opinion. It is therefore worth examining Augustine's analysis of the will, not least because the understanding of human nature informing More's *Utopia* is in many respects 'Augustinian'. Augustine's deliberations on free will[13] are formulated in conjunction with his consideration of the origins of evil, his critique of the Stoic interpretation of the 'foreknowledge' of an eternal God, his treatment of the neo-Platonic principle of illumination, and his development of the theory of predestination.

Augustine postulates that happiness is delivery from sin and that this is to be discovered in the perception of truth identifiable as God. Hence the question of whether the will of fallen Man is capable of adhering to the objective of attaining this beatific good. This is turn raises the issue of whether, given the possible occurrence of sin, the bestowal of free will is itself a good, and what is to be construed of God if the endowment of free will disbenefits Man. As is the case with a number of such considerations, Augustine's response here is essentially Platonic. That is to say, he believes free will to be an intermediate good; it is not itself bad but want of its proper use is. The essential issue to which Augustine's analysis moves is that of causation.

If foreknowledge is an attribute of an omnipotent God, is it not the case, as the Stoics held, that such a God has foreknowledge of our sin? Furthermore, if this is so, is it not also the case that, as a corollary of God's very omnipotence, Man's will is entirely in accord with God's will to the effect that sin is necessitated by a God with whom responsibility for evil must reside? Augustine's response is to deny these conjectures by stipulating as an article of faith that God's foreknowledge is consistent with the discretionary will of Man. Men can, after all, meaningfully regret their sinful actions. Here again, Augustine develops an essentially Platonic response to the problem. Good has form; sin, on the other hand, is the absence of good, is the absence of form, is nothingness, and God cannot be instrumental in creating nothingness. Thus Augustine moves to the conclusion that:

> If you try to find the efficient cause of this evil choice, there is none to be found. For nothing causes an evil will, since it is the evil will itself which causes the evil act; and that means that the evil choice is the efficient cause of an evil act, whereas there is no efficient cause of an evil choice; since if anything exists, it either has, or has not, a will.[14]

Whatever the shortcomings of this position it is manifestly clear that the prognosis for Man is not promising. On this account evil is explicitly occasioned by the perverted will. In Augustine's opinion this evident deficiency renders absurd the attempt to identify the efficient cause of evil. All this sustains Augustine's conviction that although men are by free choice fallen, they cannot be redeemed by a similar act of will. Attainment of the good is therefore to be achieved only by the predestined few who are the beneficiaries of God's grace.[15]

The social and political implications of Augustine's appraisal of the will are addressed below. At this stage it is necessary to consider the response to this psychology of the will advanced by Aquinas's treatment of Aristotelian rationalism in the context of his analysis of evil, the will, and divine providence.[16] It is immediately evident that the Thomist position affords far greater scope for the role of the intellect in discerning moral choices. Similarly, Aquinas's portrayal of God is of a Creator who allows evil in order that good may come of it.

From Aristotle, Aquinas takes the premises that natural necessity and liberty of the will are reconcilable, that choice may pertain to means rather than to ultimate ends, and that the will does not desire of necessity what it desires. Crucially, Aquinas differentiates between necessary causes as producing necessary effects and intermediate causes which occasion contingent effects. Thus Aquinas is able to develop a position established upon the contention that while free will is itself caused and is therefore necessary, it is nevertheless merely an intermediary cause productive of contingent effects such as, for example, institutional arrangements. As an intermediary facet of divine providence the will is in principle capable of initiating rationally determined actions. As a fallen and impaired faculty the will is, of course, perfectly likely to fail so to do.

In the opinion of many commentators, Aquinas's achievement was to reinstate an essentially humanistic conception of action, with all that this implies for human potential and for politics. There can be little doubt that, in writing a utopian political treatise, Thomas More was susbstantially influenced by Thomist rationalism. Yet More was not at heart a philosopher; he addressed the human condition from an essentially theological point of view and in so doing drew upon a body of doctrine which did not always demonstrate some of the philosophical incongruities occasioned by the attempt to reconcile Augustinianism and Aristotelianism. It is therefore appropriate to read More as moving between these traditions rather than utilizing a coherent synthesis. Certainly, More was swayed by the continuing influence of Augustinian psychology, a position emphasized by J.B. Korolec, who contends that:

> The most striking feature of the medieval discussions of the freedom of choice is the number of scholars who supported a moderate voluntarism, in contrast to the rationalism of Thomas Aquinas. It was voluntarism which had far the greater influence on the European mind in the second half of the thirteenth century and in the two succeeding centuries.[17]

In that More's assessment of human nature appears to exemplify this tendency it is hardly surprising that, given the indecisiveness of his approach to Augustinian and Thomist secular thought, the meaning of *Utopia* is often less clear than it might be.

5

Augustine's psychology of the will and general denigration of human potential supports an assessment of secular institutions which is to be understood only with reference to his theory of providence and the progress of history.[18] He states: 'God foreknew everything and therefore could not have been unaware that man would sin. It follows that all our assertions about the Holy City must take into account God's foreknowledge and his providential design'.[19] Augustine presents the image of a theocentric universe, ordered by its Creator, but damaged by the disorderly conduct of Man. His view of history is anti-cyclical, catastrophic and apocalyptic. He borrows from the Greeks a rendition of the fate of Man construed as *nemesis*, from the Stoic philosophers the notion of providence, and from

Pauline doctrine the idea of predestination. Comprehending history in this manner complements Augustine's theory of the will to the effect that he is able to regard the affairs of this world and of the secular realm as matters of secondary importance.

Augustine's portrayal of civil institutions as originating in and occasioned by the Fall proved vastly influential for centuries to come. On this account secular institutions serve a dual purpose; they are, as one commentator has it, both 'repressive and remedial'.[20] Institutions such as government, property and slavery emanate both from original sin and divine retribution; they are manifestations of sinfulness yet are prerequisite for the restraint of that very propensity. In effect, while refraining from the total derogation of earthly values, Augustine emphasizes the essential relativism of social rules. In the main these are merely contingent effects; 'a kind of compromise between human wills about the things relevant to mortal life'.[21] Indeed, without the City of God actual institutions may not be informed by any principle of justice whatsoever.[22] Mortal life is a pilgrimage in a hostile land.

6

The assimilation of Aristotelian rationalism by, in particular, Albert the Great and Aquinas, afforded not only a substantially more deliberative account of human action but also the prospect of a more positive role for Man in the social and political spheres. It is said of the synthesis proposed by Aquinas that 'the Augustinian understanding of fallen human nature is used to explain the limitations of Aristotle's arguments, just as the detail of Aristotle often corrects Augustine's generalizations'.[23] Let us take as an example the question of how human happiness is constituted.[24] Here Aquinas regards Aristotle's teleology as defective. For Aquinas perfect happiness is consummate and must consist in nothing other than the vision of the Divine Essence. The happiness attainable in this life is, therefore, constrained by the limitations of Man's natural powers and is thereby imperfect. Even so, Aquinas does not follow Augustine's lead in detailing the corruption and misery of the worldly existence. This, however, raises the question of precisely what degree of moral rectitude Aquinas believed men to be capable of attaining. Much turns upon how assertions such as the following, taken from the opening pages of the *Summa Theologica*, are to be understood:

> there is nothing to stop the same things from being treated by the philosophical sciences when they can be looked at in the light of natural reason and by another science when they are looked at in the light of divine reason.[25]

Under examination is the issue of how much faith Aquinas placed in the capacity of human reason to stimulate actions directed to the good and the extent to which the thinkers who followed him were influenced by the Thomist analysis. Aquinas's rationalism underpinned his conception of law which in turn informed his wider appreciation of social and political philosophy. Law, according to Aquinas, is properly a dictate of reason. Following Aristotle, Aquinas suggests that:

> the intention of every lawgiver is to make good citizens . . . the proper effect of law is to lead its subject to their proper virtue: and since virtue is that which makes its subject good, it follows that the proper effect of law is to make those to whom it is given, good, either simply or in some particular respect.[26]

Following Augustine, Aquinas asserts that the force of law is determined by the justice, construed as the accordance with the rule of reason, of the enactment. A 'law' lacking this attribute is perverse and insubstantial and is law in name only.

Clearly, in evaluating the rationality of the citizen, this theory of law appears to presuppose much. This faculty is termed by Aquinas 'practical reason'. Given that on this account 'the precepts of the natural law are to the practical reason what the first principles of demonstrations are to the speculative reason, because both are self-evident principles',[27] a good deal depends upon the extent to which citizens might be expected to act with requisite prudence as participants in the fulfilment of the eternal law.

Aquinas approaches this problem with reference to the distinction between speculative and practical reason postulated in Aristotle's *Physics*. Whereas speculative reason addresses universals which are necessarily true, practical reason pertains to the human domain of contingent truth. Thus the endeavour of practical reason to apply universal precepts in particular situations is susceptible to defective enactment. In locating the potentiality of human reason within a fourfold gradation of law (eternal, divine, natural, and positive), Aquinas attempts to accommodate both Aristotelian rationality and the Augustinian emphasis upon human fallibility. Thus although men may attempt to regulate their lives in accordance with the natural law, they will not do so unerringly:

> Consquently, we must say that the natural law, as to the first common principles, is the same for all, both as to rectitude and as to knowledge. But as to certain more particular aspects, which are conclusions, as it were, of those common principles, it is the same for all in the majority of cases, both as to rectitude and as to knowledge; and yet in some few cases it may fail . . .[28]

The number of such precepts specified are few; self-preservation and human sociability are mentioned. Other than these, the quality and content of positive law will depend upon the extent to which men's natural aptitude for virtue is trained via education and disciplined by law.

An insight into Aquinas's position is afforded by his treatment of property.[29] Here Aquinas holds that although that natural law prescribes the free and equal access to property, this does not preclude the introduction under positive law, for reasons of mutual convenience, of forms of private ownership, except in so far as those forms are not to be so exclusive as to override the rationale of 'reasonable use'. Hence, he argues, the possession of all things in common and universal freedom [is] said to be of the natural law, because, namely, the distinction of possessions and slavery [was] not brought in by nature, but devised by human reason for the benefit of human life.[30]

For the thinkers who followed Aquinas the Thomist synthesis posed a profound problem and it is this dilemma which pervades More's *Utopia*. While, ideally, men may exercise reason in accordance with the natural law, in proposing modes of government, education, ownership and so on, there remains the problem that human nature is flawed by the Fall in such a way that, even on Aquinas's account of the intellect, reason may fail to restrain the wanton will. In this respect it is the view of one critic of Thomism that even for Aquinas the central experience of human life is the recognition of Man's inability to live by the natural law.[31]

7

The detailed analysis of More's *Utopia* developed below suggests that More's social philosophy is informed by the conundrum that developed within the corpus of medieval philosophy as the issue of Man's rationality and moral capacity was addressed in light of the doctrine of the 'Fall of Man' and of the reception of Aristotelianism and particularly of the *Nicomachean Ethics*. The question of whether the Aristotelian account of action, and particularly the ethical and political corollaries of that account, should be regarded as viable, is one with which More grappled rather than one which he resolved. This is in part because of the reluctance, demonstrated in his theological speculations, to adopt a thoroughgoing voluntarism. This notwithstanding, More remained deeply sceptical of the facility of human rationality to promote the effort of will necessary for the institution of the good society. *Utopia* is, therefore an exercise in speculative rationalism and theological pessism.

That this is the case should not be particularly surprising. More wrote at a time when what has been termed the 'clerical paradigm'[32] informing the medieval view was on the point of disintegrating, to be replaced by a variety of perspectives some of which avowedly adhered to Aristotelian ethics. Others, such as the view promoted by Luther and Melanchthon, did not.[33] More's theology, examined below, is a body of work produced under pressure from the philosophical cross-currents of the age. Equally, *Utopia* reads as the work of a mind unable to decide between the case for seeing social institutions as originating immutably with the Fall and that for promoting a programme of reform inspired by Aristotelian naturalism.[34]

More's theology

1

In analysing More's theology it is necessary to take cognizance of the fact that his writings fall into three more or less distinct periods: first an essentially speculative phase in which More mused upon the human predicament and allowed himself a certain degree of latitude in proposing a solution to it (it was in this period that *Utopia* was composed); second, his polemical confrontation with various Protestant reformers; and third a phase substantially constituted by the post-controversial 'Tower works', a series of contemplative studies written at the end of More's life in which he explores many questions concerning Man and Man's redemption that assumed particular pertinence given More's immediate circumstances, and which afford a telling testament to More's mature perception of the human condition.

The evident periodization of More's writing presents certain methodological difficulties once it comes to attempting to discern coherent positions maintained and developed through the disparate situations informing his intellectual career. Quite evidently, the style and intent afforded by respective attitudes of philosophical investigation, polemical confrontation and meditative contemplation might be seen as confirming the elusiveness of the 'true' or consistent More. In particular, the value of the views expressed in More's polemical works in providing an understanding of an earlier work such as *Utopia* might be questioned. However, these writings do provide valuable insights so long as they are used advisedly and indeed selectively. Major works such as the *Response ad Lutherum*, the *Dialogue Concerning Heresies* and the *Confutation of Tyndale's Answer* are characterized by passages of coherent theological argumentation interspersed by what to the modern reader are digressionary (but to the contemporary reader pertinent), phases of vitriolic disputation and posturing. More was not a systemizer, but he did adhere to a more or less coherent body of theological principles. Thus a broad understanding of this outlook is a prerequisite to discerning the import of More's social philosophy.

Undoubtedly More's polemical writings constitute a substantial source for ascertaining his theological opinions. Although a layman, More had established something of a reputation as a theologian. Indeed, he was singled out by both Henry VIII and Cuthbert Tunstal to repulse the Protestant position.[35] The arguments proferred by the reformers on such issues as justification of faith, the salvation of a predestined elect, the reform of religious practices to reduce their ceremonial and sacramental content, and a greater lay participation and scripturalism, all prompted More to produce in reply what constitutes, to say the least, a vehement defence of Catholicism.

While More's polemical response to Protestantism caused him to express certain long-held tenets of his faith, which otherwise he might not have done, it is important to bear in mind that More was often constrained in the terms of debate by his opponents. Forced on to the defensive, More inclined to devices such as rhetoric and the dialogic form to advance what were often unmitigated and extreme assertions.[36] The weight of the responsibility assumed by More took its toll. More's polemical writings are often extremely lengthy expositions of both his and the opposed case, and consequently may have been less effective than a more pithy rejoinder.[37] Even so, once all these factors are taken into consideration More's debates with Luther, Tynedale, Barnes, Fish, Frith, and Saint-German may be profitably utilized in the reconstruction of his theological position.

2

In regard of ecclesiastical matters[38] More's cardinal idea is straightforward: the Church is invested with the Holy Spirit.[39] Christ's Church is the known Catholic Church as exemplified by its historical continuity.[40] Particularly in confronting the Protestant reformers, More betrayed anxiety to establish the case for the Catholic Church being regarded as the one unerring depository of truth amid Man's uncertain predicament. As a corollary, More wonders, 'if the spirit of truth shall dwell in the church for ever, how can the church err in perceiving of the truth'.[41] Further, More maintains that through the Church God bestows a continuing revelation upon Man.[42] Similarly, the workings of the Holy Ghost within the Church stimulate a consensus among Christians.[43] Hence because of his conviction that the congregation of the Church constitutes the whole body of the faithful who through time acknowledge Christ, More cannot conceive of anything other than a universal institution.[44] By insisting that while there is always a prospect that sinners might repent and return to God, More contends that sinners remain members of the Church. This, of course, militates against the Protestant conception of a church composed of the elect only.[45] Indeed, More asserts that only heretics stand outside the Church.

A problem of no little magnitude is encountered in attempting to relate More's ideas concerning the Church to the views expressed in *Utopia*. The absence in Utopia of fully-fledged Catholicism has led some scholars to doubt the seriousness of More's intentions in writing the piece. Even so, the tenets of utopian theology, along with aspects of their ceremonial worship, indicate at least some affinity between the religion of Utopia and More's doctrinal convictions. Indeed, much of what More says on ecclesiastical matters in *Utopia*, some of which is highly rhetorical and ironical, can be seen as an advocacy of the internal reform of contemporary Catholicism, and particularly of clerical conduct. The coming of Protestantism certainly caused More's public statements on formal religion to take a conservative turn. Elements of speculation and even flippancy, discernible in *Utopia*, are no longer to be found. Such a reaction was not untypical among Humanists, many of whom contributed either consciously or inadvertently to the first seeds of both Reformation and Counter-Reformation. Quite evidently, at the time of writing *Utopia* More did not anticipate the dissolution of the universal Church. Consequently, his desire for internal reform prompted him to include in *Utopia* a highly satirical commentary on aspects of contemporary clerical ife.[46] It is hardly surprising, then, that such a critique is considerably more vehement than anything More said on clerical matters once his polemical confrontation with Protestantism had commenced.

The range of his writings indicates that More experienced great difficulty in isolating the precise location of sovereignty within the Church. His inability to clarify the nature of the Church's constitution is not unique in the early sixteenth century. In More's case this uncertainty is explained partly by his more immediate concern than with the locus of authority within that body. More's position on the question of Papal primacy might have remained even less definite had not the issue erupted as a matter of major importance during the course of his political career. The turn of events certainly caused More to clarify his ideas,[47] although his own ultimately perilous position necessitated considerable reticence in the wording of whatever public pronouncements he inclined to make concerning what he seems to have regarded as the undecided question of the Pope's role within the Church. Undoubtedly, as the Reformation developed More inclined, at least so far as the *Responsio ad Lutherum* indicates, to the defence of a restrained Papal authority.[48] Some years later, in a carefully drafted letter to Cromwell, More admits to a shift of position during the period of controversy.[49] Even so, although More's stance on the question of Papal primacy is not unimportant, it seems that in considering the overall question of the authority of the Catholic Church he attached far less significance to this one particular issue than did many within the contemporary political elite.

More's irresolution on issues such as the constitution of the Church should serve to dispel assumptions that his was an absolutely dogmatic theology. Pre-Tridentine Catholicism was often more speculative than is sometimes supposed.[50] The very universality of the Church meant that intellectual disputation was normally internalized. Particularly in the period preceding the Reformation More was party to this mood. This was the spirit in which Erasmus advanced his telling critique of the Church and its roll in society and in which More wrote *Utopia*. In 1516 More was prepared to speculate upon the ideal of the Christian way of life. Such latitude could not be afforded once the confrontation with Protestantism was under way. In looking back upon the last days of albeit faltering doctrinal unity More spoke of Erasmus's *Praise of Folly* and his own *Utopia* with considerable contrition. In view of the events of the intervening period More felt compelled to reply that:

> I wolde not onely my derlynges bokes out myne owne also, helpe to burne them both wyth myne owne handes, rather then folke sholde (though thorow theyr own faute) take any harme of them, seynge that I se them lykely in these days so to do.[51]

This is the statement of a man who, having written an extremely subtle book, came to realize that it had become an anachronism in an age of polemicism. It is a further reminder that More's response to Protestantism should not be construed as the sum total of his theology.

3

The conjectural element of More's pre-Reformation theology is amply illustrated by his discussion in *Utopia* of sacramental worship. By simply comparing Utopian practices to More's avowed views on the sacraments it might be concluded that the two positions differ substantially. According to More, a fundamental property of the Church is its monopoly of the administration of the sacraments.[52] Thus, in contending that, except in cases of deadly sin, repentence should restore the prospect of salvation, More refers to the sacraments as media for the expression of contrition and as instruments of faith.[53] One purpose of sacraments is to

> purge and clense our soules by confession, contricion, and penance, with full purpose of forsakyng from thenseforth, y proude desyres of the deuyll, the greedy couetise of wretched worldly welthe, & the foule affection of the fylthy fleshe . . .[54]

From all this it is evident that More regarded communion with the Catholic Church as a necessary condition for salvation. This should not, however, lead to the rigid conclusion that *Utopia* is devoid of serious discourse occasioned by More's preoccupation with Man's redemption. It can quite legitimately be contended that sacramental worship is a feature of daily life in Utopia. For instance, Utopians are 'shriven' by confessing their sins to the patriarchal head of their household,[55] who is responsible for the general spiritual welfare of the family. The point here is that an observation which in 1516 could appropriately be interpreted as an instance of humanistic concern for lay religiousity (as expressed indeed in the conduct of More's own household) might a decade later be cited as a instance of Reformist advocacy of a priesthood of all believers. This illustration reiterates not only the mutual ancestry of Protestantism and Counter-Reformation, but also the need to distinguish carefully between what More could freely discuss in 1516 and what, as an ardent champion of Catholicism, he would willingly publish in the 1520s and 1530s.

4

Among the points at issue between More and the Protestant reformers, the correct use of scripture loomed large. More's rejection of the principle of solifidianism (of which more below) was one reason for his emphasis upon the continuing revelation informing the oral tradition within the Catholic Church, and particularly the necessity of recourse to the Fathers as a source for scriptural interpretation.[56] In effect, the use to which thinkers such as Winstanley would one day put the Bible epitomizes More's worst fears concerning the consequences of the Protestant emphasis upon *sola scriptura* and individual interpretation on the part of the laity. Hence More's affirmation that scripture and the teachings of the Catholic Church could never contradict one another. More accounts for this concord by arguing not only that the Church is the repository of the written word,[57] but also that the Church is the only infallible interpretative authority concerning scriptural matters.[58] Consequently, More warns of the potential dangers of private interpretation and recommends that the unlearned should look to the help and guidance of the Church if they are to receive a correct understanding of scripture. Towards the end of his life More assumed a decidedly authoritarian stance on this matter, arguing that

> the people may haue euery necessary trewth of scrypture, and euery thynge necessary for them to know, concernynge the saluacyon of theyr soules, trewly taught and preached unto theym, though the corps and bodye of the scrypture be not translated vnto them in theyr mother tonge.[59]

Prior to this More had not been in principle opposed to vernacular translations of the Bible, but had remained adamant that such ventures must be overseen by the Church.[60] More insisted that even for learned men such as himself the Bible could only be comprehended with the interpretative assistance of the Fathers. In essence, More concluded that a concentration upon scripture alone would be insufficient for salvation. An individual must also look to prayer, natural reason, the writings of the Fathers and the ministrations of the Church.[61]

5

More sustains the belief that although God could be known to men by faith and reason,[62] He is ultimately inscrutable in His wisdom.[63] Thus God is not constrained to act in accordance with the limitations of human wisdom, and can therefore perform miracles.[64] Most significantly, God is implacable in his justice and mercy.[65] More argues that these characteristics are evinced by God's judgement of Adam,[66] and will be manifest in the judgement of all men. That all men should suffer the temporal consequences of Adam's maleficence is in accordance with God's justice. However, in His mercy God has provided men with the hope of redemption. Ultimately More regards this prospect of exoneration as an inexplicable mystery. Thus God's mercy is confirmed by the cleansing of men's sinfulness through Christ's passion.[67] Consequently, God punishes men for their sinful conduct rather than for their inheritance of original sin.[68] So, because God would have all men saved, damnation is the result of choices freely made by men themselves.[69]

6

More identified sin as not only an expression of the relationship between Man and God but also as a pervasive aspect of human interaction.[70] The prevalence of both reason and faith as elements of More's theology is confirmed by his assertion that sin results when men lose 'the natural light of reason and the spiritual light of faith'.[71] In order to appreciate the complex juxtaposition of optimism and pessimism in More's view of the human condition, it is necessary to be clear about his differentiation of original sin and act of sinning. In the *Treatise on the Passion* he speaks first of

> the fylth of original synne (with wych euerye manne borne into this world, by natural propagacion, is infected in the vicious sinful stocke, in that we wer all in of Adam . . .[72]

Yet, subsequently, More is to be found arguing that

> no man to be perpetually dampned by sensible feeling of the fyre of hel, for originall synne contracted withoute his witting but onely for actually synne freely committed by hys owne vicious wyl.[73]

Here are certain reminders of the position formerly advanced by Aquinas,[74] although More is perhaps even less convinced of man's natural virtue than Aquinas had been.

More's basic premise is essentially pessimistic. He argues that all men are tainted by original sin. This is a condition into which men are born, it is innate and ineradicable. Nevertheless, in believing that in His mercy God would not punish men for original sin More's theology admits a glimmer of optimism. Yet More offset's this with the cautionary contention that God acts in accordance with retributive justice by punishing men for their actual sins. Further still, More's conception of human nature assumes that men will sin prolifically. But yet again, from this potentially abject assessment of Man's predicament More outlines in *Utopia* plans for a society intended to eradicate a number of the means by which men could express their propensity for sinfulness. So ultimately, More's social theory is characterized by profound ambivalence as to what men might achieve.

More's categorization of a hierarchy of the various forms of sinfulness is an important aspect of his perception of the human condition. He regularly analyses the seven deadly sins of 'pryde, enuy, wrath, and couetice, glotony, slothe and lechyrye'.[75] On such occasions More's prose is invariably graphic. He describes envy for instance as 'the first begotten daughter of pride, begotten in bastardy and incest by the devil, father of them both'.[76] Typically, More's identification of covetousness as the irrational fear of want[77] complements the view expressed in *Utopia* that the sin of covetousness could be stifled only if the grounds of such insecurity were removed. More is quick to point out that covetousness impelled Judas to betray Christ.[78] Similarly, he cites the appetite which drove Eve to partake of the forbidden fruit as the most notorious instance of gluttony.[79] Indeed, such was the extent of More's preoccupation with human sinfulness that he was given to regarding sleep as a form of sloth.[80]

Within this hierarchy of sin, pride predominates. Not surprisingly, digressions upon the subject are common within More's writings.[81] The discussion of pride contained in *Utopia* is quite typical. More states that: 'This serpent from hell entwines itself around the hearts of men and acts like a suckfish preventing and hindering them from entering on a better way of life.'[82] More regards pride as the source of all other sinfulness. He verifies this conclusion both historically, pride being 'the first of all synes, begon among the angels in heauen',[83] and empirically, in his analysis of 'the very head and root of all sins, that is to wit, pride, the mischevous mother of all manner of vice',[84] Pride assumes such consequence in More's theology because he conceives of this sin as that forsaking of God which has led men to succumb to both initial temptation and to the multifarious sinfulness that follows.[85] Thereupon More confidently predicts that 'the person of them that in pride & vanite passid the tyme of his present life, & after that so spent passed hens into hell'.[86] In this context it is interesting to recall that in the Middle Ages humility was emphasized as the basic countervailing Christian virtue.[87] It is apparent, however, that More doubted whether most men could achieve the degree of humility necessary for their salvation. Hence, in *Utopia*, the proposal of a number of institutional bolsters to Man's faltering humility via provision for the subjugation of pride.[88]

More's perception of the human condition is influenced by his acute awareness of the immediate danger to each individual posed by the cosmic battle raged between immanent forces of good and evil. More maintains that 'our enemy the devil constantly prowls like a roaring lion looking everywhere for someone who is ready to fall because of the weakness of the flesh'.[89] More's belief in the pervasive influence of the devil, 'the prince of this world, nor is there any power on earth like him',[90] is obviously germane to his conception of sin and temptation. According to More, to sin is to offend God by succumbing to temptation and thereby wilfully breaking His command to resist such temptation. More also conceives of sin as a condition of bondage into which men might fall.[91] Even so, although Christians can fall into sin, More argues that choices are still available to them. Either men may repent and return to God, or continue to sin and be damned.[92]

These considerations are of relevance to the understanding of More's social theory, for not only did More recognize human sinfulness as the basis of all social evil, but he also believed that existing social institutions presented a continuing temptation which most men were incapable of resisting. In effect, sinful men had established institutions which would only perpetuate the corruption of their own morals. Therefore, most men remained in a state of sin. Further, it seemed to More unlikely that men would extricate themselves from the bondage of sin by repenting of their own volition. As a corollary, men could attain salvation only if temptation were first to be removed. Given this, it was evident to More that social institutions required radical amendation. Consequently, in *Utopia*, More is to be discovered proposing a series of alternative arrangements such as communism which, he hoped, might remove the temptation to sinfulness presented by existing institutions such as private property.

7

The function of faith in the process of salvation was a central issue in the confrontation between More and his Protestant adversaries. In the main the writings of the reformers are heavily imbued with the teachings of St Augustine and thereby argue for the predominance of faith. For More, faith is certainly necessary but could not be sufficient.[93] The ultimate point at issue here is the scope and nature of Man's free will. In pointing to the insufficiency of works in appeasing God, the Protestants regarded as inadmissable the notion that degenerate Man could influence the destiny of his soul. So ultimately the reformers argue that men must reconcile themselves to the fact that the selection of the few, who through no merit of their own could be saved, is predetermined arbitrarily by an omnipotent God.

As Protestant theology, chastened by the misconstruing of this doctrine by anarchist tendencies, took a conservative turn,[94] it came to be concluded that the performance of works was symptomatic of election. It appears that More was largely unaware of this development. Thus he construed the doctrine of justification of faith as a form of antinomianism constituting a prescription for anarchy.[95] By retracing what he took to be the logic of the Protestant case More accused Tyndale of arguing that god was the author of sin by attributing

> our sin to the necessity and constraint of God's ordinance, affirming that we do not sin for ourself by any power of our own will but by the compulsion and handiwork of God. And that we do not the sin ourself, but that God doth the sin in us Himself.[96]

More was equally alarmed by what he took to be Luther's proposition that the elect could never sin. Similarly, again in confronting Tyndale for his 'frantyke heresyes agaynst free wyll',[97] More expresses concern over the apparent political implications of Protestant doctrine.[98] Thus he contends that Protestantism threatens the established correlation between religious ideas and social conduct. More believed that men's actions should always be guided by the assumption that their conduct would influence God's eventual judgement of them. So in an age that dreaded the unleashing of chaos and disorder, More argued that the doctrine of predestination not only presumed upon God's mercy,[99] but also posed the threat of libertinism and anarchy.[100]

For More, faith is certainly prerequisite to works but cannot itself determine the moral worth of the individual's conduct. Thus faith is simply the first stage in a progression towards salvation.[101] Indeed, it is an article of faith for More that men, with their limited powers of comprehension, must accept the seemingly illogical doctrine that God's grace and Man's free will are necessary for salvation.[102] As a corollary, More maintains that Protestant opinions strike at the dignity of man by derogating free will and the performance of good works. Rather typically, by regarding predestination as trap set to lure men to their damnation, More ascribes the concept to the devil.[103] Instead, More affirms that men can in some sense 'choose' to love God,[104] and that 'man may by his free wyl by good endeuoure of hym selfe, be a worker wyth god toward the atteynyng of fayth'.[105] Faith could be a product of the will[106] which, once attained, brings with it God's comfort of a quiet conscience.[107]

8

More's evaluation of human reason extends beyond his theology to his general apprehension of the human condition. This facet of More's thought is characterized by the form of difficulty likely to attend any attempt to appreciate the relationship between reason and the will. More is to be found contending that Man possesses a twofold nature, consisting of the earthly body and the 'reasonable soule'.[108] He thus regards reason as an antidote to the sensuality and sinful inclinations of the fleshly body. However, More also suggests that 'reason' constitutes an absolute standard according to which human conduct, the result of men exercising free will, can be assessed. At this juncture More's thought exhibits its strongest affinities to the natural law tradition. More maintains that when an individual turns away from God by sinning, he must be aware of what he does:

> his wyll fallynge from the followynge of his reason, to the fulfyllyng of his fleshely desyre & beestly luste and deuelysshe appetite, accomplyssheth his detestable dede nat from any lacke of wyt and reason, but thorowe a faute of the frowarde wyll wyttyngly workynge for pleasure agaynste reason.[109]

Yet, conversely, More maintains that the exercising of reason alone is insufficient for men to attain salvation. In order to fulfil their full potential men must also benefit by God's grace and the gift of revelation.[110]

The problem of coming to terms with More's analysis of the human condition is occasioned in large part by his ambivalent conception of reason. On the one hand, More is fully aware that because this faculty has been weakened it had become unlikely that men would use reason to their advantage. More concurs with conventional opinion by believing that Man's reasoning faculties had been radically impaired at the Fall. Thus he contends that in the original condition man's soul had possessed 'three great gyftes, memory, vnderstanding, and wyl'.[111] Originally these faculties funtioned in unison, but as a consequence of the Fall the balance had been disturbed in favour of the will. So actions, determined by the will, could no longer be expected to accord with the dictates of reason, whereas before the Fall man's 'bodies wer far from al filthi tokens of sin. Their sensual partes conformable vnto reason.'[112] Afterwards, 'reason' became hard pressed to restrain the evil inclinations, originating in the sensuality of the body, of men.[113] Even so, on the other hand, More insisted that although it was certainly detrimental, this impediment did not leave men without responsibility for their conduct. Indeed, More argued that reason taught men to provide for their self-preservation once they had been cast out of paradise.[114] For all that, More always remained aware of the frailty of human reason as manifested by its inability to prevail consistently over the will, and through that prevalence to control and restrain action.

More's theology posits an ideal conception of the balance between reason, the will, and faith to the effect that,

> if reason be suffered to run out at riot, and wax over high-hearted and proud, she will not fail to fall in rebellion towards her master's faith. But on the other side, if she be well brought up and well-guided and kept in good temper, she shall never disobey faith, being in her right mind. And therefore let reason be well guided, for surely faith goeth never without her.[115]

Given this, it is possible to approach More's position concerning reason and the guidance afforded by faith and revelation. Throughout *The Confutation of Tyndale's Answer* More contends that it is impossible to reach God through reason alone. He illustrates his argument by suggesting that the reformers had allowed their will to promote their reasoning faculties to the extent that they presumed to advance doctrines which went beyond the revelation embodied in the teachings of the Catholic Church.

9

It is evident that the notion of free will employed within More's theology must be afforded extensive consideration. More claims, for example, that Man's will had been responsible both for the horrible sins that had brought about the Fall,[116] and for the propensity to sinfulness that came to follow.[117] According to More, all human conduct, whether it be sinning and falling from grace or resisting the devil and turning to God, is the result of voluntary choice; 'for there is no such man y doth any suche dede agaynste hys will'.[118] More argues that men must necessarily face the trial of temptation and must resist by the strength of will. Conversely, in assessing mankind's actual predicament More categorically places 'the fawte of hys fall in the frowardnesse of hys owne wyll'.[119] Hence More's contention that it is the individual's own responsibility to seek pardon for and the remission of his sins.[120] More's notion of the spiritual autonomy of the individual is exemplified by the assertion that men defy God through their own wilful malice. Although God desires that salvation of all men, He does not impose redemption upon unwilling malefactors.[121] More effectively summarizes his assessment of the workings of faith, reason and free will in stating:

> he that wyll be conformable and walke with goddes grace, may fynde good cause inoughe to captyue his reason to the belefe and yet nat so great and vrgent causes,

but that he whiche wyll be yll wylled and frowarde, may let grace go, and fynde his selfe cauellacyons prowdely to rest upon his owne reason agaynste the worde of god.[122]

More's discussion of free will indicates an optimism limited in its extent by his impression of the manner in which contemporary men actually exercised their will. Hence More's position has been evaluated by one commentator as displaying 'moderation, scepticism and grudging hope'.[123] More's understanding of free will is relevant to the interpretation of *Utopia*. Given the assumption that, if left to their own devices, individuals are unlikely to exercise their will judiciously (that is, by using it to turn to God and thereby to attain salvation), More posits in *Utopia* a set of social institutions designed to reduce temptation, limit available choices, and channel the will in a requisite direction. The question of whether by living under such constraining institutions individuals nevertheless exercise *free* will is not developed by More to the extent that it might be. This problem is not, of course, unique within the history of political philosophy. Clearly these issues raise difficulties not dissimilar to those posed by Rousseau in *The Social Contract* in suggesting that men might be 'forced' to be free.[124] The essence of More's utopianism is his belief that institutional arrangements could regulate human conduct. It seems that More had reason to believe that to exercise the will in the desired manner, albeit under the constraint of an institutional environment, constitutes a greater good than to allow the will free reign given the inherent perils occasioned by Man's inclination to sin. It is significant that both More and Rousseau resort to the literary device of the lawgiver-legislator as the means of imposing rules which otherwise may not have been voluntarily invented or assumed. Furthermore, both More and Rousseau provide an account of the process by which Man has acquired the capacity for immoral action.[125] Rousseau sees the republican institutionalism of *The Social Contract* as affording an albeit partial and momentary respite from moral torpor. More also has in mind an institutional regime capable of rectifying such a situation in terms of an improvement in human *behaviour*. However, the issue of whether *Utopia* proposes a lifestyle that is of *moral import* is compounded by More's appreciation of human motivation, one facet of which is his understanding of the idea of 'grace'.

10

For a thinker of More's disposition to conceive of an ordered relationship between reason, freedom of the will, faith, grace and meritorious good works is essentially to maintain a comprehensive view of human nature and Man's potential. Thomas Aquinas deals with these issues in addressing himself to the question of whether Man is capable of willing and doing good without the intervention of divine grace.[126] Aquinas's position illustrates the order of difficulty occasioned by the free will issue within medieval philosophy and theology. Aquinas argues that several attitudes are possible, depending on particular conceptions of Man and of the good. Man is fallen; certain of his faculties, including reason, are impaired. Thus human nature may be considered from two perspectives according to whether it is viewed as 'intact' or 'spoiled'. In both cases, believes Aquinas, divine grace is the ultimate prime-mover in Man's performance of actions constituted as morally good. For obvious reasons this is especially so of 'spoiled' human nature. Yet even in this state individuals may autonomously perform good actions proportionate to their potential. For instance, individuals might produce artefacts. However, for men to accomplish the supernatural or transcendant good, divine assistance is required. According to Aquinas, deliberation can never be independent of at least one crucially important causal factor. Ultimately, concludes Aquinas, retracing the stages of the process of deliberation leads to the realization that individuals are motivated to will morally good actions by the inspiration of divine grace. So even in the positive or intact position individuals are not absolutely self-sufficient moral agents. Human nature has to be complemented by divine grace if men are to be capable of performing virtuous actions.

In his own analysis of these considerations, More argues that God's grace is a unified phenomenon. However, in order that it be bestowed or put into effect, the process of *preuencyon*,[127] 'grace' is subdivided along the following lines.[128] *Gratia gratum faciens* is the grace by which the individual becomes acceptable to God. *Gratia praeueniens* is the grace by which God instigates the individual's facility to do good. *Gratia cooperans* is crucially important, being the grace by which God and individuals work together. *Gratia subsequens* is granted for the individual's good use of the foregoing grace. Finally, *gratia consummans*, the final grace, completes the sequences by which Man attains perfection.[129]

More deals with the problems associated with the initiation and the precise moment of choice to perform the good by invoking the doctrine of *preuencyon*. In this sense, grace assumes an anticipatory function by predisposing men to turn to God. Thus, it seems that men are incapable of wholly autonomous virtuous sentiments. At the very least, some minimal divine assistance is always required. Nevertheless, More is anxious to assert that in bestowing faith and grace God is concerned not to detract from Man's meritorious potential.[130] The manner in which More reconciles these two conditions, namely *preuencyon* as grace anticipating the individual's moral actions and the actual merit attending those actions, might well be regarded as one of the least satisfactory aspects of his entire understanding of human potential. Logical or causal clarity and doctrinal truth are not always easily accommodated. This is especially true of passages in which More explains,

> when men endeuoure them selue towarde so good a thynge they maye then make them selfe sure, that God have preuented theym wyth hys grace, for elles they could not so so . . .[131]

According to this apprehension, then, the attainment of grace and virtue, and the performance of moral action, is evidently the result of a willing co-operation between Man and God. So although God desires Man's salvation this is not to be effected without Man's willing conversion, which in turn requires 'preuencyon and concurraunt helpe of goddes especyall grace'.[132] God's grace also 'preuenteth our good workes'[133] and ensures that good people are capable of resisting the temptations of worldly life.

The doctrine of *preuencyon* must be seen in the light of other tenets upon which More reveals himself as absolutely insistent—the view that reason can incline the will to co-operate with God's grace, the belief that faith can be infused as a result of such co-operation, and the conviction that the receipt or the rejection of God's grace is always left to the discretion of the individual.[134] This emphasis upon co-operation as an exercise of will is evident in More's assertion that even an individual who enjoys God's grace should continue to will to co-operate with God because 'the spyryte dwelleth in hym and helpeth hym to contynue such as longe as the mans wyll by the applyenge of hys owne wyll contynue with the spyryte'.[135] Given all this, it is perhaps not surprising that the Protestant reformers felt easier with a position which elevated the role of God's grace to the extent that their perception of individual free will was somewhat derisory. Not so More, who in reply continued to assert that although faith is certainly a gift from God, its bestowal is not entirely dependent upon God's grace, but is also to be attained by an element of individual endeavour.[136] Thus, according to More, grace must be earned through merit; turning to God is an act of labour.[137] Individuals must submit their will to God's will by praying for grace.[138] The problem, of course, is that More is obliged to uphold the view that none of this is possible without the initial impetus provided by the availability of grace in the form of *preuencyon*. God remains omnipotent, just and merciful, Man his dignified and meritorious servant and dependant.

In general, thinkers such as More, who are concerned by the problem posed by the relationship between grace and freedom of the will, seem happier arguing from the counterfactual by contending that individuals have discretion to do other than accept grace. This is quite probably explained by the consideration that the counterfactual affords greater scope for stressing the autonomy and responsibility of the individual.[139]

In response to the reformers, who emphasized the omnipotence of divine grace, More regularly stressed that Man's free will must be of considerable consequence simply because it is obvious that individuals actually *defy* God by deliberately choosing to sin, thus falling from grace.[140] Similarly, More stresses that an act of repentance must be a deliberate choice determined by the will. However, at this juncture the whole problem of individual autonomy re-emerges. In discussing 'the health-giving grace of repentance',[141] More asserts that just as grace is necessary for an individual to resist temptation, some divine assistance is also involved in the act of repentance.[142] Again, in discussing the possibility of sinners being 'borne of god agayne by grace thorowe penaunce',[143] More commits himself to the view that men co-operate with God to perform the good. If men choose to respond, they may be called to grace through tribulation and sacramental penance.[144]

11

More's insistence that men must exercise some element of free will is based upon his assertion that salvation is attainable only through merit. With the issue of good works in mind, More believed that by emphasizing the sufficiency of faith for salvation the reformers had made a fundamental error. Again this prompted More to develop his view on the manner in which men must conduct themselves.[145] He discerns that by subscribing to the doctrine of justification by faith an individual might be tempted to complacency and inactivity. Hence More's contention that the mere avoidance of sin is an insufficient basis for salvation. Instead, men must also actively endeavour to do good.[146] The requisite attitude of mind called for both works and faith.[147] More's counsel is therefore that it would be presumptuous for men to trust in God's goodness as the sole means of attaining redemption. The main hope of salvation resided with the individual endeavouring to co-operate with God.[148]

Quite evidently, the performance of good works must presuppose the appropriate disposition of the will. More asserts that in order to avoid pride and the temptings of the devil, works must be carried out in a condition of humility. Pride and humility are seen as quite antithetical bents of mind. More argues that just as pride caused Lucifer to be cast out of heaven so humility represents the only means of gaining access thereto.[149] However, a residual difficulty arises: because Man's reason is impaired he is prone to the proud attitude of trusting in the validity of his own works. So More re-emphasizes that humility is the requisite stance for offsetting innate pride and goes on to affirm that should individuals achieve this attitude they will not presume to overestimate the value of their works.[150]

The individual's perception of his own works has been an enduring problem for Christian thought.[151] More seems to have attempted to negotiate this issue by contending that although an individual should never presume to attribute value to his own works, his deeds would make manifest to others his standing as a child of God or of the devil.[152] Thus More concludes that 'good wurkes wrought in fayth, hope, and cheryte, be very profytable towarde obtaynynge of forgyuenesse and getynge reward in heuyn'.[153]

12

One of the most profound aspects of More's view of the human predicament is his sensitivity to the transience of life itself. To More the imminent prospect of death constituted a pervasive facet of the human experience.[154] Hence his belief that the choice between heaven and hell could not fail to impinge on Man's choice of social arrangements. The imagery and stark frankness with which More discusses death is likely to be unpalatable to modern tastes. To take an example: in the poem 'A Ruful Lametacion' More has Elizabeth, the recently deceased wife of Henry VII, address the world from the grave on the themes of death the leveller and the futility of worldly affairs.[155] Similarly, in 'The Four Last Things' More develops the theme of the inevitability of death and also gives vent to his view that the condition of the soul ought to be the primary concern of mortal men. There is here no counsel of comfort: 'thou mayest look upon death, not as a stranger, but as a nigh neighbour'.[156] Preoccupation with the 'dance of death' not only led More to bemoan the possible plight of the soul, but also to dwell upon the physical decomposition of the body.[157] The unpredictability and the suddenness of the time of death prompted More to reiterate the dangers of being caught in deadly sin at the moment of death.[158] More is seldom more evocative in discussing the human condition than in stating:

> Mark this well, for of this thing be very sure, that old and young, man and woman, rich and poor, prince and page, all the while we live in this world we be but prisoners, and be within a sure prison, out of which there can no man escape.[159]

While pondering on the insecurity of life More is thus inclined to infuse his discussion of heaven and hell with a sense of immediacy. It is perhaps in accordance with the spirit of the age that although More often contrasts the joys of heaven with the pains of hell, he tends to dwell upon the latter.[160] More is resolute in repeatedly warning that judgement waits all men. While hell will be the lot of those who live their lives in sin[161] grace remains available to all. This is the basis of More's assurance that 'there is no dampnacyon vnto them that be in Chryste Iesu'.[162] The fate of the individual soul is the direct result of how the individual chooses to conduct himself during his lifetime. Hence More's rueful observation that 'they that now lye in hell for their wrechid livyng here do now perceve their foly in the more payne they toke here for the lesse pleasures'.[163] (Accordingly, More is ever confident that the heretical Protestant reformers are doomed.)[164]

Within More's theological system the fine calculations that balance sin against eternal reward or punishment, along with his conception of the justice and mercy of God, sustain a fervent belief in the existence of purgatory.[165] Again, the strength of this conviction is indicative of More's concern with the problem of attaining salvation. More contends that because God is just He is committed to the punishment of sin, either in this life in the form of tribulation,[166] or after death in purgatory or hell. However, because God is also merciful, purgatory represents a means of punishing sin without resorting to eternal damnation.[167] More describes the purpose of purgatory as 'abiding and enduring the grievous pains and hot cleansing fire that fretteth and burneth out the rusty spots of our sin, till the mercy of Almighty God . . . vouchsafe to deliver us hence'.[168] Purgatory, argues More, should make an impression upon the living. The righteous should pray and celebrate Mass in order that the dead be relieved of their torment. More further defends the doctrine of purgatory on the grounds that it supplements the prospect of hell as a sanction upon sin and thus upon social conduct.[169]

During the period in which More wrote *Utopia* it is known that he had cause to meditate upon 'whatever is necessary for salvation'. His conclusion, to the effect that whatever had 'been handed down to us in abundance, first of all by Sacred Scripture itself, then by their ancient interpreters, furthermore, by the common practice handed down from the Early Fathers, and finally by the sacred decrees of the Church',[170] constitutes an authoritative pronouncement on this concern. More conceives of salvation as the end to which all human effort ought to be directed. For the individual the question of his own salvation is the great intangible; it is as perilous to presume that one is saved as it is to despair of ever being redeemed.[171] Salvation, More asserts, is attainable only through obedience to God. During the course of a lifetime an individual might have to contend with many tribulations. However, More assures himself that God in His mercy tests men so that they might reflect upon their sins and seek pardon for them.[172] Thus More's conclusion that:

> suche as were good men receyued theyr grace by the fayth and bylyefe of oure savyour that after sholde come, and were by vertue thereof made able to resyste the relyques of orygynall synne and inclynacyons of the flesshe towarde actuall synnes, & ther by were after Crystes passyon saued . . .[173]

The question of mankind's salvation pervaded More's life and writings. In regulating his own affairs he endeavoured to ensure that every other consideration became subservient to salvation. Similarly, in his theory and consideration of the human condition More identifies Man's redemption as the central concern. More maintains that the predicament incurred as a consequence of the Fall is essentially permanent. In directing his political thought to the problems posed by such a situation More arrives at two broad conclusions: first, that institutions should be arranged in such a manner as to ease the burden imposed upon men by their predicament; second, that the organization of the polity and the regulation of Man's earthly conduct would directly affect the salvation of souls. Hence the significance of works such as *Utopia*.

The Fall and the human predicament

1

More's view of the original condition constitutes a facsimile of the situation he understood men to have forever forsaken at the Fall, a position regarded by More as of considerable privilege. As he points out, in the pristine condition Man was not afflicted with death, enjoyed authority over beasts and his own offspring and, most importantly, because reason was able to curtail the will, benefited from the restraint of sensuality.[174] This prerogative was granted on condition that Man should not break God's commandment. Because God had created Man to compensate for the loss of the proud and fallen angels, and because God hoped to prevent Man succumbing to the same sin of pride that had caused Lucifer's downfall, He placed Man in the Garden of Eden. However, as a safeguard, God exacted some measure of obedience from Adam and Eve. Thus, He ordered that they 'be occupied and worke in the keeping of that pleasant garden'.[175] Such unexacting labour was also designed to counter any possible disposition to sloth.[176] So, in paradise as in Utopia, there was an obligation to labour stipulated according to the objective of frustrating the inclination to pride. However, a crucial difference occurs in that in Utopia the duty to labour is underwritten by the need associated with the curse brought about by Man's recalcitrance in complying with the original obligation to God.

In comparison to later versions advanced by thinkers such as Gerrard Winstanley, More's account of the Fall is conventional. More argues that in creating the angels God endowed them with free will so that they might either accept or reject His grace.[177] The fall from heaven of the rebellious Lucifer is thus attributed to the fact that his 'pryde made hym so frantyke, that he boasted that he would be goddes felow in dede'.[178] In looking back upon this event More comments that 'Lucifer, created by God as the most eminent among the angels in heaven, became the worst of the demons after he yielded to the pride which brought about his downfall'.[179]

The banishment of Lucifer, his being cast down to earth, is followed by the creation and placing of Man in the Garden of Eden. These events, according to More, marked the inception of the cosmic battle between good and evil in which the devil was eventually prompted to use the cause of his own ruination, pride, to tempt Man away from God. Astute in his cunning, Lucifer 'would not begyn at the man, whom he perceiued to be wiser and more hard to begyle'.[180] Instead, recognizing that even in the original condition the natural weakness of woman would make her more susceptible to his wily machinations, the devil utilized Eve's pride to initiate the 'Fall of Man'. Eve's pride was essentially manifested by her desire to develop an awareness of the knowledge of good and evil.[181] After giving way to temptation, Eve proceeded to entice Adam to do likewise.[182] In keeping with his overall evaluation of reason and the will, More emphasizes that Adam freely exercised his own will in committing the original sin.[183] Further still, Adam compounded his injudicious conduct by failing to confess to and ask forgiveness of God.[184] As a result of this transgression, and in accordance with God's just nature, divine judgement settled on all men in perpetuity. There can, therefore be little doubt that More regarded the Fall as a momentous event in the history of Man, one superseded only by Christ's Passion.

As the punishments meted out following Adam's original sin were in keeping with the just aspect of God's nature, Christ's Passion exemplifies for More the munificence of God's mercy.[185] The language employed by More to describe the Passion befits his undoubted awe at the inestimable magnitude of this gesture. More is anxious to stress that not only did God offer His son for Man's salvation but also that Christ withstood the enormous tribulations of the Passion, despite the frailties attributable to the human aspect of His nature. More stresses that it is important to be clear that Christ as a man atoned not merely for the sins of all men, but in particular for the original sin of Adam.[186] Crucially, More maintains (especially in the *De Tristitia Christi*) that Christ resisted all temptations to the contrary and, as an act of free will 'wyth hys bytter passion paye the price of our redempcion, and restore the kinde of man vnto thenheritaunce of the kingdom of heauen',[187] paid Man's ransom.[188] More expends considerable energy in expressing constant amazement at the consequences of this act for the vistas of Man's potential. He is quite certain that 'the redempcion of man after his fall was a greater benefite vnto him, then was his creacion'.[189] Although Man had not been restored to the original condition and the situation in this world remained precarious, the possibility of salvation offered the prospect of a condition above and beyond anything previously known in the human experience—eternal life to be enjoyed in heaven.[190] An underlying purpose of More's social thought is, therefore, to examine the precise means by which this end might be attained.

2

Since one purpose of this book is to evaluate the proposals for the amelioration of the human predicament advanced in *Utopia* it is necessary to take into consideration More's thoughts on the consequences of the Fall. Evidently, More recognized that, as a result of the Fall, Man had subsequently to endure a series of inescapable obstacles to the attainment of happiness on earth. In keeping with the essentially Augustinian tone of this account, More conceives of these hindrances as, at one and the same time, obligations with which men are required to comply if they are to secure the best possible earthly condition, circumstances permitting. Thus, an important underlying presupposition of More's thought is the notion that the punishment for original sin should be to some extent remedial. This may be illustrated with reference to a number of examples germane to the reading of *Utopia*.

It has already been noted that More understood that because of the Fall Man is cursed with the need to labour in a manner less congenial than that undertaken in paradise. Consequent upon his injudicious conduct, Man is cast 'oute of that pleasant paradyse, into the wretched earthe'.[191] The cost of being excluded from Eden is that Man has henceforth to endure scarcity and to provide for his own subsistence. Thus More cites Genesis 3:19: 'In the sweate of thy face shalt thou eate thy breade, tyll thou returne agayne into the earth'.[192] It is significant that More's design for a utopian economy aims to minimize this form of work while at the same time responding to scarcity and guaranteeing the subsistence of each individual.

In response to the role played by Eve in the Fall, More argues that it is in accordance with divine justice that women in general should endure not only the pains and sorrows of childbirth, but must also 'be vnder the power of the man, and he shalbe the Lord ouer thee'.[193] Even so, here, without ever attempting to disavow what is seen as an inevitable situation, or indeed to mitigate Man's punishment, More attempts to make the curse more bearable by stressing its remedial facet. Thus a degree of emancipation, especially with regard to education and sexual morality, is proposed in

Utopia.[194] Nevertheless, More remained convinced of what he saw as the inherent inferiority of the female sex.

More asserts that the flesh was wrenched from the control of reason when sensual concupiscence was introduced at the Fall. Hence the need felt by Adam and Eve to hide their nakedness as 'they felt such filthy sensual mocions of concupiscence, ryse and rebell againste reason in theyr fleshe'.[195] Man was now exposed to the prospect of temptation and deadly sin. By contrast, More responds to this situation in *Utopia* by positing a strict moral code which, despite offering little in the way of alleviating personal frustration, is undoubtedly intended to reduce the opportunities for individuals to transgress God's will by succumbing to temptation.

More presses the point that the pre-lapsarian awareness of the knowledge of good and evil, as a consequence of which 'thei lost the good that they had & got but euill alone',[196] had not so much brought about a moral sense as created a considerable debility. This awakened consciousness of evil prompts More to offer a response in *Utopia*. Here the form of religion, the philosophy of pleasure, and the educational system are intended to inculcate a comprehension of virtue.

Finally, More asserts that as the ultimate result of the Fall, men are not only doomed to die but are impressed with the constant awareness of their mortality and of life's afflictions.[197] Again, More is concerned to ameliorate, so far as is possible, the consequences of this fate. The diligent standards of medical care as prescribed in *Utopia*[198] are evidently intended to reduce the distress Man is constrained to endure during his earthly existence. Even so, More admits that in all probability, because death had been introduced at the Fall, most men would endure the wretchedness of anticipating damnation.[199] However, whereas this attitude prevails in contemporary Europe we are assured that, in startling contrast, the Utopians face death with equanimity and are confident of their redemption.[200]

In keeping with the concerns of the present chapter, it is gratifying to discover that More also believed that 'it is worthwhile to pay close attention to the constant revolutions and vicissitudes of the human condition'.[201] Indeed More is to be discovered contending that most facets of the human predicament are ultimately attributable to the Fall. Hence this succinct description of the situation:

> They lost their innocency, and became sinneful: Gods fauour thei lost and fell in his displeasure, his visitacion thei reioysed not, but were afeard to some neare him: eche of them ashamed to beholde the other or them selfe either: al beastes wer at warre with theym, and eche of theym with them selfe, their owne bodies in rebellion and battaile against their soules, thrust out of pleasaunt paradise into the wretched earth, theyr liuing goten with sore sweate, their chyldren born wyth paine. Then hunger, thurst, heate, cold, syckenes sundry and sore. Sure sory looking, for the vnsure time of deathe: and dread after al this, of the feareful fire of hel, with like paine and wretchednes to al theyr ofspring for euer.[202]

It is to this lamentable position that the institutional recommendations of *Utopia* are addressed, not with the intention of affecting an earthly restoration—given his appreciation of Christ's Passion and understanding that redemption could only be attained by means of God's grace, More regarded a restoration on earth as an impossibility—but in the hope of encouraging improvement in human behaviour.

Tudor England as the fallen condition and More's analysis of private property

1

Towards the end of his life More stated that 'no Christian especially, as one who hopes for heaven, should pursue the contemptible glory of this world'.[203] There is no reason to believe that More felt any differently nearly two decades earlier when he wrote *Utopia*. Indeed, commenting in *Utopia* upon the considerable disparity between the teachings of Christ and the prevalent morality of the times, More reflects that 'if all the things which by the perverse morals of men have come to seem odd are to be dropped as unusual and absurd, we must dissemble almost all the doctrines of Christ'.[204] The text goes on to state that:

> The greater part of His teachings are far more different from the morals of mankind than was my discourse. But preachers, crafty men that they are, finding that men grievously disliked to have their morals adjusted to the rule of Christ . . . accommodated His teachings to men's morals as if it were a rule of soft lead that at least in some way or other the two might be made to correspond. By this method I cannot see that they have gained, except that men may be bad in greater comfort.[205]

If, as seems reasonable, it is appropriate to regard More as a thinker genuinely convinced of the fact that corrupt morality sustained the existing social order by effectively repudiating teachings bestowed upon men as a guide to redemption, then a question arises as to how Books I and II of *Utopia* relate to one another. The secondary literature is replete with claims to the effect that Book I was intended to be regarded as an open condemnation of contemporary mores and institutions. Similarly, very many scholars argue that Book II ought to be understood with this view of Book I in mind. However, over the years Morean scholarship has not achieved a consensus as to precisely how Book II is informed by the social critique advanced in Book I. Even a broad agreement in recent years upon the point that Book II was written prior to Book I[206] has not been attended by any decrease in the amount of analysis devoted to the question of whether, and in what manner, Book II should be read as a prescriptive treatise dealing with the issues addressed in Book I. The position of the present study will become evident as our consideration proceeds. First, we must examine More's appraisal of early Tudor society—an impression ascertained in the main from Book I of *Utopia* and reinforced by pieces written at or around the same time as *Utopia*.

2

More's appraisal of the condition of contemporary Christendom is characterized by his inclination to integrate themes. For example, according to More the contemporary nobility not only coveted private property but was also the class which devoted itself to warfare.[207] More also notes that the nobility are impelled by pride to pursue material gain, and on achieving it to flaunt their affluence by openly comparing their situation to the wretchedness of others.[208] Thus More provides an indication of the manner in which the distributive system detailed in Book II would eradicate scarcity by remarking of the contemporary nobility that 'these evil men with insatiable greed have divided up among them all the goods which would have been enough for all the people'.[209] More anticipates Winstanley by contending that even during periods of famine the granaries of the rich will invariably remain well plenished.[210] Predictably, the rich are taunted by the reminder that the acquisition of material goods is seldom a means to a sound conscience.[211] The Utopian distributive system is proferred by contra-distinction to the situation prevalent in Christendom.

During the course of his legal and public careers More gained first-hand insight into the chicanery to which the nobility and gentry often had recourse. Hence his claim that nobles exploited the law and the legal system in order to appropriate property, and to ensure a constant supply of cheap labour.[212] More states in this respect that he can 'see nothing else than a kind of conspiracy of the rich, who were aiming at their own interests under the name and title of the commonwealth'.[213]

A further and fundamental charge levelled against the nobility and gentry is that they are idle in that while living a life of luxury and grandeur and posing a threat to good order they and their retinue fail to perform any productive labour.[214] More also condemns as false pleasures the manner in which the rich utilize their ill-gotten leisure time in hunting, gaming and whoring. Hence his contention that scarce land is often wasted by being devoted to the breeding of game.[215] More, in Book II, expresses the preference that pleasure should be intellectually rather than materially resourced, thereby avoiding the absorption of valuable goods.

The invective against war contained in Book I is an indictment both of the warrior class and of their ethic of chivalry. This critique echoes humanist ideals such as those expressed in works like Erasmus's *The Education of a Christian Prince.* More is adamant in his description of 'war as an activity fit only for beasts yet practised by no kind of beast so constantly as by man'.[216] In this vein a penetrating analysis of martial society is advanced. More warns of the harmful repercussions of warfare upon the general standard of morality; if a state regularly goes to war its people will become accustomed to violence and disdainful of their obligations under the law.[217] Concern over the impoverishment likely to be occasioned by the maintenance of standing armies prompts More to contend that if war becomes a major item of national expenditure, it leads to illicit revenue-raising activities and to corruption of the judiciary, as the state attempts to supplement its income through fines.[218]

3

Although in Book I of *Utopia* More satirizes not only the contemporary state and political elite but also the Church, his criticism of the latter is levelled not so much against the actual institutions of the Church but in the light of an ideal informing the indictment of those occupants of clerical office who manifest a marked propensity to sin. At a time when pious laymen felt increasingly inclined to condemn those members of the clergy who failed to live up to the standards expected of them, More was quite prepared to draw attention to clerical misdemeanours. However, once Protestantism began to pose a threat to the unity of Christendom, More's writings display his willingness to stand as a wholehearted apologist for the clergy. Even so, an essential consistency is sustained by statements to the effect that 'as for vyce, I hold yt myche more dampnable in a spyrytuall person that in a temporal man'.[219]

In one of his most trenchant considerations of these issues, the letter *To a Monk*, More writes with disillusion of the corruption of the clerical ideal. He refers to the infiltration of 'the cunning enemy' (the devil) into the cloister and of the resultant depth of clerical impiety. Hence More warns the clergy to beware of a devil who, 'being God's adversary in all things, he endeavours to make evil of our good works'.[220] In another epistle More also diplays a typically humanistic impatience with clerical educational standards.[221] More is not averse to claiming that many clerics are ignorant even of the scripture but are prompted by pride pretentiously to profess their great learning.[222] Again typically, More accuses the religious orders of being too readily inclined to pursue material gain by, for example, enclosing pasture every bit as rapidly as the laity.[223] This essentially poor opinion of clerical standards is most blatantly evident in More's portrayal in *Utopia* of a friar as a vain and ignorant buffoon.[224]

4

The extent to which More was on occasions quite capable of abstracting himself from his own immediate circumstances, and thereby of facilitating a critical appraisal, is exemplified by his dispassionate assessment of the legal system. As a lawyer who subsequently became Under-Sheriff of the City of London and eventually Lord Chancellor, More was evidently an outstanding legal practitioner of his day. This did not inhibit his adverse reaction to many aspects of contemporary jurisprudence. There is certain evidence to suggest that in his professional capacity More witnessed the onset of a phenomenal expansion in litigation,[225] later to be diagnosed by Winstanley as a major social ailment. For his part More was readily prepared to recognize that lawyers, 'who cleverly manipulate cases and cunningly argue legal points',[226] retained an interest in opposing proposals for the reform of the law and therefore inflicted considerable damage upon the commonwealth.

One obvious area of contention with which the law was increasingly called to adjudicate was that of land use and rights of access. It may be that the impact of the process of enclosure upon Tudor society has been exaggerated,[227] but this, if correct, suggests More's acute sensitivity to the social issues attending the movement to pasturalism. Indeed, possibly the best-known passages in *Utopia* are those dealing with the issue of enclosure; a practice presumably regarded by More as a prime manifestation of covetousness. More somewhat sardonically remarks that 'your sheep, which are usually so tame and so cheaply fed, begin now, according to report, to be so greedy and wild that they devour human beings themselves and devastate and depopulate fields, houses and towns'.[228] In keeping with this awareness of a developing social malaise, More indicates that he was conscious of the first symptoms of a food price rise, the responsibility for which he saw fit to attribute to the greed of a few.[229] Increased prices, More argues, force people to reduce the size of their households and consequently to contribute to the increasing number of vagrants in society.[230] So, in his analysis of contemporary social ills, More expresses concern over what to him appeared to be an almost inevitable and logical progression from eviction, through unemployment, to vagrancy, criminality, theft and ultimately the gallows. Not suprisingly, therefore, great play is made in Book II of *Utopia* of the facility of communalism successfully to counteract these problems.

It is readily apparent that More's insights into the workings of the law must profoundly have affected his conception of crime and punishment. In this respect More notes that because even the death penalty constituted an inadequate deterrent, there had to be some ulterior reason for the increasing number of thieves who appeared before the courts.[231] This raises an interesting point concerning More's analysis of the human condition and his proposals for its amelioration. Clearly, More must have regarded human sinfulness as a quite basic reason for criminality and thereby as a fundamental reason for the increasing numbers of convictions. But this could not constitute the whole story. More must presumably have believed that the evil predisposition of men was becoming ever more manifest because of shortcomings in the institutional structure which was supposed to regulate human conduct. In this context More identifies both idleness and the failure correctly to educate youth as causes of crime,[232] and proceeds via his utopianism to recommend institutional remedies to the punitive practice of contemporary society. He perceives in this manner that it is both unjust and detrimental to the public good to administer 'grievous and terrible punishments for a thief when it would have been much better to provide some means of getting a living'.[233] It is interesting that elsewhere More suggests that one likely explanation of why punishments outweigh the crimes which invoke them is simply that by this means the accumulated wrath of society can be assuaged.[234]

Reading *Utopia* it is possible to arrive at the conclusion that More anticipated by nearly a century the institutional reforms towards which Tudor poor law groped.[235] Here he suggests that in many cases a system of bondage ought to replace capital punishment. This practice, he argues, is more equitable and humane in that it facilitates the restoration of goods, and provides an opportunity for the reform of offenders.[236] Predictably, we are told that this system prevails in Utopia.

More is particularly critical of the failure to differentiate between human life and private property implicit in the implementation of the death penalty for a wide range of offences, and anticipates the direction of much subsequent utilitarian jurisprudence by pointing out that the fear of being executed for crimes against property is an incentive to thieves to kill their victims or witnesses in order to avoid detection. As the law stands, argues More, thieves have nothing to lose by compounding their crimes and turning to murder.[237]

It is very significant, however, that More does not regard the common people merely as unfortunate creatures of a hostile institutional environment. They, too, are fallen. Hence More's assertion that pride constitutes as abominable a sin in the penniless as it does in persons of great estate,[238] and his willingness to castigate the poor for their improvidence because, should the occasional opportunity arise, they too are 'given to ostentatious sumptuousness of dress and to excessive indulgence at table'.[239] In this way More distinguishes the moral standing of the poor from that of the rich only in that the latter class have the means of expressing the propensity to sin more readily available to them.

5

Much of the fame of *Utopia* is attributable to More's exposition of communism.[240] His analysis of private property, therefore, provides a significant insight into the purposes of the utopian discourse. It is worth reminding ourselves at this stage that More's 'theory of property' is discernible only by inference and reconstruction. Nowhere does More provide a conceptual analysis of private ownership. His position on this issue must therefore be derived from what he has to say on the virtues of communism, from the few direct references he makes to the nature and basis of private ownership, and from what it is reasonable to assume his position to be in the light of the intellectual influences and languages to which he was susceptible.

More's conception of private property appears to be informed by two fundamental propositions. First, he argues (in the *Responsio ad Lutherum*) that whatever justification there might be for private ownership must be located essentially in positive law:

> For the law of the gospel does not apportion possessions, nor does reason alone prescribe the forms of determining property, unless reason is attended by an agreement, and this is a public agreement in the common form of mutual commerce, which agreement, either taking root in usage or expressed in writing, is public law.[241]

Second, it seems that although More understood there to be no incontrovertible support for private ownership to be derived from natural law, he did not *necessarily* assume the institution to be contrary to natural law. Even so, despite the apparent moral neutrality of private ownership, More appears certain as to the inadmissability of the institution on the grounds of its representing an institutional expression of corrupt human nature. More's position would, therefore, appear to be as follows. Natural law is neutral as to the most appropriate form of ownership; neither common nor private ownership is ruled out by natural law. Thus, in principle, private ownership may constitute an appropriate institution under which men can live; in practice, however, it cannot. The reason for this is that men are innately and irrevocably fallen and hence destined to use private property to ill effect. This realization informs the injunction to communal ownership exemplified by the lives and practices of Christ and the Apostles, and contained in the Gospels. Thus communism is contrary neither to natural law nor to revelation. It is worth pointing out that this appraisal, if correct, entails the corollary that, in practice, private ownership could not be satisfactorily reconciled to natural law because prior to the Fall communism prevailed whereas thereafter, although private ownership came into being, it was inevitably abused by fallen men. These nuances are not examined by More in any detail. One possible reason for this is that, as a political conservative at heart, More was wary of countenancing attacks upon private ownership that might also extend to political authority. More envisaged that after the Fall, communism could obtain only in relation to the context of a strict and even authoritarian range of civil institutions.

In due course we shall have cause to return to More's contention that private property was founded upon positive law and that, under certain conditions, it could be replaced by communal ownership. However, at this juncture it is worth stressing that More's belief that in actuality only human law and contrivance sustained private property encouraged him to criticize the contemporary prejudice in favour of private ownership.[242] Certainly, it is the case that More readily emphasized the obligations of Christians to obey the jurisdiction upon which private property was founded. Such assertions were inspired by More's apprehension of an anarchical disregard for private property. But it is equally the case that while More advanced this conventional version of political obligation, doing so did not entail the approval of specific laws, such as those pertaining to property, maintained by existing regimes. More's views on the relationship of private property to positive law are therefore in accordance with his support for a *regulated* form of communism. More's contention is that there is neither a basis in the gospels for the *existing distribution of private property*, nor any foundations in reason for such a system. This identification of private property and positive laws accords with More's utopianism in that he was in a position to argue that the institution of a society founded upon communism lay within the scope of human artefact, and that such a system would conform to individual and to divine law.

More's account of the detrimental impact of private property upon morality suggests that he believed, particularly with regard to the post-lapsarian predicament, that communism would fulfil more adequately the intent of natural law. In pointing to the folly of acquisition in a transitory world, More regularly complains of proud and misguided individuals who had made 'their goods their God'.[243] At one point, he states quite clearly that 'worldly goods are either downright harmful, or else by comparison with that one benefit, the merest trifles'.[244] Equally, by further arguing that 'wherever you have private property and all men measure all things by cash values, there is scarcely possible for a commonwealth to have justice or prosperity'.[245] More implies that the abolition of the exchange market would be conducive not only to higher standards or morality, but might also be justified in a more straightfowardly utilitarian sense. He consistently maintains that the general welfare could be promoted only if there first existed an absolute equality of goods. More is certain that individual appropriation not only establishes a juxtaposition of wealth and poverty, in which few actually appear to prosper, but also that the existence of substantial holdings of property impairs the overall prosperity of society.[246] As he ironically comments, 'poverty, which money alone seems to make poor, forthwith would itself dwindle and disappear if money were entirely done away with everywhere'.[247] More is sure that scarcity and need are essentially consequences of inefficient distribution, and to that extent avoidable. Hence the distributive system accredited to the island of Utopia appears as a response to More's assertion that he was 'fully persuaded that no just and even distribution of goods can be made and that no happiness can be found in human affairs unless private property is utterly abolished'.[248]

3
The Utopia of moral conduct

Book II of *Utopia* constitutes Thomas More's proposal for the institutional means of restraining sinful conduct. More's pronouncements on the manner in which an economy ought to be regulated, on the role of communal and familial life in guiding the individual, on the educability of Man, and on a range of spiritual and ethical considerations, amounts to an appraisal of the extent to which social order and spiritual well-being might be attained despite the moral incapacities occasioned by the 'Fall of Man'.

The disposition towards elements of both profound pessimism and relative optimism identifiable within the amalgam of theology and social commentary that constitutes More's 'philosophy' often makes *Utopia* waver between expressions of confidence in and negation of human potential. This disposition is ultimately attributable to More's understanding of the conditions prerequisite to Man's salvation. In that More suspected that the ideal of the reasoning faculties disposing the will to the good would almost invariably be frustrated by the mutually reinforcing shortcomings of moral laxity and social mismanagement, *Utopia* emerges as a work which identifies the essential difficulty of the human predicament without, however, providing a philosophically cogent proposal for its resolution. It is, nevertheless, important to stress that the very manner in which More perceived the essence of the human predicament, that is to say the problem of attaining salvation, necessarily precluded such a proposal. Hence *Utopia* represents a scheme for the regulation of human *conduct* which leaves open the question of whether More truly believed that behaviour of the kind informed by Utopian institutionalism would fully satisfy the prerequisites for salvation.

Communism and the Utopian economy

1

Communism appears as the fundamental institutional recommendation of *Utopia*. The Utopian economy is designed in such a way as to effect the regulation of wants, the accordant satisfaction of demand, and the efficient use of labour, in order to facilitate a 'fair' allotment of goods and spare time among the populace. Nevertheless, many scholars, and in particular those associated with the school of thought which might be termed the 'Catholic Apology', have sought to suggest that More was never anything other than an advocate of the pre-positive natural right to private ownership. Such opinion, which is traceable back to More's sixteenth-century apologists, has more recently been fervently canvassed in association with the beatification (1886) and subsequent canonization (1935) of More and his co-religionist John Fisher. The essence of this appreciation is that More's position accords with the conventional understanding of the role of communal ownership. So it is argued that as a consequence of the inclinations of fallen Man, the restraining influence of private property is evident and was so to More.[1] Thus, communism is elevated as an ideal sustainable only by those few individuals who voluntarily enter religious orders. The traditional Catholic analysis maintains that the mass of men are insufficiently virtuous to maintain such a system.

The position argued below is at variance with the Catholic Apology. As a facet, it will be contended, of his utopianism, More perceived the property regime as being susceptible to institutional amendment, an understanding borne out by More's contention that the foundations of private property lay in positive law.[2] This is of enormous consequence because although More did not deny that the conduct of the citizen should be regulated, he regarded communism, rather than private ownership, as the more appropriate institution for the achievement of this end. Further, communism appeared to possess the additional advantage of being recommended by natural law and by the gospels.

Utilizing an argument similar to the appreciation of utopianism which assumes that the good society is attainable only by regenerate men, the traditional Catholic view holds that the establishment of a communist ideal must depend upon the initial voluntary impetus given to such a regime by virtuous individuals. However, More accepted degenerate human nature as a constant, yet still proposed an alternative institutional fabric founded upon communal ownership. He agreed that only a small minority of righteous individuals might *voluntarily* renounce private property, an understanding which explains his pessimism concerning the autonomous assumption of communism in Christendom.[3] That communism was *imposed* upon the Utopians is not in dispute; we are told that the institution was established in Utopia following the conquest of the island by the lawgiver Utopus. But neither can it be disputed that More conceived of communism as the ideal way of life for Christians. What is at issue is the *means* by which he believed that such a system could be supported. The conventional Catholic case concludes that More believed communism to be sustainable only by a minority of naturally virtuous individuals. It will be suggested below that More held that, once established, communism would in many respects be self-perpetuating because of its capacity to sponsor public virtue and thereby the inclination to sustain the system.

There is, then, an obvious tension between conventional appreciations of the regulatory function of private property and the view that, as a means of establishing social harmony and human felicity,[4] God in fact commended the abolition of private property. Apostolic communism is the most renowned enactment of this decree. In this light it is plausible to believe that after assessing the failure of private property to achieve the objective attributed to it, More dismissed the traditional view and concluded that, contrary to expectations, private property merely encouraged human sinfulness.[5]

More did not regard communism as the forsaken opportunity of a lost golden age, nor merely as a political device designed to correct malfunctions. Instead he conceived of communism as a vehicle for the retrieval of a moral and righteous social order.[6] In this sense it is admissible to suggest that *Utopia* depicts a 'holy' community because the avowal of communism contained therein embodied fundamental Christian virtues such as charity.[7] Indeed, the Christian way of life has appropriately been described as 'the ideological context which explains More's educative, humanistic, and satirical book.[8] A great paradox of *Utopia* would appear to be that this exemplary social order had evidently been achieved without the formal guidance of Christian revelation. The issue of *Utopia*'s rationalism and espousal of natural religion is one to which we shall subsequently turn. Suffice at this point to comment that scholars critical of the inference that More was committed to communal ownership have almost invariably sought to distance More from the suggestion discernible in *Utopia* that religious truths might be deduced by the exercise of pure reason.

2

Much of the meaning of *Utopia* can be determined by analysing the economic system outlined therein. Care and caution is necessary in reconstructing More's position. It is, for example, a mistake to argue, in the manner of Karl Kautsky, that by exploring possibilities for utilizing labour more efficiently More prophesied the socialist ambition of curtailing working hours.[9] This is to miss the stand taken by More against contemporary attitudes to work. Indeed, such was More's assiduousness in anticipating traditional 'Aristotelian' objections to communism,[10] that he was constantly at pains to assert that in the communist economy of Utopia production would be adequate to eradicate scarcity as he understood it. It is at this juncture that the work ethic extolled in *Utopia* plays such an important part in More's argument. A few years after writing *Utopia* More reiterated his attitude to work and labour, arguing that 'surely the things coming of the earth for the necessary sustenance of man, requireth rather the labour of the body than the care of the mind'.[11] This is not to suggest that More excluded mental activity from the category of work and labour, but in *Utopia* he certainly emphasizes an almost universal obligation to obtain subsistence by performing manual labour. In effect, as an alternative to private property and the frenzied delineation of fortune associated with it, More is to be found advocating a system of communism founded upon the obligation to work.[12]

In his account of Utopian history More has the lawgiver Utopus come upon natives blighted by a pronounced distaste for hard work. It is unnecessary to stress that this outlook is reminiscent of More's account of attitudes to work in his own society. Similarly, More affirms that the island of Utopia does not possess an idealized environment but, like England in this respect also, is poorly endowed as regards natural resources.[13] We are told that in Utopia neither the climate nor the land are particularly conducive to agricultural production. In view of these adversities More is thereupon obliged and able to argue that in order to sustain the economy and to compensate for unpropitious natural circumstances, a fairly intensive injection of labour is required. More's resistance to the temptation to endow Utopia with an idealized environment means that the problems associated with Man's struggle for subsistence, given the scarcity of both resources and goods, are addressed with appropriate candour. More does not therefore envisage an environmental panacea in which scarcity and competition between men could be eradicated by abundance. Instead, he concentrates upon proposing a series of institutional reforms designed to optimize the economic situation. For example, More suggests that much of the drudgery could be removed from labour by adhering strictly to the universal obligation to labour, thereby reducing the labour time assigned to any one individual. Thus, More comments, the Utopians do not sustain a socially disparaging attitude to work. Although More appears to have accepted the idea of work being an inevitable curse visited upon fallen men, he nevertheless attempts to avert its worst consequences. This emphasis upon optimizing a situation attended by unpropitious circumstances is very much in keeping with the underlying theme of *Utopia*.

The equitable distribution of labour is a crucial aspect of Utopian economic viability. We are told that Utopia's economy is established primarily upon domestic industry, a factor possibly informed by More's awareness of agricultural underemployment in Tudor England. More is emphatic that all citizens be taught a craft, with the proviso that such occupations be in keeping with the natural needs of the community rather than being responsive to the demands of conspicuous consumption.[14] Women, too, are to learn a trade, albeit performing the lighter tasks. Women are also expected to work by rota in the communal dining halls.[15] In order that none be continually burdened with the type of work identified by More as the hardest form, it is stipulated that each citizen is required to fulfil a minimum two-year period of agricultural labour. Similarly, at harvest time Utopian townsfolk, who after such an initiation would presumably be adequately skilled, provide supplementary agricultural labour. In contrast to the more *ad hoc* market arrangements of contemporary society, the Utopian system is apparently so efficient that crops are usually gathered in one day only.[16]

It is significant that More and Winstanley share a concern to eradicate idleness from the human condition. In Utopia there is no place for such elements of More's own society as the clergy, the rich nobility and gentry, their retainers, 'lusty and sturdy beggars',[17] and members of the legal profession, who must have constituted a substantial proportion of Europeans performing little or no consistent productive labour. In Utopia only five hundred officials and clergy per city are excused manual labour, and even here, in order to set an example, the members of this intellectual and administrative elite invariably labour voluntarily. This universal obligation to contribute to the common good by labouring in some capacity, be it manual or intellectual, is one means by which More responded to potential difficulties concerning communism and the resolution of scarcity.

Given the equitable distribution of work and labour effected in More's ideal commonwealth, it seems that More proposes a working day shorter than the norm for contemporary England. However, a number of factors, particularly the universal obligation to labour,[18] indicate that in Utopia the average number of man hours per annum would probably be greater than that of More's own society. The maximum duration of the working day is six hours, although the satisfaction of production quotas could reduce the demand upon labour time still further.[19] Working days are divided into short bursts of intensive labour. Holidays, held only upon the first and last days of every lunar month, represent a vast reduction from the time 'lost' to economic production in Tudor England. From all this it seems reasonable to conclude that in *Utopia* More intended that citizens should work harder and to greater effect than was generally expected in Tudor society. Of equal significance is More's insistence that despite the fact that all Utopians are compelled to labour none would be constrained to endure the privations of those who shouldered the burden of work in his own society, where, according to More, 'such wretchedness is worse than the lot of slaves'.[20]

There may appear to be a degree of contradiction present in the fact that even though More believed men to be irrevocably fallen and thereby cursed to labour, he nevertheless attempts in *Utopia* to amend attitudes to labour. This is typical of the theme of optimality and the disavowal of abject fatalism which pervades the work. In *Utopia* More seeks to make the best of an ineradicable situation.[21] Even so, labour is depicted as necessary and on occasion even distasteful. The chief function of local officials such as the syphogrants is to remain vigilant against idleness.[22] Hence More's affirmation that in Utopia 'nowhere is there any license to waste time, nowhere any pretext to evade work'.[23] In their annotation to the text, Erasmus and Bude comment on the contrast between this situation and that current in Europe. Christians are implored to emulate the Utopian work ethic. Indeed, More would later comment that in Europe sloth had become so commonplace as to be rarely recognized as a sin at all.[24]

The moral implications of the Utopian work ethic are self-evident. In his account of the Utopian attitude to work, and its distinction from leisure, More renders a crucial insight into what he regards as the achievement to be attained by adopting the practices outlined in the ideal commonwealth. He states that:

> The people in general are easy-going, good tempered, ingenious, and leisure-loving. They patiently do their share of manual labour when occasion demands, though

otherwise they are by no means fond of it. In their devotion to mental study they are unwearied.[25]

This outlook evidently did not prevail in contemporary Europe, where, despite a changing intellectual climate, many noblemen and gentlemen would have regarded the Utopian pleasure of pursuing a humanistic education as an onerous chore.

3

More does not press a distinction between various conceptions of work and labour. It may be the case that because he believed that *all* citizens should contribute to the common good by performing productive labour, More was disinclined to digress at any length upon the relative utility of various forms of work and labour. Certainly, in *Utopia* there is no discrimination posited between the dignity attending manual and mental work. Both are appreciated as contributing to the common weal. Such an ethic might well have been intended to accommodate the ideal of the Christian-humanist serving society by becoming a member of the governing class, yet doing so within the division of labour.[26] Although mental activity is regarded as a fundamental form of pleasure in Utopia it could also constitute work, if undertaken for the benefit of the community, as in the case of government officials fulfilling their duties[27] or of scholars delivering public lectures. The view that in the absence of provisions for personal acquisition More sought to resolve the problem of providing an incentive to work by eradicating the drudgery from labour, would appear accurately to encapsulate More's position.[28] As an alternative incentive to personal gain, More proposes a system which distributes the opportunity to engage in appropriately construed 'pleasure', a reward intended to reconcile the individual to the necessity for hard work.

In the absence of a money economy goods in More's ideal commonwealth are subject to distribution according to 'natural' needs.[29] More does not explore the manifold difficulties that might be occasioned by so seemingly simple an assumption. Instead he asserts what to him appear the evident advantages of such a distributive system. Hence his comments on the eradication of conspicuous consumption and the consequent reduction in the demand upon labour time this might be expected to afford.

More assumes that labour time can be devoted to the production of goods which satisfy the needs rather than the unnatural wants of the community. His analysis of needs and wants is closely related to his views on the role of the Utopian economy in restraining human sinfulness. In that More maintains that as a consequence of the Fall men are constrained to provide for their own subsistence, it is reasonable to assume that this condition would be fulfilled upon needs being met. More's assumption that only in the pre-lapsarian condition were Man's needs and wants identical undoubtedly informs his belief that as a consequence of the Fall men are inclined to pride, covetousness and gluttony and thus are likely to articulate wants above and beyond their natural needs. This differentiation of 'natural needs' and 'unnatural wants' is also an aspect of the philosophy of pleasure which constitutes an important part of the ethical disposition outlined in *Utopia*. Thus the disparity between needs and wants evinced in More's own society is not evident in Utopia. The Utopians despise the gold and jewellery so coveted by Europeans.[30] It seems that as a consequence of restricting the distribution of goods to the satisfaction of needs as opposed to unattenuated wants More believed that an economic system such as that advocated in *Utopia* would contribute both directly and indirectly to the neutralization of Man's propensity to sin.

4

In approaching the scarcity issue and in responding incidentally to opinion which might have remained dubious as to whether a system of communism could deliver sufficient goods, More is to be discovered seeking a balance by regulating Utopian attitudes to both production and demand. Again, in so doing, More's radical utopian stance effects the amendment of contemporary values. This is certainly not an achievement destined to advocate, as one commentator has it, 'a mercantilist paradise'.[31] Nor is there evidence in *Utopia* of a scheme designed to attain such abundance that More's ambitions were to sponsor a commonwealth close to 'the higher phase of communist society'.[32] Indeed, even thinkers such as Karl Kautsky and A.L. Morton have on occasion been obliged to comment upon the unusual frugality of life in Utopia. This somewhat confounds the case for regarding the work as presaging many elements of modern socialist thought.[33] More defends his advocacy of communism by contending that private property militates against general prosperity, and by remarking that within the Utopian economy 'though no man has anything, yet all are rich'.[34] Thus we are told that Utopia is capable, for example, of producing a surplus of agricultural goods for use either in compensating for harvest failures or for export.[35]

More advocates a work ethic structured to ensure an adequate supply of labour, a provision intended to go part of the way towards meeting the demands upon the commonwealth's productive capacity. Other means by which More seeks to resolve the scarcity problem include the needs-orientated distributive system, and in particular the abstemious nature of Utopian patterns of consumption. Hence More's assertion that in Utopia 'they are all busied with useful trades and are satisfied with fewer products from them'.[36] More suggests that an excess of productive labour over consumption might result in an abundance of commodities; more, that is, than would be required to satisfy natural needs. Communism, More maintains, by guaranteeing the satisfaction of demand originating in needs, could eradicate such fear of want that generates unreasonable accumulation. By emphasizing communal welfare rather than the particular interests of the individual, More advances a radically different conception of prosperity from that current in the prevailing system of private ownership. Thus More cites the physical health of the Utopian people as testimony to their genuine prosperity,[37] a form of well-being differentiated from contemporary conceptions by virtue by its emphasis upon communal interests reflecting 'natural' gratification rather than selfishness and distorted wants. Similarly, More is able to recommend the sturdiness and utility of Utopian buildings in which glass is apparently commonplace, yet relate this to the needs of shelter and warmth.[38] It is important to recognize that, while More regarded social conditioning as a factor in sustaining unwholesome wants and expectations, he could never by any means absolve Man from a substantial degree of direct and indirect culpability in maintaining what he perceived as illegitimate patterns of ownership and consumption. Thus More saw avarice and greed as both cause and consequence of the fear of want; a disposition which he believed to be substantially rooted in Man's innate pride. Realizing that this trait might ultimately find expression in conspicuous consumption, More remained resolute: 'this latter vice can have no place at all in the Utopian scheme of things'.[39] It is, therefore, one purpose of Utopian institutionalism to stifle such tendencies. By concentrating directly upon the prosperity of the common weal, rather than upon that of the individual citizen conceived independently of civil society as a whole, More clearly hoped to convince that economic structures which benefited society in general would best secure the interests of the individual citizen.

5

More contends that the principles of distribution described in Utopia accord with the dictates of reason.[40] He assumes, somewhat readily, that if only distribution were to respond to needs, poverty, fear of want, and greed might be eradicated.[41] As has been intimated, this all presupposes that 'need' can be clearly discerned and, presumably, that it can be assessed according to some reasonable, equitable, and universally applicable standard.[42] Not surprisingly the expression of demand in Utopia is not left entirely to the discretion of the citizen. The opportunities for an individual to be tempted into covetousness or to express unnatural wants are limited. Much of the responsibility for the evaluation of demand resides with the local community. This predisposition typifies an underlying objective of Utopian social arrangements. A general principle of communal life in Utopia is that mutual surveillance should prevail. The vigilant scrutiny of the individual by the community is intended to divest him of the occasion to sin. Consequently, there is no buying or selling in Utopia.[43] Instead, food is conveyed from centralized 'markets' for preparation in communal dining halls. Each quarter of a Utopian city possesses such a market where a series of storehouses is arranged to accommodate particular types of commodity. To these depositories each family is required to convey the produce of its own trade, and from them the head of each household collects what each family requires for the pursuit of its daily life.[44]

The thoroughness of More's communism and principle of equitable distribution is amply illustrated by the convention that houses, of an essentially uniform type, are nevertheless subject to exchange according to decennial lottery.[45] More may be presumed to have seen in this process a means of guaranteeing that, despite all the precautions taken in Utopia, families should not assume a private property in their abode. A major point of distinction between the conception of communism outlined in *Utopia* and that promoted by Winstanley in *The Law of Freedom* is that Winstanley condones the form of domestic ownership specifically discouraged by More. The extent of the barriers to the assumption of private property evident in *Utopia* is indicative of More's belief that, whatever the institutional environment, fallen men would always possess an innate inclination to private ownership. It is evident that More believed that, should this predilection be condoned, it would be to the detriment of both the individual's soul and the social fabric. Hence More's specification that an *absolute* form of communism should prevail.

6

It is evident that, on the one hand, the obligation to labour and, on the other, the distribution of goods and leisure time are elements in More's vision of an integrated economy. Such a system is designed to achieve the specific end of stifling the inclinations of fallen men towards aggrandizement. Whether More's proposal could ever have constituted a viable system is undeniably open to some doubt. The equilibrium sought by More might be regarded as a recipe for economic stagnation. However, given his understanding of what the optimal economy should accomplish it is fair to assume that 'stagnation' is precisely what More aspired to. More's treatment of factors of production and distribution illustrates graphically the rationalism informing his utopian institutionalism.

A primary purpose of *Utopia* is to outline a scheme of civil institutions capable of curtailing Man's sinful propensities. Accordingly, More's design is on one level a direct assault upon sinfulness. The communism of *Utopia* advocates the eradication of private property which, in contemporary Europe, constituted a vehicle for the manifestation of sin. By determining to ensure the satisfaction of 'natural needs', More trusted that the impetus to appropriate goods would also be stifled. Consequently, by orientating the problem of scarcity to needs rather than to wants the whole question of demand was to assume less daunting dimensions in the ideal commonwealth than in Tudor England. More argues that in Christendom wants are often generated by corrupted tastes. Conversely, the wants advanced and met in Utopia are informed by 'natural desires' and thus correspond to 'needs'. Hence demand could be satisfied adequately, albeit within a context of frugality. By a considerable feat on institutional engineering, More theoretically eradicated the immoral principles of the property regime from the human condition.

The state and the Utopian polity

1

The question whether the author of a utopia can be all that seriously interested in politics as an ongoing facet of life is a contentious one. The view undoubtedly exists that utopianism posits the elimination of the political in the sense of politics being a sphere of life informed by a greater or lesser degree of contention. There is a good deal of truth in this appreciation of utopianism. The evaluation of the Utopian state and its 'politics' reveals a series of processes which the modern reader might be excused for regarding as essentially administrative. However, this should not be taken as an indication that More's purpose in writing *Utopia* is markedly disimilar to the objectives informing the 'civic humanist' tradition,[46] or those of a thinker such as John Calvin who conceived of political theory as an *ars* given over to the identification of the *Christiana politia*,[47] or indeed of thinkers as late chronologically as Thomas Hobbes. A distinguishing characteristic of Renaissance and early modern political thought is the concern to isolate that series of institutions and social structures capable of withstanding what was perceived as the inherent facility of human affairs to tend towards conflict and dissolution. The mark, therefore, of the successful polity is regulation. Rarely if ever in the early modern period was politics conceived as an activity containable within a series of conventions. The fear was always that politics had a disturbing tendency to get out of hand. Thus, in writing *Utopia*, More accorded with the thinking of the times by theorizing upon the design of a self-perpetuating system capable of sponsoring the common weal while minimizing active political conflict.

The structure of the polity detailed in More's ideal commonwealth is indicative of his concern to establish the legitimacy of Utopian communism. More is aware that the advocacy of a system of communism exposes the theorist to the conventional retort that proposals for the eradication of private property constitute a prescription for the dissolution of political authority. Thus More might have found himself on the horns of a dilemma, particularly in maintaining that in contemporary Christendom Man's innate sinfulness is evinced through the media of wealth *and* power. By regarding communism as prerequisite to the dissipation of the distorted values of the property regime, More needed to justify such a position by supporting the establishment of a polity capable of maintaining order and of regulating day-to-day activity. In effect, More was required to confound apprehension that *Utopia* was an anarchical document. Further still, More had also to ensure that the exercise of political authority deemed necessary to contain human sinfulness would not be corrupted by that very propensity. So More may be read as regarding political authority as at once a necessity, but also as a potential threat to the Utopian achievement. The construction of the Utopian political system is therefore an astute endeavour to manipulate institutions in order to avert the abuse of power.

More's attitude to the connection between political authority and private property was consolidated during his polemical confrontation with Martin Luther. There is an obvious temptation to deduce, as a number of More's Catholic apologists have done, that because he became apprehensive that Luther had unleashed a prescription for disruption and anarchy, More's own social philosophy took a conservative turn. In particular, it is assumed in these circles that More adhered to the conventional association of private property with political authority and must therefore have regretted (and consequently retracted) his earlier conception of communism. However, More's response to Luther is markedly more consistent with the analysis of private property and political authority advanced in *Utopia* than this appreciation allows. More takes Luther to believe that the Christian's first obligation is to his own conscience rather than to legitimately constituted magistrates or to civil laws. In fact, More somewhat misapprehends Luther's position, but in so doing is prompted to clarify his own case. It is entirely in accordance with the purpose of *Utopia* that More should warn that,

> even if we could live in common with far fewer laws, we could still not live altogether without laws. For the obligation to work would have to be prescribed for certain classes, and laws would be needed to restrain crimes which would run riot even in that kind of life.[48]

Further, that More's constitutionalism is based upon the rule of law rather than upon the will of magistrates[49] is typical of his fundamental distrust of human nature.

It is evident that More believed that, ideally, men should live according to both secular (positive) law and divine law, and that the latter ought to be embodied in the former. Thus in a well-regulated society, civil law ought to promote a situation conducive to Man's highest end—that of salvation.[50] More argues that it is a necessary but not a sufficient condition of the character of a Christian jurisdiction that it should embrace charity. But he also contends that some form of political authority is necessary, with the capacity to perform functions above and beyond the charitable disposition of individual men.[51] Implicit in this decidedly Thomist stance is the view that the state is indispensible both to prohibit vice and to promote virtue. This understanding is pursued in *Utopia*, where More assumes that however altruistic the actions of men *might* become, the dispersal of political institutions could never be envisaged because a well-regulated polity would be necessary in the first instance to initiate beneficent conduct among men, and thence to sustain it. As a corollary of this proposition it is fair to conclude that whereas More was dubious of the facility of private property to avert discord, this doubt did not extend to his appreciation of political authority. Consequently, More should be seen as attempting to endow Utopia with a degree of constitutional stability capable of defying men's worst inclinations.

2

The exact nature of the Utopian polity is somewhat difficult to ascertain, but an insight can be gleaned from the various sections of the discourse which deal, often in passing, with the state and civil society. The electoral system in Utopia is indirect,[52] and is apparently based upon the principle that each family should possess a vote. The ultimate aim of this procedure is to elect three 'old and experienced' delegates from each city to meet annually in the capital. The major function of this 'Senate' is to administer the economy.[53] As a testimony to the potential of his institutional proposals More comments on the fact that, compared to contemporary England, life in Utopia is far less litigious.[54] This benefit arises as a consequence of the omission of private property, a consideration which also dispenses with the numerous legal accoutrements of the property regime. More maintains that a society founded upon communism would require far less regulatory legislation than one sustaining private property. It is presumably the case not only that is the economy easier to control, but also that the improved social conduct facilitated by communism results in reduced demands upon the legislative process.

While accepting that formal governmental institutions would be necessary in the ideal commonwealth, More is clearly anxious to avert the possibility that any one individual might acquire and abuse power, or exercise it on his own behalf rather than for the good of the community. Thus More includes stipulations to ensure that only the most suitable citizens may attain positions of authority. Even so, More maintains that given Man's inherent moral frailty, even the worthiest official might be susceptible to the corrupting influence of power. Therefore, any person so ambitious as to solicit votes disqualifies himself from holding public office.[55] Honour is not to be sought in Utopia; rather it is to be conceived and conferred as an indication of the natural and spontaneous communal approbation of the individual. Just as indulgent self-consciousness on the part of the performer of the good work taints the act, in a tradition of thought traceable to classical sources More believes that he who is fit for public office must be solicited but must not solicit. Diffidence rather than ambition is characteristic of the virtuous Utopian.

In keeping with his general apprehension over the potentially detrimental effects upon the individual citizen of wielding authority, More stipulates that, in principle, office-holding should be restricted to a duration of one year. In Utopia, the only exceptions to this rule are the 'governors' who, unless suspected of tyranny, hold office for life. Similarly, the middle-ranking 'tranibors' are elected annually, but are not replaced without good reason. By this means, More presumably intends to ensure the continuity and stability of government.

3

The Utopian legislative process is evidently designed to eliminate the prospect of political corruption and intrigue. In Utopia it is required that all political debate should take place entirely in the public forum. Further, three days' careful deliberation is obligatory prior to any proposed legislation being ratified.[56] By these means provision is made for objections to be raised. Thus the possibility of legislation being rushed through to the benefit of a self-interested minority is avoided.

In Utopia, private political discussion constitutes a capital offence. This pertains especially to matters affecting the common interest.[57] Such a condition reflects More's concern to avoid two quite different contingencies. First, it places a considerable sanction upon tyrannous and oppressive practices by the officers of the commonwealth, and second, it betrays the contemporary Tudor concern with political disorder and subversion. In Utopia no little peril attends the initiation or even contemplation of group insurrection.

It is reasonable to assume that the nature of 'democracy' in Utopia is profoundly affected and constrained by the proscription of political discourse outside the legislature and by the disqualification incurred by the soliciting of votes. Clearly, any notion of elections requiring declared candidates, meetings and campaigns is antithetical to the Utopian ideal. The election of officers would therefore appear to depend upon some expression of a 'general will', or at least the mutually sympathetic consensus of a majority. There is, as has been indicated above, no shortcoming of logic or feasibility to More's stance on these matters. The virtuous individual simply cannot advance his own claims to public office and More would not have expected citizens to be able to do so. The meritorious individual might be consensually recognized, but could never be certain of his own good standing in the eyes of the community. The whole concept of 'politics' in Utopia seems to be submerged by the essentially static atmosphere of Utopian society. The internal affairs of the island appear so well regulated that few decisions of a 'political' nature are necessary. Interaction with the outside world and questions relating to foreign policy might occasion greater demands of the decision-making machinery of Utopia, but even here it is not unlikely that More anticipated a broad consensus of outlook.

In marked contrast to the European situation which concerns More in the 'Dialogue of Counsel' of Book I, all Utopian governors, ambassadors and priests, are chosen as proven individuals from the company of scholars,[58] a situation prompting the conclusion that More's ideal polity would be governed by persons not unlike his own Christian-humanist associates.[59] Undoubtedly, a form of elitism pervades Utopia, but this is not preserved by a hereditary principle. Instead, access to the elite is determined by a combination of intellectual prowess and moral rectitude. As More remarks, 'no official is haughty or formidable. They are called fathers and show that character.'[60] Only by continuously fulfilling such requirements may individuals preserve their membership of the elite.

While a substantial element of secular coercion exists in Utopia, so, too, does a countervailing system of honours to encourage men to virtue. Such is the extent to which the operation of authority in Utopia is calculated to accord with More's conception of human nature. Those citizens whose conduct is constrained to the extent that they fulfil the ends for which the commonwealth is designed might be expected to find life in Utopia reasonably felicific. Those who remain recalcitrant may experience the retribution of the state and ultimately of God.

4

Utopia has been cited as classic example of a work embodying the principle that law ought to be founded upon reason,[61] and indeed More endows Utopia with a strict and thoroughgoing legal code which takes natural law, as opposed to contemporary positive law, as its point of reference. Hence More's conviction that the intention to transgress is as grievous an offence against natural law as the actual commission of a crime. Throughout his life More remained a consistent advocate of this principle. In *Utopia* he is to be found arguing that 'to tempt another to an impure act is no less punishable than the commission of that impure act'.[62] Similarly, in the *Confutation of Tyndale's Answer* More contends that the crucial consideration is the will to sin rather than the actual perpetration of the act. This emphasis upon intention informs More's belief that if action 'be done without the wyll it is not synne'.[63] From this it is reasonable to deduce that More regarded the facility of the state to regulate conduct as extending in some way to the concern to instill virtue.

Indicatively, More, so often the self-critical lawyer, excludes the practitioners of his own profession from Utopia. He remarks that the Utopians have 'very few laws because very few laws are needed for persons so educated—all laws are promulgated to remind every man of his duty'.[64] More is particularly concerned to elevate the principle of equity within the legal processes of his ideal commonwealth.[65] Thus he argues that as a consequence of the brevity of and publicity afforded to the legal code, rather than resorting to lawyers all Utopians should be in a position to plead their own cases. Furthermore, a repercussion of More's critique of the contemporary punitive system is his concern in *Utopia* to ensure that the punishment of crimes for which no stipulated penalty exists should be determined according to principles of equity.[66] Again, this provision implies More's preparedness to appeal to natural law as the absolute standard of legal reference. Positive law should be evaluated accordingly. It is typical of the ethical foundations of Utopian jurisprudence that excommunication is identified as the ultimate punishment.[67]

The family and the community

More's thinking on the subject of social organization and grouping is compounded by his tendency to indulge in an implicit and somewhat inconclusive examination of a range of possibilities. The consequence is that More's commentary on family life and the role of the community might appear curiously inchoate. The humanist audience for which *Utopia* was intended would, however, have recognized that More was toying with a variety of juxtaposed views on the most appropriate mode of human association—the Platonic communal ideal as opposed to the Aristotelian structuring of society upon the household, monasticism versus patriarchalism, the *vita contemplativa* or the *vita activa*. Ultimately, More leaves the reader better convinced of the complexity of balance informing the combination of factors required to sustain the civic humanist ideal of the virtuous citizen than of the exact constitution of such a balance.

1

Despite devising social theories which inverted various prevalent institutional arrangements, neither More nor Winstanley abandoned the concept of the patriarchal family. The role of the family as a socializing agency, as a locus of authority, and as an institution affecting economic life and the Form of distribution and ownership, is well attested by early modern thinkers. The attitudes assumed by More and Winstanley towards the family afford an insight into the purpose each had in mind in writing about an ideal commonwealth.

Interestingly, More regarded patriarchal authority as a grant from God to Adam [68] which, despite the Fall, necessarily continued. As such, patriarchalism constitutes the non-elective facet of the Utopian authoritative hierarchy and is incorporated by More into the Utopian design for the restraint of human nature. As one commentator has it: 'the family provides a powerful cohesive force for the whole commonwealth both as a coercive institution and as a training place for citizens'.[69] In *The Republic* Plato proposes the abolition of the family.[70] In *Utopia* More, whose own love of and devotion to family life undoubtedly finds expression in the work,[71] makes a conscious departure from the Platonic ideal.

We are informed that the household is the basic unit of the Utopian city.[72] Each household is subject to the authority of the eldest male occupant, unless that person is a dotard. Such household units are extended and contain from ten to sixteen adults. The size of these families is adjusted by means of the transfer of individuals from one household to another as, for instance, in the case of girls marrying and becoming members of their husband's family. In the rural areas of Utopia families are larger; each farm being composed of forty adults and two serfs who are subject to the authority of 'a master and a mistress, serious in mind and ripe of years'.[73] Throughout Utopian familial relationships one paramount principle expresses the patriarchal idea: 'wives wait on their husbands, children on their parents, and generally the younger on their elders'.[74] Not only is such deference intended to maintain the structure of social control, but also, if strictly applied, these practices would presumably obviate the need for household servants. (The retention by Winstanley of servants in his utopian ideal suggests that his attitude towards patriarchalism was orthodox as compared to More's.)

In identifying the family as the basic unit of Utopian production More simply adheres to the contemporary economic norm. Not only is the

Utopian household expected to be to some degree self-sufficient by, for example, doing its own tailoring, but it is also required to devote itself to a craft and to produce commodities for the common stock.[75] It is assumed that sons will be naturally inclined to follow the craft of their fathers. However, as a sop to individualism, More provides for the possibility that those not so inclined may 'be assigned to a grave and honourable householder',[76] under whose tuition they might be taught an alternative trade.

The anticipation that authority permeates downwards is common to both *Utopia* and Winstanley's *The Law of Freedom*; in both instances the family is perceived as the basis of governmental hierachy.[77] However, by implying that the entire family is to have a voice in political affairs (by, for example, contributing to the decision on how the patriarch's vote should be cast), More adds an element of progressivism later missing from Winstanley's conception of family life. Besides playing a role in politics, the family has a displacement within Utopian religious beliefs and practices. Before attending religious services Utopians are 'shriven' by confessing their sins to and begging the pardon of their familial superiors; 'wives fall down at the feet of their husbands, children at the feet of their parents'.[78] While such spiritualization of the household is generally associated with Protestantism, it is worth recalling that domestic devotions were regularly practised within More's own household.[79]

Although More was often quite radical in his view of patriarchalism, he nevertheless regarded the family as an inviolable institution. Apart from his obvious moral objections to pre-marital sex and promiscuity, he is to be found seeking to discourage such behaviour on the additional grounds that immoral conduct undermines family life and thereby poses a threat to the stability of the commonwealth.[80] Even so, within the family unit More advocates certain 'progressive' attitudes which would ultimately, in centuries to come, lead to considerable tension and to the questioning of patriarchal authority. For example, More's objections to wet-nursing[81] is symptomatic both of a developing recognition of the very concept of childhood and a growing fastidiousness over educational methods.[82]

2

More did not emphasize patriarchalism as an institution essential to the functioning of society to the extent subsequently voiced by Winstanley. Such a disparity is explained in part by Winstanley's advocacy of patriarchalism as a factor in the social encouragement of spiritual regeneration. More's predominant concern, however, is with the subjugation of the worst characteristics of human nature. He tends, therefore, to regard communal life rather than the closet of the family as a more appropriate medium for the attainment of this end. Yet certain undeniable tensions would appear to be occasioned by More's advocacy of various practices which seem inimical to strong patriarchal authority. For example, More is an ardent advocate of marital 'love'; this in marked contrast to the system of arranged marriages often associated with the dominance of the patriarchal householder. The reader is informed that in Utopia, in a spirit of intense pragmatism, would-be marriage partners are ceremoniously displayed naked to each other before undertaking any vows.[83] The objective in mind is that of ensuring compatibility and familial harmony; but presumably an element of discretion is by this means extended to the parties of the proposed union. So although More subscribes to the contemporary norm that a man should marry only after completing an apprenticeship, by enhancing choice for participants, More may have proposed conventions likely to detract from patriarchal authority. Arranged marriages imply a substantial degree of parental control. By challenging this practice, the Utopian principle of catering for the emotional needs of sons and daughters might well have imposed obvious limitations upon patriarchalism. Even so, irrespective of these elements of ambivalence the institution is clearly an important factor in More's ideal commonwealth, particularly with respect to economic activities and to the moral tenor of society.

3

The emphasis placed by More upon communal activities has naturally prompted suggestions to the effect that 'More was concerned to enquire whether the monastic virtues could be made to work outside the monastery'.[84] There is undoubtedly credence in the view that the personal dilemmas of More's life, which turn upon his lingering affiliation to monasticism as an ideal to which he could not entirely commit himself, find expression in the pages of *Utopia*. While More probably did regard monasticism as an exemplar it is also evident that his analysis of the human predicament prompted him to conclude, independently of any deference to the monastic ideal, that communal life would be to Man's benefit.

The communal facet of life in Utopia pertains not only to economic considerations but also to the system of surveillance necessary for the frustration of men's evil inclinations. With this objective in mind More extends the notion of community to include an additional sanction upon conduct by stipulating that the Utopians' belief 'in the personal presence of their forefathers keeps men from any secret dishonourable deed'.[85]

Certain disjunctures appear to compound More's professed concern with patriarchal familialism alongside the advocacy of communalism. It appears, for instance, that most activities, with the exception of tradescraft, are undertaken in groups larger than the family. The strength of the anti-proprietorial communal ethos is evinced by the revelation that in Utopia all domiciles are completely open to access,[86] a practice designed both to militate against the assumption of private property in the dwelling place and to exemplify the moral rectitude of citizens.

Each street in Utopia is composed of thirty households, the members of which attend a communal dining hall. We learn that while individuals are not compelled to attend communal meals a powerful social sanction against abstention arises from distrust of the motives of those who prefer privacy.[87] The seating arrangements at such meals are revealing. The young are constantly watched over in the expectation that 'the grave and reverend behaviour of the old may restrain' them 'from misbehavious freedom'.[88] The provision for readings 'conducive to morality'[89] as accompaniment to meals is a reflection of the practice of monasteries, the Inns of Court and More's own household.

In Utopia other communally based institutions are prominent. For example, nurseries provide for the care of infants while hospitals—to which patients go voluntarily, in marked contrast to the contemporary norm—are maintained for the benefit of the sick.[90] In general More appears anxious to stress not only the efficiency of communal provision but also the moral benefits enjoyed by the individual through actively participating in the affairs of the community.

4

A further pervasive motif of life in Utopia is uniformity, which is manifested in a wide variety of ways and is essentially intended to fulfil a twofold purpose: first, it is an important factor within the process of stifling human sinfulness; and second, uniformity and the consequent eschewance of conspicuous consumption reduce the demand for goods and hence the labour required for the production of commodities. There are numerous examples of the applications of these utilitarian principles in Utopia. For instance, streets and houses are described as substantial, hygenia and identical.[91] This in contrast to the innovatory building boom of More's own time which represented the epitome of European conspicuous consumption. Rather than standing the cost of constantly rebuilding, the Utopians save on both time and labour by keeping their existing property in good repair.[92]

More is anxious to affirm that styles and fashions in Utopia have remained static throughout the history of the commonwealth and will continue to do so. His attitude to the whims of fancy is decidely disparaging. Some years after writing *Utopia* More attempted to deflate the pride taken by his fellows in fine clothes by pointing out that 'a poore shepe ware it on her backe before it came vpon his: al the while whe ware it, wer her wull neuer so fine, yet was she pardie but a shepe'.[93] Not surprisingly, in Utopia utility is the sole criterion by which clothing is evaluated. The Utopians are 'dressed unpretentiously in leather or hide, which lasts for seven years'.[94] Similarly, they prefer linen to wool[95] (presumably thereby avoiding being overrun by sheep).

Given that ownership of a horse represented a considerable status symbol in early modern England[96] the virtual absence of horses from Utopia might be read as affording a further insight into More's purpose.[97] More, perhaps somewhat illogically, seems aware that had he made horses readily available in Utopia, he would have risked providing a vehicle for the expression of pride and vainglory. This is an interesting instance in which More appears to have momentarily lapsed by allowing the perverted mores of European society to threaten the socialized standards of Utopia, for presumably the

Utopians could have had no preconceived awareness of the social implications of horse-ownership.

More relates the principle of uniformity to the question of demand and consumption by postulating that 'universal behaviour must of necessity lead to an abundance of all commodities. Since the latter are distributed evenly among all, it follows, of course, that no one can be reduced to poverty and beggary'.[98] It is important to recall that More was not primarily concerned to increase the production of goods. The term 'abundance' is used here to describe the prosperity of the common weal as compared to contemporary society. It is worth stressing once again that More feared that inequitable distribution and affluence would be detrimental to Man's well-being because of his belief that such a situation inevitably stimulates conspicuous consumption and its attendant moral evils.

More's basic intention of identifying a social regime capable of averting Man's inclination to sin is discernible in almost every detail of Utopian life. Thus he finds himself in a position to claim that 'nowhere is there any license to waste time, nowhere any pretext to evade work—no wineshop, no alehouse, no brothel anywhere, no opportunity for corruption, no lurking hole, no secret meeting place'.[99] Throughout the description of the ideal commonwealth More instances a variety of ancillary means by which the citizen is to be diverted from temptation. For example, gold and silver are employed in Utopia to make the most mundane of utensils and, poignantly, as chains for slaves.[100] That the Utopians use gold to stigmatize wrongdoers is a somewhat cumbersome and ironic articulation of More's belief that the value attributed to 'precious' metals is a product of Man's corrupt nature and of unnatural wants. In the *Treatise on the Passion* More states:

> How proud be men of golde and syluer, no part of our self, but of thearth, and of nature no better then is the poore coper or tinne, nor to man's vse so profitable, as in the poore mettall that maketh vs y plough share, and horse shoone, and horse nayles.[101]

More similarly deprecates precious stones.[102] In order to drive home this emphasis of use value More places the Utopians in a position in which they are obliged by geological circumstance to export gold in exchange for iron.[103] Once again, the natural needs of the community and of utility determine what More perceives as *real* value. Implicit in this disapprobation of gold and jewellery is the assumption that fallen men will inevitably covet wealth, even in forms which are intrinsically worthless. Not surprisingly, when the badly-briefed Anemolian ambassadors, 'being more proud than wise',[104] parade through the streets bedecked in all their finery, they are ridiculed by the simply and uniformly dressed Utopians.

5

More is at pains to exclude from his ideal commonwealth the brutality of everyday life and its accompanying insensitivity. So it is that he includes a somewhat inconsistent proviso to the effect that 'they do not allow their citizens to accustom themselves to the butchering of animals, by the practice of which they think that mercy, the finest feeling of our human nature, is gradually killed off'.[105] Such work is reserved for slaves, who are considered to have sacrificed the right to be regarded as reasonable men.

Several further features of life in Utopia reflect More's desire to construct a society in which individuals are constantly under scrutiny. The restriction on travel advocated in *Utopia* may well have been a measure of the Tudor dread of vagrancy. Given that Utopian cities are more or less identical, curiosity cannot possibly constitute a motive for wanderlust. Consequently, the desire to travel requires not only the provision of an adequate pretext and the securing of a permit but also, invariably, a communal journey and the performance of labour on the way.[106] Even an apparently innocuous country walk is not free from suspicion and requires the approval of the individual's father and/or wife.

Apart from the differentiation of the priesthood the only distinctions of styles of clothing evident in Utopia are those identifying marital status.[107] This is a further condition which presumably lends itself to the scrutiny of potential immorality. Perhaps the most coherent example of the Utopian preoccupation with the exclusion of every opportunity to sin is the punitive reaction to pre-marital sex. Not only are those found guilty of the offence forbidden to marry, but also the father and mother of the household in which the offence is committed are punished for their dereliction of duty—to guard over the conduct of the young.[108]

The education of the virtuous citizen

1

A pivotal aspect of the Christian-humanist project is the conviction that, despite the constraints of innate incapacities, Man is still to a marked degree educable. *Utopia* is a graphic example of the currency of this belief. In *Utopia* More intends education to serve a dual purpose. Not only does he assume that education encourages moral character, but he also conceives of education as a substantial form of pleasure and thereby as and end in itself.

The most obvious reason for More's interest in learning is his appreciation of education as a technique vital to bringing about changes in conduct. More suggests that although the state may, by essentially coercive means, extract the performance of duty, it was vastly preferable to entice the co-operation of the citizen. Self-discipline could be induced by education.[109] Thus, in Utopia, education contributes to political socialization. As one critic has correctly observed, education secures 'the propagation of the ideal state'.[110]

It appears that More saw in education a means of compensating for the ignorance and frailty of reason inherent in the fallen condition of Man. In the *Dialogue Concerning Heresies* More echoes the earlier thoughts of *Utopia*, arguing that liberal studies are conducive to the reasoning faculties.[111] All this had led commentators to contend that 'to be good through humanist knowledge is the Utopian ideal'.[112]

Given More's concern to design institutions which would profit man in the quest for salvation, his conception of education, as one means of inculcating certain indispensable moral values, affords an insight into the overall purpose of the piece. Even critics doubtful of the seriousness of the Utopian discourse recognize that the educational provisions of *Utopia* are intended to encourage an enlightened piety of a Christian form. It is notable that More's close friend Erasmus maintains that one function of education is to provide men with access to a lifestyle which might enable them to approximate Christ's example.[113] More himself expresses the view that, although education is not absolutely necessary for salvation, it might nevertheless be of benefit because by this means the soul is trained in virtue.[114]

2

In More's ideal commonwealth the learning of a craft is considered imperative if an individual is to avoid the sinfulness associated with idleness.[115] This injunction to work is complemented by a form of education recommended by More on the grounds that it promotes morality.[116] The Utopia concern for morality and virtue is as substantial as that for the advancement of learning. Hence More's assurance to his audience that:

> They take the greatest pains from the very first to instil in to children's minds, while still tender and pliable, good opinions which are also useful for the preservation of their commonwealth. When once they are firmly implanted in children, they accompany them all through their adult lives and are of great help in watching over the condition of the commonwealth. The latter never decays except through vices which arise from wrong attitudes.[117]

The preservation of the commonwealth is, however, something of an ancillary rationale for More's educational programme. More's own household constituted an experiment in humanist education, and the inspiration for this accorded with More's objectives in writing *Utopia*. In a letter to his children's tutor, William Gonell, More counsels that his own children are

> to esteem most whatever might teach them piety towards God, charity to all, and modesty and Christian humility in themselves. By such means they will receive from God the reward of an innocent life, and in the assured expectation of it will view death without dread.[118]

The fundamental point at issue is articulated by More's insistence that 'the more do I see the difficulty of getting rid of this pest of pride, the more do I see the necessity of getting to work at it from childhood'.[119] Clearly, the educational regime specified in *Utopia* is intended to serve such a purpose.

In his more confident moments More sees in education an institutional means of determining individual conduct. The question of whether moral education teaches *virtue* or mere habit, and the form of the relationship between conduct and behaviour, would at first sight not appear to have struck More as being particularly problematical. There is, however, cause to regard *Utopia* as an intellectual enterprise every bit as concerned with identifying the circumstances of 'autonomous' action as was Aristotle's *Nicomachean Ethics* or, indeed, more recent work in the philosophy of education.[120]

The ends of life: ethics and religion

1

More's political philosphy is informed by a keen awareness of the influence exerted by civil institutions and social mores upon the nature and purpose of human existence. The causal nexus of such influence is, of course, by no means simple. More's utopianism represents an attempt to break into the very tight circle sustained by what he saw as the mutually reinforcing factors of social structure and human disposition. In essence, having discarded the prospect of any transformation of innate human proclivity, More came to identify the reformation of social institutions as the only means of rectifying Man's predicament. This having been established, the onus of the problem of reform shifted to the question of how institutional restructuring could be brought about. Given More's retention of an implicit awareness that human nature would always militate against radical institutional amelioration, the utopian genre in which More's political treatise is couched is testament to his identification of what he regarded as the essential political problem and the meagre prospects of its solution. It is from this perspective that those parts of *Utopia* dealing with rationalism and religion, ethics and aestheticism, are most appropriately analysed.

The passages referred to are, to say the least, often bemusing, and have occasioned prolonged and acrimonious controversy among scholars. Of the plethora of positions assumed with regard to this aspect of More's thought the following broad synopses are discernible:

I. 'Catholic' interpretations.

(a) Strong version: sustaining the view that any attempt to accommodate the *controversia* alluded to in *Utopia* must ultimately compromise the doctrinal basis of More's life and work. These aspects of *Utopia* are therefore either

  (i) explicable in terms of More's avowed distaste for what is discussed or

  (ii) inexplicable.

(b) Weak version: accepts as a premise More's doctrinal concern and commitment, but holds that either
   (i) at the time of writing *Utopia* More articulated in an exaggerated manner facets of real and acknowledged doctrinal uncertainty or
   (ii) he intended the Utopian discourse to exemplify the appropriate relative displacement of reason and revelation; shortcomings occasioned by the neglect of reason in Christendom and the absence of revelationary guidance in Utopia are thus evident and thought-provoking.

II. 'Humanist' interpretations.
Are generally sympathetic to position I.b.ii, but assert more thoroughly the view that it was with the neglect of 'reasonableness' in contemporary Christendom that More was most directly concerned. Thus the significance of revelation within More's theology is somewhat played down.

III. Anticipatory socialism.
Finds this aspect of *Utopia* of least interest. More, it is argued, was constrained by the social and intellectual context in which he wrote in such a way that he was incapable of realizing the full potentialities of social ownership. He retained, therefore, a marked interest in matters religious. The passages are either neglected or considered anachronistic.

IV. Utilitarianism.
The nineteenth-century development of this version of moral philosophy identified More, often as a cautious disciple of Epicurus, as providing a very early instance not only of the awareness that the institutional environment affects the prospects of human happiness but also that it should do so positively.

From an analytical perspective, that is to say from the point of view of an approach which seeks to evaluate the *full implications* of More's position, two points are of considerable relevance to the examination of what is said concerning religion and ethics in *Utopia*. The first is that More acknowledges that the revelation of Christianity is superimposed upon the religious and moral rationalism described in Book II, but does not elaborate upon the likely effects of that revelation in terms of the nature and objectives of Utopian society. Evidently, conversion to Christianity would require that the Utopians discard certain beliefs and practices, but this still leaves open to question More's thoughts on the type of society likely to emerge from the amalgamation of residual religious rationalism and Christian conviction.

The second consideration that should inform the analysis of religion and ethics in *Utopia* is that whereas More could accept as an article of faith the prescriptions of Christianity concerning the point and purpose of human existence, this did not necessarily entail a disavowal of a rationalist approach to such issues. Where the reasoning disposition yields areas of incongruity, faith and doctrine provide an alternative response. *Utopia* is very much concerned with the limitations of philosophy and reason in coming to terms with the human condition. The major area of concern, one which has been the source of much consideration throughout the history of philosophical enquiry, and one which is evaluated by More in *Utopia*, is that of human motivation, or, to use a term more appropriate to this particular case, the 'free will' problem. Taking this factor into account should be enough to discourage hasty assumptions as to what conclusions More arrived at in so meditative a work.

2

The discussion of religion presented in *Utopia* generates a problem not least because we are informed that although they do not subscribe to full-fledged sixteenth-century Catholicism, the Utopians follow a religion that in terms both of its doctrines and its externals maintains several important prescriptive recommendations relevant to the salvation of Christians. Thus, a straightforward dichotomy between 'Christian' Europeans and 'heathen' Utopians is unsatisfactory.

To take an example of the order of difficulty posed by Utopian religion, Catholic critics have been swift to claim that *Utopia* is replete with statements that More simply would not have made other than in a *jeu d'esprit*. One example is the Utopian claim that it is ludicrous 'to pursue hard and painful virtue and not only to banish the sweetness of life but even voluntarily to suffer pain from which you expect no profit'.[121] This assertion is clearly contradicted by what is known of More's own asceticism; for much of his life he wore a hair shirt and devoted himself each Friday to private contemplation and mortification.[122] The Catholic school has correctly concluded that More could not have sincerely advocated the opinions on asceticism held by the Utopians. However, the Catholic position is quick to point out that Christian revelation had not been bestowed upon the Utopians.[123] Whereas both these premises hold true it is of the utmost significance that the former is a corollary of the latter. Thus More's overall position maintains an essential consistency; without Christian revelation the Utopians could have no assurance that asceticism could enhance the individual's prospects of salvation. The crucial consideration here is that it is a mistake to deduce from this instance and others like it the general proposition that Utopian natural religion and Christianity are fundamentally dissimilar.

The basic principles of Utopian religion, 'which is serious and strict, almost solemn and hard',[124] are more than a series of purely rational propositions; they would have been identifiable as a set of defensible religious tenets by More's contemporaries, who possessed the additional reference of revelation. For example, the Utopian belief in miracles would have seemed perfectly orthodox to Europeans. Furthermore, the rationalist Utopians' derision of superstition might have been applauded rather more by contemporary Catholic theologians than by many European laymen.[125]

More expands upon the themes that the existence of God and the nature of certain divine truths are ascertainable philosophically, arguing that 'reason first of all inflames men to a love and veneration of the divine majesty, to whom we owe both our existence and our capacity for happiness'.[126] The prevalent Utopian conception of God would have been familiar to the contemporary European mind. In Utopia, God is regarded as

> a certain single being, unknown, eternal, immense, inexplicable, far above the reach of the human mind, diffused throughout the universe not in mass but in power. Him they call Father. To him alone they attribute the beginnings, the growth, the increase, and the end of all things as they have perceived them. To no other do they give divine honours.[127]

Such an ontological conception of God's existence and nature accords with the view of a perceptible yet ultimately inscrutable being developed in More's explicitly theological writings.

We are told that irrespective of an element of religious toleration in Utopia, all citizens are expected to adhere to certain religious tenets which, significantly, are essential to the one dominant religion that has come to surpass all others in its facility of 'reasonableness'. Here again, contemporary European opinion would have experienced little difficulty in identifying such ideas. These tenets are, first, that 'the soul is immortal and by the goodness of God born for happiness';[128] second, that 'after this life rewards are appointed for our virtues and good deeds, punishment for our crimes';[129] and third, an appreciation of divine providence as reflected in the notion that 'there is one supreme being, to whom are due both the creation and providential government of the whole world'.[130] A subscription to these precepts is deemed in Utopia prerequisite to human dignity.[131] Furthermore, such apprehensions are regarded as sanctions which contribute to the substance of laws.[132] It is worth recalling that in the Middle Ages the individual's uncertainty of his fate at judgement was valued not least because it represented an important constraint upon daily conduct.[133]

In *Utopia* More is not merely concerned to elucidate the eschatological standing of the virtuous heathen; his task is considerably more prescriptive. It is worth noting that the Utopians clearly exceed More's conception of the minimum requirements for the redemption of the virtuous heathen. In the *Treatise Upon the Passion* More expresses the opinion that judgement would seem unduly harsh if individuals who were born into original sin but lived out their lives ignorant of Christ and his message should inevitably be damned as a consequence. He goes on to argue that

> it was sufficient for their saluacion to belieue those two points onelye which saynt Paule here reherseth, that is to wit, that there is one God, and he wyl reward them that seke him. And those two pointes be such, as euery man may attayne by natural reason . . .[134]

The Utopians evidently satisfy these conditions. However, it is of some importance to observe that More avails readers of *Utopia* of the following information:

> after they had heard from us the name of Christ, His teaching, His character, His miracles, and the no less wonderful constancy of the many martyrs whose blood

freely shed had drawn so many nations far and wide into their fellowship, you would not believe how readily disposed they, too, were to join it, whether through the rather mysterious inspiration of God or because they thought it nearest to that belief which has widest prevalance among them. But I think that this factor, too, was of no small weight, that they had heard that His disciples' common way of life had been so pleasing to Christ and that it is still in use among the truest societies of Christians.[135]

More's expression of consternation at the Utopians' receptivity to Christian revelation is rhetorical; More describes in *Utopia* a society primed for the reception of revelation and ready to convert to a social exemplification of that message.

3

The practices and externals of religious observation are apparently of less moment to Utopian theology.[136] Certainly, the formalities of medieval Catholicism are reflected in Utopian practices.[137] On this facet of religious life More's position is undoubtedly speculative.[138] It is evident that at least a certain amount of revision would be necessary to accommodate some of these offices to the introduction of Christianity.

More's description of the Utopian priesthood is one instance of an institution which simultaneously reflects elements of Catholicism while providing an example to the benighted standards of contemporary Europe. More informs us that Utopian priests 'preside over divine worship, order religious rites, and are censors of morals'.[139] They are elected by secret ballot, are even by Utopian standards exceptionally virtuous, and number only thirteen per city; all considerations clearly intended to reinforce More's indictment of the idleness and licentiousness of many European clerics. Even so, in a number of respects Utopian priests differ radically from their European counterparts. For instance, in Utopia there is no rule of celibacy and priests are allowed to marry. Elderly widows are admitted to the priesthood. Most impressively, Utopian priests go to war with the intention of curtailing bloodshed.[140] While the clergy are invited to comment as appropriate, the punishment of offenders in Utopia is the responsibility of the civil authorities. Nevertheless, the most dreaded sentence is 'ex-communication'—the exclusion of the individual from divine service.

It has been noted in connection with Utopian working practices that in comparison to contemporary Europe very few holy days are observed in the Utopian calendar. Not only might this provision be seen as facilitating increased output, but also restricting holidays may have been intended as a response to the loose morality for which such events had become notorious. Not surprisingly, the primary purpose of holy days in Utopia is to enable citizens to attend religious services. Despite emphasizing a simple piety More is obviously concerned to provide for certain external stimuli to devotion; practices which were often derogated by other humanists such as Erasmus.[141] The only decorative garments ever seen in Utopia are those worn to divine service by the priesthood. More is notably keen to assert the mystical aspect of such 'vestments'.[142] Similarly, the splendidly furnished temples and resort to petitionary prayer[143] contribute to a religious aura evidently influenced by the externals of contemporary Catholicism.

4

Perhaps the most telling facet of the discussion of religion contained in *Utopia* is that dealing with the issue of death and the prospect of eternity. The preoccupation of More's age with these matters, usually from a decidedly apprehensive perspective, is discussed above. In contrast to the abject pessimism of parts of More's devotional works, the Utopians maintain a rudimentary outlook which differs markedly from the spirit of the age. More points out that

> almost all Utopians are absolutely certain and convinced that human bliss will be so immense that, while they lament every man's illness, they regret the death of no one but him who they see torn from life anxiously and unwillingly.[144]

The obvious inferences of this qualification are that only those plagued by a bad conscience are reluctant to face their judgement and that in Utopia such persons are not commonplace. We are intended to presume that the general confident expectation of redemption is testimony to the calibre of moral life sustained in Utopia. Indeed, Utopians pray to be relieved of life and to be reconciled with God at the earliest opportunity.[145] Elsewhere, More recommends such a mode of thought as an ideal to which Christians should aspire.[146] Evidently then, for most men, life in Utopia is conductive to 'salvation'. The question remains as to whether More conceived of the institutions and philosophical principles of *Utopia* as a means towards the redemption of all men.

5

The view of asceeticism advanced in *Utopia* is an interesting instance of the difference between, on the one hand, the pure rationalism of Utopian religion, and, on the other, More's own convictions.[147] Those Utopian ascetics who eschew learning,[148] a socially esteemed pleasure, are believed to have taken to extremes the principle that the rejection of an immediate pleasure might promote greater felicity in the future (in this case eternal bliss). Such Utopian ascetics pursue an active life and voluntarily perform the hardest labour in the hope of securing happiness after death. Thus, their 'works' involve a charitable disposition to bolster the economy and further the common good. Consequently, others are provided with additional leisure time.[149] More maintains the consistency of Utopian philosophy by revealing that of the two forms of ascetic the 'celibates', who dismiss all forms of pleasure, are esteemed as the holier, while those who marry and reject pleasure only when it threatens to interfere with labour, are regarded as the saner.[150] Clearly, this is an instance in which the dictates of natural reason diverge from contemporary understandings of revealed admonition. More leaves the reader to suppose that the inception of Christianity in Utopia would resolve the issue by amending indigenous attitudes in favour of the dictates of revelation. The discussion of asceticism affords a medium through which More is able to evaluate religious considerations in conjunction with an appreciation of pleasure and 'happiness' as ethical objectives.

6

For a thinker as obsessed as More was with Man's fallen condition the question of how the citizen should while away time was certain to prove intellectually exacting. From More's point of view it was necessary to postulate circumstances in which certain of the objectives of productive labour, the benefit yielded to the individual soul and to the communal economy, would be promoted throughout the individual's conscious hours. Just as labour should discourage sinfulness so should those activities undertaken in leisure time. It was More's general understanding that in the fallen condition recreation could only be justified once the prior obligation to labour had been fulfilled.[151] Thus More's observations on the Utopian philosophy of pleasure draw together various facets of the Utopian discourse—economic practices and objectives, the quest for moral propriety, the educative function, the aesthetic appeal, and the overall conception of the 'good life'.

More's treatment of the philosophy of pleasure in *Utopia* has prompted nearly as much contention as that occasioned by his evaluation of natural religion. More's portrayal of the Utopian conception of human happiness is sufficiently rationalistic as to have attracted the attention of nineteenth-century devotees of Utilitarianism.[152] By the same token, Catholic opinion has sought quite strenuously to distance More from a position which can be construed, superficially at least, as elevating pleasure above virtue.[153] It is fair, therefore, to conclude that any treatment of the philosophy of pleasure as outlined in *Utopia* must be sensitive in particular to the relative displacement of pleasure and virtue within the argument and to More's qualitative differentiation of forms of pleasure.

The recognition that men would incline towards the pursuit of pleasure made it imperative for More to be able to argue that such a propensity need not be at a cost to the prospects of the individual's salvation. Within the Utopian philosophy of pleasure, and indeed general ethical outlook, the relationship between Epicureanism and Stoicism is complex and interesting —a situation that has prompted one scholar to remark that the Utopians possess 'a Stoic ethic and an Epicurean psychology'.[154] Certain aspects of Epicureanism are discernible in *Utopia*. The principles that pleasure is the highest good, that it is a derivative of either bodily health or the tranquility of the soul, and that superficial pleasures are often prejudicial to the achievement of higher forms, are all integral to the Utopian philosophy of pleasure. However, in *Utopia* More does not follow Epicurus by eliminating from the philosophy of pleasure the belief in an eventually supernatural judgement. A belief in retribution is clearly likely to effect certain limitations upon earthly conduct and the unrestrained pursuit of pleasure. Furthermore, it is also evident that Utopian Epicureanism is offset by the considerable emphasis placed upon the Stoical promotion of virtue. By means of this 'reconciliation' of two seemingly contradictory positions the Utopians are seen as enjoying pleasure and behaving virtuously at one and the same time.[155]

Scholars have been quick to comment upon More's admiration for the proximity of aspects of Stoic philosophy to the Christian ethic.[156] Even so, *Utopia* remains an example of the humanists' 'rehabilitation' of Epicurus. Subject to revision according to the three religious tenets of *Utopia*, Epicureanism emerges not so much as a philosophy of sensualism as a set of principles defining the form of pleasure accessible only through a good conscience. In his loyalty to the traditional Catholic interpretation of *Utopia*, E.L. Surtz argues that More intended Utopian philosophy to provoke contemporary Christians into serious deliberation on the nature of pleasure.[157] However, there is a case for supposing More to have intended something rather more substantial and prescriptive. Surtz clearly regards Utopia as a society in which communism and natural religion both sustain hedonism.[158] Hence the contention that More's eclectic definition of pleasure entails a spectrum of sensations ranging from physical gratification to the contemplation of God.[159] This leads Surtz to surmise that the Utopians predispose to bodily pleasure and practice virtue only in order to attain such satisfaction. Consequently, the Utopian ethic maintains that virtue is both subsidiary and ancillary to pleasure.

While Surtz's appreciation recognizes the assimilation of Epicureanism and Stoicism accomplished in *Utopia* it is clear that his intellectual sympathies colour his interpretation to the effect that it emphasizes unappeased Epicureanism. More, it is argued, presented the impression that pleasure is the sole end of life in *Utopia*. Surtz's position, then, and it is not unrepresentative of a substantial body of opinion, asserts that More was far from identifying any possible synonymity of virtue and pleasure. Acceptance of this position entails the corollary that in *Utopia* certain ends to which pleasure appears to have been a means are negated. In the minds of some critics, then, *Utopia* is a tract intended to caution against unmitigated hedonism. This view is challenged below.

7

Given that More was so hypercritical of the often debauched leisure-time activities of his own society and believed that men should be subject to the closest social scrutiny if they were not to succumb to temptation, the discovery that he endowed *Utopia* with a philosophy of pleasure might justifiably occasion consternation. The nature of this ethic is therefore deserving of close examination.

In accordance with More's belief that, in the fallen condition, recreation could be justified only if the prior obligation to labour had been satisfied, the Utopian economy is organized in such a way as to afford an ample and equitable distribution of leisure time. These arrangements are designed to regulate wants and to satisfy demand, to minimize the requirement upon socially necessary labour time, and to facilitate a just and fair allotment of 'spare' time among the entire population. More is naturally concerned that this time should be used to maximum advantage; the Utopian philosophy of pleasure thus represents a further means of redirecting fallen men to the good. Effectively, in Utopia 'pleasure' guides men to salvation; this in marked contrast to the situation in contemporary Europe where, assumed More, it all too often sent them to damnation. The devotion to the full and active use of time which is so evident an aspect of the Utopian discourse may well be an expression of a commonplace Christian-humanist ideal, reflected in the decision made in 1504 by More himself to pursue an active as opposed to a contemplative life.

Critics have generally been agreed upon what one scholar has termed More's 'mode of distribution of the means of pleasure'[160]—the equitable allocation of such leisure time as More deemed necessary for the moral and intellectual development of all individuals. More's analysis of the nature of pleasure is thus an issue of some consequence. He defines the Utopian conception of pleasure as 'every movement and state of body or mind in which, under the guidance of nature, man delights to dwell'.[161] More's citation of 'nature' as the appropriate criterion of reference is the clue to the essence of his position in that *Utopia* sustains a thoroughgoing dichotomy of 'true' and 'false' pleasures. More conceives of false pleasures as indulgences informed by the perverted values of fallen men. In *The Four Last Things* More asserts that 'our soul can have no place for the good corn of spiritual pleasure as long as it is overgrown with the barren weeds of carnal delectation'.[162] By constantly intimating that spiritual sensation constitutes a higher form than 'sensual and fleshly' pleasure,[163] More reiterates the theme that lies at the heart of the Utopian philosophy of pleasure. His awareness that the corruption of public opinion generates the promotion of false values[164] led More to mistrust popular consensus as to the defining principles of true pleasure.[165] By working upon the Aristotelian belief that men are guided by habit, but questioning whether this necessarily sustains virtue, More is able to contend that institutional constraints might be necessary both to jolt men out of their degenerate ways and to keep them interested in virtuous pleasures.

In accordance with his conception of 'true pleasure', More is anxious to assert that the abundance of leisure time available in Utopia should not be construed as a licence for idleness.[166] Much of this time is to be devoted to serious intellectual activities, attendance at edifying public lectures being the custom. Alternatively, the mood would be set at communal dinners by enlivening music and the burning of incense because 'no kind of pleasure is forbidden provided no harm comes of it'.[167] Conversely, More is repeatedly critical of conventional European values. He describes the prevailing conception of honour as a 'counterfeit pleasure'.[168] This distinction between true and false pleasure finds typical expression in More's sanctioning of the admiration of beauty, but rigid disapproval of cosmetic decoration.

8

We are told that the Utopian conception of pleasure is central to the ethical outlook prevailing on the island. The major issue with which Utopian ethical enquiry is concerned is the nature of *happiness*.[169] The conclusion reached is that pleasure is the principal constituent of happiness. However, this general proposition is qualified by the assertion that happiness can be located only in those varieties of pleasure to which human nature is attracted by virtue.[170] Several years later, writing in *The Four Last Things*, More affirms this opinion as his own, arguing that

> if it be true, as it is indeed, that our sin is painful and our virtue pleasant, how much is it then a more madness to take sinful pain in this world, that shall win us eternal pain in hell, rather than pleasant virtue in this world, that shall win us eternal pleasure in heaven?[171]

Clearly, it is reasonable to surmise that More saw the Utopian ethic as antithetical to the European habit of deriving 'pleasure' from practices to which men are enticed by their fallen nature.

Virtue is defined in *Utopia* as living according to nature and to the dictates of reason. Thus, given Utopian religious sentiments, the ultimate form of virtue is to act in accordance with God's will.[172] The three basic tenets of Utopian religion (the immortality of the soul, judgement in the hereafter, and the existence of divine providence), obviously represent something of an arduous sanction upon the pursuit of pleasure. At the very least, these injunctions might be expected to reinforce the Utopian communal ethos to the effect that individuals would not seek pleasure at a cost to the well-being of their fellow citizens. It is no coincidence that the laws of distribution in Utopia accord with the belief that 'humanity', the concern for the welfare of others, is a very substantial virtue.[173] Thus the emphasis upon communal activities appears as a factor intended to alleviate tensions that might arise as a consequence of the persistent admonition to live within the confines of mutual constraint.

The understanding, current also within more recent conceptions of utility and welfarism, that a lesser pleasure should be forgone if this is likely to result in the attainment of a greater pleasure, prompts the Utopians to question an assumption familiar within the Christian ethos, namely that of 'deferred satisfactions'. The Utopians contend that the pursuit of virtue at a cost in terms of pain, or at the expense of pleasure, is contradictory to the dictates of reason. For all this, it is significant that the pleasure to be derived from a good conscience (having, for example, served one's fellow through the performance of one's duty) is represented in *Utopia* as the supreme form:

> they cling above all to mental pleasures, which they value as the first and foremost of all pleasures. Of these the principal part they hold to arise from the practice of virtues and the consciousness of a good life.[174]

For experiencing such natural pleasure, an individual might expect to be rewarded by God.

9

Utopian citizens incline towards a 'Christian' way of life because they live according to certain well-promulgated ethical principles which are in turn sustained by a sharp differentiation and gradation of various forms of pleasure. Just as true pleasures typically include music and intellectual board games such as the popular favourite 'vices versus virtues',[175] false pleasures, as defined by the Utopians, number dicing, the delight in fine clothes, honours, jewellery and hunting.[176] All these, of course, are peculiarly reminiscent of the preoccupations of the European nobility. In Utopia, these are concerns to which slaves, who are deemed to be deficient in reason, are attracted. More roundly condemns such predispositions as being sanctioned only by the futile consensus of fallen men. According to More, once men are left to exercise their own discretion they will almost certainly be detrimentally influenced by their imagination[177] and thereby defy 'nature'—only to discover that their perverse and evil desires cannot instill happiness.

In evaluating the nature of 'true pleasure' More provides supplementary subdivisions. The satisfaction of the senses and ultimately the consciousness of possessing good health,[178] although of value in their own right, are ancillary to mental pleasures 'which they value as the first and foremost of all pleasures'.[179] More regards bodily pleasure as belonging to a lower order because he sees such forms as being more susceptible to adulteration than intellectual or spiritual pleasure.[180] Even so, More's exaltation of good health as the primary bodily pleasure is indicative of his awareness that the body could be abused by indulgence in false and sensual pleasure. It remains reasonable to assume that because More includes the maintenance of a sound conscience alongside intelligence and the contemplation of truth in the category of higher pleasures, he derives his principles of pleasure as much from theological as from philosophical foundations.[181] In accordance with his underlying intentions in writing *Utopia*, More concludes his consideration of Utopian philosophy in terms similar to his last works on Utopian religion, presaging the acceptance of Christian revelation:

> This is their view of virtue and pleasure. They believe that human reason can attain no truer view, unless a heaven-sent religion inspire man with something more holy. Whether in this stand they are right or wrong, time does not permit us to examine—nor is it necessary. We have taken upon ourselves only to describe their principles, and not also to defend them. But of this I am quite sure, that whatever you think of their ideas, there is nowhere in the world a more excellent people nor a happier commonwealth.[182]

Beneath this rather cryptic passage, it is apparent that More portrays the Utopians as leading an essentially virtuous existence. It is left to the reader to discern whether the evangelism of Hythlodaeus's group of adventure would cause the Utopian lifestyle to become as 'perfect' as any to which men could aspire.

10

The ethical position attributed by More to the Utopian commonwealth maintains a series of beliefs and practices which are, to say the least, incongrous to the period or, for that matter, to most other circumstances. These attitudes, which include an attenuated form of religious toleration, the facility of divorce for individuals wronged within the marital contract, medical euthanasia, the admission of women to the priesthood, clerical marriage, the cremation of the dead, a subscription to the doctrine of the 'just war' bordering on *Realpolitik*, colonial settlement as a means of alleviating population pressure and the holding in a condition of servitude of criminals and prisoners of war, have provoked a remarkably varied critical response.

Catholic scholars have discovered in *Utopia*'s enunciation of the extremes of rationalism within religious and ethical conventions an opportunity, evinced by the absence of revelationary restraint, to distance More from aspects of the book's contents. Even so, a certain ambivalence has prevailed. The treatment of 'heretics' in Utopia, informed esentially by admonition and counselling, has been cited as typifying More's position on this subject by writers uneasy at his reputation as a vigorous prosecutor (even persecutor) of Protestant heresy.[183] The essential point, it is argued, is that More distinguished between heretics confused as to doctrinal truth, and those who threatened the violent disruption of public order.[184] However, the argument that More was no bigot, and indeed in 1516 was critical of bigotry within Catholicism, fits ill with the condemnation by avowedly Catholic opinion of other aspects of Utopian religious rationalism.

Other facets of the Utopian way of things have occasioned considerable bemusement. This is particularly true of the related issues of Utopian foreign policy and slavery. More has, for example, been identified as countenancing a 'Machiavellian' prosecution of the objectives of the Utopian state.[185] Others have rushed to More's defence, asserting his championship of the ideal of Christendom, adherence to received understandings of the doctrine of the just war and intention only of exposing the hypocrisies of contemporary foreign policy.[186] Similarly with the question of slavery, an institution which has variously been rationalized in terms either of Utopian paganism[187] or a level-headed approach to punishment and penal servitude.[188]

Scholarly appraisal of *Utopia* should now be sufficiently mature as to render ingenuous ready and straightforward 'solutions' to the incongruities thrown up by the book. It is possible, of course, to rehearse a series of feasible explanations of what might have exercised More's mind in attributing such attitudes to Utopia. Undoubtedly More utilized these often extraordinary positions to imply the fallacious potential of unrestrained human reason, but what as the conviction that More was an affirmed rationalist. The truth lies somewhere between these two positions. The interpretation currently being developed suggests that there are reasons for supposing that More was himself unsure as to the facility of men to exercise reason in the successful regulation of social affairs.

11

More's social philosophy is more consistently in accord with his theology than is often supposed. This impression is confirmed by reviewing the relationship between the philosophy of pleasure, the Utopian practice of communism and More's ultimate purpose of providing an institutional basis for the salvation of Man by neutralizing the sinful propensities of fallen human nature. Within this scheme of things, communism is ultimately perceived as contributing to Man's salvation in two ways. First, communism directly affects the process of redemption by frustrating the sinfulness More associates with the desire for private ownership. Second, communism is also an indirect means towards the deliverance of the individual from sin because it facilitates an equitable distribution of time and allows for the performance of good works. Further, free time in Utopia is devoted to intellectual activities and to the contemplation of truth and virtue. Effectively, communism makes for a sound conscience, and makes such a condition available to all. In Utopia the opportunities and facilities for salvation are distributed equally.

More's belief that a good conscience may derive every bit as much from a virtuous active life as from a contemplative one has a considerable bearing upon the internal coherence of *Utopia*. More argues that an individual could derive satisfaction, and presumably a sound conscience, from the scrupulous discharge of his duties. More thus reconciles work and labour to the principle of true pleasure, a feat which obviously augurs well for the Utopian economy.

But further, the *vita activa* and the *vita contemplativa* are available to all Utopian citizens. As we have seen, the Utopians conceive of the stimulation of their reasoning faculties as a higher form of pleasure. Yet exercising reason also lies at the heart of Utopian religion. So because 'pleasure as reasoning' is equitably distributed, the contemplative life effectively embraces the entire Utopian citizenry. In Utopia, therefore, spiritual contemplation is not the prerogative of a relatively privileged minority set apart from the remainder of society. The combination of works and contemplation which permeates life in Utopia is informed by More's apprehension of the human predicament. It is apparent that in *Utopia* More seeks to resolve certain dilemmas related to the salvation of Man. Although a degree of 'utilitarianism' is evident in *Utopia*, More's religious philosophy, which maintains that true pleasure is objectively discernible by right reason, provides a restraint upon hedonism. Men subject to *both* revelation and the rationally constituted institutions of *Utopia* may therefore lead to something approximating a truly Christian way of life.

The Utopian worldview

1

The intellectual outlook portrayed as prevailing in the ideal commonwealth is to a considerable degree a reflection of More's purpose in writing *Utopia*. To take an example, More's discussion of the education programme epitomizes the task he set himself. More proclaims the range of benefits to be derived from a sound education policy. Education is contributory to economic production, the improvement of social behaviour and the attainment of pleasure. The popularity of intellectual activity among the Utopians stands in marked contrast to the disdain of such pursuits exhibited by a substantial proportion of the European elite. Thus the Utopians are endowed with an attitude to education reminiscent of the outlook of More's mentors, Colet and Erasmus. The Utopians prove receptive to the great humanist programme, the learning of Greek.[189] However, More is obliged to recognize that the cerebral gifts of individuals vary. So within the division of labour he provides the opportunity for those not given to intellectual exertion to occupy themselves, and to serve the community, by performing manual work. The intellectual elite are in principle at least granted perpetual freedom from manual labour so that they may contribute to the common good by constituting the governing class.[190] Hence it appears that in the island of Utopia at least, a dialogue on the sagacity of accepting public office, such as that contained in Book I of *Utopia*, would be redundant. There, intellectuals of a Christian-humanist disposition could assume office without any qualm. That education constitutes both a moral good and a major pastime in Utopia explains More's insistence that both men and women partake of it. *Utopia* is to this extent a document of quite radical reform.

2

More's analysis of science and technology is informed by a series of presuppositions which prove interesting when compared to Winstanley's evaluation of similar themes. More believed that the Fall and its consequences had placed a severe restriction upon the degree to which the human condition could be amended. This, in turn, profoundly affected More's conception of progress. For More to have believed in an untramelled degree of scientific advance, which might in turn have ameliorated aspects of Man's predicament, would have required him to abandon the basic tenets of his worldview. One crucial difference between the respective positions maintained by More and Winstanley is that the citizens of Utopia appear berefit of the aggressively experimental attitude towards the predicament advocated in *The Law of Freedom*. In essence, Winstanley's conception of progress exceeded anything More could possibly have contemplated.

Although More states that the objective of technology in Utopia is to 'promote the advantage and convenience of life',[191] the Utopian attitude to scientific advance evinces a ready acceptance of innovation rather than a rigourous endeavour to discover and apply new technology. So whereas they are prepared to accept the printing press introduced by Hythlodaeus, the Utopians are not endowed with any system of institutions or techniques likely to favour home-bred technical innovation.

The essential passivity of outlook conceived in *Utopia* is complemented by More's attitude towards the experimental investigation of the natural world, a consideration which raises the issue of 'forbidden knowledge'. More points out that while the Utopians 'think that the investigation of nature, with the praise arising from it, is an act of worship acceptable to God'[192] they perceive such enquiry essentially as a source of pleasure,[193] in a manner suggesting a non-progressive, almost dilettanteish, approach to science.

This impression is confirmed by More's condemnation of 'that infamous and deceitful divination by the stars',[194] astrology. Elsewhere, in speaking of 'false astrologue and devynatrice'.[195] More presses the view that Man's predicament is so frought with perilous temptation and the prospect of an inevitable death that any attempt to prophesy the future is utterly futile. Instead, More advises men to look to the more immediate problem of the conditon of their soul. All this may seem rather inconsequential; yet once it is recalled that astrology was an activity which attempted to counter the immediate sensation of helplessness often promoted by contemplation of the predicament, the significance of the activity becomes apparent. In a rather absurd distortion of logic, contemporaries were given to the assumption that by divining the future, any necessary corrective or evasive action could be taken to amend the shape of things to come. Apprehensions of this type enjoyed widespread support during the early modern period.[196] It is also significant that astrological investigations prompted certain ancillary astronomical observations and mathematical techniques which contributed to the discovery of the new cosmology.[197] Clearly, wittingly or not, More closed the door on all of this. That he eschewed astrology provides one indication of his resignation to the impossibility of any dramatic improvement in Man's earthly circumstances.

Far from using *Utopia* to remonstrate with his contemporaries for the extension of natural philosophy in Christendom, an analysis of the terms employed by More in the work suggests to the contrary that More adhered to the dominant worldview of the time by conceiving of natural philosophy as the means to progress of a strictly limited form. More's belief that ultimately Man's fallen condition would prohibit any substantial change in the predicament, and his understanding that whatever moderate improvement might be effected would be achieved by institutional rather than by scientific means, are a measure of the purpose of the discourse. So More's worldview was very much a factor of his diminution of worldly affairs. By concentrating attention upon the issue of Man's spiritual redemption, More propounded a philosophy of resignation which conceived of Man's earthly situation as an essentially immutable condition.

Freedom and moral behaviour in *Utopia*

1

The problem of political obligation brings to the fore the question of how the individual placed in a social context such as that promoted in *Utopia* might 'freely' exercise the will in a manner appropriate to the attainment of the good. The facility of a society such as that outlined in *Utopia* to enhance the status of man as citizen is brought into question by J.C. Davis, who contends that More's concern with the pursuit of moral certainty means that 'in preventing uncertainty by restricting the freedom of men to an extreme degree, he might jeopardise their whole status as moral agents'.[198] According to Davis, More's concern to foster social stability and to achieve the harmony of positive law and individual conscience led him to develop a social philosophy that was in effect at odds with the participatory ideals of classical republicanism. Social stability was therefore secured in Utopia through the thoroughgoing institutional restraint of individual action. This theme is not unfamiliar to students of More's work.[199] However, in assessing the Utopian achievement Davis speaks of 'a discipline which is totalitarian in its scope and denial of human individuality', and goes on to argue that 'if we mean by moral behaviour a free choosing of the good rather than the bad when both alternatives are available, the Utopian's area of choice is so limited that he is almost incapable of moral behaviour'.[200]

The contention that the institutionalism of *Utopia* would militate against the individual attaining moral autonomy is one which begs two important questions: first, whether More shared the conception of moral behaviour, founded on a particular understanding of what is meant by freedom of choice, utilized by scholars such as Davis; and second, whether More, failing an adherence to this outlook, could ever have been persuaded to accept it. It seems unlikely that More's understanding of individual freedom was of a form capable of supporting the apprehension that the social determinism implied in *Utopia* would constitute an unwarranted constraint upon individual action *according to More's perception of the concept*. In considering the first question it is necessary to explore More's apprehension of Man's potential for moral action, a view that recalls aspects of his theology. In turning to the second question, it is necessary to extend the logic of More's position in order to discover precisely what he understood by the idea of freedom.

To accept that freedom is in some sense related to choosing is to presume a good deal of individual ability. In a positive sense, persons may be regarded as being free only to the extent that their capacity to choose and to act accordingly are manifest. Thomas More's views on Man's ability to choose and act are manifest in his theological and spiritual writings and it is to these views that critics concerned with the problem of moral behaviour in *Utopia* must turn. To recapitulate: in essence More believed the human predicament to be described and informed by the 'Fall of Man' and that Man's ultimate potential of salvation had been secured by Christ's Passion. More's social and political thought was therefore devoted to the question of precisely how the predicament might be withstood while affording the best opportunity of developing human potential.

It is evident that Davis's critique of the social determinism he believes More to have upheld in *Utopia* is informed by a particular conception of moral action, a view which assumes that individuals enjoy sufficient freedom of choice to ensure that their actions fulfil the necessary criteria of 'moral behaviour'. Several conditions, including the principle that 'ought implies can', and the availability of at least one alternative to do other than the good, broadly satisfy this conception of moral behaviour. Those versions of this approach advanced by (among others) Aristotle, Kant and G.E. Moore are familiar.[201] So, to reiterate, according to such a conception of moral behaviour not only must a range of choice be available to agents, but the *ability* of agents must also be such that they can consciously choose between alternatives. This ability is often defined in terms of 'free will'. Thus, determined action seems to imply some degree of moral incapacity on behalf of the agent(s) in question. Equally, cases of determined action where the 'cause' is identifiable as an 'external impediment' would seem to imply that the potential of the individual for moral conduct is frustrated.

It is clear that a close examination of precisely how and what More believed persons to be capable of choosing is required. It is also necessary to ascertain More's understanding of Man's *responsibility* for his choices. One of the most interesting aspects of More's understanding of freedom of choice is the existence of a disparity between his conception of how and what men are *capable* of choosing, and his view on the extent to which they might be *responsible* for their choices. This appreciation turns upon More's conception of the 'Fall of Man' and his understanding of the conditions prerequisite to salvation. Basic to More's apprehension of the human condition is his conviction that although the Fall had left the individual morally incapacitated, salvation would require the individual to act in a manner which to some degree at least counteracted the consequences of the Fall. More's understanding of this problem is informed by the complexities of his position on divine grace and freedom of the will, a position which is ultimately unclear as to the precise point at which the individual exercises responsibility for his own salvation. Thus, it appears that More conceived of Man's predicament as one according to which he is required to exercise a form of moral responsibility while seeming unable to do so. Quite obviously, such discord between ability and responsibility is some distance from the conception of moral action presumed by Davis. The problem More faced in dealing with the evident and potential abilities of mankind is but one aspect of the conundrum which is integral to his analysis of the human condition.

2

In confronting the problem of the extent of individual liberty within the constraints entailed by the social arrangements outlined in *Utopia*, analysis must turn to More's perception of what it is to be a person. It is quite apparent that More's conception of Man's potential for autonomous action differs markedly from the view informing Davis's interpretation. The crucial point at issue is that although More maintains that persons are capable of acting virtuously and meritoriously by exercising freedom of the will, he also insists upon the further element of grace as an essential facet of virtuous action. Whatever the logical shortcomings of this position More was adamant that this provision would not constitute any contradiction of Man's potential. 'God does not impart grace to men in such a way as to suspend for the moment the functions and duties of nature.'[202] Each individual agent is attributed with responsibility for his own moral actions.

A consideration central to the interpretation of *Utopia* is that More's conception of divine grace complements rather neatly the conundrum that is his apprehension of human nature. Man fallen and depraved, yet retaining some potential to act freely and virtuously. This feeling is captured in the following:

> For syth euery man that seketh for the bylyefe, and endeuoreth hym self therto, purposeth therby to seke the way to saluacyon; the corrupte nature of man can neuer begyn to entre into that iournaye, nor walke forth one fote therin, by yf he be bothe fyrste preuented by grace, and haue it walke wyth hym styll. For our sauyour sayth, wythout me can ye nothynge do.[203]

Persons are so corrupt as to be incapable of fully autonomous moral actions. Thus they require the assistance of divine grace. Nevertheless, this does not entail the assumption that individuals are not held responsible for their actions. This curious apprehension of moral responsibility, as a notion bereft of a fully-fledged concept of moral autonomy, constitutes a crucial element of More's conception of individual liberty. It must constantly be borne in mind that More oscillated between two positions—on the one hand, the admission that men are incapable of absolutely autonomous or self-determining moral action, and, on the other hand, the convention that despite this limitation men would be held responsible *as if* they were capable of such conduct. In this lies the basis of More's conception of responsibility, an understanding which in turn informs his appreciation of freedom of choice.

The difficulties encountered by some scholars in analysing the relationship between the individual and the state prescribed in *Utopia* often arise from a failure to recall that More was influenced by an intellectual tradition according to which Man is perceived as a responsible moral agent without being entirely autonomous in the sense familiar within the sort of moral and political discourse informed by the analysis of causal determinism proferred by 'modern philosophy'. Hence, the problem of attempting to discern precisely what notion of freedom occupied More's attention. The crucial consideration appears to be that More was concerned less with the problem of freedom of choice as such, although he certainly believed this to be important, and more with the *substance* of the choices which individuals actually make. The problem of whether More was so aware as he might have been of the view that the moral calibre of choice is often informed by the manner of choosing is discussed below. However, at this stage it is important to stress that More's conception of Man and Man's potential was such that he did not regard the role of grace in moral choice as an abrogation of individual autonomy. Rather, More emphasizes that, as responsible moral agents, individuals will be held accountable for the actual choices that they make. This is important because grace, according to More, is a benevolent gift and is a necessary factor if men are to choose the good. More does not regard grace as an imposition upon individual autonomy because he believes that human potential can be realized only by choosing the good. Thus conceived, grace is not an impediment but a facility to morally responsible choice. This having been established, it is appropriate to move on to the question of whether other similar, although obviously less efficacious, bolsters to Man's capacity for determining upon the good, the sphere of human artefacts of which politics is a form, can be seen in the same light.

3

It has been said of the relationship between the state and the citizen described in *Utopia* that 'unless the spirit of willing obedience animates the individual citizen in Utopia, the liberty of democracy becomes for him the tyranny of the many in the servile state'.[204] No digression into theories of authority, consent and political obligation is required to remind us that such a problem is not peculiar to *Utopia*. Nevertheless, remarks such as these are undoubtedly inspired by what a number of scholars have identified as the unusual punctiliousness of the Utopian state in regulating the affairs of its citizens. The uncomfortable feeling is that such a presence is precisely what More intended Utopian society to sponsor. Presumably, More expected to discover 'the spirit of willing obedience' among those Utopian citizens whose propensity to evil had been subverted to the extent that their natural virtues could be exhibited.

More's assessment of the depravity of human nature informs his belief that individuals might be capable of correct behaviour on a sustained basis only as members of a society in which conduct is precisely regulated by institutional means. His advocacy of communism is but one aspect of this line of thought. This reasoning extends to his views on the state. Effectively, in *Utopia* 'Augustinian' Man is to be redeemed by a 'Thomist' polity. Yet once again, the major problem with this position arises from the moral estimation of the apparently determined action that Utopian political institutions appear to posit.

It is apparent that More does not regard the direction or channelling of the individual will by the state as a significant or unjustifiable curtailment of the freedom of choice of the citizen. Clearly, More attributes criteria of value to various forms of liberty. More's conception of the human predicament seems to lead to the conclusion that it is extremely unlikely that the individual could sustain himself as a truly self-determining agent in the sense that he would invariably or even regularly choose the good. For one thing, Man inhabits a universe in which the powers of evil are immanent. More maintains that Man's reasoning faculties are impaired by the Fall. Hence the contention that Man's capacity to exercise the will in choosing the good is also damaged. Beyond the Fall Man can never be entirely 'free'. He can, of course, exercise free will in choosing to sin; but More conceives of the condition of actual sin as a form of bondage. Against this, More must be seen as regarding societal compulsion in directing the individual towards the good as a lesser evil. Indeed, More may be regarded as understanding that the Utopians are 'freed' from the bondage of actual sin to achieve the higher end of salvation, and that in this lies the only means of redeeming the integrity of Man.

It is possible to deduce that More's treatment of the concept of liberty is distinguished by an implicit assumption which attributes value to two forms of liberty.[205] However, for reasons that will become evident, More experienced difficulty in applying this distinction specifically. The first form of liberty in question is freedom of choice or the exercising of free will. The second is that freedom from sin necessary to do the good. More seems to suggest that freedom from the bondage of sin is intrinsically good, but that this condition is valueless unless it is freely and consciously chosen, and that such choice is valuable because it affords the opportunity to choose good as opposed to evil. At this point it is important to recall that the balance between the value of the freedom of choice and the value of specific alternatives is defined, according to More's logic, by the consideration that Man's moral responsibility is not, in fact, absolute and free but will be assessed as if it were. It is therefore interesting to speculate on whether More regarded freedom of choice as intrinsically valuable. It seems unlikely that he did. He is more likely to have argued that freedom of choice is instrumentally valuable, but may have intrinsic value imputed to it, because it is the means of securing ulterior objects or conditions which *are* instrinsically valuable. Although for More freedom from sin is obviously intrinsically valuable it seems that he also wished to suggest that moral value is derivative of the psuedo-free manner in which it is chosen.

These points have a considerable bearing upon how the political prescriptions of *Utopia* ought to be regarded. If the value of choice (in this case the choice to act virtuously) depends upon the exercise of a relatively unconstrained choice between alternatives, then it is possible to contend that More may have placed the Utopian citizen in an unenviable position. As has been observed, Utopian society placed many restraints upon men's conduct, and in particular, sought to reduce the opportunity to sin. Were not this impression created More would have failed in his intentions. Nevertheless, and paradoxically, such success in institutional design has been regarded as reducing the moral significance of choice because of the apparent suggestion in *Utopia* that the opportunity to choose evil might be largely precluded.

Even so, the existence of a punitive system in Utopia[206] indicates that More expected evil to persist and that choice must thereupon be to some extent 'real'. Indeed More is clearly indicating that, whatever the institutional environment, the very depravity of human nature guarantees that the value of choice between good and evil will always be maintained. Further, More must also have believed that the adoption of Utopian institutions in contemporary Europe would not only constitute a morally significant choice in itself, but would also secure the moral significance of a good proportion of all future choices. In a reformed Christendom, the collective and presumably publicized recollection of the possibility to do greater evil in the pre-reform system would continue to enhance the moral calibre of collective choice in a restraining society. Although More designed Utopian institutions to be self-perpetuating he must also have recognized that their maintenance in Christendom would have depended to some significant degree upon a continuing decision to that effect. Even so, had he been presented with this argument More might well have responded pessimistically—playing down the prospects of his contemporaries voluntarily opting for an alternative institutional regime. Again, this conundrum stands at the centre of the fundamental dilemma of More's conception of the human condition and the social theory he advanced as a solution to it.

Analysis along these lines ultimately returns to the question of precisely how More's moral actor chooses to do the good. There appears to be no way out of this difficulty other than to argue that the logical incongruities pervading More's ideas concerning Man's facility for free will yet accompanying reliance on divine grace are also evident in his appreciation of the respective value of freedom of choice and actual determinate choices. So, although More's understanding of the doctrine of *preuencyon* ultimately involves a regress to divine grace as prime mover, More is also anxious to speculate on the reciprocal and co-operative relationship between divine grace and Man's free will. Similarly, although More ultimately identifies the substance of choice as the paramount value, he is reluctant to stand by hard determinism. In this sense, it seems fair to argue that More regarded freedom of choice as at least instrumentally valuable and, circumstances permitting, as occasionally intrinsically valuable. More's nagging problem, and this is manifest in *Utopia*, is that he could never comfortably accept the view that persons might sustain their appointed role in this complicated system. If his thinking on divine grace is representative of More the soft determinist, his utopian institutionalism betrays More the hard determinist. We are never far from the conundrum that pervades his understanding of mankind's predicament.

4

More's eclecticism and assimilation of ideas from various intellectual currents contributed to his often ambivalent appreciation of the human predicament. His view of Man suggests that More was largely sympathetic to an essentially 'Augustinian' conception of human nature. Nevertheless, although he maintained that worldly affairs are of secondary importance to the condition of the soul, More did not subscribe wholeheartedly to St Augustine's deprecatory attitude to the affairs of the world. Neither did More succumb to the ideas derived by Luther from Augustine's view of the depravity of Man. Had he done so, the appreciation of the human condition and appropriate remedy posited in *Utopia* might have attained greater logical consistency, albeit at a cost to the doctrinal affiliations of his theology. Instead More modified his Augustinianism by incorporating several Aristotelian and 'Thomist' ideas and concepts. An essential theme of *Utopia* is that men should conduct their wordly affairs as closely as possible in accordance with the harmony of reason and revelation. By pointing to the inadequacies of positive law in his own society, More demonstrated the ineffectual exercising of reason by his own contemporaries. While this fault is addressed in *Utopia*, where the substance of positive law is intended to accord with natural law, More is also anxious to assert that without reference to the sanction of revelation, individuals could never be confident of exercising reason correctly. Grace and revelation are necessary supplements to reason if the will is to incline to the good. Ultimately, however, More's belief that persons could use their reason to discern the optimal form of life in the fallen condition is clouded by his sensitivity to the corruption of human nature. More never successfully resolved this dilemma. Thus his own utopianism is appropriately regarded as an instance of the application of reason by one person to the problems arising from the human predicament. As a result, the institutional recommendations of *Utopia* were designed to direct men away from sin and towards virtue. Yet his conception of human nature caused More to view the prospects for the adoption of his ideas by the mass of the unregenerate with profound pessimism.

Despite his testimony to the ameliorative potential of the institutionalism of his ideal commonwealth More remained convinced of the inherent sinfulness of Man. So he assumed that society was unlikely to originate the optimal commonwealth without some ulterior prompting. It appeared to More that, although once implemented his institutional proposals were capable of subjugating human nature, Man's own sinfulness would prejudice him against their adoption. Consequently, More expressed his political treatise in the form of a utopia, and within this format accounted for the foundation of the state by arguing that the fallen islanders had been conquered by the lawgiver Utopus.[207] This literary device is clearly demanded by More's awareness of the disparity between the ideal evinced in *Utopia* and the reluctance to initiate reform in his own society.

More is anxious to assert that, even after 1760 years,[208] Utopian institutions remain ever vigilent because people would always retain the innate and ineradicable propensity to sin. So although the Utopians conduct themselves in the best possible manner this is not attributable to any superior characteristic of their nature; they are inherently the same as all men. However, because their laws, social mores, and education suppress Man's tendency to sin, and encourage his capacity for good, the Utopians conduct themselves more virtuously than their European counterparts.

Presumably, the reader is intended to gain the impression that this remains the case only so long as they stay within the institutional domain of Utopia. Should they be relieved of the restraining influence of Utopian society they will inevitably degenerate into the abyss of sinfulness that typifies contemporary Christendom.

More's conception of the human condition is not totally despondent. Despite his tendency to emphasize the depravity of human nature, he also believes persons to possess certain natural desires and affections which could lead them to the good. However, More insists that such virtues are likely to be manifest only in a corrective social environment, and particularly in conditions of equality. Hence his arrival at the following categorical conclusion:

> Nor does it occur to me to doubt that Man's regard for his own interests or the authority of Christ our Saviour—who in His Wisdom could not fail to know what was best and who in His goodness could not fail to counsel what He knew to be best—would long ago have brought the whole world to adopt the laws of the Utopian commonwealth, had not one single monster, the chief and progenitor of all plagues, striven against it—I mean Pride.[209]

According to More's perception of the human condition it emerges that Man, exercising reason and free will as an autonomous being independent of divine grace, is potentially capable of achieving a good; but that good is an artefact—the civil society described in *Utopia*. The artefact is the means of attaining an ulterior end—the supernatural good of salvation. More emerges as a 'positive libertarian'; for him the alternative of the self-sustaining moral actor is simply unrealistic. Every day he observed the use to which Man put the 'freedom' reposited in contemporary Christendom—in the corrupt abyss of sinfulness that he saw in his own society.

Part III

4

Gerrard Winstanley's conception of the human condition

Winstanley's theology

1

On the occasion of the dispersal of the Digger colony in 1650 Winstanley stated that: 'True religion, and undefiled, is to let every one quietly have earth to manure, that they may live in freedome by their labours.'[1] This seemingly trite pronouncement, blending as it does secular with spiritual concerns, takes us to the very heart of the debate over the role played by religious ideas within Winstanley's thought. Scholarly disputation centres upon the issue of whether Winstanley's intellectual development is most appropriately regarded as demonstrating a consistent preoccupation with theological concerns or whether, at some stage, Winstanley more or less abandoned spiritual considerations in favour of an essentially secular appreciation of the human condition.[2]

In this section, the main principles of Winstanley's theological position are scrutinized. This task is complicated by the aforementioned developmental nature of Winstanley's writings and by the radical and often innovative form of the speculations contained therein. Even so, whereas it is not possible to assume that Winstanley adhered to a fundamentally consistent body of doctrine in the manner of a thinker such as More, it remains the case that any systematic analysis of Winstanley's social philosophy cannot ignore his concern with religion because theological notions form the basis of Winstanley's assessment of Man's predicament.[3]

Winstanley's spirituality and conception of religious truth is in part experimental: 'if a particular branch of mankind desire to know what the nature of other men and women are, let him look not abroad, but into his own heart, and he shall see'.[4] Propositions of this kind sustain the method, blending experimentalism and introspection, recommended by Winstanley for the analysis of the human condition. Yet Winstanley often drew upon an amalgam of received opinion, such as the doctrine of the Fall, before reinterpreting such ideas to accommodate his own concerns and preoccupations.

The difficulties encountered in attempting to evaluate Winstanley's religious ideas are immediately apparent once his understanding of an entity or concept such as 'God' is afforded consideration. On the question of the nature of the deity, Winstanley's thought developed rapidly. Initially, Winstanley perceived of God as a just and essentially merciful ruler of men.[5] However, with an increasing insistence that experience constituted the only valid foundation for religious knowledge, Winstanley came to argue that individuals who had not been enlightened by God could not possibly understand Him.[6] So although Winstanley describes God as 'the onely one infinite being', who is distinguished by His 'incomprehensiblenesse',[7] he recommends that men should

> not look for a God now, as formerly you did, to be a place of glory beyond the Sun, Moon and Stars, nor a Divine being you know not where, by [but] you feel him ruling within you, and not onely in you, but you see and know him to be the spirit and power that dwells in every man . . .[8]

Throughout, Winstanley is certain that individuals who attain such true perception are impressed by God's most essential characteristic—His *reasonableness*. So he ultimately defines God as:

> the incomprehensible spirit, Reason; who as he willed that the Creation should flow out of him: so he governes the whole Creation in righteousnesse, peace and moderation: And from hence he is called, The Lord, because there is none above him: And he is called, The Father, because the whole creation came out of him . . .[9]

An important presupposition of Winstanley's thought is the understanding that the harmony of the Creation relates directly to the prevalence of reason among men. As a corollary, Winstanley affirms that universal harmony is to be accomplished only through the realization of the true nature of God by all men.[10] Thus, although Winstanley tends to substitute the terms 'God' and 'Reason', he does so not because of a desire to abandon belief in the deity,[11] but because he wishes to endorse his conception of the true nature of the controlling power of the universe.

Winstanley's contention that God could be known only through spiritual experience laid the foundation for his theory that individuals might be restored to a condition of righteousness. From the outset, Winstanley is to be discovered claiming that 'you cannot say the spirit is your God, till you feel, and see by experience that the Spirit doth govern your flesh'.[12] Even in what is commonly acknowledged as his most secular work, *The Law of Freedom*, Winstanley remains adamant that 'God is an active Power, not an imaginary Fancy'.[13] Much of Winstanley's thought is devoted to the problem of how individuals would come to experience such righteousness within. As we shall see, the development of his social philosophy was inspired in part by his transition from the view that men must passively await such an awakening to the belief that righteousness could be induced by institutional means.

Winstanley conceives of reason as existing in two basic senses, and argues that a correspondence of the two will render the Creation harmonious by reconciling Man to God. On the one hand, Winstanley refers to the 'Spirit Reason' in the sense of a synonymity to God. On the other hand, Winstanley professes a belief that men are endowed with a faculty identifiable as 'Reason'. He argues, therefore, that the deeper men descend into the fallen condition of moral degeneracy the greater the antagonism between 'God-as-Reason' and Man. Winstanley maintains that, ideally, the actions of the individual ought to be guided by the Spirit Reason.[14]

As is the case with so much of his thought, Winstanley's position on the question of right reason is a complex amalgam of both established and incipient intellectual viewpoints: the spiritual, the moral and the secular. One of the challenges facing any reader of Winstanley's works is to tease out the intricate array of ideas which blend a concern with the nature of God, spiritual well-being, rational action and moral conduct, social utility and Man's relationship to the natural environment. Only in relation to this range of concerns can the full significance of Winstanley's obsession with the nature of labour and with property rights be fully appreciated. To take labour as an example: here Winstanley believes that only if appropriate arrangements attend the process of labour may Man attain not only moral and spiritual enlightenment but also the forms of production and distribution necessary to obviate those social injustices sustained by the prevailing mode of property holding.

The appeal to *right reason* as a principle for the justification of social conduct is, of course, a disposition which gathered momentum as the seventeenth century progressed. During the Civil War such appeals were especially prevalent among radicals, the social theories of the Levellers providing an obvious case in point. The potentially restorative effects of right reason are an oft-repeated element of Winstanley's writings. In one instance, he speculates that:

> it is Reason that made all things, and it is reason that Governs the whole Creation, and if flesh were but subject thereunto, that is, to the spirit of Reason within himself, it would never act unrighteousness (*sic*) . . .[15]

Winstanley's contention that men could only perceive reason experimentally, which so typifies the general tenor of his religious ideas, prompts him to the confident assertion that any individual who experienced the spirit of reason 'may be said to be a perfect man'.[16] In the sensation of reason Winstanley sees the recovery of what men had forsaken in the Fall.

An important principle of contemporary psychology was the appreciation that reason could restrain 'imagination' and thereby inhibit immoral or selfish actions.[17] Winstanley accords with this view, suggesting that reasonable conduct is also to be known intuitively. Again, this aspect of his evaluation of Man's potential influences Winstanley's social theory. He argues, for example, that reason and the practice of communism are integrally related because:

it hath a regard to the whole creation; and knits every creature together into a onenesse; making every creature to be an upholder of his fellow; and so every one is an assistant to preserve the whole.[18]

The identification of the harmony of the Creation with communism recurs throughout Winstanley's writings. Thus he uses 'reason' in a sense intended to confirm the spiritual implications of his social recommendations:

Reason makes a man to live moderately and peaceably, with all; he makes a man just and righteous in all his actings; he kills forwardnesse, envy and pride in a man: and why? where lies the Reason? Because this man stands in need of him; and therefore makes a man to doe as he would be done unto.[19]

2

Winstanley's conception of reason is closely related to his understanding of what he terms 'the spirit', a notion which in turn constitutes an important facet of his consideration of experimental religion. The spirit is usually portrayed in Winstanley's writings as a restorative agent. He claims, for example, that 'the power oi [of] the Spirit, who is the King of righteousnesse within every man, treads down the flesh, and sets the creatures free from Hell, Death, and Devil'.[20] So, before men can become righteous they have first to attain an awareness of 'the spirit'. In this manner, the individual will be brought into communion with the guiding spirit of the entire Creation. Winstanley confirms that such an experience bestows upon the individual an inner tranquility capable of withstanding the disruptions of the world without.[21] This line of argument informs Winstanley's pronounced anti-intellectualism, whereby the idea of 'the spirit' rather than formal learning is advanced as the essential element of true religious knowledge.

Although not oblivious to the historical role of Christ, who as 'God manifest in the flesh'[22] was for Winstanley the perfect man, he is evidently more concerned to stress the potential influence of the *spirit* of Christ upon society. Winstanley conceives of Christ as the mediator destined to remove sin from the world,[23] a redemption to be attained as individuals experience the resurrection of 'Christ within'. Hence Winstanley is prompted to describe Christ as 'not a single man at a distance from you: but . . . the wisdom and power of the Father, who spirits the whole creation, dwelling and ruling King of righteousnesse in your very flesh'.[24] It is perhaps not surprising that Winstanley is at greater ease in discussing the spirit of Christ than in accounting for the corporeal presence of Christ on earth. His 'historical' exposition of the resurrection and ascension of Jesus is, to say the least, complex and unconvincing.[25] However, in anticipating the 'Second Coming', Winstanley is more confident about what to expect:

if you look for him under the notion of one single man after the flesh, to be your saviour, you shall never, never taste salvation by him . . . if you expect, or look for the resurrection of Jesus Christ, you must know, that the spirit within the flesh is the Jesus Christ, and you must see, feel, and know from himself his own resurrection within you, if you expect life and peace by him.[26]

This emphasis upon the spiritual return of Christ as something which could in principle be experienced by all men, is a profoundly influential determinant of the nature and direction of Winstanley's social philosophy.

In the discussion to follow, of Winstanley's account of the 'Fall of Man', the consideration will be emphasized that Winstanley placed particular weight upon what he conceived as the conflict between 'the spirit' and 'the flesh' within Man.[27] More than once Winstanley asserts that by exhibiting, most notoriously, unwholesome concerns with private property, commerce and sensual gratification, individuals succumb to the temptings of the flesh and incline to prefer material gratification above spiritual fulfilment. Nevertheless, Winstanley contends that as the son of righteousness and 'inner light'[28] Christ will come to dwell within Man and will destroy 'inner darkness'.[29] Again, the implications of such a line of thought for Winstanley's social and political position are considerable. Not only does he invoke this line to explain the existing condition of human nature and the social arrangements presently sustained by men, but according to it Winstanley also posits the prospect of an improvement in men's manners. In his early pamphlets Winstanley expresses confidence that the coming of Christ will lead to far-reaching social reform. Yet, after a period of deliberation occasioned by setbacks in the practical implementation of his ideas, Winstanley arrived at the conclusion that institutional reform must itself be accomplished prior to men experiencing the inner light; 'when your flesh is subject to the spirit of righteousnesse, as the flesh of Christ was, and this is to believe in Christ'.[30] Christ within would restrain thought and action so that men might recover their true liberty by renouncing materialism.[31]

Winstanley infers that because the reasonableness and righteousness of God are perceptible to Man, the characteristics of His adversary the devil are also evident within Man, in the form of sinful human nature. As a consequence, he states that 'the Devil is not the third power between God and man, but he is the curse in flesh; and the power of utter darkness in this'.[32] As a result of God's dispensation of wrath, fallen men are conscious of their sinfulness to the extent that 'pride of the flesh, envy, slavish fear, distrust, hypocrisie, carnall thoughts, self love, and the like, are particular Devils'.[33] Winstanley also suggests that such bondage of the soul might appropriately be described as 'hell'.[34] His rejection of the notion of an immanent devil is of considerable importance to his general appraisal of Man's potential and as such is a further factor in shaping his social theory. In believing that both evil and the illusion that the Devil actually exists as a discreet entity are actually attributable to corrupt human nature, which is itself eradicable,[35] Winstanley was, when engaging in political debate, able to conceive of a form and degree of social progress unconstrained by a cosmically independent party devoted to the destruction of human well-being.

As an extension of his beliefs concerning the experimental bases of spirituality, Winstanley contends that 'heaven and hell' are merely internal sensations. Throughout his writings the experience of God and Christ within is identified as 'heaven'. Hence the following distinction:

And what is this heaven? Why truly, as the firmament is called Heaven in the history, because the created Sun, Moon, and Stars, those glorious lights are seated there; so wheresoever God dwells, who is the light of lights, that is called Heaven in the mystery.[36]

Implicit here is the arresting assumption that by experiencing the spirit within, men could be restored to a condition of righteousness and thus be redeemed during the course of their earthly existence.

In contradistinction to his view of heaven, Winstanley portrays 'hell' as that condition of despair and unrighteousness from which men are restored by experiencing Christ within.[37] Accordingly, hell is the 'death' and sorrow endured by all descendents of Adam prior to their being redeemed.[38] He claims that 'if the selfish power rule your heart; then as you live now upon uncertainties, in confusion and vexation: so this manifestation of hell, darkness and sorrows, shall multiply within you'.[39] By implication, it is apparent that Winstanley envisaged the transformation of human nature as the means by which men would experience 'heaven' on earth. A startling feature of Winstanley's thought, therefore, is that his social theory was advanced with this objective in mind. Winstanley ultimately came to assume that by regulating life in accordance with certain social institutions such as communism, men might conceive of their earthly existence as a 'heavenly' experience.

The connection between conceptions of heaven and hell and the organization of society is also evident in Winstanley's suspicion that the prospect of heaven and the fear of hell were notions promulgated by the clergy with the deliberate and self-interested intention in mind of constraining the liberty and rights of the common people. Such sanctions, Winstanley surmised, were designed to reinforce the existing structure of society and were consequently perpetuated to disadvantage the common people. Hence, in keeping with his general disposition towards the cloth, Winstanley is to be discovered taunting clergymen for their reluctance to depart forthwith to the attractive after-life depicted to the laity. In essence, Winstanley insists that there can be no certain knowledge of first causes,[40] and impudently argues that

If there be a local place of hell, as Preachers say there is, besides this I speak of, time will make if manifest but as yet none ever came back from the dead to tell men on earth, and till then, men ought to speak no more than they know; what I speak, I speak from what I have from some measure seen within me, and as I have received from the Lord in clear light within myself.[41]

Once again, Winstanley confines 'certainty' in the spiritual realm to knowledge ascertained experimentally.

3

A feature of his promotion of experimental religion is Winstanley's differentiation of the 'gospel' from 'scripture':

First, The Gospel is the Spirit that ruled in the Prophets and Apostles, which testified to them, that in the latter daies the same Spirit should be poured out upon all flesh. Secondly, then their writings is not the Spirit; but a report or declaration of that law and testimony which was written within them.[42]

Winstanley goes on to contend that the gospel, or immediate perception of the spirit, is truly understood only at the point at which peace is brought into men's souls and that should this occur, the curse would be lifted and men would be reconciled to their maker.[43]

Certain commentators regard Winstanley's citation of biblical passages as little more than an appeasement of contemporary convention.[44] An examination of Winstanley's attitude to scripture, however, invalidates this conclusion. In Winstanley's opinion the scriptures constitute a 'record of experimentall testimony';[45] the Bible is in effect an exposition of individual experience. Hence Winstanley's eagerness to distinguish the literal knowledge of scripture, which could be acquired at a university, from the actual spirit of truth, which was only to be appreciated by individuals enjoying direct experience. Hence the contention that 'it is not the Apostles writings, but the spirit that dwelt in them that did inspire their hearts, which gives life, and peace to us all'.[46] The scriptures report the gospel which is in turn the experience of the spirit by Christ, the Apostles and the Prophets.[47] By implication, Winstanley would have the reader believe that were the same spirit to infuse an individual in contemporary society, that person would become capable of interpreting the scriptures correctly.[48] Given Winstanley's belief that the bulk of his fellows were fallen, and that this was particularly the case with the university-educated clergy, his anti-intellectual understanding of spiritual enlightenment assumed, at least in the short term, an exclusive element. So he was prepared to assert that

if the same anointing or power and wisdome of God dwell and rule in you as did appear in the Prophets and Apostles that writ, then you can see into that mysterie of the Scripture (which is God manifest in flesh) and so can speak the minde of the Scriptures, though you should never see, hear, nor read the Scripture from men.[49]

Winstanley regularly attributed the mistranslation and corruption of biblical texts to the fact that interpretation was left to formally educated individuals who lived according to the flesh. In that Winstanley insisted that the lower orders of society would be first to appreciate the spirit within, the radical implications of his position are clear.

4

That Winstanley's analysis of sin is by no means as comprehensive as that of a thinker such as More is perhaps indicative of his more optimistic appreciation of human potential. This notwithstanding, Winstanley equates sin with the characteristics of fallen human nature, often by arguing that the crux of human sinfulness lie in pride, hypocrisy, self-love and covetousness.[50] He accepts that the origins of sinfulness are located in the Fall; 'when the whole earth is filled with this disobedience, so that you cannot meet with a branch of mankinde; but hee lives upon the objects of the creation, and not upon the spirit'.[51] Evidently, Winstanley attributes social malaise to human sinfulness. He frequently associates sin with 'darkness' and with 'the flesh', suggesting the tone and influence of Augustinian ideas transmitted through the medium of contemporary preaching. Nevertheless, and this is a crucially significant consideration, the fabric of Winstanley's social philosophy presupposes a rejection of conventional appreciations of original sin. Winstanley should be regarded not simply as a religious radical who advanced a heretical view of human sinfulness, but instead as a thinker of some considerable sophistication who was influenced by a changing conception of the human condition, one which appeared increasingly valid as the seventeenth century progressed, in that there developed in this period a reluctance to see human potential as constrained by either the reality or the doctrinal orthodoxy of original sin.

Alongside his substantive analysis of the nature of 'sin', Winstanley advances arguments suggesting an acute awareness of the manner in which the idea of sin was sustained as an object of social utility, in that the restraint of conduct might turn upon it. The rationale here is similar to that informing contemporary invocations of 'heaven' and 'hell'. In Winstanley's opinion, so much discourse on the nature of sin was simply devoid of any genuine moral content. Indeed, he regularly maintains that the utilization of socially recognized conceptions of 'sin' to suggest threatened penalties was itself reprehensible and therefore truly sinful because, for example, by this means private property was preserved and extended.[52] Thus, by inverting conventional assumptions, Winstanley insists that the real sinner is not the individual who challenges institutions such as private ownership, but

> he, that restraines the liberty of the outward man, not suffering him to have a free enjoyment of his portion in the Earth; making such actions to be a sinne, which that righteous creating Spirit made not a sinne.[53]

Winstanley concludes, therefore, that actual sin is constituted by the covetousness which impels men to deprive their fellows of their birthright by using as a sanction the notion that to demand those very rights is a sin.

5

Winstanley's concern with the condition of society turned in good part upon the need to account for the origins of private property and to explain its persistence. In providing a rationale for the *origins* of private ownership, the 'orthodox' account, which placed the responsibility for the instigation of private property with Adam, stood Winstanley in fairly good stead. However, received opinion on the *persistence* of private property, which cited the congenital sinfulness of Man as a fundamental cause, was always likely to be incompatible with Winstanley's belief that contemporary patterns of ownership need not be maintained into the future. Orthodox understanding of the continuation of private property therefore represented a powerful argument requiring a substantial disclaimer. As we shall see, what Winstanley's response lacked in simplicity it made up for in innovative acumen in that, whereas the traditional account placed great emphasis upon the irrevocable depravity of human nature, Winstanley took as his starting point an alternative perspective on Man.[54]

Before examining Winstanley's account of the 'Fall of Man' it is necessary to clarify what he understood and meant in using the term 'Adam'. Within Winstanley's writings this name is used in several ways.[55] On numerous occasions Winstanley accords with conventional wisdom by calling the first man to fall 'Adam'. However, Winstanley also employs the term as a typological concept which refers to all men; this because he understood all men subsequent to the historical Adam to be in some sense destined to endure a similar spiritual catastrophe. Thus Winstanley claims with all sincerity that 'we may see *Adam* every day before our eyes walking up and downe the street'.[56] Winstanley would not be distinct in adopting this typology were it not for the fact that he attributed the common moral defects of men not to congenital inheritance, but instead to shared psychological dispositions. This subtle difference carries much of the burden of Winstanley's perception of the human condition.

Winstanley often refers to the collective of fallen individuals as the 'first Adam'. Alternatively, he also maintains that the 'Self is the first *Adam* that falls from the Spirit'.[57] Effectively, Winstanley uses the term in this sense when discussing the condition of human nature resulting from men living according to the 'flesh' by seeking material gratification. This position is summarized in statements to the effect that 'every particular branch of mankind, living upon the objects of the creation, and rejecting their maker, are linage or generation of the first man: yea, being bound up all together, they make up the one first *Adam*'.[58] Winstanley would have his readership believe the time allotted to the ascendancy of this phase of human nature to be necessarily limited. Hence the confident prediction of the first Adam being succeeded by the 'second Adam', and of Man being restored to righteousness by living according to reason. Identifying quite when and how this transformation might occur is the fundamental point at issue within Winstanley's writings.

As he set about constructing a theory of human history, the conventional doctrine of the Fall provided Winstanley with a number of useful premises. Even so, Winstanley did not adhere to the implicit constraints placed by traditional belief upon Man's future. So it is crucially important to emphasize that although Winstanley recognized the existence of an individual named 'Adam' as a person who once perpetrated an historical act, the 'Fall of Man', he also understood the uniqueness of this one event to be much exaggerated. For Winstanley, the most that could be said of the historical Adam was that his experience provided an indication of what was to come.

In analysing Winstanley's appraisal of the 'Fall of Man' it is essential to remain aware of the consideration that his views on the matter were not fixed. From an initial and fairly orthodox version of the story of the Fall,

Winstanley gradually developed an interest in the implications of this event as an exemplar for the conduct of successive generations. Hence his developed understanding of 'the Fall', an eventuality he believed to occur within the life cycle of each and every individual, described the fundamental problem which Winstanley, intent upon the amelioration of the human condition, hoped to resolve by means of his proposals for social and political reform.

6

Winstanley's conception of the 'salvation of mankind' is that of a restoration capable of taking place on earth. He is, therefore, ever anxious to juxtapose his own views on the requirements for salvation against those of more orthodox, and to his mind misinformed, opinion. In discussing the spirit of Christ he stipulates that

> you are not saved by believing, there was such a man, that lived and died in Jerusalem, for though you believe there was such a man, yet it is not saving faith to you, till you feel the power of a meek spirit come into you, and reign King.[59]

Once again, emphasis is placed upon the mystical experiences of the individual rather than on any subscription to preordained beliefs and practices. In this context the process of 'anointing' is of great consequence, so much so that Winstanley writes:

> when the same Anointing or Spirit that was sent downe into that body [Christ's]; is sent down into yours, changing your vile bodies and making them like that glorious body, killing all the cursed powers in the flesh; making your flesh subject to the Spirit; now you are become one with Christ and with the Father, which is your salvation.[60]

As our analysis proceeds we shall see that Winstanley's thought passed through a series of stages, each of which involved a differing theory of how this process might occur.

7

This section has provided a brief analysis of the core of Winstanley's religious ideas. In turning shortly to Winstanley's appreciation of the 'Fall of Man', and beyond that in relating his views on the Fall to his social theories, it will become evident that Winstanley's theological deliberations provide the foundation for the conception of Man's predicament addressed by his social analysis. Just as Winstanley saw a correspondence between living according to the dictates of the flesh, resorting to formal religious practices and received opinion, and turning to material gratification to satiate the desires of fallen human nature (in particular, by accumulating private property), he supposed that, were men to be guided to the spirit of righteousness, they would acquire such peace of mind as to enable them to become spiritually self-sufficient. Accordingly, individuals would then trust in experimental knowledge and thereby sustain social institutions centred on communism.

The Fall of Man and the Myth of the Norman Yoke

1

Much of Winstanley's social theory is devoted to the problem of how certain conditions he supposed to have obtained prior to the Fall might be restored. Thus the image depicted by Winstanley of an ideal society to be established by means of institutional reform bears marked resemblance to his conception of the pristine condition. The overall structure of his thought is therefore informed by Winstanley's appraisal of Man's pre-lapsarian situation. For example, Winstanley maintains that just as universal love had prevailed before the Fall, the Restoration must, by implication, turn upon the recovery of the law of righteousness.[61]

His writings indicate the consistency of Winstanley's belief in the certainty that Man's spiritual condition will be influenced by two aspects of social existence, namely the status of work and labour, and the mode of distribution of private property. In evaluating the 'curse' occasioned by the Fall, Winstanley emphasizes that, with regard to the moral connotations of both work and property, a marked degeneration occured as a consequence of the remove from the original condition. So too, argues Winstanley, had Man's capacity to dominate the environment. Thus he advances the impression that originally all men participated in harmonious natural environment:

> in the beginning of time the whole Creation lived in man, and man lived in his Maker, the spirit of Righteousnesse and peace, for every creature walked evenly with man, and delighted in man, and was ruled by him; there was no opposition between him and the beast, fowls, fishes, or any creature in the earth: so that it was truely said, The whole Creation was in man . . .[62]

2

As his pamphleteering career proceded, Winstanley became increasingly aware that, especially as his advocacy of communism became more vehement yet economically astute, an equally ardent defence of the virtues of hard labour was absolutely prerequisite. Initially, however, in examining the role of 'work' in the pre-lapsarian condition, Winstanley had argued in a rather traditional vein that 'after God had made Adam, he put him into a Garden called Eden, which was full of Trees, Hearbs, Creatures, for pleasure and delight, that he should dresse it, and live contentedly in the use of all things therein'.[63] Some months later, in attempting to justify the communal cultivation of the commons to Fairfax, Winstanley appears to be maintaining a similar position by pointing out that 'before the Fall, Adam, or the Mañ id dresse the garden, or the earth, in love, freedome and righteousnesse'.[64] However, by this time Winstanley had elaborated upon a very much more sophisticated appreciation of the nature of labour and, commensurately, realized that the claim that Man in the original condition had not been constrained to provide for his subsistence might generate certain discordant theoretical implications, not to say embarrassing personal affronts, should it be juxtaposed to his rationale for digging. So Winstanley amended his erstwhile position, contending that 'when he consented to that Serpent covetousnesse, then he fell from righteousnesse, was cursed, and was sent into the earth to eat his bread in sorrow: And from that time began particular propriety'.[65]

As Winstanley deduced the establishment of private property, particularly in the form of landownership, to be one aspect of the curse, he argued that *hired* labour was another. Thus he came to distinguish hired labour from the 'natural' and free working of land that was not privately owned:

> *To subdue the Earth.* And this implies, plowing, digging, and all kind of manuring. So then observe. That bare and simple working in the Earth, according to the freedome of the Creation, though it be in the sweat of mans browes, is not the curse.[66]

Such propositions are consistent with Winstanley's assertion that the strenuous activity of digging, and the obligation to labour detailed in *The Law of Freedom*, would be spiritually restorative. Ultimately, Winstanley even suggested that Man could *labour* to reinstitute the dominion over nature.[67]

3

Winstanley's observations on the nature of property before the Fall are more consistent and explicit than is the case with his discussion of labour. He maintains quite categorically that in the original condition all objects had been held, or at least were designed to be held, in common. Consequently, before the Fall there had been no private property. With regard to the act of Creation, Winstanley asserts that as God 'made mankinde to be Lord of the Earth, so he made the Earth to be a common Treasury of livelihood to whole mankinde without respect of persons'.[68] The idea that the Earth was once, and ought still to be, a 'common treasury' developed as an integral theme within Winstanley's writings. Winstanley remained insistent that all men possessed a birthright to partake of the common treasury.

> In the first entrance into the Creation, every man had an equall freedom given of his Maker to till the earth, and to have dominion over the beasts of the field, the fowls of heaven, and fish in the Seas.[69]

The evolution of Winstanley's social ideas witnessed a hardening commitment to the view that this 'creation right' had been abrogated with the introduction of private property, and continued to be withheld from the common people by social and political arrangements originating in the main with the Norman Conquest. By maintaining that the Civil War had been fought to overthrow Normanism, Winstanley felt confident in asserting that the birthright to cultivate the land (or at the very least the wastes and commons) ought to be restored immediately.

Contemporary thinking on the pristine condition often emphasized Man's former dominion over nature.[70] As Winstanley drew upon this notion, the radical implications of it became evident to him. Thus he is to be discovered asserting that 'mankind in all his branches is the lord over Beasts, Birds, Fishes, and the Earth, and was not made to acknowledge any of his owne kind to be his teacher and ruler'.[71] By extension, Winstanley used his ideas concerning the 'common treasury' and on the original form of labour to contend that whereas Man had once exercised dominion over animals alone, and that consequently 'not one word was spoken in the beginning, That one branch of mankind should rule over another',[72] after the Fall men were themselves subject to the dominion of other men.

It is not uncharitable to suggest that Winstanley's thoughts on the origins of labour, and the manner in which he amended his position, were often coloured by his impression of what in ideal circumstances the future might hold. Even so, optimistic as Winstanley's utopianism appears, it cannot be said that Winstanley brushed aside certain apparently intractable aspects of the prevailing predicament. Thus, whereas Winstanley took exception to *hired* labour and *private* property in land, his vision of the future nevertheless stipulated the *obligation* to labour alongside the equitable distribution of the goods thus produced. Winstanley's account of the past and of what was 'natural' stresses the righteousness of 'unalienated' labour and the birthright to enjoy the 'common treasury', the common ownership of productive resources and the equitable apportionment of produce. In regarding land as the fundamental form of property, Winstanley assumes that the reintroduction of the 'common treasury' would facilitate the restoration of men to a condition not dissimilar to the original harmonious condition. Individuals would thereby be relieved of the oppressive attentions of their fellows.

4

The case for identifying Winstanley's understanding of the 'Fall of Man' as the fulcrum of his thought is compelling. Winstanley's writings demonstrate such a consistent preoccupation with the Fall that it appears evident that his consideration of the event, particularly as a historical entity, is considerably more important to the overall structure of his thought than some scholars allow.[73] Despite a sophisticated use of allegory and imagery (the 'tree of life' for universal love, the tree of the knowledge of good and evil for Man's imagination, and the serpent for the role of imagination in introducing dominion and lordship),[74] Winstanley stands by the conviction that Man in general had fallen from a pristine condition, and that this had distanced him from God. In applying these ideas, Winstanley often alludes not only to his own spiritual trials but also to the moral redundancy of Man as a whole. That Winstanley's is in many respects an unorthodox appreciation of the Fall is not to be disputed; but the very precise connections between this facet of his thought and important aspects of his social theory should not be doubted.

It has been observed that Winstanley saw in the law of reason a principle without which men could not hope to live in a condition of righteousness. The law of reason informed the harmony of the Creation.[75] Winstanley understood the Fall to be the process by which this law was broken by men, an aberration accounting for the desperate state of human nature. Hence the contention that,

> if there had been no Law, there had been no transgression, if there had been no binding law of reason to require him to cleave only to his maker, and to eye and own him principally; then he had not done evill though he had placed his delight in the objects of the earth, his fellow creatures.[76]

Similarly, Winstanley at one point argues that the Fall entails Man's 'revolt from the spirit, in making choyce to live upon the creation, and not upon the spirit: and hereby now the law of Reason is broke'.[77] Crucially, Winstanley's interpretation of the 'Fall of Man' affords not only an evaluation of the original transgression and its consequences but also examines the continuing and repeated defiance of the law of reason by each individual.

Although ultimately Winstanley arrived at the conclusion that the single most important aspect of Adam's fall was its significance as a psychological exemplar for future generations, he intially propounded a relatively traditional and historical version of the circumstances attending the original sin.[78] In this account Winstanley begins his description of 'the Garden of Eden, the History'[79] by arguing that Adam had once possessed a pure nature. However, because Adam was created to exist as an entity distinct from God, he inevitably inclined to self-love, and the aspiration to be God's equal. The inviolability of the 'forbidden fruit' became the crucial point of contention between the will of God and that of Man. The recognition of the sanctity of this object stood as the test of Man's free will and wilful subjugation to God. However, Adam, being self-loving and proud, transgressed God's command and assumed for himself the knowledge of good and evil. Delighting in his profanation and wickedness Adam fell from communion with God into a condition termed by Winstanley 'death'. What all this implies with respect to the attributes of God is a problem not examined by Winstanley. Even so, while in this early treatment of the matter Winstanley adheres to a fairly orthodox rendition, the allegorical implications of his testimony are never far from the surface. This is particularly evident in the assertion that 'this selfishnesse in the midle of the living garden, Adam, is the forbidden fruit, and this is called the Serpent, because it windes itself into every creature'.[80]

5

Although Winstanley's evaluation of the Fall is not devoid of relatively orthodox foundations, the most peculiar and significant characteristic of his rendition is the conception sustained therein of the means by which evil is perpetuated to the effect that Man remained in the fallen state. Instead of subscribing to more conventional accounts purporting the transmission of guilt by means of innate and original sin, Winstanley insists in his developed theory that all subsequent men will during the course of their own lifetimes emulate Adam's injudicious conduct. One of the most radical propositions to be found in Winstanley's writings is, therefore, the stipulation that 'the Fall' was not an experience confined to the first historical Adam.

In maintaining that 'this Adam is within every man and woman',[81] Winstanley sought not to emphasize the congenital transmission of sin, but instead to draw attention to the individuated and internalized essence of the Fall. Thus, he conceived of the Fall as, in part, a crucial factor in the life cycle of each and every person. In this context he asserted:

> when a man fals, let him not blame a man that died 6000 years ago, but blame himself, even the powers of his own flesh, which led him astray; for this is Adam that brings a man to misery . . .[82]

Winstanley believed the historical Adam to be distinct therefore, only in that he was the first man to experience the Fall. Accordingly, he maintained that human nature remained depraved because men had subsequently and repeatedly fallen. So Winstanley did not subscribe to the notion of innate and original sin advanced in orthodox and traditional accounts of the Fall.

A digression of this kind brings with it a number of important consequences. For one thing, implicit within Winstanley's individuated version of the Fall is the assumption that men are capable of rectifying their predicament by amending to some degree the circumstances informing the transgression of individuals; effectively the social arrangements which tempted successive generations to succumb to, and remain in, a condition of sinfulness. However, an unwillingness to accept that men are innately sinful entails the corollary that some other reason must account for continuing evil. In effect, the overall coherence of Winstanley's social philosophy presupposes his ability to provide an account of human nature and human history capable of locating the reason for both continuing evil and the belief that evil is eradicable.

Despite constituting one of the most significant aspects of Winstanley's thought, his account of the precise process by which successive individuals fell remained somewhat unresolved and clouded. By arguing that 'Adam's innocency is the time of child-hood',[82] Winstanley was able to suggest that as each individual approached an increasing understanding of the world about him he would confront a choice between the righteous path, on the one hand, and moral depravation, on the other. Informing this situation was the conflict between the spirit and the flesh. Winstanley has his readers believe that, certainly in a society established upon the principle of private ownership, the flesh would inevitably triumph, as individuals sought 'self-propriety, which is the curse'.[83] This emphasis upon self-gratification is a fundamental factor within Winstanley's appraisal of the individuated moral trangression. Thus, selfishness is cited as the 'forbidden fruit'[84] as Winstanley claims that the 'serpent' entices all men to reject the spirit and instead to appease the flesh by absorbing the material objects of the Creation.[85] In like manner, Winstanley states that 'if you delight more in the objects of the earth, to please selfe, then in the spirit that made all things, then you eat the forbidden fruit, you take the Apple, and become naked and ashamed'.[86]

6

Winstanley's use of the term 'apple', in denoting material objects, is both interesting and significant. He explains in *The New Law of righteousnes* that:

> The Apple that the first man eats, is not a single fruit called the Apple, or such like fruit; but it is the objects of the Creation; which is the fruit that came out of the Seed, which is the Spirit himself that made all things: As riches, honours, pleasures, upon which the powers of the flesh feeds to delight himself.[87]

This rather esoteric statement carries considerable weight. It was evident to Winstanley that no one man owned the apples in the Garden of Eden. In the pristine condition the 'ownership' of material objects ultimately resided with God. The Earth was, after all, His creation, the product of His labour. This proposition aligns quite neatly with what Winstanley says concerning the 'common treasury'. The material objects of the Creation, particularly property in the form of land, argues Winstanley, had been bestowed by God upon all men for their common use rather than for private appropriation. Thus all men should enjoy an equal right to cultivate land in order to obtain subsistence, but none had sufficient right to appropriate the means to life as a private property. All this seems to be in keeping with Winstanley's conviction that, to borrow the Lockean phraseology, sufficiency and spoilation limitations could be ensured only by a communist distributive system, and that goods should only become the private property of any individual once they had been allocated to him for immediate consumption.[88] So, unlike Locke, Winstanley was not exercised to expound a rationale for the individual appropriation of tracts of the Creation. In fact, quite to the contrary, Winstanley's concern was to establish the illegitimacy of precisely this form of appropriation.

In looking at Winstanley's writings it becomes evident that his appraisal of various considerations including, human nature, the account of human history informed by the Fall and the evaluation of property and ownership, are intricately linked. Thus, a basic premise supported by Winstanley's individuated account of the Fall is that on breaking with the law of reason individuals are motivated to appropriate property. As, therefore, the individual forsakes righteousness, 'then appears pride, covetousnesse, forwardnesse, uncleannesse springing in his heart'.[89] Hence it follows that in order to derive at least some (albeit ephemeral) peace of mind, all men would emulate the historical Adam by attempting to acquire particular objects from the Creation. So private property was sustained and even extended. Because Winstanley regarded the Earth as a 'common treasury' he was primarily concerned with the assumption of private property in the form of land and therefore commented adversely upon the propensity of fallen men to enclose parcels of land and to declare a particular property therein.[90] Clearly, Winstanley believed that the cumulative social implications of all this had been quite devastating. Accordingly, he was moved to state that as

> man began to look after the objects of the earth, delighting himself to live upon or among fellow creatures more then the spirit; and so chose to himself another livelihood and protection . . .
> . . . but when he fell off, and delighted to follow the lusts of his eye, the lusts of his heart, and guidance of the flesh, then he governed al in unrighteousnesse, and so pulling death and curse upon himself, and upon the earth.[91]

It is passages such as these which establish the undoubted centrality of Winstanley's evaluation of the Fall within his social philosophy.

7

The dual conception of the Fall with which Winstanley operated, on the one hand as an historical entity and on the other as an enduring psychological phenomenon, throws considerable light upon one of the most bemusing aspects of his thought: the difficulty entailed in attempting to isolate his views on the exact causal relationship pertaining between the Fall and the institution of its social manifestations—private property, political authority and hired labour. Basically the intellectual dilemma informing Winstanley's social philosophy is quite straightforwardly stated, but it required him to develop an extraordinarily complicated theory of the Fall and of the prospective moral regeneration of Man. Winstanley wished simultaneously to maintain several positions that were always going to be difficult to accommodate within the one general theory: that the 'original sin' was indeed a historical occurrence; that the predicament described by the Fall still prevailed; that evil would to some extent continue to obtain; that the social institutions conventionally regarded as necessary restraints upon conduct had been corrupted and thereby rendered useless; and that irrespective of all this men could attain spiritual restoration during the course of their earthly existence. Effectively, whereas Winstanley remained aware of the utility of the orthodox account of the Fall in sustaining certain of his own premises, particularly in describing the ultimate origins of evil, he could not accept the full implications regarding human potential of the traditional version.

Given the complexity of his position, it is not surprising that Winstanley often appears unclear as to the exact causal relationship between the Fall and the creation and appropriation of private property. This is in part because of his tendency to allude to the historical and 'internalized' versions of the Fall concurrently. In the latter form, material objects, particularly in the form of private possessions, were often cited as 'causes' of the fall and spiritual degeneration of individuals. This conception of private property and its link with character, as a consequence of the historical Fall but also as a cause of the transgressions of subsequent individuals, has prompted certain commentators to advance somewhat unqualified assumptions. T.W. Hayes, for example, argues that 'to Winstanley, the Fall is not an abstract, timeless, generality, but an historical phenomenon originating in the creation of private property and the commodity character of the division of labour it produces'.[92] Christopher Hill initially presented a similar although slightly more cautious appraisal, claiming that 'Winstanley reversed the order: covetousness and private property are the causes, not the consequences of the Fall'.[93] The position originally adopted by Hill highlights the difficulties occasioned by Winstanley's theories, because Hill is here forced to identify an attribute of fallen human nature (covetousness) and an institution sustained by such a characteristic (private property) as the joint causes of the Fall.

Elsewhere, Hill appears to be aware of this problem and accordingly revises the wording of his argument by stating that 'this reverses the orthodox view that private property, inequality, and the state which protects them, were consequences of the Fall. For Winstanley the establishment of private property was the Fall'.[94] In this extract Hill seems to abandon the question of identifying a causal nexus in favour of advancing the simple assertion that Winstanley merely correlated the institutions of private property and the Fall. Such reluctance to confront the question of causality is again evident in a more recent treatment of the matter by Hill. By attributing reticence to become embroiled in 'chicken and egg' arguments to Winstanley, Hill himself appears to evade this crucially important issue. Again, Hill implies that Winstanley saw the Fall and the establishment of private property as coincidental, arguing that 'Winstanley always associated the Fall exclusively with the origin of private property, even when he was using the biblical myth'.[95]

Winstanley's position is more intricate than such impressions allow, but it is nevertheless discernible. Winstanley believed that, historically, the Fall had given rise to the institution of private property.[96] Adam had appropriated what was rightly God's. Subsequently, the existence of private property tempted successive generations of individuals to transgress and thereby to descend into the fallen condition. This elucidation highlights the ambiguity of Hill's rather sweeping assertion that 'there is no evidence that the later Winstanley believed in "man's universal moral fall", separate from and prior to the origin of private property: and much evidence that he regarded the two as inseperably linked'.[97] Here, Hill's choice of words is guarded. Even so, there are grounds for believing that Winstanley's overall position is even more complicated than the later Hill recognizes.

Winstanley reveals a telling similarity to the orthodox line in arguing that once the detrimental step had been taken towards the institution of private property, the resultant insecurity experienced by all men, that occasioned by competitive appropriation, simply perpetuated the process. Thus the Fall heralded the inception of particular interests which were subsequently maintained. As Winstanley claims,

> this is the beginner of particular interest, buying and selling the earth from one particular hand to another, saying, This is mine, upholding this particular propriety by law of government of his own making, and thereby restraining other fellow creatures from seeking nourishment from their mother earth.[98]

Moreover, Winstanley contends that once an individual was fallen, he would inevitably seek to appropriate simply because 'Covetousnesse begets Fear, least (*sic*) others shall crosse them in their Design, or else begets a Fear of want, and this makes a man to draw the creatures to him'.[99] Hence, communism is regarded by Winstanley as the solution to such fear of want identified as both cause and consequence of the displacement of private property in the structure of contemporary civil society. Winstanley sees private property as stimulating such antagonism between men that the whole reprehensible edifice of buying and selling, and the multiplication of lawsuits, could be directly attributed to it. Ultimately, Winstanley denounced warfare as the most pronounced manifestation of the competitiveness initiated at the Fall.[100] The Diggers attempted to defy the curse through pacifism.

8

Winstanley's theory of the psychological internalization of the cosmic drama sustains quite profound general implications for his social philosophy. Not only does he profess the belief that the impulse to appropriate private property is characteristic of fallen human nature, but he also suggests that as men endeavour to secure their own interests they are certain to compete for social and political power. In identifying this facet of human nature Winstanley echoes the thought and expression of his great contemporary, Thomas Hobbes.[101] Of fallen men, Winstanley has this to say: 'all that *Adam* doth is to advance himself to be [the] one power: he gets riches and government into his hands, that he may lift up himself, and suppresse the universal liberty'.[102]

Winstanley insists that, consequent upon all this, fallen men would abuse authority in order to advance their own interests. Inevitably, 'every one that gets an authority into his hands, tyrannises over others'.[103] Winstanley is thus led to the conclusion that 'the Monarchical spirit is the power of darkness'.[104] His correlation of fallen human nature and the existing structure of politics adds weight to his ultimate identification of the cause of institutional reform with the spiritual regeneration of Man.

9

There can be little doubt that one of the great demands placed upon social thinkers in the seventeenth century was to produce a sufficiently cogent explanation, often in terms of what God had originally intended for Man, of the contemporary distribution of private property and of the structure of labour relations and political authority attendant upon the property regime. For thinkers such as Winstanley, who related the issue back in time to the original pre-lapsarian condition, the great imponderable was the question why the world knew of evil. Conventional accounts of the Fall might simply assert that in some way the responsibility for evil ultimately devolved upon Man. However, the logic of Winstanley's position seems to extend beyond the seeming superficialities of traditional explanations. The important point to be grasped is that Winstanley accorded with some of the most radical thinking of the era, thought which accepted that evil was and would remain inevitable, but which nevertheless recognized the prospect of at least some improvement or modification in the human condition.

With this in mind it becomes easier to comprehend the significance of two major threads within Winstanley's thought. In the first place the Fall (not only of Adam but of all subsequent generations) 'explains' continuing evil and the seeming inevitability of at least some malevolent disposition among men. Men are undoubtedly flawed and demonstrate a potential selfishness and covetousness which is manifest and brought into light when stimulated and tempted by the proximity of private property. In the first instance, the Creation, the product of God's labour, is God's own. God may have intended the 'common treasury' to be regarded as usufruct, but the original Adam saw it as the property of another and thus sought to appropriate a portion of it to himself. A second extension of Winstanley's position, one that is certainly not explored in any depth by Winstanley, is that God envisaged the likely consequences of placing an independent being (Man) upon a property (the Creation), and thus either intended the Fall to occur, or overestimated the moral rectitude of Man. Making a mistake of the later magnitude hardly seems consistent with the notion of a rational and beneficent omnipotent power. Thus, it would appear that the God of this logical extension must in some sense have 'intended' the Fall. Whether or not Winstanley actually appreciated speculation of this kind is a matter of extreme conjecture. However, the truly important and genuinely radical insight arrived at by Winstanley is his belief that the Fall was originally a consequence of Man's rejection of God's intended principle of usufruct. Thus it appeared to Winstanley that Man's spiritual restoration would depend upon the re-establishment of this same principle. It is also evident that, as time passed, Winstanley grew in the conviction that Man must endeavour to restore the pristine scheme by his own unaided efforts.

10

There is, then, a compelling case for believing that Winstanley regarded the Fall in both the historical and internal psychological senses as fundamental to the human condition. In keeping with more traditional accounts of the Fall, Winstanley recognized that Man's perception of his own situation warranted lamentation. This despair is captured in the following terms:

> But when Mankinde begins to look within himself, and see his pride, Envie, Covetousnesse, Lust of the flesh, anger, hypocrisie, and nothing but darknesse and discontent; and begins to say with himselfe; oh what have I done, how am I falne? all outward content in objects flies away, and I am left naked, and want Light, life and rest within.[105]

Despite the admittedly esoteric facets of his understanding of the Fall, Winstanley's adherence to the general notion and to aspects of more orthodox opinion on it is evidence of his essential absorption into the spirit of the age. Winstanley is repeatedly to be discovered citing Man's own pride, selfishness and covetousness as causes of his predicament.[106] Similarly, he argues that in transgressing God's ordinances Man had disrupted universal harmony; 'he put the Creation out of order, by forsaking his Maker, and by acting according to the flesh'.[107] A significant feature of Winstanley's account of the human condition is therefore his insistence that if men would only understand how they had brought about their own predicament, a process of abstraction and rationalization would begin,[108] whereby they would be capable of rectifying the situation. Winstanley's theology and account of the Fall did not merely colour his view of the world as it stood. The latent assumptions contained therein ultimately determined his impression of what a future social order might look like. This will become more readily apparent once we have discussed Winstanley's adaptation of the myth of the Norman Yoke.

II

Winstanley employed the theory of the Norman Yoke to exemplify the worst aspects of the human condition in such a way that, especially as his social philosophy grew more complex and sophisticated, he occasionally failed to maintain a well-defined distinction between the impact of the Fall and that of the Norman Conquest. Certainly however, Winstanley regarded Normanism or 'kingly power' as the most abject social manifestation of fallen human nature. Thus, for example, he attributed the actual Conquest and the resultant 'enslavement' of English commoners to the covetousness of the Normans.

In his authoritative essay 'The Norman Yoke' (which significantly opens with a discussion of the Fall)[109] Hill points out that the theory of the Norman yoke was in many respects historically inaccurate. Even so, the vision of a 'classless' Anglo-Saxon society, supposedly destroyed at the historical watershed of 1066, yet partially recovered through the concessions wrested in Magna Carta, was deeply imbued in the consciousness of Englishmen up to and beyond the seventeenth century. As Hill says, 'within the theory English patriotism, Protestantism, and the defence of representative institutions all seemed closely linked'.[110] Like the Bible, the theory of the Norman Yoke became a sanctuary for thinkers reluctant to base their appeals for social reform solely upon reason or utility.

In the earlier part of the seventeenth century reference to the Norman Conquest was used to validate, or invalidate as the case may be, a variety of constitutional theories. For instance, apologists for the royal prerogative argued that the monarch's power over landed property, and the arbitrary right to exact taxation, were justified by the initial conquest. But conversely, as Pocock eruditely argues

> since there was an increasing tendency to claim sovereignty in the full sense for the King, it was natural that those who sought to defend threatened privileges or liberties should emphasize in return that their rights were rooted in a law which no King could invalidate.[111]

Hence the status and conception of common law became the crucial point at issue in these constitutional debates. As Pocock demonstrates, in an attempt to establish the continuity of English law and to deny thereby the disruptive impact of the Conquest, many common lawyers appealed to immemorial custom.[112] However, the discovery that feudal law had been introduced into England *after* the Conquest suggested to some minds at least that the Norman regime had been illegitimately founded.[113] One proponent of this revisionary view was the eminent legal theorist, Edward Coke, who attacked the concept of royal prerogative by arguing that the Norman Conquest had impaired and infringed the common law by introducing an element of arbitrary will into the legal process.[114] Gerrard Winstanley, who appears to have possessed some detailed knowledge of Coke's writings,[115] went one stage further. By appealing to a pre-Norman ideal, Winstanley claimed that the existing common law had actually been imposed by the Normans.

It seems that Winstanley may well have derived his ideas on the Norman Yoke from pamphlets produced by the extreme wing of the Leveller movement.[116] During the course of the civil conflicts many radicals, but particularly the Levellers, not only deployed the theory of the Norman Yoke alongside their conceptions of natural right (by appealing to the 'reason' supposedly embodied in Anglo-Saxon law) but also fused, as Hill puts it, 'Biblical and constitutional theories'.[117] Winstanley adopted a similar position.

For radicals living under the Commonwealth, the apparent retention of 'Norman' social institutions became disconcerting. The spirit of their frustration is captured in S.E. Prall's view that 'the conclusion was that justice once had been abroad throughout the land and only had to be restored. Utopia lay not so much in the future as in the past.[118] The Diggers responded by advancing what Hill terms 'the most comprehensive and drastic statement of the social version of the Norman Yoke theory'.[119] In supporting this claim Hill appropriately cites the Diggers' critique of the vestiges of feudalism, their revaluation of agrarian relations, and their proposals for the abolition of copyholding. We now proceed to demonstrate that other aspects of Winstanley's ideas, particularly concerning the moral regeneration of Man, are in part a corollary of his concern with Normanism.

12

The full significance of Winstanley's resort both to the 'Fall of Man' and the Norman Conquest as explanations of the human condition is seldom adequately appreciated. In essence, this conjunction ultimately enabled Winstanley to formulate in institutional terms his theory of the spiritual and consequent moral recovery of Man. Latent within Winstanley's analysis of Man's predicament is the proposition that the restoration of Man from the fallen condition would require a commensurate reform of social institutions. As the Norman Yoke provided Winstanley with a constitutional facet to his appreciation of the fallen condition, any attempt on his part to resolve the problem of how Man could be redeemed was likely to direct Winstanley towards an appreciation of the need to amend such institutions as labour, property and political authority. A concentration upon institutionally based reforms is therefore a principle characteristic of Winstanley's utopianism.

In considering Winstanley's intellectual development it must always be recalled that his social theory was inspired by his concern with the spiritual restoration of Man. To elaborate, after initially anticipating a form of millennium (through which the regeneration of human nature was also to be expected). Winstanley eventually arrived at the conclusion that institutional reform would provide the best means of facilitating an improvement in morals. Because the theory of the Norman Yoke was an integral element in Winstanley's evaluation of the human condition, his practical and analytical consideration of how this condition could be ameliorated caused him to abandon millenarianism for the practicalities of the Digger experiment, an undertaking that was itself superseded by Winstanley's institutionally orientated utopianism.

Hill argues that Winstanley possessed an ideal of pre-lapsarian righteousness which transcended the institutions of the Norman Yoke.[120] Similarly, Pocock contends that appeals to the 'immemorial' encouraged the perpetuation of myths suggesting the existence of a golden age at some time in the past.[121] Accordingly, radicals pressed their claims for the restoration of those liberties which had supposedly been the right of all men. Although Winstanley does not confuse the pre-Conquest era with the pristine condition, he certainly suggests that the coming of the Norman Yoke *exacerbated* the effects of the Fall. Hence his preparedness to assert that the Norman Conquest had unleashed an unprecedented degree of chaos into the Creation.[122] More particularly, Winstanley maintains that the extent and evil effects of private property, especially the ownership of land, became more pronounced after the Norman invasion. Thus he believed that the Normans had established all other social institutions upon the basis of private property. Not surprisingly, Winstanley's response proposes a return to the virtues of communalism.

13

Consideration has already been afforded to the problems generated by the causal relationship pertaining between Winstanley's understanding of the

Fall as a historical occurrence, his view of the introduction of private property and its perpetuation, and his theories concerning the nature of an internalized-cum-individuated conception of human moral transgression emulating the experience of the Fall. These difficulties are extended once Winstanley's introduction of the Norman Yoke into his discussion of the generation of private property is brought into account. Winstanley variously attributes the instigation of private property in the form of landownership to the historical Adam and to the Norman Conquest.[123] He argues, for example, that although enclosures had certainly existed before the Conquest, these had been appropriated by the Normans.[124] Winstanley then insists that the Normans extended propriety in land by converting existing enclosures to freehold and by introducing an extensive system of copyholding.[125] Despite the occasional ambiguities of his case, it is plain that Winstanley identified a correlation between the Conquest and the consolidation and extension of private property.

14

Winstanley's belief in the instrumental role played in the individuated process of the Fall by private property eventually informed the commensurate conviction that communism might instigate Man's spiritual restoration. Winstanley regarded the existence of private property in land as the most significant aspect of the curse to have befallen Man after Adam's historical fall,[126] and similarly concluded that if private property was the curse then it related closely to the idea of 'bondage' in the sense of men being subjected to illegitimate and coercive political authority.[127] However, Winstanley contended that while the condition of bondage entailed the abrogation of individual freedom, the term also implied a condition of sinful depravity endured by all individuals who had fallen. Thus, as we have already observed, Winstanley accorded with a general impression of seventeenth-century psychology[128] by arguing that in fallen human nature, unrestrained imagination was likely to prevail over right reason. His conclusion was that fallen men possessed such an insatiable craving for material objects that every person would pursue 'inclosures proper or peculiar to himselfe'.[129]

By elaborating upon the widespread view that both political authority and the preservation of private property were necessary contraints upon Man's fallen nature, Winstanley advanced the dissenting proposal that the existing law

> is the extremity of the curse, and yet this is the Law that every one now adayes dotes upon: when the plaine truth is, the Law of propriety is the shamefull nakedness of mankinde, and as farre from the Law of Christ, as light from darknesse.[130]

Hence my contention that Winstanley's social theory relates closely to his conception of Man's spiritual welfare and is concerned with 'the battell, that is fought between the two powers, which is propriety on the one hand, called the Devill, or covetousnesse, or community on the other hand, called

Christ, or universal Love'.[131] In his social philosophy Winstanley turned his intellectual powers to prescribing and accounting for the victory of the latter.

Stuart England as the fallen condition

1

Winstanley's association of the Fall with the Norman Yoke, and his persistent tirades against the continuation of Norman institutions of 'kingly power' would suggest that it would be worthwhile to examine what he described as 'the present condition mankind lies under, and this is darknes or the fall'.[132] Winstanley intimates that by merely observing the condition of the world its faults were easily recognizable. His concern with the evident discord prevailing in contemporary society was not unique. Similar disquiet was elegantly and somewhat more systematically registered, to markedly different effect, by Hobbes. Even so, Winstanley's analysis of the causes of so troubled a predicament and his proposals for the resolution of it are highly original.

According to Winstanley the regime of 'kingly power' *was* the fallen condition. Hence statements stressing the synonymity of the 'Norman Yoke, and Babylonish power'.[133] Similarly, Winstanley asserts that: 'The Kingly power is covetousness in his branches, or the power of self-love, ruling in many over others, and enslaving those who in the Creation are their equals'.[134] It is illuminating to examine the range of institutions and beliefs to which Winstanley attributed the sustenance of kingly power—those associated with the clergy, lords of manors and lawyers.

Winstanley presents a decidedly disparaging evaluation of the contemporary clergy. His anticlericalism, abhorrence of tithing and anti-intellectualism are pronounced. Indeed, the vehemence of his anticlericalism prompts Christopher Hill to identify Winstanley as the most extreme and systematic exponent of this view to have emerged during the Civil War, 'for Winstanley, the English state church was antichristian'.[135]

Much of Winstanley's anatagonism towards the clergy was informed by what he took to be the experimental basis of his own religious beliefs, views that convinced him of the role of the poor in constituting the vanguard of the redeemed. Popular anticlericalism, as defined by J.F. McClear, amounted to 'the ancient folk distrust of clerical ambitions and its hatred of priestly domination, corruption and greeed'.[136] According to this appreciation, the incidence of such feeling was widespread, Winstanley being the most thoroughgoing critic of the clergy's role in society.[137] Anticlericalism could emanate from a number of factors, considerations often exemplified in Winstanley's writings. For example, many 'Puritans' developed a contempt for conforming clerics who fell short of the intellectual standards being attained by pious laymen.[138] Alternatively, the exclusive educational background of the clergy and the enforced payment of tithes could often precipitate something akin to class-based anticlericalism. As with other popular beliefs, the expression of anticlerical feeling reached its apogee during the course of the civil disorders. The morale and self-preservation of sectarian groups opposed to Presbyterian authoritarianism often leant heavily upon this outlook.[139]

By extending the reaction against perceived clerical abuses to an attack upon the very concept of the clerical vocation, anticlericalism could blend into a more amorphous anti-intellectualism.[140] Again, this disposition, coupled with the impression that the clergy actively maintained the *ancien régime*, found bountiful expression in Winstanley's pamphlets. Take, for instance, his contention that the clergy regularly sought the assistance of the coercive instruments of secular authority to compel the people both to attend services and to maintain the clergy through the payment of tithes.[141] Much of Winstanley's distaste for the clergy was inspired by the suspicion that 'it is not the zeale of God which sets them to work, but the desire and sweetness of a temporal living'.[142] Thus, the self-interest of the clerical branch was preserved by a unified state church which propagated 'one outward lazie, formall, customary, and tyth-oppressing way of pretended Divine worship, which pleases the flesh'.[143] So Winstanley is to be found ever willing to stress that whereas established forms of religion gratified the flesh, his own experimental version catered for the needs of the spirit.[144] Ultimately, Winstanley's contempt for the clergy led him to doubt the existence of any scriptural justification for their eminence. He provides, therefore, a sweeping indictment of the contemporary church:

> But the Ministers of England, and such as follows them in the practise of praying, preaching, sprinkling of children, breaking bread, sabbaths, Church societies, & Ministers maintenance, as they practise in their customary way of performances, which they call God's ordinances; had neither Reason nor Scripture to warrant them.[145]

Addressing the clergy quite forthrightly, Winstanley proclaims: 'you are none other but Witches and Deceivers'.[146]

During the Civil War anticlericalism was bolstered by an intensification of the latent controversy concerning the payment of tithes. Radicals were particularly prone to incorporate this debate into their programmes for social reform. Understandably, it has been pointed out that proposals for the abolition of tithes were often regarded as a threat to the very sanctity of private property.[147] Given the post-dissolution sale of impropriations to lay owners, whereby in many parishes the right to exact tithes had assumed the form of a private property largely dissociated from the original religious function, such alarm may well have been quite appropriate. Furthermore, lay impropriators often retained the right to present the local minister. This was pertinent to the whole disputed issue of clerical finances. It was generally agreed that whoever funded the Church effectively controlled it, a concern especially worrying to those who assumed, rightly or wrongly, that the Church was a vital organ of society which via its pulpits could provide a medium for the dissemination of government propaganda. Proposals by self-financing and independent sectarian groups for the abolition of tithes were perceived, therefore, as a challenge to both private ownership and to political authority. Among conservatives, such ideas naturally caused consternation. Clearly, in his analysis of contemporary society as the fallen condition, the close links forged by the issue of tithes between the clergy, landowners and the state were not lost upon Winstanley.

In keeping with the tone of this aspect of his thought, Winstanley's rejection of tithing is cited in the literature as the most vehement expression of popular feeling on the issue.[148] It is interesting to speculate that Winstanley may have sensed that disputes over the payment of tithes had proliferated during the Laudian period and had contributed to an increase in litigation, a trend also wholeheartedly condemned by Winstanley. In accordance with this anticlerical perspective, Winstanley addresses his remarks to 'You Norman-Clergy, oppressing Tith-mungers',[149] who, he claims, are possessed by 'the spiritual Power of Covetousness and Pride'.[150] By further referring to the clergy as 'they that take Tythes to tell a story',[151] Winstanley betrays the anti-intellectual facet of his conviction that the clergy were purely mercenary. Perhaps Winstanley expected to strike a chord with popular anti-Papal sentiments by claiming that the retention of tithes indicated that Protestantism had not as yet divested itself of a typically Catholic practice.[152] Furthermore, Winstanley confronted the clergy with the accusation that 'if the people refuse to give you tithes, you tell the Magistrate, it is his duty to force them, all which is not warrantable, either from Reason nor Scripture'.[153] By arguing in this manner, Winstanley asserted his belief in the mutually reinforcing nature of the oppressive institutions of contemporary society.

In discussing the clergy and its place in the hierarchy of 'kingly power', Winstanley's essential proposition is that William the Conqueror had bestowed tithes upon the clergy as a gift in return for their undertaking to preach up the regime.[154] Thereafter, in order to preserve this income, the clergy had been prepared to support and condone the ruling elite—whatever its confessional persuasion. By accusing the clergy of using the fear of hell to exact political obedience from the people, and thus to preserve their livelihood,[155] Winstanley displays an acute awareness of one intended function of clerical preaching. In all, Winstanley consistently regarded such activities as an instance of fallen men corrupting religion in pursuit of material advantage.

2

Winstanley's anticlericalism was related to another popular attitude, one involving a reaction against clerics, lawyers and university teachers, namely anti-intellectualism. This outlook in turn extended to the ancillary notion pertaining especially to lawyers, that of 'anti-professionalism'.[156] Winstanley proved particularly keen in his distrust of the legal profession. In many respects, anti-intellectualism represented the inversion of the Calvinist assumption that, as Hill puts it, 'necessarily only a select group has the economic status, the education, the leisure to master this theology: only a minority can be free, only a minority are the elect'.[157] Instead, anti-intellectualism stressed what is termed the 'indwelling presence of the Holy Spirit rather than formal learning'.[158] Even so, this provision could be similarly exclusive, especially when applied to a minority group of saints.

Winstanley's emphasis upon universal salvation, as L.F. Solt points out, placed him outside the antinomian tendencies often associated with anti-intellectualism.[159] Consequently, it is difficult to see how Winstanley could have anticipated the rule of the saints in the form of an exclusive and elect minority, a conclusion which obviously casts considerable doubt upon the suggestion that Winstanley was a thoroughgoing millenarian. Winstanley's anti-intellectualism was genuine enough, but his association of it with a commitment to the hope of universal salvation and to an egalitarian social theory counts against the concept of 'Digger saints' [160] as privileged counterparts to the Fifth Monarchists.

Winstanley's verbal assault on formal learning is often highly charged. He is to be discovered referring to the universities as 'standing ponds of stinking waters',[161] and contending that 'the secrets of the Creation have been locked up under the traditional Parrat-like speaking, from the Universities, and Colledges for Schollars'.[162] Predictably, the clergy, who emanated from such institutions, are arraigned by Winstanley for their imaginary teaching power and their 'booke-studying, University, Divinity, which indeed, is Iudas Ministry'.[163] Rather poignantly, Winstanley maintains that formal education is tantamount to the 'engrossing' of experimental knowledge ascertained by the efforts and industry of others. The juxtaposition of received ideas and experimentalism is an important aspect of Winstanley's thought which prompts him to advance claims of the following type:

> there are so many Hypocrites amongst professors, they know much in the letter, as man teaches them; but they know nothing in spiritual power, which is the way that God teaches.[164]

> The Scriptures of the Bible, were written by the experimentall hand of Shepherds, Husbandmen, Fishermen, and such inferior men of the world.[165]

Clearly, an inference to the effect that the contemporary lower orders might be capable of emulating this feat is a potentially powerful stimulus to social radicalism.

By perceiving many prevailing intellectual norms as those of fallen Man and by relating anti-intellectualism to experimental knowledge, Winstanley identifies one means of fostering Man's spiritual regeneration. This impression is confirmed by Winstanley's understanding of the Fall as an occasion

> when a studying imagination comes into a man, which is the devil, for it is the cause of all evil, and sorrows in the world; that is he that puts out the eyes of mans Knowledg, and tells him, he must not trust to his own experience.[166]

Instead, Winstanley categorically asserts that:

> Men must speak their own experienced words, and must not speak thoughts.
> —thoughts, and studies, and imagination of flesh.[167]

The distinction posited by Winstanley between the potential spirituality of the common people and the insubstantial standards set by state-endorsed religion is phrased in terms reminiscent of More's discussion of Utopian religiousity:

Qu. Thus the heathen walked according to the light of nature, but Christians must live above nature?
Ans. The English Christians are in a lower and worser condition, then the heathens, for they doe not so much.[168]

Eventually, in his ideal commonwealth, Winstanley prescribed that men should be allowed to follow experimental religion free from the constraints of a formal state structure.

3

Besides the clergy and the intelligentsia, Winstanley obviously believed that the landowning classes possessed a vested interest in perpetuating the fallen condition of Normanism. He assumed that the lords of the manor in particular were every bit as culpable as the clergy of preserving 'kingly power'. As an aspect of his theory of the Norman Yoke Winstanley contends that lords of the manor were the descendants of William the Conqueror's colonels and favourites,[169] and that, consequently, their titles to their property were illegitimately founded upon the initial conquest and the continuation of the king's arbitrary will. Similarly, Winstanley regards freeholders as the descendants of Norman soldiers.[170] Hence his conclusion that, within this structure of landownership, the tenantry are nothing else but 'poor enforced slaves',[171] maintained in a condition of perpetual bondage by the refusal of landlords to allow them to live apart by cultivating the wastes and commons.[172] Typically, Winstanley accuses the landlords of overstocking the commons with their own animals and thereby depriving their tenants of a supplementary form of livelihood.[173] For such immoral actions Winstanley subjects the landlords to a savage indictment. He accuses them of effectively transgressing divine commandments against killing and stealing.[174] An interesting appendage to this facet of Winstanley's thought is his sympathetic response to the plight of younger sons, including those of landed families. Winstanley deduces a conspiratorial significance in the clerical endorsement of primogeniture,[175] and claims that the younger sons of landowners are deprived of their birthright in a manner similar to the duplicity worked on the common people.

4

In one of his most celebrated passages Winstanley states that 'England is a Prison; the variety of subtleties in the Laws preserved by the sword, are bolts, bars, and doors of the prison; the Lawyers are the Jaylors, and poor men are the prisoners'.[176] This suggests considerable ill-feeling towards a further element of kingly power, the law and its practitioners. Significantly, Winstanley perceived that the legal system was particularly instrumental in the process of identifying and preserving private property.[177] In evaluating the plight of the poor and needy, Winstanley is ever willing to condemn the legal system for its failure to react equitably. At one point he says of the destitute:

> if they steal for maintenance, the murdering Law will hang them; when as Lawyers, Judges, and Court Officers can take Bribes by whole sale to remove one mans Propriety by that Law into another mans hands: and is not this worse theevery then the poor man that steals for want?[178]

In general, Winstanley's account of the contemporary legal system is verbosely endowed with devilish connotations.[179]

Throughout his writings Winstanley displays a considerable knowledge of both jurisprudence and of legal institutions. Indeed, his complaints concerning the shortcomings of the fallen condition in respect of the operation of the law are reflected in the detailed proposals for reform contained in *The Law of Freedom*. Prior to this, a matter of months after the execution of Charles I, Winstanley was asking 'whether all Lawes that are not grounded upon equity and reason, not giving a universal freedom to all, but respecting persons, ought not to be cut off with the King's head?'[180]

Winstanley regularly lists a series of telling indictments of prevailing legal practices. He points out the anomaly of juries being composed of 'Norman' freeholders rather than of the peers of the defendant.[181] He also insists that the law effectively confirms its oppressive qualities by enforcing the payment of tithes.[182] Further grievances concern language. Legal proceedings in early modern England were conducted in Latin or in Law French (the Norman tongue),[183] a practice which aroused the indignation of the anti-intellectual Winstanley, who complained that, as a self-interested professional class, lawyers were only too ready to exclude the common people from an understanding of the rules according to which public conduct was regulated. In a similar vein, Winstanley criticized the centralization of the legal system and the expense of litigation, particularly in 'those Nurseries of Covetousness, The Innes of Court',[184] In Winstanley's opinion, lawyers were simply monopolists and profiteers who would not allow individuals such as himself to plead their own cases.[185] So he was forced ruefully to conclude that 'the Law is the Fox, poore men are the geese; he pulls off their feathers, and feeds upon them'.[186]

5

The correlation identified by Winstanley between the Fall and private property led him to perceive that the covetous disposition of fallen men caused them to seek their own advantage by indulging in commerce. Thus, he regarded 'buying and selling' as an institution peculiar to the fallen condition and believed that only the restoration of an essentially communal lifestyle could eradicate such practices. One possible reason for the attention afforded by Winstanley to 'buying and selling' is the fluidity of the contemporary land market, by which the commodity that he regarded as prerequisite to Man's very subsistence was subject to exchange.[187] It has been noted that during this period, because land was regarded as the fundamental form of property, capital accumulated in economic activity other than agriculture was channelled into the land market.[188] Winstanley emphasized his abhorrence of commerce by predicting that in the reformed society gold and silver would become mere utility metals.[189]

The prospect of a restoration on earth

1

Perhaps the most striking feature of Winstanley's social philosophy is that it is informed throughout by the belief that Man possesses a potential for spiritual and moral regeneration. Winstanley's indefatigable confidence in the eventual attainment of such a restoration is exemplified in his consistent reiteration of the theme. From the outset, in *The Mysterie of God*, he insists that the curse incurred at the Fall is merely a temporary penalty to be remitted with the restoration of the entire creation.[190] Subsequently, in *The Saints Paradice*, he affirms that the regeneration of human nature is a very real possibility.[191] In *The New Law of Righteousnes* he advances, albeit in a somewhat abstract manner, the contention that the curse afflicting the creation might be removed by the suppression of covetousness. Thus men await the restoration of righteousness.[192] Even so, Winstanley's patience soon begins to waver. On commencing the communal cultivation of the commons, a project inspired by the attempt to anticipate the restoration, Winstanley stresses in his writings that regeneration will only be effected by the subjugation of the flesh to reason. Soon afterwards, Winstanley asks Fairfax:

> Whether the work of the restoration lies not in removing covetousnesse, casting the Serpent out of heaven, (mankind) and making man to live in the light of righteousnesse, not in words only, as Preachers do, but in action, whereby the Creation shines in glory? I affirm it.[193]

Certainly, Winstanley regarded digging as just such a practical step towards inaugurating the restoration. Once the Digger experiment was well advanced, Winstanley assured his readers that 'there is a promise of restoration and salvation to the whole creation, and this must be wrought by a power contrary to darkness'.[194]

It is perhaps to be expected that in the more overtly theological *Fire in the Bush* Winstanley should discuss Man's predicament in terms of the Fall and of restoration. However, it is indicative of the panoramic scope of Winstanley's mode of thought that he should conclude that the power of 'the restorer, Saviour, Redeemer, yea and the true and faithful Leveller'[195] would arise to dispel the evil consequences of the Fall. Even when intimating that digging had failed to achieve the promised restoration of all men, Winstanley took solace in his undaunted anticipation of 'the universall restoration of Man-kind to the law of righteousness, from whence he fell'.[196]

The communist implications of Winstanley's theory of a restoration are evident in ruminations upon the subject of

> the restoring of Mankind to his originall righteousnesse, and that they shall be brought to be of one heart, and of one mind: and that they shall be freely willing to let each other enjoy their Creation-rights, without restraining, or molesting one another; but every one doing as he would be done by.[197]

Ultimately, this ideal was effectively realized in the utopian institutionalism of *The Law of Freedom*.

2

As his pamphleterring career progressed Winstanley discovered that his fundamental difficulty was to explain precisely the processes by which the restoration would come about. This problem arose as a consequence of his understanding that the spiritual regeneration of Man and the reform of social institutions would be causally linked. In attempting to ascertain the exact nature of this connection Winstanley found himself facing a dilemma turning upon the issue of whether human nature or social institutions would respectively either cause or effect the restoration. A further possibility was that some spontaneous and simultaneous transformation of nature and institutions might transpire. We shall demonstrate that although Winstanley initially expected an improvement in the nature of social institutions to arise as a consequence of the redemption of human nature, he ultimately contended that only extensive institutional reform could bring about moral regeneration. In *The Law of Freedom* Winstanley prescribed the means to this effect. Quite obviously, to have effected so dramatic a change of perspective Winstanley must have undertaken an intellectual reappraisal of some magnitude. An analysis of Winstanley's intellectual development is undertaken in the next chapter.

5
The development of Gerrard Winstanley's thought

Between 1648 and 1652 Gerrard Winstanley's thought passed purposefully through a number of distinct but interrelated phases. This is readily apparent from even the most superficial comparison of his first pamphlet, *The Mysterie of God* and his last, *The Law of Freedom*. The former is a complex and often emotional exposition of Winstanley's mystical spirituality. The latter is a comprehensive scheme for an institutional utopia, related directly to the societal ailments of the Interregnum. Such a juxtaposition has prompted a number of commentators to suppose that at some point in the development of his thought Winstanley crossed a great divide, to the effect that the ideas evinced in his earlier pamphlets are but tenuously linked to the concerns of his subsequent writings.[1] It will be demonstrated below that Winstanley's intellectual development, although possessing a momentum, can be broken down into a series of logically coherent responses to his appreciation of the human condition.

Premises and propositions

1

Winstanley's conception of the human condition and his understanding of the prevailing national predicament, as appraised in terms of the Fall and the prospect of a restoration, is outlined in the predominantly theological writings produced prior to the establishment of the Digger community. These works exemplify the peculiar tone of Winstanley's millenarianism. Far from constituting, as one critic claims, 'undistinguished genre literature',[2] these tracts reveal Winstanley's sincere anticipation of the transformation of human nature, and ultimately of the universal redemption of Man. After spending a number of months in this state of relative passive expectation, Winstanley's patience gave way to disquiet and to a more active approach to the question of Man's spiritual redemption. In the course of this transition Winstanley can be seen elucidating a developing social theory that remained, however, markedly influenced by his established apprehension of the human condition.

Winstanley's first pamphlet, *The Mysterie of God Concerning the Whole Creation Mankinde* (1648), is addressed to his 'beloved Countrymen in the County of Lancaster'.[3] A characteristic of Winstanley's early pamphlets is that they are, in part, spiritual autobiographies. In *The Mysterie of God* Winstanley anxiously assures his readers that although he had once felt himself to be under the bondage of sin, God had nevertheless rescued him from the fallen condition.[4] Winstanley attributes this recovery to spiritual enlightenment received directly from God.[5] Clearly, this sensation of personal redemption contributed substantially to the formation of Winstanley's general theory of experimental religion.

From the very outset Winstanley devotes considerable attention to the analysis of Man's predicament. In *The Mysterie of God* he adopts a relatively 'orthodox' account of the Fall to explain the existing state of human nature. Yet, already, Adam's personality is equated with that of all subsequent generations, and so Winstanley claims that 'after the fall he became envious, disobedient, full of all lusts and concupiscence of evill, even as we find by experience our bondage'.[6] Thus Winstanley concludes that, as a consequence of the Fall, Man's inclinations have not necessarily been directed to just actions.[7]

The guiding principle of Winstanley's thought is his assurance that men would not persist in the fallen condition. In this belief Winstanley remains consistent; what does change are his assumptions concerning the means by which Man's bondage might be terminated. In his early writings Winstanley's hopes are formulated into an aspect of millenarian expectation. Thus he maintains that 'the mystery of God is this, God will bruise this Serpent's head, and cast that murderer out of heaven, the human nature'.[8] Winstanley explains a commonplace millenarian image, that the seed would bruise the serpent's head, by arguing that Christ in the flesh had conquered inner selfishness, and, as the spirit within all men, would produce the same effect. This essentially optimistic appraisal prompts Winstanley to calculate that the last days of the beast's reign were shortly to be expected. He attributes the troubles of the times to 'the rage of the Serpent . . . because his time growes short'.[9] So Winstanley assures his readers that the serpent's head is about to be bruised and that all men are to be redeemed.[10]

The universal salvation of Man is the goal which impels Winstanley along an intellectual voyage in search of a solution to Man's predicament, a journey destined to bring him to land with the idea of utopian communism. By contrast, in the formative stages of his thought, Winstanley does little more than to *assert* that all men are to be saved, because 'Christ gave himself a ransome for all'.[11] According to Winstanley, the mystery of God is the means by which Man's redemption from darkness and bondage will be effected. Thus he states that human nature will be transformed to the extent that the 'Spirit of truth that dwels and rules in Man, may be God himselfe'.[12] God will take man up into Himself and in the process individuals will 'be delivered from Corruption, Bondage, Death, and Pain'.[13] Winstanley stresses that the prospect of redemption has been made known to him experimentally. So he takes it upon himself to inform his fellows that,

> as God did dwell bodily in the Humane Nature, Jesus Christ, who was the first manifestation of this great mystery of God, so when his work is compleated, he wil dwell in the whole Creation, that is, every man and woman without exception.[14]

As God had once appeared in Christ, He was now returning to the saints.

Winstanley was not unaware that by advancing a theory of universal salvation, his views might be misconceived as an apology for unrestrained lasciviousness. However, throughout his writings Winstanley remained the ardent proponent of sobriety. Thus, perhaps somewhat paradoxically,[15] he was constrained to retain, as a sanction upon conduct, the idea of sin being met with divine retribution. In order to facilitate this claim without abrogating the contention that all would be saved, Winstanley adapted the essentially Calvinist concept of 'the elect'. Instead, however, of maintaining that the elect were the few who had been singled out for redemption, Winstanley argues that the members of the 'City of Sion' whose names are inscribed in the 'Lambs Book of Life' will be taken up directly into God.[16] Sinners, meanwhile, might be judged and condemned to a period in the 'lake of fire'. Resting in the assurance that this prospect should dissuade the presumptuous, Winstanley goes on to assert that ultimately God's wrath would ensure that 'the Serpent only shall perish, and God will not loose a hair that he made, he will redeeme his whole creation from death'.[17] Sinners will eventually be delivered from hell.[18]

Throughout his writings Winstanley fails to explore the obvious incongruities sustained by the defence of notions of universal salvation or spiritual restoration alongside adherence to some conception of 'election', even in the relatively moderated sense of a privileged minority destined to enjoy the rewards of restoration prior to the remainder of man. There are parallels between this position and Winstanley's subsequent presumption that the Diggers constituted a select minority of spiritually restored individuals who were soon to be joined in the communal cultivation of the land by the mass of men. Similarly, the officer class (and in general individuals who had attained full citizenship) described in Winstanley's ideal commonwealth constitute a minority. Here again, Winstanley suggests that eventually each individual could aspire to membership of this righteous elite. As a further aspect of this disposition, by believing that his native land was assigned the prior position in the history of world redemption, Winstanley is to be found subscribing to the concept of the 'elect nation'.

Many of the arguments advanced in *The Mysterie of God* may appear to be at some distance from the eventual form of Winstanley's social theory. It remains important, however, to consider these latter ideas in the broader context of Winstanley's intellectual development. As he grew impatient with his earlier thinking on the redemption of Man, Winstanley developed a greater interest in secular concerns. In the initial phase of his thought, however, Winstanley was content to argue that in the last troubled days of the resolution of God's design, the saints must endure oppression patiently, in the confident expectation that God was about to redeem mankind: 'If thou lie under sorrowes for sins, now know, that it is God's dispensation to thee, wait patiently upon him, hee will work an issue in his time, but not in thy time.'[19] Social philosophy has been enriched because Winstanley proved incapable of heeding his own exhortations.

2

His second pamphlet, *The Breaking of the Day of God* (20 May 1648), sees Winstanley providing further insights into the spiritual regeneration he felt himself to be experiencing. He accomplishes this largely by comparing his former entanglement 'in riches, in friends, in self-satisfaction, in my pride, covetousness, and contents of my flesh',[20] to the encouragement he had received from the discovery that 'the love, the self-denial, the inward rejoicing of my heart to advance God above all things, is Christ, the Anointing in me'.[21] At this stage in his intellectual development Winstanley retains the optimistic assumption that the world will be renewed as each individual experiences a similar metamorphosis.[22]

The Breaking of the Day of God is Winstanley's most chiliastic pamphlet. It is therefore opportune to include at this point a brief synopsis of the millenarianism exemplified by this tract. It is clear that Winstanley adapted a number of prevalent millenarian themes to suit his own particular purposes. For instance, the general proposition of *The Breaking of the Day of God* is that universal redemption would be secured by millenarian means. The substance of this long and extremely involved argument is as follows.

The Beast lies within Man and is manifest in social institutions. Thus, 'ignorance, pride, self-love, oppression and vain conversations acted against Christ'[23] influence the character of Church and state. As prophesied, two witnesses are to appear to confront this Beast. According to Winstanley, these two witnesses are 'the Anointed and the Anointing, Christ and his Spirit',[24] or Christ and the saints. Similarly, these witnesses are the seed of the woman that will ultimately bruise the serpent's (Beast's) head.[25] As this purpose nears fruition, Babylon, 'the multitude of fleshly inventions arising from the spirit of self-love',[26] and Antichrist will tremble and fall. In the last days of the Beast, the bottomless pit, or 'the corrupt heart and flesh of man',[27] will open to allow the Beast to slay the two witnesses. Hence the saints must endure present adversity.

Naturally, all this fervour of expectancy prompts Winstanley to advance a series of involved calculations intended to predict the timing of the last days of the Beast. Accordingly, he estimates that fortunately 'his time, times, and dividing of a time, are upon the point of expiring'.[28] Winstanley hopes that England, Scotland and Ireland will constitute that tenth part of the City of Babylon which is to be the first to fall from the Beast.[29] Thus he views the present discontents as cause for certain optimism. With all these considerations in mind, Winstanley assumes that the process of anointing is under way and that God is burning up the drosse of men's flesh.[30]

Despite his assertion of pure experimentalism, Winstanley was far from being reluctant to take on board received ideas. Many relatively orthodox or popular notions are to be found incorporated into Winstanley's theory. Three themes affirm this impression. First, Winstanley speaks at considerable length and in a fairly conventional manner of God sending His only son into the world and of Christ freely facing death in order to absolve men of their sins.[31] Second, the martyrdom of saints in times past is attributed by Winstanley to the reaction against them for elevating humility above pride.[32] Third, Winstanley is clearly influenced by the contemporary fear of popery, by claims that the Papacy, 'this Ecclesiastical Bastardly power',[33] is Antichrist, and that the oppressive power of this Beast had been most pronounced in 'Queen Maries dayes'.[34]

The contention that Winstanley's evaluation of the human condition, in both a spiritual and a secular sense, determined the eventual form of his social theory is corroborated by the claims advanced in *The Breaking of the Day of God* to the effect that fallen human nature is reflected in contemporary institutional arrangements.[35] For example, Winstanley asserts that 'Ecclesiastical power' continues to defy the spirit of Christ.[36] Furthermore, he argues that the predisposition of fallen men to follow the dictates of the flesh causes them to misapprehend truth and thereby to maintain corrupt constitutional standards, authoritarian political structures, and oppressive laws. In asserting that ill-founded and perverted laws encourage rather than suppress human wickedness, Winstanley shares More's doubts as to the efficacy of conventional institutional values. Even at this early stage Winstanley urges 'the reformation and preservation of Magistracy in Common-wealths . . . it being God's Ordinance'.[37] The proposition that the institutions of civil society might play an instrumental role in the recovery of moral rectitude is already evident in this pamphlet. Indeed, Winstanley goes so far as to envisage a situation in which 'the Magistrates shall love the people, and be nursing Fathers to them'.[38]

Despite this initial sortie into the realms of institutionalism, Winstanley retains the conviction that the poor, oppressed, and despised sectors of society will be the first to experience the spirit of righteousness and will consequently enact God's will by initiating social reform. He injects considerable force into this argument by comparing the reaction against the contemporary saints 'that are branded Sectaries, Schismaticks, Anabaptists, Round-heads'[39] to the persecution of Christ and His immediate followers. In blatantly evocative terms Winstanley insists that Christ's anointing, as experienced by 'Shepherds and Fishermen, or Tradesmen',[40] is quite as apposite to the position of the lower orders of his own day as it had been originally. Yet, as Winstanley ruefully comments, in both eras the true followers of God were restrained in their mission by a ministry authorized only by human ordination. It is apparent to Winstanley that a lesson is to be learnt from the past, when

> the purity of the Scriptures of the Gospel was corrupted, and the practice of it quite altered, and the invention of selfe-seeking flesh set up in the room of it, and sharp punishing laws were made to forbid Fishermen, Shepherds, Husbandmen and

Tradesmen, for ever preaching of God any more, but Schollars bred up in human letters, should onely do that work.[41]

Winstanley's primary concern in *The Breaking of the Day of God* is to elucidate his belief that the gradual restoration of human nature is commencing. So he repeats the claim that 'the great Mystery of God is this: He will cast the Serpent out of men; subdue that corrupt flesh under his feet, & dwell in man himself.'[42] Accordingly, Winstanley contends that the eventual universal salvation of Man will be achieved via the dissemination of God's strength through mankind—'by the plentifull increase of the Saints', and by the destruction of the Beast of self-love.[43]

Winstanley believed that the turmoils of the day indicated that this process to be under way.[44] For the moment, because of the constraints extending from an essentially millenarian perspective, Winstanley saw no immediate need to consider institutional matters in any depth. He was merely content to claim that the current national crisis corresponded, on the cosmic scale, to the last days of the *ancien régime* which was soon to be replaced by a new order, form unspecified. Thus he is to be found assuming that 'when this sort of righteousness and love arises in Magistrates and people, one to another, then these tumultuous Nationall stormes will cease'.[45] Effectively, men had only to await their restoration.

From this standpoint any temptation actively to anticipate mankind's restoration was necessarily muted. This attitude sets the tone for the first phase of Winstanley's intellectual progression. His counsel of patience was in part an attempt to sustain the morale of the saints during their exacting adversities. Hence Winstanley's persistent reiteration of the opinion that the period of oppression was about to end.[46] Such an essentially encouraging apprehension of Man's potential affords a clear indication of the state of development of Winstanley's incipient social philosophy. His position is quite categorical. At this stage Winstanley anticipated that the restoration of human nature would be *accompanied* by a similarly extensive reform of social institutions:

in the effecting of his great work, God shakes, and will yet shake, Kings, Parliaments, Armies, Counties, Kingdomes, Universities, humane learnings, studies, yea, shake rich men, and poore men, and throwes down every thing that stands in his way opposing him in his work.[47]

Winstanley confidently proceeded to assume that 'the pure reformation of civill Magistracy would soon appear'.[48]

The anxiety, belied here, to intimate that he is not a mere anarchist, is prescient of Winstanley's ultimate appreciation of the utility of civil institutions. However, whereas in his final pamphlet, *The Law of Freedom*, Winstanley was to insist upon the necessity of civil institutions for the restraint of the citizen's conduct, in *The Breaking of the Day of God* Winstanley retains a considerably more benign appreciation of the connection between the conduct of the individual and the influence of civil society. Thus he argues that once men are spiritually restored 'we shall have Laws and Governments according to truth, love and delight to be executing justice, for the good and safety of the Commonwealth'.[49] Crucially, it is evident that in this initial phase Winstanley did not believe the achievement of these results to be susceptible to human discretion; 'all that I shall say in conclusion is this, Wait patiently upon the Lord'.[50] The retention of such a conception of divine providence obviously impeded the development, for the while at least, of any substantial sophistication of Winstanley's social theory.

3

In the third of his tracts, *The Saints Paradice* (1648),[51] Winstanley maintains the general tenor of his previous writings while at the same time introducing a number of interesting new themes such as an exploration of the nature of God in association with the concept of reason and a developing interest in the moral basis of political authority. These ideas are early signs of matters destined to concern Winstanley more fully as time passed. For the moment Winstanley remained convinced that an immediate experience of the spirit of righteousness was the one necessary and sufficient condition for comprehending God, and that his own experience stood as an example to the remainder of mankind. So Winstanley recounted his claim that while he had relied solely upon received ideas he had 'lived in the darke, being blinded by the imagination of my flesh'.[52] Subsequently, the direct experience of God had fostered such spiritual enlightenment that Winstanley was able to resist the temptation to sin to which he had once succumbed so readily.[53] He seems to have regarded this privileged insight into matters spiritual as consolation for the loss of property and companionship.

Winstanley's acute sensitivity to the nature of a spiritual crisis prompted him to advance a lengthy account of the inner conflict integral to the 'Anointing', the process entailing the restoration of the individual to righteousness. Winstanley suggests that while men lived according to the flesh and upon the objects of the Creation, they would be capable of attaining only a somewhat bestial felicity. Thus the initial sensation of righteousness would be a time of spiritual trial as the individual would inevitably be torn between the self and God.[54] Winstanley employs a series of images to describe this condition. He speaks of God 'burning up thy drosse',[55] and of the spirit burning up the unrighteous flesh.[56] He also uses the analogy of the 'Sun' and the 'Son of Righteousness'—as the light that would dispel the darkness within Man.[57] The essence of the restorative theory is captured by Winstanley's reference to 'the Anointing, or that Son of God ruling, A King of righteousness and peace within you, that sets you free'.[58] As God would penetrate the individual soul so the individual would become absorbed into Him.[59] In *The Saints Paradice* Winstanley once again asserts[60] the imminence of the salvation of mankind by means of a restoration on earth and states that:

Now the Father is beginning to work a great mysterie, and that is, to pull Adam out of the selfish-flesh again, and to plant him into the pure spirit, and to bring him into the most fruitful Garden of Eden.[61]

Winstanley contends that by this means Man could recover his dignity by being restored to that state of reasonableness which had once distinguished men from beasts.[62] Thus Winstanley is able to envisage transformed human nature as 'Love, Humility, Patience, Meeknesse, Joy, and a sweet resting of heart in God'.[63]

It is in *The Saints Paradice* that Winstanley introduces the notion that God and Reason are synonymous. He seems apprehensive lest this conception should meet with disapproval. So he maintains that it is imperative for men

to know that this spirit which is called God, or Father, or Lord, is Reason: for though men esteem this word reason to be too mean a name to set forth the Father by, yet it is the highest name that can be given him.[64]

This departure is of the utmost importance because the identification of God and Reason provided Winstanley with an opportunity to free himself from the intellectual strait-jacket in which he had erstwhile been constrained by his essentially millenarian approach.[65] For the first time he was prepared to suggest that as men approached perfection by becoming absorbed in the spirit of God, they might be distinguished by attaining a capacity to live according to 'the light of reason'.[66] Eventually, by inverting this argument, Winstanley would postulate that reasonable conduct should itself be construed as evidence of spiritual regeneration. So, whereas previously he had assumed that the restoration of Man must be determined exclusively by the will of God, he is now to be found moving to a position that would enable him, should he so desire, to argue that men might be induced to act reasonably by means other than divine providence. This being the case, Winstanley was also in a position to argue that, by implication, spiritual righteousness and moral regeneration were attainable via institutional restructuring. Although these propositions would remain latent within Winstanley's thought for some time, ideas of this sort ultimately developed into a rationale for activism of the kind represented by the establishment of the Digger colony and, indeed, Winstanley's construction of an ideal commonwealth.

In *The Saints Paradice* Winstanley takes up once again the issue of the 'Nationall hurly burlies'.[67] He accounts for 'the discontent that appears generally in mens spirits in England, one against another',[68] by arguing that God was cleansing England of its sinfulness. Hence Winstanley's derivation of solace from the conviction that God was in complete control of the situation and had in fact chosen England as the elect nation.[69] Although earlier pamphlets reveal a highly impressionistic analysis of contemporary institutional affairs, *The Saints Paradice* contains thought of a somewhat more systematic kind. Certain of Winstanley's subsequent preoccupations are anticipated. For example, it is in this tract that Winstanley first refers to 'kingly power', by issuing the following challenge: 'assure your selves, you Kingly, Parliamentarie, and Army power, and know this, that all unrighteous powers and actions must be destroyed; the Father is about this work, and his hand will not slack'.[70] Only in subsequent months would Winstanley arrive at the conclusion that men might remove political oppression by their own volition. Similarly, Winstanley was soon to extend the conviction that men might live in 'community with him who is the Father of all things',[71] by proposing, not a chiliastic solution to the predicament, but instead the understanding that this end could be achieved through the recovery of reasonableness within a community of property.

Despite these incipient developments Winstanley remained convinced for the time being that Man's predicament could only be altered by divine intervention. However, a touch of anxiety had begun to permeate Winstanley's exhortations for endurance amidst the persecutions and oppression of the times. In citing the case of Job—who according to Winstanley had been tested by God in order to foster righteousnes,[72] Winstanley indicates that despite anticipating 'the restored state which the Father hath begun to work, and which his people wait for compleatness of',[73] his resilience and patience were wearing thin.

4

As the title suggests, *Truth Lifting Up Its Head Above Scandals* (16 October 1648) is an apologia. In it, Winstanley writes not only in self-defence but also in an attempt to exonerate his new-found associate William Everard,[74] who had recently been incarcerated on a charge of blasphemy. Winstanley's response is a tract intended to extol the essential religiousity of both Everard's and his own theological statements. Consequently, Winstanley seeks to provide a coherent exposition of his spiritual ideas, one in which his anticlericalism and advocacy of experimental religion are well to the fore. In particular, he expands upon his belief that the universal harmony destroyed at the Fall might yet be recovered.

Winstanley's notion that only a reassertion of the law of reason could restore the harmony of the creation[75] receives close attention in *Truth Lifting Up Its Head*. The ideal of men living 'in community with the Globe, and . . . with the Spirit of the Globe',[76] which was maintained throughout his intellectual career, is again developed. In this formative period he argues that:

> The spirit of the Father is pure Reason: which as he made so he knits the whole creation together into a one-nesse of life and moderation: every creature sweetly in love lending their hands to preserve each other, and so upholds the whole fabrique.[77]

Evidently, Winstanley believed that he would be able to identify the means by which the human condition could be ameliorated by analysing the disruption of this unity.

In this pamphlet Winstanley advances the interesting theory that, after burial, the corpses of fallen men would necessarily pollute the earth,[78] because men are composed of the same four elements ('fire, water, earth, and aire'[79]) as the entire creation. Winstanley also discusses the notion that

as the body of the first man was a representation of the whole Creation, and did corrupt it; so the body of Christ was a representation of the whole Creation, and restores it from corruption, and brings it all into a unity of the Father again.[80]

Winstanley's position here is a little obscure because he fails to explain why further restoration was required after the death and burial of Christ. Presumably, he supposed that the ascension terminated the restorative vigour exuded from Christ's body. Winstanley seems to have assumed that the rejuvenation of the physical world would recommence once the spirit of Christ had restored Man to righteousness.

Up to this point Winstanley remained content to assure his fellow men that the coming of the spirit would rectify human nature. So, once again, he counsels patience in awaiting this event.[81] Although Winstanley confidently predicts the imminence of changing times, he limits himself to the assumption that such a restoration is to be effected by some form of millennium.[82] However, by this time this aspect of his thought had become increasingly esoteric. Even so, he confirms that events were to 'change times and customs, & fil the earth with a new law, wherein dwels righteousness and peace'.[83] Within a matter of months Winstanley would be prepared to be a little more categorical, particularly in predicting the likely social manifestations of the new order.

5

The New Law of Righteousnes (26 January 1649) is very much a transitionary piece in that in this pamphlet Winstanley resumes his ongoing analysis of the human condition while at the same time serving notice of the amelioration of that situation. The reader of this tract can have little doubt that the incipient law of righteousness presumes the instigation of a society founded upon communalism. Winstanley readily confides that:

As I was in a trance not long since, divers matters were present to me by sight, which here must not be related. Likewise I here these words, Work together. Eat bread together; declare this all abroad.[84]

Despite the intimation that divine revelation lay at the source of all his ideas it seems quite likely that Winstanley drew considerable inspiration in the clarification of his social thought from *Light Shining in Buckinghamshire*,[85] a tract published shortly before *The New Law of Righteousnes* by a nearby group of 'True Levellers'.

Winstanley's millenarianism has already been discussed. Two conclusions regarding this aspect of his thought have emerged. First, it seems that although initially Winstanley maintained an affinity to certain millenarian insights, his emphasis upon universal salvation and the transformation of human nature was exceptional, and contributed to his peculiar adaptation of millenarianism. Second, it is apparent that as Winstanley turned to communal cultivation and eventually to utopianism, he abandoned the core of his millenarian tendencies. In *The New Law of Righteousnes*, however, Winstanley still evinces an interest in the millennium.[86] For example, he speaks in a manner reminiscent of *The Breaking of the Day of God* to the effect that

> the Lord he gives this Beast a toleration to rule 42 months, or a time, times and dividing of time; and in that time to kil the two Witnesses, that is, Christ in one body, and Christ in many bodies; or Christ in the first and second coming in flesh, which is Justice and Judgement ruling in man. Rev. 11. 2, 9 Rev. 12. 14[87]

Even here, it is apparent that, from the assumption that 'the greatest combate is within a man',[88] Winstanley is adapting a millenarian vocabulary to accord with his own spiritual ideas, his views on human nature, and his conception of Man's predicament.

Much of this pamphlet is devoted to a lengthy consideration of the Fall of Man and to his salvation or restauration rather'.[89] Hence Winstanley expounds the view that all men have emulated Adam's experience. Yet in arguing that 'perfect man shall be no other but God manifest in flesh'[90] (as humility overcomes pride), he envisages the prospect of the regeneration of human nature. Winstanley's prediction of the redemption of all men is sustained by the belief that the 'King of righteousnesse . . . shal save his people from their sins, and free them from all distemper of the unrighteous flesh. This is the only spreading power that shall remove the curse, and restore all things from the bondage every thing groans under.'[91] Although *The New Law of Righteousnes* is transitionary in the sense that in this piece Winstanley achieves a clearer appreciation of those aspects of the human condition to which his social theory was to be addressed, he remained for the moment irresolute as to the *precise* means by which this would be accomplished. So Winstanley expresses concern over the continuing 'large distance between Christ and the bulke of man-kinde'.[92] As we might anticipate, Winstanley's social philosophy was soon required to address the question of how this gap might be bridged.

Winstanley expected a series of reforms to transpire as a result of the regeneration of human nature. Quite obviously, the most fundamental of these was the anticipated restoration of the 'common treasury'. Winstanley appears convinced that the process of spiritual regeneration had already commenced, particularly among 'the lowest and despised sort of people'.[93] Clearly, he believed that institutional reform would ensue. It is important to reiterate that such an assumption is dialectically opposed to the principle feature of the form of utopianism ultimately adhered to by Winstanley, namely the propensity to emphasize institutional reform without necessarily presupposing the prior moral regeneration of Man. The most significant aspect of Winstanley's intellectual development is his inclination towards such utopian institutionalism.

As yet, Winstanley remained content merely to speculate upon the secular consequences of the spiritual restoration of Man. Hence his prediction that once the law of righteousness had restored all men 'none shall desire to have more than another, or to be Lord over other'.[94] Winstanley also assumes here that the cessation of aggrandizement inspired by the newly discovered moral rectitude would produce a more equitable society in which 'the distribution of dominion in one single person over all, shall cease'.[95] Even so, Winstanley remains adamant that the means to social reform would be of divine origin. Hence the contention that

when the spreading power of wisdome and truth, fils the earth man-kinde, he wil take off that bondage, and give a universall liberty, and there shal be no more complainings against oppression poverty or injustice'.[96]

This optimism inspired Winstanley to believe that the existing legal system, which he condemns as corrupt and inefficient,[97] might be relinquished, because the restoration of human nature would mean that 'there shall be no need of Lawyers, prisons, or engines of punishment one over another, for all shall walk and act righteously'.[98] By the time he came to write *The Law of Freedom* Winstanley's confidence had been tempered. The increasing sophistication of his social thought led Winstanley to recognize that the regeneration of human nature would not be achieved in an instant. So in the last of the phases into which Winstanley's writings are divisible—utopianism—he would come to argue that individuals might be restored to spiritual righteousness only gradually and during the course of the life cycle. Thus he ultimately accepted that the retention of a punititve system would be necessary to curb the actions of malefactors.

During the Digger period Winstanley found himself required to dispute, in an increasingly complex manner, the claims of landlords to a private property in land. He eventually challenged the constitutional basis of this property right by utilizing the theory of the Norman Yoke. However, before this, in *The New Law of Righteousnes*, Winstanley used purely ethical arguments to attack 'that devil (particular interest)'.[99] In this pamphlet Winstanley develops his case for the proposition that 'the earth was made by the Lord, to be a common Treasury for all, not a particular Treasury for some'.[100] He asserts that landlords have no right to appropriate or to assume a property in land because to do so is to transgress the law of reason. Thus he maintains that:

'The rich man tels the poor, that they ofend Reasons law, if they take from the rich; I am sure it is a breach in that Law in the rich to have plenty by them, and yet wil see their fellow creatures men and women to starve for want; Reason requires that every man should live upon the increase of the earth comfortably; though covetousnesse fights against Reasons law.'[101]

This statement is indicative of Winstanley's maturing propensity to perceive these matters in terms of natural law and natural rights. Winstanley's position in this respect will be analysed in greater detail in a later chapter. At this juncture it is enough to stress that Winstanley was by now quite certain that a system of communalism was prerequisite to the spiritual restoration of Man.

By early 1649 Winstanley had developed his social thinking to such a degree that many of the issues to which he would soon devote considerable attention are discernible in *The New Law of Righteousnes*. To elaborate, by this stage in his intellectual development Winstanley had attained a fairly detailed conception of the equation between economic and socio-political power in contemporary society. Thus the claim that:

> The man of the flesh judges it a righteous thing, That some men that are clothed in the objects of the earth, and so called rich men, whether it be got by right or wrong, should be Magistrates to rule over the poor . . .[102]

So Winstanley contends that the abuse of political authority would cease only once the spirit of righteousness impelled men to reinstate the 'common treasury'. To this end he advances several ideas relevant to the practice of communism. For example, he introduces the idea of 'storehouses', eventually to become the focal point of the distributive system in Winstanley's ideal commonwealth. Winstanley predicts that should storehouses become operative 'there shall be no buying nor selling, no fairs or markets, but the whole earth shall be a common treasury for every man'.[103] Even at this early stage, Winstanley was sensitive to the type of argument likely to be weighted against his proposals. So he attempts to dispel the notion that communism encourages idleness and even the sharing of women.[104] Instead he asserts that communism is capable of inaugurating 'a new heaven, and a new earth, wherein dwells righteousnesse'.[105]

In *The New Law of Righteousnes* Winstanley discloses an attitude to the issues attending the hiring of labour and the expropriation of land which in its potential was extraordinarily radical.[106] Given that a good deal of the impact of Winstanley's social thought turns upon this analysis the question obviously deserves detailed consideration. In general, the full significance of Winstanley's proposals is not fully appreciated. Often this reaction arises as a consequence of regarding *The New Law of Righteousnes* as a purely theological piece.[107]

When he wrote *The New Law of Righteousnes* Winstanley felt sufficiently unconstrained as to propose the subversion of the hired labour upon which landlords were to a marked degree dependent for the preservation of the economic viability of their estates.[108] Tactical considerations attending the public defence of the Digger colony, always perilously perched on the margins of existence, caused Winstanley subsequently to temper his public pronouncements concerning this question.

Winstanley's rejection of the principle of hired labour is derived from the proposition that the institution effectively sustained the regime of private property, which in turn had led to the establishment of the coercive and illegitimate political authority which oppressed the common people who continued to labour under it.[109] Winstanley expresses the cruel irony of the situation: 'The poor people by their labours in this time of the first Adams government, have made the buyers and sellers of land, or rich men, to become tyrants and oppressours over them.'[110] The close affinity of Winstanley's spiritual concerns and his social theory is evident in his affirmation that the incipient restoration of Man would entail the abolition of hired labour.[111]

This argument is symptomatic of the type of dilemma Winstanley confronted during the course of his intellectual development because, on the one hand, he clung to the conviction that social reform would be guided by divine providence while, on the other, he was swayed by an evolving supposition that men could *actively determine* their social and spiritual condition. Thus, in recognizing that his case might be misconstrued as an apology for the forceful dispossession of the propertied classes and of anarchy in general, Winstanley is anxious to stress that:

> I do not speak that any particular man shall go and take their neighbours goods by violence, or robbery . . . but every one is to wait, till the Lord Christ do spread himself in multiplicities of bodies . . . [112]

Conversely, Winstanley also warns that:

> Whosoever it is that labours in the earth, for any person or persons, that lifts up themselves as Lords & Rulers over others, and that doth not look upon themselves equal to others in Creation, The hand of the Lord shall be upon that labourer . . . [113]

By arguing that both labourers and proprietors would incur God's wrath if they persisted with existing social arrangements, Winstanley effectively suggested that men were capable of choosing their institutional environment.

It is of the utmost significance that Winstanley argued that hired labour and private property constituted the curse shortly to be withdrawn. Thereafter, men could be restored only if they obeyed God's ordinance to desist in either hiring out or employing labour. The radical and even subversive implications of Winstanley's theory are most apparent in the following statement:

> Therefore if the rich wil stil hold fast this propriety of Mine and thine, let them labour their own Land with their own hands. And let the common-People, that are the gatherings together of Israel from under that bondage, and that say the earth is ours, not mine, let them labour together, and eat bread together upon the Commons, Mountains and Hills.
>
> For as the inclosures are called such a mans Land, and such a mans Land: so the Commons and Heath, are called the common-peoples.[114]

This is a declaration of intent. Winstanley had come to envisage a society in which 'no man shal have more land, then he can labour himself, or have others to labour with him in love, working together, and eating bread together'.[115] It seems, therefore, that Winstanley regarded the withdrawal of hired labour as an appropriate means to the establishment of a predominantly communist system of ownership.

Further aspects of Winstanley's views on this matter are worth taking into account. In an oft-quoted statement Winstanley claims:

> Divide England into three parts, scarce one part is manured: So that here is land enough to maintain all her children, and many die for want, or live under a heavy burden of povertie all their daies: And this miserie the poor people have brought upon themselves, by lifting up a particular interest, by their labours.[116]

In this passage the threads of three closely related arguments are entangled: first, Winstanley's thesis that hired labour is contributory towards sustaining the contemporary hierarchical distribution of property and power; second, that sufficient land is available for the common people to cultivate should they refuse to work for landlords; and third, that the extension of cultivation beyond its present limits will alleviate suffering and want by increasing production and thereby the general prosperity of the nation. Even were this estimate to be accurate, Winstanley must presumably have realized that the landowners would attempt to claim some form of property right in the uncultivated tracts of land to which he alludes. This leads to the interesting question of how Winstanley expected the landowning classes to react to the imminent spiritual restoration and attendant reformation of social institutions and practices here predicated.

The occasional ambiguity of Winstanley's position in *The New Law of Righteousnes* is illustrated by his evaluation of the manner in which the propertied classes might be expected to respond to the forthcoming restoration of social and spiritual harmony. We have established that Winstanley posited a general correlation between the extent of the individual's holding of private property and the depth of that person's descent into the fallen condition. Winstanley anticipated that the poor would be the first to be restored. Nevertheless, in arguing as follows he confidently predicts that the spirit of reason might even inspire the rich: 'When the universall law of equity rises up in every man . . . every one shall put to their hands to till the earth.'[117] Alternatively, in a more pragmatic and possibly deferential moment, Winstanley suggests that

> he that is now possessour of lands and riches, and cannot labour, if he say to others, you are my fellow creatures, and the Lord is now making the earth common amongst us: therefore take my land only let me eat bread with you, that man shall be preserved by the labour of others.[118]

So it appears that Winstanley understood that the restoration might ultimately include the propertied, who in their newly-discovered righteousness would relinquish their claims to private ownership in land and would restore it to the 'common treasury'. Nevertheless, we have seen that Winstanley held in reserve the more drastic suggestion that less enlightened landowners would eventually be constrained by circumstance to abandon their claims to private property. In a situation in which labour might become scarce and thus difficult to hire, landlords could be expected to encounter problems in maintaining the economic viability of their estates. In this light, Winstanley warned landowners of the retribution they were liable to face:

if thou wouldst find mercie, then open thy barns and treasuries of the earth, which thou hast heaped together, and detains from the poor, thy fellow creatures. This is the only remedy to escape wrath.[119]

6

Communal cultivation in the form of 'digging' constituted an active response to the intellectual premises established in this, the first of the phases into which Winstanley's thought is divisible. The call to action succeeded and in many ways contradicted Winstanley's confident assurances on the inevitability of the law of righteousness: 'the whole earth shall be filled with the knowledge of the Lord, and of his Dominion there shall be no end . . . it draws near to be made manifest, wait for it with patience'.[120] Hence this period was very much one of 'waiting for a restoration by Christ the King and law of righteousnesse, who is the restorer of all things'.[121] In his conviction that 'it must be the hand of the Lord alone that must do it'.[122] Winstanley appears resolute as to the futility of any active attempt to precipitate the restoration and even intimates that such a course might be detrimental to the divine purpose. Men could not attempt to transform the world by anticipating the coming of reason.[123] As yet, contends Winstanley, only a few individuals have been restored. He concludes *The New Law of Righteousnes* with a plea to the effect that the unregenerate should patiently await their restoration: 'O my dear friends in the flesh, despise not this word I speak; wait upon the Lord for teaching; you will never have rest in your souls till he speak in you.'[124] Such pacificism obviously represented a constraint upon Winstanley's thought and action. Even so, particularly in terms of his analysis of the practice and consequences of hiring labour, Winstanley already had to hand a body of social analysis capable of enabling him to effect the fundamental change of intellectual position that resulted in the commencement of digging.

The Digger experiment

1

Recalling that 'the manifestations of a righteous heart shall be known, not by his words, but in his actions . . .',[125] the inception of the communal cultivation of the common lands obviously marked a crucial reformulation of Winstanley's approach to the problem of achieving Man's spiritual restoration. According to his own account, visionary guidance prompted Winstanley to commence digging on (the conveniently proximate) St George's Hill on 1 April 1649. By tilling the land in order to institute the recovery of the 'common treasury' Winstanley had by this time determined actively to anticipate the restoration.[126] Soon afterwards, Winstanley and his chief associate, William Everard, were twice interviewed on apparently amicable terms by Fairfax.[127] These meetings coincided with the publication of the first of what proved to be a long series of pamphlets which both defend and explain the activity of digging. Despite apparently satisfying Fairfax that they constituted a relatively innocuous group, the Diggers were subjected to an array of violent attacks and legal proceedings instigated by the local populace whose activities were orchestrated by a representative of the gentry in the person of one Mr Drake and of the clergy in the guise of one Parson Platt.[128] The Diggers endured this intimidation patiently. However, despite relocating, financial straits brought an end to the colony after a troubled one-year existence. Nevertheless, during this period, Winstanley's thought concerning the wider issues of Man's predicament was engrossed with the immediate destiny of the Digger colony.

2

The critical evaluation of Winstanley's writings suggests four possible explanations of digging. These might profitably be considered.

Keith Thomas is one of a number of scholars[129] to regard digging as essentially a consequence of scarcity and necessity. As Thomas states:

> 'the whole Digger movement can plausibly be regarded as the culmination of a century of unauthorized encroachment upon the forests and wastes by squatters and local commoners, pushed on by land shortage and the pressure of population.[130]

Clearly, there is considerable plausibility to this 'necessity and pressure of population' account, but, as Thomas appreciates, it is not an *entirely* convincing explanation of the cultivation of St George's Hill. Digging was squatting of a unique nature in which the occupation of the wastes and commons was justified by arguments that are central to an intricate social theory. It is noteworthy that Winstanley did not emphasize the argument from necessity until well into the Digger period, at which point the colony was actually threatened by extinction.[131]

Often attendant upon this position is the second explanation, which asserts that the Diggers were determined to claim the commons for the poor and thereafter to differentiate these communes from the enclosed holdings of the gentry.[132] Thus, it is assumed that the Diggers envisaged a situation in which two ways of life, that is to say communalism and the adherence to a system of private ownership, could peacefully coexist. The obvious shortcoming of this explanation is its failure to take full account of Winstanley's ideas on the subversive withdrawal of hired labour and the collapse of landlordism such action might precipitate.[133]

A third view, the 'millenarian' explanation, argues, for example, that Digging represented the anticipation of the lifestyle Winstanley believed the millennium would inaugurate.[134] An alternative within this view holds that digging constituted an 'outward millennium' according to which the 'inward regeneration' of human nature was sought.[135] By accommodating some consideration of his spiritual concerns these views provide some clues as to Winstanley's reasons for digging. However, this explanation is impaired by the dogmatic insistence that while he tilled the commons Winstanley still sincerely awaited the millennium.

The final, somewhat more satisfactory, explanation of digging postulates a connection between communal cultivation and Winstanley's conception of the restoration of Man. Thus Perez Zagorin, for instance, relates Winstanley's adoption of practical communism to his earlier assumptions about the origins of evil and the recovery of moral rectitude. Yet Zagorin also contends that digging was merely a *symbolic* action.[136] It seems more likely, however, that with the foundation of the Digger colony Winstanley understood that, for the participants at least, the process of restoration had actually begun. As G.H. Sabine argues, Winstanley

> believed, naively no doubt, that a life of Christian love was about to transform the whole economic and political organization of society, but he expected also a complete transformation of human nature.[137]

Thus digging constituted a remedy for Man's fallen condition. It becomes, therefore, admissible to maintain that by this stage in his intellectual career Winstanley had developed a concern for, as P. Elmen has it, 'possible changes in the outward structure of laws and institutions'.[138] Thus Winstanley's intellectual progress is characterized by his gradual recognition of the potential utility of institutional reform in restoring Man's spiritual esteem. As will be demonstrated below, Winstanley's Digger pamphlets are the depository of the seeds of his utopian institutionalism, rather than the consummation of his millenarianism.

3

We now turn to an examination of the pamphlets written by Winstanley during the Digger period. The first of these tracts, *The True Levellers' Standard Advanced* (20 April 1649) is concerned with three major themes. These are, first, an evaluation of Man's current predicament and the prospect of restoration; second, the failure of the new government to institute thoroughgoing social reform; and third, the explanation and justification of digging.

With regard to the first of these themes, the analysis of the human condition, *The True Levellers' Standard Advanced* contains substantial evidence to confirm that Digger communism was informed by Winstanley's preoccupation with the moral and spiritual welfare of Man. The elements of continuity within Winstanley's intellectual position originate in his sustained endeavour to evaluate the 'Fall of Man' and to postulate a means of effecting a restoration. Hence he opens the first Digger tract by discussing the pristine condition and its implications for existing circumstances:

> 'In the beginning of Time, the great Creator Reason made the Earth to be a Common Treasury, to preserve Beasts, Birds, Fishes, and Man, the lord that was to govern this Creation; for Man had Domination given to him, over the Beasts, Birds

and Fishes; but not one word was spoken in the beginning, That one branch of mankind should rule over another.[139]

This discussion is developed into an analysis of various notions commonplace to Winstanley's outlook (including the bondage of Man represented as 'Adam', the correlation of pride and political oppression, and property as the curse). A degree of millenarian terminology is retained within Winstanley's expostion of the restoration. Thus he advances the familiar claim that 'the Seed out of whom the Creation did proceed, shall bruise this Serpents head, and restore my Creation again from this curse and bondage'.[140] Perhaps more significantly, Winstanley retains his preoccupation with the 'rule of righteousness' by adapting it to the Diggers' predicament. He advises men to 'Do, as you would have others do to you; and love your Enemies, not in words, but in actions.'[141]

The True Levellers' Standard Advanced was dedicated but three months after the execution of Charles I, an indication in itself of the profound impact that this event had upon thinkers of a radical bent such as the understandably impetuous Winstanley. This consideration stimulated the second of the pamphlet's themes. Even after so short a time, Winstanley advanced the nascent supposition that the new government was not exerting itself to restore that liberty and freedom identified by Winstanley as every Englishman's birthright.[142] Thus Winstanley expresses concern over what he sees as the continuation of oppression beyond the time of the tyrant's execution. Winstanley was to become increasingly disillusioned during the course of the ensuing year and would in the process develop this notion into a more detailed analysis of 'kingly power'. That Winstanley reacted so quickly and so critically to the shortcomings of the new regime suggests a growing impatience fuelled by his anticipation of the restoration and its attendant social reform.

Thirdly, and finally, Winstanley's most obvious reason for writing *The True Levellers' Standard Advanced* was his desire to vindicate the communal cultivation of the commons. Although in the tract Winstanley claims to be advancing six arguments in defence of digging, he effectively presents only three. The first of these is that the Diggers were responding to visionary guidance bestowed upon himself.[143] That the Norman Yoke was a vestige of Babylonish power, that particular interests were the curse, and that landowners had breached the Lord's commandments against killing and stealing; all this apparently had been revealed to Winstanley in a trance. By defining liberty in terms implying that the poor should be free to cultivate the commons, Winstanley was able to argue that 'this is one Reason for our digging and labouring the Earth one with another, That we might work in righteousness, and lift up the Creation from bondage'.[144] Similarly, Winstanley goes on to maintain that a voice in a trance had directed him to declare communism through his words, writings and actions, and thereby to reintroduce the 'common treasury'.[145] He again speaks with assurance that any individual culpable of sustaining the existing social structure by hiring out his labour, would face divine retribution. Winstanley even insists that the precise location for the establishment of the Digger colony had been indicated in a dream.[146]

The second argument lies in the citation and interpretation of scriptural authority, a form of argument suggesting that Winstanley conceived of the cultivation of the commons as possessing a spiritual foundation. Thus Winstanley offers a long list of Biblical citations culminating in Acts 4: 32, the admonition to Apostolic communism.[147]

Winstanley would eventually develop his third reason for digging into a proposition which, in an amended form, constitutes a central theme of *The Law of Freedom*. This is the notion that labour, especially if entailing the communal cultivation of land, must be integral to the spiritual restoration of the individual. Hence Winstanley's claims to the effect that the Diggers had been invested with the spirit of righteousness,[148] and through their communal life were privy to considerable tranquility of spirit.[149] By arguing that digging must be fundamental to the resurrection of the spirit within,[150] Winstanley suggests that the colony was in the process of laying the foundations for the restoration of Man.

4

Their second pamphlet, *A Declaration From the Poor Oppressed People of England* (1 June 1649), is witness to the ebullient mood of the Diggers during the first few months of the colony's existence.[151] From the proposition that the earth had been created as a 'common treasury' the tract goes on to emphasize the guilt and intransigence of the lords of the manor in depriving the common people of their livelihood.[152] By means of a series of anti-intellectual assertions the belief that the Diggers had indeed become enlightened is vigorously advanced.[153] Hence the contention that by perceiving that the land was originally intended for communal cultivation, the Diggers were heralding the reinstatement of the spirit of righteousness.[154] Furthermore, by contending that the Diggers were motivated by 'the inward law of Love'[155] to discredit private property, the suggestion is again made that the colonists were already experiencing a regeneration of spirit. This essentially theological justification for digging is supplemented by the contention that the freedom of the common people to cultivate the land originates in their birthright.[156] The case for regarding armed conflict as a process by which the people sought to recover lost freedoms is developed by invoking an argument to the effect that, in accordance with the 'National Covenant' (the Solemn League and Covenant of 1643), the sacrifices of life and property volunteered by the common people to the cause of overthrowing the king effectively constituted a contractual undertaking. In due respect to the sanctity of this contract, it is argued, the people should be regarded as having recovered their lost birthright, a situation that would be confirmed only once the government committed itself to the cause of social reform.[157] Hence the claim that by cultivating the commons, the Diggers were merely acting within the terms of a long-standing agreement.

It is evident from this pamphlet that the Diggers were animated by one particularly sensitive issue—the proprietorial status of woodland—the implications of which were not insignificant. It appears that, notwithstanding any theoretical abhorrence of commercial transactions, the Diggers had been constrained to compromise their ideals by selling wood gathered from the commons in order to sustain themselves until such a time as their crops ripened.[158] This enterprise had met with the disapprobation of local landowners who maintained that their property rights were being infringed by the Diggers. The Diggers repsonded by elaborating upon the claims they saw themselves as advancing on behalf of the people. Hence the following stipulation:

> Therefore, we requrie, and we resolve to take both common Land, and Common woods to be a livelihood for us, and look upon you as equal with us, not above us, knowing very well, that England, the land of our Nativity, is to be a common Treasury of livelihood to all, without respect of persons.[159]

5

On 20 April 1649 Winstanley and Everard visited Whitehall in an attempt to exonerate the Diggers' actions and to explain their social philosophy to the man they regarded as the *de facto* head of state, Lord General Thomas Fairfax. On 26 May Fairfax actually inspected the St George's Hill colony. This event seems to have strengthened Winstanley's conviction that digging was of immense consequence not only to the destiny of England but also within the entire cosmic scheme of things. Soon afterwards Winstanley is to be found writing of his understanding that 'our digging upon the Common, is the talk of the whole Land'.[160] It appears that relations between Winstanley and Fairfax had proceeded amicably enough. For his part Winstanley was able to convince Fairfax that the Diggers did not pose a subversive threat to the newly established Commonwealth, while Fairfax seems to have given the Diggers a sympathetic hearing and to have remained tolerant of their experiment. Fairfax's somewhat paternal attitude inspired Winstanley to look to him for protection against the various violent attacks that the Diggers were obliged to endure.

A letter written by Winstanley to Fairfax (9 June 1649) indicates that by this time Winstanley's confidence in the conviction that the project would succeed and proliferate was at its height.[161] Despite certain assaults upon the colony from its less endearing neighbours,[162] Winstanley reports a gradual conversion of the local populace to the Digger cause.

In this letter Winstanley takes the opportunity to clarify some of his basic ideas. Thus he reminds Fairfax that the cultivation of the commons is every Englishman's birthright,[163] that the Civil War had been successfully prosecuted largely as a result of the 'covenant' between Parliament, army and people,[164] and, as a corollary, that the contractors should remain united in confirming the victory by bestowing upon the common people a share of the spoils—in the form of free access to the common lands.[165] Similarly, Winstanley outlines for Fairfax's benefit his interpretation of the Fall and of 'the burthen of the Norman yoke',[166] alongside his understanding of digging as an activity capable of recovering the 'common treasury' and thus as an integral aspect of the cosmic battle and of the spiritual restoration of Man. The relationship, postulated by Winstanley, between the Fall and the Norman Yoke is demonstrated in the following conclusion:

the Reformation that England is now to endeavour, is not to remove the Norman Yoke only, and to bring us back to be governed by those Laws that were before William the Conqueror came in, as if that were the rule or mark we aime at: No, that is not it; but the Reformation is according to the Word of God, and that is the pure Law of righteousnesse before the fall, which made all things, unto which all things are to be restored: and he that endeavours not that, is a Covenant-breaker.[167]

Winstanley's suggestion that by advancing the Digger cause Fairfax might further this reformation, marks the germination of an important new stage in his intellectual development because ultimately, in *The Law of Freedom*, Winstanley would conclude that *only* civil institutions could actively promote the spiritual restoration of the individual.

In view of the direction his thought was destined to take with regard to the whole issue of institutionalism, it is perhaps ironical that a significant feature of this letter turns upon Winstanley's discussion of the limited circumstances in which government would be necessary and might indeed be justified. His apology for the insular anarchism[168] of the Digger colony is phrased thus:

we were not against any that would have Magistrates and Laws to govern, as the Nations of the world are governed, but as for our parts we shall need neither the one nor the other in the nature of Government; for as our Land is common, so our Cattell is to be common, and our corn and fruits of the earth common, and are not to be bought and sold among us, but to remaine a standing portion of livelihood to us and our children, without that cheating entanglement of buying and selling, and we shall not arrest one another . . .[169]

He adds: 'we have chosen the Lord God Almighty to be our King and Protector'.[170] These affirmations corroborate the impression that, certainly at the time of communicating with Fairfax, Winstanley's confidence in the utility of digging had culminated in a profoundly optimistic appreciation of human potential. Hence his assumption that the moral regeneration of the Diggers enabled them to dispense with private property and to live without the restraint of any form of political authority. By eradicating, at this stage, both private property and political authority from his scheme of things, Winstanley precluded two institutions traditionally associated with concern to subjugate the evil inclinations of fallen Man.

In the event, Winstanley failed to maintain his anarchical assurances.[171] As time went on Winstanley became less confident of the facility with which the moral reformation of Man would occur. Thus he became obliged to disavow the luxury of anarchism. Eventually he would confront with considerable alacrity various issues germane to the institutional restraint of the citizen's conduct. In the most systematic exposition of his mature social theory, *The Law of Freedom*, Winstanley proposes various institutional arrangements designed to achieve this end. It is nevertheless important to note that whereas in the Digger period Winstanley repudiated a jurisdiction ('kingly power') which he conceived as corrupt, in his latter period of utopianism he insisted that the institutions of state must defer to the law of righteousness.

6

In *An Appeal to the House of Commons* (11 July 1649) Winstanley brings to maturity his theory of the *de facto* convenant involving the new regime and the people. The tract represents a detailed plea for the thoroughgoing reformation of society through the extirpation of the institutions associated with 'kingly power'. During the course of the pamphlet Winstanley recites several of his standard arguments. For example, he rails against both the centralization and linguistic obfuscations of the Norman legal system.[172] The law, Winstanley insists, should instead accord with reason and equity. In this context Winstanley's claim that the Norman Conquest and the concessions subsequently extracted via Magna Carta were among the most important events to have occurred 'since the fall of man from that righteous Law'[173] assumes evident significance. From this standpoint Winstanley maintains that the Diggers were trespassing only if God had granted an exclusive property right in the common lands to the lords of the manor.[174] Winstanley consistently doubted the veracity of this assumption.

Occasional bouts of repetition notwithstanding, Winstanley uses *An Appeal to the House of Commons* to expand upon his theory of the National Covenant. Accordingly he argues that the civil disorders had been brought to a successful conclusion largely as the result of an undertaking in which the common people had contributed both blood and money to the war effort on the understanding that once victory was assured their birthright of the 'common treasury' would be restored to them.[175] Yet, as Winstanley points out, despite this arrangement, the selfishness and pride evident in the nature of those who assumed control of the Commonwealth impelled them to retain 'kingly power' even after their disposal of the king. So Winstanley states that

> it will appear to the view of all men, That you cut off the King's head, that you might establish yourselves in his Chair of Government, and that your aym was not to throw down Tyranny, but the Tyrant.[176]

In recommending the House of Commons to take such measures as would be necessary to rectify this situation Winstanley is typically forthright:

> The maine thing that you should look upon is the Land, which calls upon her children to be free from entanglement of the Norman Task-masters, for one third part lies waste and barren, and her children starve for want, in regard the Lords of Manors will not suffer the poor to manure it.[177]

Winstanley attempts to convert the House to the view that it is party to a contract to restore the conditions that had existed prior to the Conquest and before the Fall. He warns that failure to fulfil this undertaking will not only confirm the suspicion that Parliament continues to subscribe to Normanism, but would also be in defiance of the will of 'Almighty God'.[178] Further, Winstanley predicts that such a crisis of confidence might eventually prompt the poor to turn in retaliation against the House of Commons.[179]

An Appeal to the House of Commons is also the pamphlet in which Winstanley discussed in greater depth the rousing suggestion that that land might be partitioned; the enclosures remaining with landowners, and the commons being relinquished to the people. So he includes the following proposition:

> Let the Gentry have their inclosures free from all Norman enslaving intanglements whatsoever, and let the common people have their Commons and waste lands set free to them, from all Norman enslaving Lords of Manors . . .[180]

This delineation assumes considerable significance in view of Winstanley's earlier proposition of the eradication of hired labour.[181] As was noted, Winstanley presumed that the success of this objective would depend upon the willingness of the people to withold their labour from the landowners, and instead to cultivate communally the wastes and commons. It seems unlikely that so tenacious a thinker as Winstanley could have forgotten these ideas during the six months that had elapsed between their exposition in *The New Law of Righteousnes* and the publication of *An Appeal to the House of Commons*. However, it seems considerably more likely that in the changed situation pertaining in the summer of 1649 Winstanley considered it inexpedient to discuss overtly his proposals for the elimination of hired labour.

The contention advanced here is that during the Digger period the withdrawal of hired labour was a latent assumption attendant upon Winstanley's advocacy of the partition of the land. The full significance of this eventuality is evident in statements of the following kind:

> we, amongst others of the common people, that have been ever friends to the Parliament, as we are assured our enemies wil witness to it, have plowed and dig'd upon Georges-Hill in Surrey, to sow corn for succour of man, offering no offence to any, but do carry our selves in love and peace towards all, having no intent to meddle with any mans inclosures, or propriety, til it be freely given to us by themselves . . .[182]

This extract begs the question of why Winstanley expected the landlords to relinquish their property. There seem to be two possible answers. First, Winstanley might have presumed that the lords of the manor would eventually undergo such moral regeneration that they would adopt a charitable disposition towards the commoners. However, we have already seen that as a result of his exasperation in passively awaiting the reform of human nature Winstanley turned to a policy of activism. Digging, he believed, would instil spiritual righteousness; but the landowners were not digging. However, the call to action is the clue to the second and more plausible explanation of Winstanley's position. Digging the commons was in accordance with his theory of the withdrawal and subversion of hired labour. As Winstanley confidently expected digging to spread he must also have anticipated the possibility that the landlords would be deprived of adequate sources of labour. So presumably, their estates would no longer be economically viable, and they would therefore be constrained to throw in their lot with the common people.

7

The tone and construction of *A Watch-Word to the City of London and the Armie* (26 August 1649), indicates that events were beginning to catch up with the Diggers. Thus, in confiding that 'I feel my self like a man in a storm, standing under shelter upon a hill in peace, waiting till the storm be over to see the end of it',[183] Winstanley confesses to a certain unease and to the dissolution of his fleeting tranquility. Such deepening anxiety was sufficient motivation for Winstanley to attempt once more to warn the nation of the perils attending the perpetuation of 'Norman' institutions. Parts of this pamphlet appear hastily constructed, the latter section in particular being interspersed with details of the immediate situation. In this case, Winstanley expresses concern over the welfare of some cows he has been herding, and which have been confiscated in lieu of the payment of a fine. The autobiographical content of the piece is therefore substantial. Once more, Winstanley asserts that the imperative to restore the 'common treasury' has been revealed to him experimentally.[184]

A Watch-Word deals particularly with a charge of trespass brought against Winstanley, and with the details of the molestation of the Diggers by the local population. Consequently, two themes emerge: first, the tract constitutes Winstanley's most thoroughgoing analysis of 'Norman' legal institutions; and second, because Winstanley is by this time clearly on the defensive he once again offers a justification for digging.

Effectively, the legal reforms eventually advanced in *The Law of Freedom* constitute a direct response to complaints such as those lodged by Winstanley during the Digger period. For example, in *A Watch-Word* Winstanley argues that the charge of trespass brought against him for cultivating the commons could be upheld only as a consequence of sustaining 'kingly' law.[185] In referring, as the point of contrast, to the 'law of righteousness' Winstanley reiterates the right to cultivate the 'common treasury'. Hence his apprehension lest England should succumb to an even stronger form of Norman power.[186] Typically, Winstanley asserts that the law ought to be founded upon equity and reason,[187] and expresses his blatant distrust of lawyers (who are dismissed as agents of Normanism), by arguing for the right of each individual to plead his own case.[188] In the same vein, Winstanley protests that under the existing system juries are packed with freeholders (the descendants of William the Conqueror's soldiers) who also retain an interest in upholding the Norman law.[189]

The second major theme of *A Watch-Word*, the vindication of digging, possesses two aspects. First, Winstanley reaffirms his notion that the earth is to be restored as a 'common treasury' and utilizes his conceptions of the Fall, of mankind as Adam, of the power of darkness and of the Norman Yoke to support this claim. He contends that 'kingly power' is not necessarily peculiar to any one individual, and that tyranny could outlive the monarch because

> the Prerogative Lawes is Belzebub, for they are the strength of covetousnesse and bondage in the creation, lifting up one, and casting down another: the Atturneys, and Priests, and Lawyers, and Bayliffs are servants to Belzebub, and are Devils, their Prisons, Whips, and Gallows are the torments of this Hell, or government of darknesse . . .[190]

Winstanley's second justification for digging rests upon his representation of the 'contract' to which he attributed victory in the Civil War. He uses these assumptions to argue that the people should henceforth be permitted to cultivate the commons: 'all sorts, poor as well as rich, Tenant as well as Landlord, have paid Taxes, Free-quarter, Excise, or adventured their lives, to cast out that Kingly Office'.[191] Thus 'those from whom money and blood was received, ought to obtain freedom in the Land to themselves and Posterity, by the Law of contract between Parliament and people'.[192] Again, this supposition prompts Winstanley to advocate a division of the spoils:

> as the Free-holders claime a quietnesse and freedom in their inclosures, as it is fit they should have, so we that are younger brothers, or the poore oppressed, we claime our freedome in the Commons, that so elder and younger brother may live quietly in peace . . .[193]

Here Winstanley discreetly omits any explicit reference to his earlier evaluation of the likely consequences of the withdrawal of hired labour.

8

In December 1649 Winstanley renewed his correspondence with Fairfax,[194] but now wrote with less optimism and assurance than he had done previously. The hostility of the local populace was obviously having its intended effect upon the Diggers.[195] Hence, following the destruction of a number of the Diggers' houses by a party of soldiers, we find Winstanley pleading with Fairfax to intervene on behalf of the colonists. True to form Winstanley is particularly anxious to impress upon Fairfax the case that the 'covenant' undertaken as a matter of 'ioynt consent' to eject Charles I was underwritten 'by the law of contract'[196] and thereby entitled the people to their liberty to cultivate the commons. Winstanley confirms that the Diggers have fallen on hard times and supplements his usual ideological apologies for digging with claims based upon the more mundane motive of sheer necessity.[197] Thus he maintains that the Diggers are cultivating the commons because of the need to provide for their subsistence. Similarly, he suggests to Fairfax that only large-scale cultivation of the wastes and commons could reduce the endemic poverty evident throughout the land. Hence the claim that, rather than accepting charity, the poor would prefer to labour and that fortunately there could be found 'wast land enough and to spare to supply all our wants.'[198]

9

Winstanley's lengthiest apology for the Diggers' cause is *A New-yeers Gift for the Parliament and Armie* (1 January 1650), in which the claim is pursued that whereas the authorities to whom the pamphlet is addressed had formerly agreed to oust 'kingly power' they were not reluctant to perform this duty, a shortcoming attributable to the moral defects of their constituent members.[199] Hence Winstanley's contention that the failure of Parliament and the army to consent to digging[200] is tantamount to their sanction for kingly power for the 'prerogative' rather than of the 'righteous' form.[201]

Once again, Winstanley bases his arguments upon propositions central to his conception of the Fall and of the Norman Yoke.[202] Indeed, the pamphlet contains Winstanley's most coherent analysis of the structure of Norman power. Thus the respective functions of the lords of the manor, the clergy, and lawyers are scrutinized in considerable detail. Similarly, institutions such as 'buying and selling', freeholding and copyholding are accounted for with reference to the Norman Conquest.[203]

From this reconstruction Winstanley proceeds to advance his analysis of the significance of the Civil War.[204] Again, he insists that the removal of the king had been undertaken as a mutual enterprise by Parliament, the army and the people.[205] So, on behalf of the common people Winstanley reminds the other parties to the 'contract' that 'Kingly power is like a great spread tree, if you lop the head or top-bow, and let the other Branches and root stand, it will grow again and recover fresher strength'.[206] In effect, although Charles I had been executed, the institutions that had sustained his prerogative still thrived.

Winstanley clearly felt that his case could be reinforced by the citation of two recent pieces of legislation; the first providing for the abolition of the monarchy (17 March 1649) and the second for the establishment of the Commonwealth (19 May 1649).[207] According to Winstanley, the same Parliament that had passed these laws obviously possessed the power to proceed further, and was therefore obliged to eradicate the institutional remnants of the Norman Yoke. So Winstanley even resorts to a well-worn argument by maintaining that the failure of Parliament to act accordingly constituted a transgression of the commandments against killing and stealing pronounced in the Decalogue.[208] In essence, Winstanley contends that although Parliament is endowed with requisite power, it manifestly lacks the will to transform society.

That he was prepared to appeal to such an essentially conservative body is indicative of two developing tendencies in Winstanley's thought: the first is a growing despair that digging might not achieve the success in terms of transforming men and society once predicted of it; and the second is Winstanley's developing acceptance that, properly reformed, the institutions of civil society could be instrumental in achieving these ends.

In *A New-yeers Gift* Winstanley again repeats the suggestion that in the *post-bellum* settlement land ought to be partitioned. He declares: 'we want nothing but possession of the spoyl, which is free use of the Land for our livelihood'.[209] However, on this occasion, by bringing to bear his understanding of the Civil War, Winstanley produces a more integrated argument to the effect that

> from hence we the common people, or younger brothers, plead our propriety in the Common land, as truly our own by vertue of this victory over the King; as our elder brothers can plead proprietie in their Inclosures; and that for three reasons in Englands law.[210]

The substantiating reasons in question are: the 'contract' between Parliament and the people; the 'right' of conquest over the king; and recent legislation abolishing the monarchy and establishing the Commonwealth. With regard to his conception of the social contract, Winstanley is moved to go so far as to contend not only that the people have effectively *purchased* their freedom to cultivate the commons, but also that the Parliamentary and army leadership had become 'Servants to the commons of England'.[211] Once more, Winstanley evades the issue of exactly how beleaguered landowners were to cultivate their portion without the availability of hired labour.[212]

The inference that Winstanley was beginning to doubt the universal restorative qualities of an anarchical form of communal cultivation is supported by his recourse to a proposition that, in terms of his overall appreciation of such matters, seems quite extraordinary. This argument relates to Winstanley's proposals for the partition of land, which he had apparently begun to regard as a form of equitable apportionment. In defence of digging, Winstanley advances the somewhat defensive contention that

> no man yet hath bestowed any labour upon the Commons that lies waste; therefore the Diggers doth take no mans proper goods from them in so doing, but those that by force spoyls their labours, takes their proper goods from them, which is the fruit of their own labours.[213]

By suggesting that land remains in the pristine condition or state of nature until it is cultivated and becomes the property of the labourer, Winstanley appears to advance an almost Lockean justification of appropriation. An obvious disparity between Winstanley here and Locke's position in Book V of the *Second Treatise* is that Winstanley speaks always in terms of a straightforward correlation of land, labour and proprietorial rights. Nowhere is there to be found any suggestion of countenancing the ownership of turfs cut by servants.[214] Winstanley remains consistently antithetical to hired labour. Even so, he does propose that the Diggers are in effect *first occupants*. It is paradoxical, therefore, that Winstanley enters the realms of a more conventional trend within political theory in order to discover an argument capable of vindicating the establishment of *communal cultivation*. Presumably, and this is very important, Winstanley's proposition was intended to convince the authorities that they should regard the Diggers' labours as an act of appropriation establishing the land in question as the property of *the colony*. Clearly, Winstanley could not have condoned the practice of such a principle of appropriation by *individuals* within the Digger community. All this suggests that as the hostility to their activities gathered momentum Winstanley was brought to an awareness that digging had not proliferated. As this perception of isolation grew, Winstanley was constrained to think beyond the immediate situation.

From the forgoing analysis of the major themes of *A New-yeers Gift* it may appear that Winstanley had all but abandoned his spiritual concerns. This is far from being the case.[215] For example, he defiantly asserts that by their actions the Diggers fulfilled biblical prophecy:

> I tell you, and you Preachers, that Scriptures which saith, The poor shall inherit the earth, is really and materially to be fullfilled, for the Earth is to be restored from the bondage of sword proprietie, and it is to become a common Treasurie in reallitie to whole mankind, for this is the work of the true Saviour to doe, who is the true and faithfull Leveller . . .[216]

Similarly, in evaluating landlordism as an aspect of the Norman institutional fabric, Winstanley concludes that 'if any sort of people hold the earth to themselves by the dark Kingly power, and shut out others from that freedom, they deny God, Christ, and Scriptures'.[217] With these two statements Winstanley confirms, in the former directly and in the latter by implication, that even as he was entering a period of intellectual uncertainty, his social theory and his theology remained closely aligned. Still, Winstanley sustained a belief in universal salvation and remained insistent that, as the elect nation, England must disover the means of effecting reform—by destroying private property.[218]

During the course of *A New-yeers Gift* a number of issues are raised that anticipate certain subsequent concerns. Winstanley denies, for instance, that the common people wish to repudiate *all* forms of government, and instead he petitions for *righteous* government.[219] It seems, therefore, that Winstanley was in the process of moving away from his earlier conviction that men might ultimately live without the restraining influence of the state. Anarchy, for Winstanley, was now assuming more insidious dimensions, a reappraisal that may well have been informed by his abhorrence of and desire to repudiate any suggestion that the Diggers were influenced by Ranterism.[220] The popular association of the Diggers with the Ranters inspired an anxiety that would become manifest in Winstanley's subsequent writings. Hence his denial that the Diggers stole goods (as Ranters reputedly did). Similarly, he denies suggestions that the Diggers' economic ethic extended to the communal use of women. Instead, Winstanley responded to 'such a unrationall excesse of female communitie',[221] by affirming his belief in monogamy. Ultimately, Winstanley rebuts accusations to the effect that by their beliefs and actions the Diggers questioned the very existence of God. Indeed, Winstanley took to the offensive by describing the adversarious Parson Platt, who seems to have been the source of these slanders, as a fallen man—'for covetousness, pride, and envie hath blinded his eyes'.[222] This impression would shortly be confirmed to Winstanley, as Platt set about organizing the ostracism of the Diggers.

10

The four months following the publication of *A New-yeers Gift* were the most frenetic of Winstanley's troubled career. During this period the Digger colony moved from St George's Hill to nearby Cobham,[223] but this did not stave off its collapse. Such trauma is reflected in the diverse nature of the writings published by Winstanley at this time. This consideration might count against the attempt to analyse Winstanley's intellectual development in terms of its periodization. However, suggestions of apparent discontinuity may be dispelled once it is appreciated that Winstanley had begun to anticipate the direction his thought would take some time prior to the actual dissolution of the community. So, during the early months of 1650, Winstanley can be seen forlornly defending the Diggers while at the same time reconsidering his overall strategy and intellectual position. For this reason the publications pertaining to digging[224] produced by Winstanley during these few months will be analysed in this section while the remainder[225] will be held over to the next section.

The brief pamphlet *A Vindication of Those, Whose Endeavors is Only to Make the Earth a Common Treasury, Called Diggers* (4 March 1650) is devoted entirely to the task of refuting accusations that to dig was tantamount to becoming a Ranter. So, by portraying the Diggers as regenerate and the Ranters as fallen, Winstanley maintains the antithetical nature of the Digger ethic and Ranter lifestyle. Winstanley came to regard the profound irritant of Ranterism as the epitome of that human sinfulness which stood against the restoration of righteousness.[226] Hence his condemnation of the Ranters as covetous, unwholesome, idle and deceitful. In summarizing this degenerate nature Winstanley states:

> It is a Kingdome that lies in objects; As in the outward enjoyment of meat, drinke, pleasures, and women; so that the man within can have no quiet rest, unlesse he enjoy those outward objects in excesse; all which are vanishable. Therefore it is the Devills Kingdome of darknesse, and not the Kingdome of heaven or true peace within.[227]

Clearly, the Digger ethic sought to rectify these mistaken values.

11

The pamphlets published by Winstanley in the early months of 1650 betray a steady worsening of Digger fortunes. As a result of their intense economic plight and of local hostility the Diggers had been forced to decamp from St George's Hill to Cobham Heath. As the covert enmity of the local tenantry increased so, too, did Winstanley's disenchantment at the failure of digging to spread, a trait that is particularly evident in *An Appeale to All Englishmen* (26 March 1650). In this tract, Winstanley somewhat plaintively sees failure in terms of the reluctance, attributable to fear and intimidation, of the poor to become Diggers.

Once more, Winstanley holds that victory in the Civil War should effectively have overthrown Normanism. On this occasion, however, Winstanley is prompted to incite the common people to act accordingly—by cultivating the wastes and commons. So he claims that the time is ripe for the law of righteousness to be actively inaugurated, that is, rather than allowing 'slavish fear, possesse the hearts of the poor, to stand in awe of the Norman Yoke any longer, seeing it is broke'.[228] In order to entice the commoners to act, and to stimulate morale, Winstanley points out that both scripture and recent legislation effectively authorize the communal cultivation of the commons.[229] So the immediate situation is assessed in such a manner that the common people are presented with the admonition that 'nothing is wanting on your part, but courage and faithfulness, to put those Lawes in execution, and to take possession of your own Land, Which the Norman Power took from you'.[230] Whereas previously Winstanley had sought to extend communal cultivation by means of the exemplar provided by the Digger colony, now, in a last desperate effort, he was apparently inciting his countrymen to take direct action. Such a recourse assumes added significance, of course, once it is recalled that Winstanley had formerly argued that the withdrawal of hired labour would ultimately eradicate the private ownership of land and thereby restore the common treasury.

It is evident that Winstanley was aware that by arguing in this manner, he was challenging a series of assumptions instilled in the popular mentality by the clergy. He is therefore to be seen questioning the belief that the poor ought to refrain from disputing the existing distribution of ownership for fear that this might impair their prospects of salvation. Hence, in this context, Winstanley is impelled to elaborate upon his appreciation of the point and purpose of tithes. Similarly, he goads the ministry by deploring its failure to perform manual labour and on behalf of the people asks 'why may we not have our heaven here (that is, a comfortable livelihood in the Earth) And heaven hereafter too, as well as you, God is no respector of Persons?'[231] Even so, despite such impudence, *An Appeale to All Englishmen* signals the dissipation of Winstanley's confidence in the apprehension that digging could effect the spiritual restoration of Man.

In a last desperate attempt to preserve the colony at Cobham emissaries were despatched through the counties around London to attempt to raise money. Would-be subscribers were encouraged to make donations in order that the Diggers might continue in their vital work of restoring freedom to the land. The urgency of the situation is reflected in Winstanley's appeal for benefactors to alleviate the plight of the Diggers before it became too late to do so, because 'in regard of poverty their work is like to flagge and droppe'.[232]

12

An Humble Request to the Ministers of Both Universities and to All Lawyers in Every Inns-a-court (9 April 1650) is the last of Winstanley's 'Digger pamphlets'. The piece came into being as a consequence of the confrontation between Winstanley and his persecutor, Parson Platt. It appears that on this occasion Platt challenged Winstanley to provide scriptural authorization for digging, and had promised that if Winstanley could successfuly accomplish this task he would abstain from further harassment. Never one to resist such a challenge Winstanley's published response not only provides an insight into the depth of his very substantial knowledge of the Bible, but also confirms how readily he conceived of digging in terms of its wider spiritual connotations.

An Humble Request contains a concise exposition of Winstanley's view of the Creation, the Fall and the prospect of a restoration. The tract also confirms the manner in which Winstanley drew upon a theory of the Norman Yoke to illuminate his conception of the fallen condition, as in the following:

> The whole Earth: By the Law of Creation, is the Common treasury of free Livelyhood, to whole Mankind. And those Lords of Manors, and others, that deny any part of mankind, this creation-freedome in the earth, are sinners in the highest degree, and are the upholders of the fall & curse of Mankinde.[233]

Even towards the end of the period in which Winstanley attempted to implement his communist ideal the essential consistency of his theological convictions remained undiminished. Similarly, the piece amply illustrates another feature of the Digger period—Winstanley's allegorical use of millenarian imagery. Take, for example, his contention that 'Mankind, in their Actings each to other, is become a Beast: And this Beastly Power was to reigne for a time, times, and dividing of times. Rev 12.14 Dan 7.25'.[234]

It is apparent from *An Humble Request* that Winstanley had resigned himself to the failure and the inevitable dissolution of the Digger colony. Although he continues here to maintain that recent legislation to oust the King and to establish the Commonwealth must simultaneously have restored the ancient and fundamental laws of the land,[235] in this mood of disillusioned resignation he is at last prepared to admit openly that Parliament and the army, along with the clergy, landowners and lawyers, were quite fundamentally antagonistic to the Diggers. The pamphlet thus culminates with a detailed account of the destruction of the Digger commune at Cobham; a catastrophe attributed by Winstanley to a conspiracy of the local tenantry instigated by Parson Platt. Winstanley's last words on the matter are indicative of the purpose of digging. *An Humble Request* constitutes an epitaph for 'This work of digging, being freedom, or the appearance of Christ in the earth'.[236]

13

During the Digger period Winstanley's association of communism with the moral regeneration of Man was not so precisely formulated as it was to become in the subsequent portrayal of the ideal commonwealth, *The Law of Freedom*. Partly because he was often on the defensive and partly because digging had clearly eased his own spiritual misgivings, Winstanley insisted that the Diggers were themselves restored: 'we rejoyce in the uprightness of our hearts'.[237] That, at the outset, Winstanley expected digging to be extended as individuals voluntarily joined in the activity, suggests that he supposed the restoration of human nature to be prescient of the establishment of a society established upon communism. However, during this period, Winstanley also advanced the related but slightly contradictory notion that participation in the communal tillage of the land was itself conducive to the spiritual restoration of the individual. Ambiguity as to the precise causal nexus relating spiritual recovery to communalism was one of the problems Winstanley believed himself to have overcome by the time he published his scheme for a utopia. As his gradualist theory, that sustaining the assumption that the communal lifestyle would enhance the prospects of moral rejuvenation, assumed greater significance within Winstanley's thought, his prior emphasis upon spontaneous voluntarism not surprisingly diminished. He therefore deduced that, rather than experiencing a relatively prompt restoration of reason, individuals might be *directed* towards their redemption by extraneous influences. This departure came to fruition with the compulsory and indeed coercive aspects of life detailed in *The Law of Freedom*.

Winstanley regarded the Digger experiment as a direct confrontation with the fallen condition of Normanism. His explanation of the foundations of the existing social hierarchy was used to lend a rationale to his defiance of it. As his hopes of success began to wane he responded to the situation by claiming that 'we endeavour to dig up their Tythes, their Lawyers, Free, their Prisons, and all that Art and Trade of darknesse'.[238] At one point Winstanley had noted that 'the Norman Camp is grown very numerous and big'.[239] It appeared that opposition to the Diggers had come to include almost every element in contemporary society.[240] The abject failure of the practical attempt to instigate a communal lifestyle did not, however, deflect Winstanley from the conviction that the spiritual and moral welfare of men could be attained only in such a context.

The interim phase of re-evaluation

1

The third of the periods into which Winstanley's writings are divisible is the interim in which he accepted the collapse of the Digger experiment as inevitable both as an economically viable proposition and as a catalyst for the spiritual restoration of Man from the fallen condition. This period preceded by almost two years the publication of Winstanley's last work, the utopia *The Law of Freedom*. Although the phase coincided with the last stages of Winstanley's vindication of the Diggers, he nevertheless appears to have maintained a reasonably clear delineation between, on the one hand, his remaining loyalties to the Digger cause and, on the other hand, his attempts to redetermine his position in light of the likely disintegration of the Digger commune.

The depth and vehemence of contention as to the dating, meaning and significance of the most substantial work published by Winstanley at this time, *Fire in the Bush*, cannot be reproduced here. To 'left-wing' commentators, who argue for the essential secularization of Winstanley's thought, the tract often proves embarrassing. The general inclination of critics so disposed has been to question the dating at least of the *original drafting* of the piece. The view offered is that Winstanley simply resurrected papers consistent with his earlier millenarian sympathies for publication at this, a later date. However, commentators opposed to the theory that Winstanley's thought underwent a process of secularization are often inclined to argue for the consistent millenarianism of Winstanley's stance. Given that *Fire in the Bush* is liberally interspersed with millenarian allusions the pamphlet has been heralded by adherents to this school of thought as testimony to the validity of their position.

There is little point in attempting to play down the analytical difficulties posed by *Fire in the Bush*. Even so, the position is far from hopeless. The interpretation of the piece advanced by Keith Thomas has much to recommend it. Thomas has not only established the date of publication of *Fire in the Bush* as 19 March 1650, but has also accurately assessed its significance.[241] In so doing Thomas maintains that arguments developed in *Fire in the Bush* are consistent with concerns recently voiced by Winstanley in the Digger pamphlets. Hence, for example, Winstanley's by now deferential attitude towards political authority and his commitment to the association of the idea of communal cultivation with that of universal love, are similarly communicated in *Fire in the Bush*. We might add that lesser matters, such as Winstanley's indignant repudiation of Ranterism, also find expression in this work. It seems reasonable therefore to believe that, faced with the probable collapse of the Digger community, it was quite natural for Winstanley's thoughts to return to a more pervasive analysis of the human condition, and to the theological bases of these ideas.

Fire in the Bush affords further confirmation of Winstanley's preoccupation with the condition produced by the Fall, and with the means of amending this predicament. Although Winstanley had initially considered that the millenium (or at least his peculiar conception of that event) would initiate such a restoration, he soon deduced that the actual establishment of a communal lifestyle might prove more propitious. Hence the foundation of the Digger movement. Because *Fire in the Bush* was written while digging was still in progress it seems unlikely that Winstanley could have abandoned the conception of the cosmic drama, which had provided the rationale for communal cultivation, in favour of an abrupt return to an essentially millenarian disposition. It is more probable that Winstanley was musing over and speculating upon the continuing human predicament. Hence *Fire in the Bush* is characterized by a restatement of his appreciation of human nature and of the social institutions preferred by degenerate men, along with a tenative and ultimately unavailing reappraisal of the mode of restoration and of reform. In these circumstances, Winstanley often expresses his analysis of the Fall and restoration in millenarian terms. Yet it is important to recall that the extent to which Winstanley is now to be seen relating these notions to his burgeoning social theory is markedly absent in his earlier and more pronounced millenarian pieces. Clearly, however plausible it may be, this conclusion is at best conjectural. *Fire in the Bush* is undoubtedly one of Winstanley's most obscure and esoteric works.[242] The tract is most appropriately viewed as an attempt by its author to reformulate his thoughts and to reassess his position.

2

Undeniably, *Fire in the Bush* contains many instances of Winstanley's adapation of millenarian terminology to illustrate his theories of the Fall and restoration. For example, the prediction that the restoration is to come in 'the fulness of the Beasts time'.[243] Similarly, the use of the millenarian notion of 'the Beast' as an allegorical device to emphasize the evil nature of Norman social institutions. Consequently, in relating the restoration to the subversion of the Norman Yoke, Winstanley stipulates that 'when the time comes for Christ to reigne, this Beast shall deliver up his Crowne, Scepter, Authority, and government unto Christ, and lay all downe at his feat. Rev 4.9 &c.'[244] Possibly the most graphic example of Winstanley's resort to millenarian imagery occurs in connection with his assertion that digging might stimulate the restoration: 'the Seed of life that lies under the clods of Earth, which in his time is now rising up to bruise the Serpents head, and to cast that imaginary murderer out of the Creation.'[245] In the same sense that Winstanley used the Bible as a textbook of human psychology, he evidently came to employ its millenarian elements as a typology of social interaction.

In contrast to the apparently hasty construction of certain of the Digger pamphlets, *Fire in the Bush* is more orderly, although only seven of the projected thirteen chapters were completed. The obvious method of analysing the tract is to follow Winstanley's chapter headings.

The first chapter, 'What the Garden of Eden is'.[246] deals with the notion that paradise and the free enjoyment of the commons are synonymous. By developing this proposition Winstanley elucidates his interpretation of the

Fall, and in particular (in the individuated form) the role of human imagination in cultivating the desire to appropriate objects from the creation. As a corollary, Winstanley assumes that the 'restoration' entails the renunciation of private property. Winstanley proceeds to affirm another of his enduring themes—that the kingdom of heaven exists within each individual, a consideration promising a form of universal salvation. Thus he reiterates his view that the spirit will spread throughout the Creation.[247]

In the second chapter, 'What the Tree of Knowledge of Good and evill is',[248] Winstanley examines the nature of the curse and of the fallen condition. In this context he draws upon his ideas concerning the internalized fall and restoration of mankind.[249] With a hint of disillusion, Winstanley comments that his own times are characterized by a superfluity of preaching and a commensurate deficiency in the experimental knowledge of Christ, all of which finds expression in the prevalence of rampant materialism.[250] On an autobiographical note, Winstanley speaks of the ostracism he has incurred as a consequence of attempting to live righteously:

> While I had no care of doing rightly, I could live. I had friends, I had peace; But since I began to do as I would be done by: friends now stands a farre off; every body hates me, and I am open to all misery; does righteousnesse bring thee to this, oh miserable wretch?[251]

The third chapter, 'What the Tree of Life is',[252] provides an admirable demonstration of Winstanley's amalgamated interpretation of the cosmic drama and of the Norman Yoke. Winstanley predicts that the resurrection of the spirit of Christ will restore Man's spiritual tranquility, and will coincide with the collapse of the type of government based upon imaginary power: 'The kingly Power, he tooke the sword to kill and conquer; and to lift up selfe, to be the Ruler; for all Lawes of the Nations are Lawes made by the will of this murderer, kingly power.'[253] This prompts Winstanley to describe the clergy, 'kingly power', the judiciary and commercial transactions as the four beasts of the Book of Daniel. On a more optimistic note than that sounded in the previous chapter, Winstanley affirms that the spirit of Christ will ultimately enlighten all men—because He is the True Leveller.

The fourth chapter, 'What the Serpent is',[254] provides an opportunity for Winstanley to vent his spleen. He fervently questions the assumption that all forms of government are ordained by God.[255] Thus he contends that the existing form of government is the serpent and is therefore devoid of true magistracy. Instead, he asserts that 'if you would finde true Majestie indeed, goe among the poore despised ones of the Earth'.[256] Clearly, this statement may imply a good deal about the quality of life within the Digger community, but it is also prescient of the social ideals embodied in *The Law of Freedom* and of the language employed therein.

The fifth chapter 'What the living Soule (Man) is, called very good',[257] again verifies the understanding of Winstanley's thought here being outlined. For instance, Winstanley reveals the radical and often allegorical nature of his religious concepts by referring to death, a condition commonly associated by contemporaries with the curse, as a 'life' devoid of righteousness.[258] Similarly, he cites Judas as the paradigm instance of a devil 'defiled and Falne by temptation'.[259] Perhaps more importantly, and this marks a significant departure, Winstanley provides a lucid account of the internalization of the cosmis battle in terms which suggest that he was beginning to conceive of the human predicament in the light of the individual life cycle:

> the Innocencie, or plaine heartedness in man, was not an estate 6000 years ago onely; But every branche of mankinde passes through it, & first is defiled by imaginary covetousnesse, and thereby is made a Devill; and then he is delivered from that darknesse, by Christ the restorer, and by him made one with the Father and the Son.[260]

In one of his most piquant passages Winstanley implies that, irrespective of the calamities that have befallen the Diggers, communal cultivation must surely be contributory to the endeavour to attain moral regeneration. He asserts that 'the life of the Spirit in sound reason lives not yet in the Sences; for pure Reason lives like a corne or wheate, under the clods of Earth, or Beast, and is not yet risen up to rule as King'.[261]

In the sixth and penultimate chapter of *Fire in the Bush*, 'What the Curse is, that doth defile the Man',[262] Winstanley predictably concludes that the curse is the bondage that has been the lot of men during the ascendancy of the power of darkness. More specifically, men have acquired a sentient appetite for material possessions; 'the pleasure of sinne enters'.[263] Obviously, Winstanley regarded the satisfaction dervied by men from holding private property as a corrupted pleasure.

The final chapter, 'What the blessing is that restores him againe',[264] suggests that, despite the disappointments of the Digger episode, Winstanley retained an essential assurance that a restoration would *eventually* occur. However, and this is extremely significant, *Fire in the Bush* is characterized by Winstanley's failure to propose, as a means of resolving the question of how this restoration was to come about, an alternative to the Digger experiment. In this light, a consideration deserving of close attention is Winstanley's conviction that early childhood constitutes a time of innocence: 'Looke upon a childe that is new borne, or till he growes up to some few yeares, he is innocent, harmlesse, humble, patient, gentle, easie to be entreated, not envious.'[265] Thus, according to Winstanley, it is only with developing maturity that, impelled by imagination, men fall—most obviously by appropriating property from the objects of the Creation, and by succumbing to the temptations proferred by 'the beauty of the female sex'.[266] In an intellectual atmosphere which still did much to preserve the belief in original and innate sin this treatment of the origins of immorality clearly manifests radical implications. Even so, it contributed nothing to the resolution of Winstanley's fundamental problem, namely that of discovering a method by which spiritual restoration and its associated social unity might be instigated. Significantly, once Winstanley came to adopt a slightly more disparaging view of human nature, his difficulties in this respect diminished. Eventually, in *The Law of Freedom*, he portrayed youth as anything but an age of innocence. Hence he came to prescribe education, apprenticeship, strict paternal supervision, and even legal penalties as curbs upon the evil inclinations of adolescence. All this would require a substantial degree of institutional organizations. So Winstanley ultimately determined upon the advocacy of forms of institutionalism which he regarded as capable of facilitating the moral regeneration of the individual. But as we have suggested, he did so in good part as the result of moving towards a more pessimistic assessment of human nature. For the moment at least, in *Fire in the Bush*, although Winstanley was beginning to turn his attention to the possibility of conceiving of moral and spiritual recovery in terms of the life cycle of the individual, he had as yet failed to flesh out these ideas to the extent that they could usefully inform a consistent social theory.

During the course of the final chapter of *Fire in the Bush* Winstanley makes an interesting reference to Mosaic Law,[267] and in the process comments upon the conventional association of private property with Man's fallen nature. Winstanley argues that although the Decalogue constitutes a reasonably equitable code, one capable of regulating the distribution of private property quite effectively, it is merely an *interim* arrangement capable only of preserving the peace between *fallen* men. What particularly concerns Winstanley is Moses' apparent admission to the effect that, 'though this be a Law, settling peace for present; yet I am not he that shall restore you to your first singleness and Innocencie'.[268] Winstanley believed that the question of precisely how Christ would effect this restoration still remained to be answered. Consequently, he confronts here an inherent dilemma of the traditional conception of private property—as both the curse and as a necessary constraint upon the actions of fallen men. In the end Winstanley was to invert this argument by contending that the curse might be physically removed and that consequently the need to curb men's actions would be commensurately reduced. Thus on both counts (as an instance of the curse and as a palliative), the redundancy of private property could be considered. In *Fire in the Bush*, however, Winstanley leaves this central problem unresolved. He can only state it:

> So then kill Covetousnesse, or that imaginary darknesse within; And the Devill is kill'd when the Tempter comes, he shall finde nothing in you; he that is free within, is moved to excesse, or unrationall action, by no outward object; but he that is not free within, is moved by every object.[269]

3

Both the Digger pamphlets and *Fire in the Bush* reveal Winstanley's underlying willingness to defer when necessary to institutions of authority, provided, of course, that these were in his view properly constituted. He is to be found affording such respect to the House of Commons, the authorities of the City of London and the army. This disposition extends to personalities; both Fairfax and Cromwell were at various times the objects of Winstanley's entreaties. Significantly, as G.E. Aylmer has shown,[270] the decline of the Digger movement coincided with a very clear assertion by Winstanley of the view that whatever its shortcomings in practice, the maintenance of the republican regime was absolutely prerequisite to the promotion of the cause of social reform. Impelled by the desire to summon support for the Commonwealth, Winstanley was thus prompted to participate in the so called 'Engagement controversy'.[271] This recommendation is contained in *England's Spirit Unfolded*, the publication of which is thought to coincide with that of *Fire in the Bush*. As Aylmer helpfully notes,[272] Winstanley attributed the prevalent lethargic attitude towards social reform not to the inadequacy of state institutions as such, but to the continuing corruption of human nature: 'that enslaving covetous Kingly power, is corrupt bloud, that runs in every man, and womans vaines, more or lesse, till reason the spirit of burning casts him out'.[273] The tone and inference of *England's Spirit Unfolded*, to the effect that institutional reform might pre-empt the spiritual regeneration of Man, is entirely in keeping with the general direction being assumed at this time by Winstanley's social thought. All this is prescient of the final stage of Winstanley's intellectual development which witnessed the publication of the utopia, *The Law of Freedom*.

The resort to utopian communism

1

Gerrard Winstanley's social theory is consistently orientated towards the fundamental problem generated by his apprehension of the human condition—the issue of how Man might be relieved of the spiritual, moral and social burdens prescribed by the fallen condition. In rejecting more conventional doctrines which argued that the aspirations of Mankind ought to be limited to the endeavour for salvation in the hereafter, Winstanley eventually turned to an examination of those social and political conditions that might be pertinent to a restoration on earth. These considerations were influential, but received a different emphasis, in each of the successive phases through which Winstanley's thought elapsed. In retrospect, Winstanley recognized that both his millenarian expectations and his confidence in the efficacy of an essentially anarchical form of communal cultivation had been misplaced. Even so, the utility of these preliminary speculations was confirmed when, as a consequence of re-evaluating these earlier ideas, Winstanley adopted the medium of utopian communism through which to advance a detailed prescription for the moral regeneration of mankind.

2

The exact time at which Winstanley wrote *The Law of Freedom* is the subject of some disagreement. Clearly, any attempt to evaluate Winstanley's intellectual development must endeavour to establish the chronological location of this crucially important piece. Much of the confusion over the dating of *The Law of Freedom* is occasioned by a statement contained in the prefatory dedication to Cromwell, to the effect that: 'It was intended for your view above two years ago, but the disorder of the Times caused me to lay it aside, with a thought never to bring it to light.'[274] If it is recalled that at the time to which Winstanley refers his confidant in high places was Fairfax rather than Cromwell, some doubt must obviously attend the accuracy of this assertion.[275] Even so, Winstanley complicates the issue further by proceeding to maintain that in the process of composing his utopia he was 'stirred up to give it a resurrection, and to pick together as many of my scattered papers as I could find, and to compile them into this method, which I do present to you'.[276] Although Winstanley's references to his earlier writings may account for the element of continuity evident in the development of his ideas, the possibility is not precluded that, at a later date, he reformulated certain of his theories. The internal evidence of the text suggests that if any part of the work was drawn from earlier drafts the most likely section in question is the first two-thirds of the introductory address to Cromwell. Indeed, at one point, the argument seems to draw to a conclusion only to recommence on an abrupt new note.[277] Up until this apparent disjunction the discourse concentrates upon the range of constitutional issues with which Winstanley had been concerned during the Digger period.[278] Thus he discusses once again questions relating to the breaking of the Norman Yoke, the contribution of the common people to the war effort, parliamentary legislation for the establishment of the Commonwealth, and the Engagement.

3

Nearly two years after the cessation of the Digger experiment Winstanley published his last work, the utopian treatise, *The Law of Freedom*. This tract represents a final pronouncement on the themes which had dominated Winstanley's career as a social theorist. As such, *The Law of Freedom* constitutes the intellectual (although obviously not the practical) solution to the problem of the moral regeneration of Man as Winstanley saw it. By coming to terms with the probability that such a recovery might be by no means inevitable, Winstanley turned his attention to the attempt to discover a method by which each individual might *gradually* be restored to a condition of reasonableness. Such a scheme is described in *The Law of Freedom*, the work which seems to have fulfilled Winstanley's evangelical aspirations, not least because its composition appears to have contributed to the resolution of his own spiritual dilemmas:

> For my own part, my spirit hath waded deep to finde the bottom of this divining spiritual Doctrine: and the more I searched, the more I was at a loss; and I never came to quiet rest, and to know God in my spirit, till I came to the knowledge of the things in this Book.[279]

The details of this project are analysed in the next chapter.

6

Winstanley's utopian institutionalism: the ideal commonwealth

Thomas More's theology and his general worldview sustained an essentially pessimistic impression of the condition of human nature and of Man's capacity to rectify that predicament. In contrast, Winstanley remained for the most part far more optimistic as to the potential of human capacity for reform. Whereas More believed that, given Man's lowly place in the universe and the state of his relationship with God, the hope of salvation defined the limits of Man's earthly aspirations, Winstanley was convinced of the possibility that Man might be restored to a condition of spiritual righteousness and moral rectitude. His major deliberations were therefore concerned with the means by which this end might be realized. The full extent to which More and Winstanley differed in their respective evaluations of human potential will become apparent as we conclude our analysis of Winstanley's social theory.

It is difficult to be sure of the depth of Winstanley's conviction that his utopian proposals might be realized. Some insight can be gleaned from the prefatory dedication of *The Law of Freedom* to 'His Excellency Oliver Cromwell'. This dedication was not a matter of mere expediency on Winstanley's part. *The Law of Freedom* was written in the somewhat euphoric atmosphere stimulated by the execution of Charles I and the institution of the Commonwealth, a heroic outlook ultimately deflated by the dissolution of 'Barebone's Parliament' in 1653. In the meantime the aspirations of social reformers had been heightened by Cromwell's seemingly messianic victory over the old order. Although during the course of 1649 Winstanley became sceptical that 'kingly power' had been completely vanquished, he seems to have recovered his trust in the nation's political leadership. The trust placed by radicals in Cromwell was by no means illusory.[1] Oliver's role in history was accommodated neatly into millenarian expectations.[2] Although Winstanley's millenarianism had abated this was not solely because of his increased confidence in 'statesmanship'.[3] Winstanley published the *The Law of Freedom* because he claimed to be responding to contemporary calls for a 'healing government'.[4] Hence he contended that the crisis could be resolved only if Cromwell instituted radical measures rather than opting for a *via media*. Statesmen should promote institutional reform.

Winstanley's reaction to Cromwell was consistent with his previous deferential atittude to authority. Even so, he continued to observe with anxiety the maintenance of the fallen condition of 'kingly power'.[5] Because his utopian scheme was designed to accomplish the spiritual restoration of Man he posited his utopia as a solution both to longer-term problems and to the current predicament. Naturally, therefore, Winstanley was particularly keen to convince Cromwell of the viability of his proposals. To this end Winstanley included the occasional commentary (and to that end, possibly misplaced) embellishment. For instance, he exaggerated his estimate of the potential productivity of the land[6] should it be cultivated according to the institutional arrangements outlined in *The Law of Freedom*. None of this was to any avail, and we are left to consider proposals which, although they failed to secure practical application, nevertheless went a good way towards satisfying Winstanley's intellectual quest for the means of attaining Man's full potential.

The communist system of The Law of Freedom

1

Winstanley clearly believed his proposals for a communal mode of production and distribution to be prerequisite to the attainment of certain fundamental ethical objectives. He defended his ideas in the following terms: 'This Platform of Government which I offer, is the Original Righteousness and Peace in the Earth, though he hath been buried under the clods of Kingly Covetousness, Pride and Oppression a long time.'[7] The ethical underpinnings of his conception of communism is also apparent in the following definition:

> That which true Righteousness in my Judgement calls Community, is this, To have the Earth set free from all Kingly Bondage of Lords of Manors, and oppressing Landlords, which came in by Conquest; as a Thief takes a true mans purse on the high-way, being stronger than he.[8]

All this suggests that Winstanley regarded communism not merely as an economic system but also as a method of sustaining the alternative organization of society which would enhance the prospects of the moral regeneration of Man.

As had been the case with More, Winstanley felt obliged to anticipate certain stock objections to communism. Winstanley calls these 'prejudices'. He admits to concern lest 'some hearing of the Common Freedom, think there must be a Community of all the fruits of the Earth whether they work or no, therefore strive to live idle upon other men's labours'.[9] In response he asserts that the communism outlined in *The Law of Freedom* should not be construed as recipe for idleness. It is a requirement of this system that all individuals should work. Furthermore, Winstanley confronts the proposition that the eradication of private property would necessarily subjugate political authority: 'Others think there will be no Law, but that every thing will run into confusion for want of Government; but this Platform proves the contrary.'[10] Winstanley advocates social arrangements designed to effect the stringent institutional supervision of the individual. Still further, and probably as a result of his desire to refute suggestions that his envisaged communist society might degenerate into the type of moral licentiousness popularly associated with Ranterism, Winstanley denies that his scheme would lead to the communal use of women.

2

In noting that 'exploitation, not labour, is the curse',[11] Christopher Hill identifies a crucial aspect of Winstanley's attitude to work and labour. Similarly, M. James, even from the point of view of an essentially materialist interpetation, accepts that in Winstanley's opinion one important consideration attending the obligation to labour is the good that might be done to the individual's soul.[12] It is evident that Winstanley was clearly influenced by ideals such as those associated with the Protestant work ethic. It is equally apparent that despite this disposition he suspected that many of his contemporaries might fail to appreciate the urgency of his advocacy of hard work and the reasons for these exhortations.

In analysing the contemporary situation Winstanley recognized the importance of labour to the productive process. For instance, in his discussion of the means by which wealth is accumulated he concludes:

> No man can be rich, but he must be rich, either by his own labors, or by the labors of other men helping him: If a man have no help from his neighbour, he shall never gather an Estate of hundreds and thousands a year: If other men help him to work, then are those Riches his Neighbours, as well as his; for they be the fruit of other mens labors as well as his own.
>
> But all rich men live at ease, feeding and clothing themselves by the labors of other men, not by their own.[13]

From observations such as this Winstanley deduced that labour ought to be utilized to sustain the welfare of the community as opposed to the prosperity of a select minority.

3

We have seen that, in relation to contemporary norms, Thomas More's utopian communism did not involve any proposals for a reduction in the amount of labour citizens were expected to perform, and indeed may very well have stipulated an increase in the average per capita workload. Winstanley appears to have adhered to this objective even more ardently. It will be argued below that work and labour were important elements in the restorative process postulated in Winstanley's schema. For the meantime we shall concentrate upon the economic implications of the utopian work ethic.

In defending his proposals Winstanley insists that 'if any say, This will nurse Idleness; I answer, This Platform proves the contrary, for the idle persons and beggars will be made to work'.[14] Similarly, Winstanley's attitude in *The Law of Freedom* is characterized by an invective against 'that now lazie generation'[15]—youth. It appears that Winstanley had tempered his appreciation of Man's early years since considering this matter in *Fire in the Bush*.[16] Thus he stipulates that every young person reared in his ideal commonwealth would be instructed in a trade or artifice. Such an obligation to work was designed not only to profit the commonwealth but also to rectify individual morality. Significantly, Winstanley retained the standard seven-year apprenticeship of early modern England. One function of the 'overseers' in Winstanley's utopian society is to supervise the training of young people, so that none could be idle.[17]

Winstanley's concern that the institutional fabric of his utopia should facilitate the moral rectitude of the citizen obliged him to think carefully about the question of economic production, without which the entire edifice would obviously stand in danger of crumbling. Anticipating the means by which the supply of goods, especially food, might be secured was clearly fundamental to Winstanley's desire to have his scheme deemed feasible. As we shall see, Winstanley advocates retirement from physical labour at the age of forty. It was therefore essential to compensate for the loss of the labour services of mature citizens[18] by ensuring that all the young should labour. Patriarchal masters were expected to keep the entire household hard at work. 'Non-productive' elements of contemporary society, such as lawyers, were excluded from Winstanley's utopia on the grounds of their social disutility. After arraigning the clergy of seventeenth-century England for their reluctance to labour Winstanley ensures that, although in his utopia 'ministers' are not expected to labour, individuals should reach retirement age before being appointed to that office. In the context of Winstanley's concern to ensure that all eligible members of society should labour it is interesting to note that other writers among Winstanley's contemporaries were discussing what has been described as 'the possibility of turning a national burden into an economic asset',[19] by proposing schemes for the compulsory and full employment of the poor. Thus it was intended to utilize an underdeveloped resource, namely unemployed labour. This provision undoubtedly constitutes a factor in Winstanley's plans to guarantee a sound basis in production for his communist economy by ensuring an adequate supply of labour.

4

Winstanley integrates into his communist economy the household basis of production typical of the day. Although each family is expected to be as self-sufficient as possible, provision is made for families to draw from the common stock goods which they are unable to produce for themselves—

and presumably these might be considerable and varied. Winstanley envisages at least some element of a division of labour. Families are expected to work both for themselves and, by contributing surplus produce, for the community. Again Winstanley echoes certain contemporary practices by assuming that all familes would assist in gathering the harvest and in conveying it to the storehouses. However, Winstanley goes further, legislating that 'every family shall come into the field . . . at seed time to plow, dig, and plant'.[20] This element of communal cultivation is an absolutely fundamental aspect of social life in Winstanley's utopia. While obviously stimulating agricultural production, communal cultivation is also regarded by Winstanley as prerequisite to the spiritual restoration of the individual.

The division of labour in *The Law of Freedom* is determined according to the physical attributes and gender of the individual. For instance, Winstanley assumes that persons who are afflicted by some form of incapacitating physical weakness, to the extent that they are unable to perform a strenuous trade, might nevertheless be gainfully employed as keepers of storehouses.[21] Further, Winstanley believes that while all boys should be taught a trade, girls should be allocated 'easier' domestic tasks.[22] By these various methods of apportioning labour, Winstanley seems to be concerned with securing the maximum output from the available labour force. His attitude to the allocation of holidays is similarly utilitarian. By restricting holidays in his utopian commonwealth to one per week he appears to have been influenced by an assumption of Puritan sabbatarianism, namely that a day of rest would facilitate and inspire greater exertions on the days of labour.[23]

5

According to D.W. Petegorsky, Winstanley supposed that 'poverty was purely an artificial product of the property system'.[24] Given that Winstanley was undoubtedly anxious to convince his readers of the economic viability of his proposals for a true commonwealth it is important to be clear about what Winstanley might have understood the eradication of poverty to involve. If we take 'poverty' to be a concept which, used comparatively, might differentiate relative degrees of wealth, some insight into Winstanley's position is afforded. Thus 'poverty' may be applied on an aggregative–distributive dimension in assessing who gets what in terms of shares from a total amount of goods. Alternatively, the concept may be used as a reference point to distinguish individuals, groups, or indeed societies. In this sense, the idea can assume an historical aspect in comparing differing aggregates. If 'poverty' is used in the first sense, as an index according to which the relative prosperity of individuals is assessed, then any inegalitarian distributive system will ensure that at least some individuals are 'poorer' than others. Clearly, on this count, by merely eradicating the institution of private property, and thereby effecting an equitable distribution of goods according to need, Winstanley could presume to be advocating the removal of poverty. However, according to the second understanding of the term 'poverty', an egalitarian society could nevertheless be regarded as 'poor' because poverty construed in terms of absolute scarcity is constituted by the failure to achieve some minimum standard of abundance.

Petegorsky fails to distinguish these two albeit contingently related senses of poverty: that which is concerned with distribution, and that which is concerned with the eradication of absolute scarcity. Obviously, it is impossible to prove whether in operation Winstanley's proposals would have eradicated the poverty, in the absolute sense, of early modern England. It cannot simply be assumed that, by effecting the redistribution of the existing supply of goods, scarcity as affecting the position of individuals would necessarily be reduced. Even so, the emphasis placed by Winstanley upon planning for the provision of an adequate supply of labour suggests by implication that productive capacity would be to some extent increased. The important point is that whatever the economic realities of the case Winstanley's true commonwealth was *intended* to be both egalitarian and more prosperous in absolute terms than contemporary society.

It is revealing to discover the means by which Winstanley envisaged that communism might relieve scarcity. We have seen that because Winstanley is conscious that communism is liable to censure for its supposed inability to ensure a sufficient supply of goods, he fervently defends his proposed mode of production. Winstanley attempts to account for the removal of absolute scarcity in several ways. For example, his insistence on the universal obligation to labour suggests that productive output would be adequate to satisfy demand of a needs-orientated form. Even Winstanley's education programme is intended in part to stimulate production.[25]

As a complement to his concern with productive capacity Winstanley insists that true magistracy could achieve such a re-evaluation of wants that demand would be restrained. In this context he comments upon the insatiable demands of certain elements of his own society: 'Indeed, covetous, proud, and beastly-minded men desire more, either to be by them to look upon, or else to waste and spoil upon their lusts.'[26] Clearly, Winstanley is not prepared to countenance such habits of consumption in his utopian commonwealth. To a certain extent all this is reminiscent of the ideas forwarded by More in *Utopia*, although, as we shall see, Winstanley did not intend to limit consumption in the manner advocated by More. Winstanley does accord with one of More's principles, arguing that the long-term demand for labour could be checked by maintaining buildings in good repair.[27] It is significant that, in keeping with his general appreciation of the possible benefits to be accrued from experimental knowledge, Winstanley appears optimistic that the discovery of the secrets of nature might eventually yield more substantial harvests.[28]

The most important aspect of Winstanley's proposals for a communist economy turns upon his desire to resolve the problem of scarcity by providing for equitable distribution facilitated by adequate production and reorientated demand. Proposals of this sort obviously sustain considerable social and political implications. Whereas Winstanley believed that only by adopting the ideas advanced in *The Law of Freedom* could society break away from the oppression of a regime in which one sector lived idly by requisitioning the produce of the labour of another, he did not regard the alternative of communalism as a negation of political authority as such. Indeed, Winstanley saw that institutional controls would be necessary to sustain the obligation to labour as an integral aspect of his system of communism.

6

The distributive facet of Winstanley's utopia is not only intended to counter scarcity and individual privation, but also, from its basis in 'reason', is recommended as the essence of the equity sustained by communalism.[29] In contrast to the situation in fallen contemporary society Winstanley sought to ensure that each individual in the true commonwealth would be obliged, and if necessary forced, to work; but that the individual would also be guaranteed the just deserts of his labours.

The distributive system outlined in *The Law of Freedom* is based on a system of storehouses of which there are two kinds. The first, 'general storehouses'[30] such as barns, hold commodities in gross. From these each family is to collect the requisite raw materials for the pursuit of its trade. The second, 'particular storehouses', are those in which the surplus manufactured produce of such trades is subsequently to be deposited.[31] Families are entitled to collect from these latter depositories those commodities that they require of necessity but are unable to produce for themselves. Just as Winstanley conceives of the institution of 'buying and selling' as a significant stage in the Fall of Man, so the omission of these reprehensible commercial procedures from his communist utopia implies a certain restorative potential.[32] The absence of the profit motive stands to encourage greater altruism in the mutual disposition of man. As Winstanley says of his proposed system of distribution:

> Now this same free practice, will kill covetousness, pride, and oppression: for when men have a Law to buy and sell, then . . . cunning cheaters get great estates by other mens labors; and being rich thereby, become oppressing Lords over their brethren: which occasions all our trouble and wars in all Nations.[33]

Clearly, Winstanley anticipated that the eradication of commerce would stimulate the moral regeneration of Man and would encourage harmonious social interaction.

It is notable that Winstanley has virtually nothing to say on the manner in which distribution from storehouses would be regulated. What is implied is that over-consumption would be avoided through a combination of factors which include the suggestion that the moral propriety supported by the true commonwealth would confound the impulses of greed and covetousness. This belief runs alongside the understanding that the utopian economy would attain levels of sufficiency capable of negating the rationale to hoard. Winstanley seems convinced that in the right circumstances distributive justice could be needs-orientated. The multiplicity of problems attending this assumption is not confronted.

7

A point of fundamental difference between Thomas More's communist scheme and that postulated by Gerrard Winstanley is that in *Utopia* communism is intended to be absolute whereas in *The Law of Freedom* there exists scope for a sphere of private ownership. This crucial variable provides a significant insight into the roles that More and Winstanley expected their respective utopia systems to play in amending fallen human nature. As we have seen, More insisted that communism should be complete because he regarded salvation on earth as an impossibility and the need to counter Man's sinful propensities as interminable. Thus the form of communism elucidated in *Utopia*, which was to be absolute, constitutes More's primary proposal for achieving the subjugation of the evil dispositions of Man. By contrast, in Winstanley's case communism is regarded as the keystone to an institutional environment intended to effect the spiritual and moral regeneration of Man. Winstanley maintains that the one criterion of the 'saved' or restored individual is his capacity to be entrusted with an element of private property, a sphere demarcated by the possessions of the family, without displaying the attributes of fallen human nature familiarly associated with extensive forms of private ownership, namely covetousness and pride.

On the rare occasions where commentators have alluded to the sphere of private property elaborated upon within *The Law of Freedom*, they have generally failed to devote much attention to it.[34] Only W.F. Murphy has given this issue any substantial consideration. Murphy suggests that the private sphere is constituted by non-productive property.[35] Although this delineation is the point upon which Winstanley is most specific, the situation is by no means as clear-cut as it might be. One obvious problem attends what Winstanley might have supposed the status of factors in production such as materials and tools to be, while they are deposited in the possession of a family. It is not so evident as it might be whether Winstanley intended objects such as tools to be regarded as private to the family or to be communally owned and possessed by the family in trust for *use* only. The ambiguities of Winstanley's position are not clarified by his suggestion that once farm buildings are allocated to a family, they should become the property of that family. Yet, by contrast, he also stipulates that each family should 'keep sufficient working tools for common use, as Plows, Carts, and furniture, according as every Family is furnished with men to work therewith: likewise Pickaxes, Spades, Pruning-hooks, and any such like necessary instrument'.[36] The provision that households should maintain tools and instruments 'for common use' suggests that Winstanley's intention is that such objects should be held as a trust or in the form of usufruct, rather than as a private property for exclusive use. This understanding is implicit in the regulation that 'every household shall keep all Instruments and tools fit for the tillage of the Earth'.[37] Again, *trusteeship*, as opposed to exclusive rights, appears to be the regulating feature of such ownership. So it seems that each family is required to engage in the productive process (which could be communally or privately orientated) by using tools, the ownership of which was indeterminate.

Ownership is an idea which admits of many grey areas, and undoubtedly Winstanley's advocacy of an attenuated mode of communism led him to stumble upon some of the many difficulties associated with restricted forms of ownership. Thomas More, by adhering to a very strict and unrelenting appreciation of communism, one which recalled the stringencies of at least the ideal of medieval monasticism, was able to avoid the nuances which are so typical of Winstanley's position.

It is clear that in *The Law of Freedom* the sphere of private property is closely related to the household, and to patriarchal authority. With regard to these considerations Winstanley is relatively precise. Thus he attempts to dispel the potential fears of his readers in the following terms:

> Shall every man count his Neighbours house his own, and live together as one Family?
>
> No: Though the Earth and the Storehouses be common to every Family, yet every Family shall live apart as they do; and every mans house, wife, children, and furniture for ornament of his house, or anything which he hath fetched in from Storehouses, or provided for the necessary use of his Family, is all a propriety to that Family . . .[38]

> every mans house is proper to himself, and all the furniture therein, and provision which he hath fetched from the Storehouses is proper to himself; every mans wife and every womans husband proper to themselves, and so are their children at their dispose till they come of age.[39]

> every house, and all the furniture for ornament therein is a propriety to the Indwellers; and when any family hath fetched in from the Store-houses or shops either Clothes, food, or any ornament necessary for their use, it is all propriety of that family.[40]

This advocacy of ownership founded upon familial need and use is extended to include one final provision which in its way typifies Winstanley's definition of the public and private sphere of property. He maintains that although 'all Publike Dayries are Store-houses for Butter and Cheese: yet every Family may have Cows for their own use, about their own house'.[41]

In *The Law of Freedom* Winstanley asserts that one of the major functions of the state and of the legal system is to protect the sanctity of this sphere of private property. Thus in the light of his reconciliation to the fact that not all individuals could be expected to act reasonably, he inserts the following clause:

> if any other man endeavour to take away his house, furniture, food, wife, or children, saying, every thing is common, and so abusing the Law of Peace, such a one is a Transgressor, and shall suffer punishment.[42]

Thus Winstanley believed that if any one individual (invariably a patriarchal householder) laid a rightful claim to an article, it should become his own property:

One man shall not take away that Commodity which another man hath first layd hands on, for any Commodity for use belongs to him that first layd hands on it for his own use: and if another come and say, I will have it, and so offences do arise . . .[43]

What we have here is Winstanley's mature position, in which he continues to insist, in particular, upon the communal ownership of land, alongside the recognition of the social utility of a sphere of private property the extent of which is to be determined by the nature and purposes of the household. The underlying objective behind Winstanley's insistence upon the preservation of a sphere of private property is explored below.

8

In *The Law of Freedom* Winstanley advances a rather exotic description of 'the abundance of peace and plenty'[44] that he expects to prevail should his true commonwealth be instituted. He anticipates a level of economic achievement capable of ensuring 'food and rayment, ease and pleasure plentiful, both for you and your brethren; so that none shall beg or starve, or live in the straits of poverty'.[45] Occasionally Winstanley's euphoria gets the better of him, as in the following extract:

If any say, This will bring poverty; surely they mistake: for there will be plenty of all Earthly Commodities, with less labor and trouble then now is under Monarchy. There will be no want, for every man may keep as plentiful a house as he will; and never run into debt, for common stock pays for all.[46]

The reference here to a reduction in labour is possibly a careless error. However, if it was seriously intended, Winstanley probably sought to imply that contemporary labourers could hope to work fewer hours and, because labour would be distributed more equitably, each individual would have to endure less really hard work. It seems unlikely, however, that Winstanley envisaged a significant reduction in the average per capita commitment to labour.

There are two possible reasons for Winstanley's claims regarding material abundance. First, he may have wished to suggest that the restoration posited by the institutional fabric of *The Law of Freedom* would recapture the pristine plenty of the original condition. Second, because he felt constrained to defend his ideas, Winstanley may have succumbed to the temptation to present a somewhat exaggerated picture of the prosperity his plans were designed to attain. This second possibility is the more likely. To take an example, he promises that his communist system would provide every citizen with free access to the *use* of a horse,[47] the possession of which would have indicated to contemporary readers evidence of substantial prosperity. It will be recalled that in the more frugal circumstances of More's utopia horses were rare. Nevertheless, the general tone of Winstanley's discussion suggests that, although he intended the standard of living in his true commonwealth to be more comfortable than the prevailing situation, it would hardly be ostentatious.

Despite these suggestions of abundance, material improvement was not Winstanley's primary objective, although some left-wing scholars such as Petegorsky have implied that it was.[48] It seems probable that Winstanley would have been wary of any semblance of luxury. In this context it is interesting to note a point made by Michael Walzer in his critique of Weber's discussion of the Puritan association of unlimited accumulation with beneficial providence and election. As Walzer argues, 'the anxiety of the Puritans led to a fearful demand for economic restriction'.[49] Thus it was deemed inadvisable and inauspicious for an individual to seek wealth surplus to his requirements. Winstanley was apparently sympathetic to restraint and sobriety of this sort. Hence the emphasis of his utopian economic system was upon sufficiency. Clearly, he assumed that by placing certain limits upon the demand for goods in general, and by discouraging the consumption of luxuries, his scheme would simultaneously ease the scarcity problem, and thereby favour the spiritual restoration of the individual.

In the next section we discuss more precisely the means by which the socio-economic system of Winstanley's utopia was expected to facilitate moral regeneration. Winstanley hoped that this final stage of his thought, utopian institutionalism, would fulfil the same ends that he had once ascribed to millenarianism and subsequently to digging. Hence, in *The Law of Freedom* Winstanley provides constant reminders that pride and covetousness, characteristics of fallen human nature, might henceforth be eradicated by institutional means. We might recall again that Thomas More's theological presuppositions caused him to applaud such restraint but dismiss the possibility of its contributing to eventual moral regeneration.

The moral regeneration of the individual

1

While through the form of a communist utopia Thomas More advocated the means of averting the worst consequences of the 'Fall of Man', Gerrard Winstanley utilized that same medium to propose institutional reforms intended to accomplish the restoration of human nature. In this section the process by which Winstanley believed such a recovery would be brought about will be reconstructed. We have already demonstrated that Winstanley's thought is permeated by a consistent conviction of the feasibility of such moral regeneration, and that both his religious and social ideas, coupled with his experience as a Digger, finally prompted him to conclude that the restoration could only be initiated by means of the thoroughgoing reform of social institutions. His proposals for such reform are outlined in their most coherent form in *The Law of Freedom*. Such 'true magistracy', Winstanley asserts, is the only viable alternative to monarchy,[50] the form of government appropriate to the circumstances of fallen Man. Consequently, Winstanley earnestly recommends his conception of true magistracy as 'the True Restorer of all long lost Freedoms . . . the joy of all Nations, and the

Blessing of the whole Earth: for this takes off the Kingly Curse, and makes Jerusalem a praise in the Earth'.[51] Winstanley dismisses the political situation prevailing since the execution of the King as a futile attempt to construct a *via media*. As an alternative, he claims that his system will fulfil the righteous law of Christ[52] by re-establishing the conditions which had been lost at the Fall. Hence he contends that 'this Commonwealths Government may well be called the antient of days; for it is before any other oppressing government crept in'.[53]

By recognizing the primacy of Winstanley's preoccupation with the restoration of Man it becomes possible to establish the nature of the relationship between the spiritual and the secular elements of this thought. Ultimately, this involves the contention that Winstanley's utopia proposes a society in which an individual could acquire sufficient reason and righteousness to rectify the spiritual damage incurred at the Fall. In effect, whereas Thomas More designed the communist economy of *Utopia* to ensure an equitable distribution of leisure time, education, virtuous pleasure, and contemplation, all of which he regarded as contributory to Man's salvation, Winstanley was concerned to advocate a system in which, on reaching a certain level of maturity, individuals could be relieved of the obligation to labour. The attainment of this condition was to be the final indicator of spiritual restoration.

Work and labour for More was a curse visited upon Man which, if adhered to and organized properly, could at least be contributory in ensuring that individuals did not use their time on earth to perpetrate immoral acts. For Winstanley, however, work which contributed to the well-being of the community would also furnish the moral well-being of the individual. Once an individual became morally regenerate the rationale underpinning the obligation to work was dispelled. The individual could therefore desist from labouring and devote his time to other activities, such as governing the commonwealth.

In *The Law of Freedom* Winstanley unfolds a theory of the several ages of Man. This suggests that he believed in some form of life cycle. These ideas appear to have been stimulated, in part, by Winstanley's conception of the individuated Fall, according to which he believed that each and every individual would experience a spiritual and moral calamity similar to that of the first man. Hence he divides the life of man into four ages, 'his childhood, youth, manhood, and old age'.[54] Winstanley maintains a decidedly protracted notion of 'youth'. He argues that this prolonged adolescence, characterized by a range of attendent moral incapacities, lasts until the age of forty. Thereafter 'from fourty years of age till fourscore, if he live so long, which is the degree of manhood and old age; they shall be freed from all labour and work, unlesse they will themselves'.[55] Not only does Winstanley argue that on attaining the age of majority, at forty, men should no longer be obliged to work, but he also contends that it could generally be assumed of individuals reaching this age in his ideal commonwealth that they would possess sufficient reason to become officers; 'for by this time Man hath learned experience to govern himself and others: for when young wits are set to govern, they wax wanton &c.'[56] From this initial proposition it becomes apparent that Winstanley conceived of the restorative process outlined in *The Law of Freedom* as a gradual progression typified by the attainment of degrees of moral and social responsibility. A life involving education, apprenticeship, labour, patriarchal mastership, and ultimately the holding of public office, was a journey towards spiritual redemption. Winstanley regards the institutions of civil society and those of the household as the two essential spheres for the provision of the facilities necessary to the cultivation of spiritual restoration.

2

If we recall that in his first letter to Fairfax Winstanley claims that the Diggers are perfectly capable of maintaining order among themselves without adopting any formal governmental institutions,[57] then the emphasis he places upon the structure of the state and the role of officialdom in *The Law of Freedom* might be regarded as an abrupt reversal of position. Certainly, by 1652 he was prepared to conceive of these matters in terms such as the following:

> A Soldier is a Magistrate as well as any other Officer, and indeed all State Officers are Souldiers for they represent power, and if there were not power in the hand of Officers, the spirit of rudeness would not be obedient to any Law or Government, but their own wils.[58]

This contention provides a clear indication of the extent to which Winstanley had amended his conception of the human condition.[59] In his earlier pronouncements Winstanley understandably believed himself to be speaking on behalf of the *regenerate* whereas in constructing his ideal commonwealth he was obliged to assume that not all members of society would possess the moral rectitude he had previously attributed to the Diggers.

In the opinion of one critic, G. Woodcock, Winstanley and the Diggers initially constituted the anarchist wing of the English Revolution. Hence the assumption that the cultivation of St George's Hill coincided with the inception of the anarchist tradition of direct action. Yet even Woodcock has been obliged to concede that Winstanley's position in *The Law of Freedom* represents a decided moderation of his views on this issue.[60] Implicit in Woodcock's analysis is the supposition that anarchism was the primary inspiration and achievement of Winstanley's earlier thought and action. Hence Winstanley's latter phase appears to constitute a 'moderation' of his position. However, this impression understates Winstanley's basic concern with Man's spiritual regeneration. From this alternative perspective it is clear that Winstanley's initial propositions concerning the method by which moral regeneration might be expected to occur, involve the corollary that any formal governmental structure would be unnecessary. Thus anarchism is merely attendant upon and ancillary to Winstanley's anticipation of the radical and prompt reformation of human nature. Subsequently, once Winstanley had revised his evaluation of the process by which men might be spiritually and morally restored, he became prepared to contend that the governmental element of his utopian institutionalism might contribute to Man's moral regeneration. Although by this stage in his intellectual development Winstanley had renounced anarchism, he did so not as a result of any immediate reconsideration of the concept, but rather as an appendage to his revised appreciation of the restoration of Man.

In considering Winstanley's analysis of the formal institutions of the state and of political authority, Christopher Hill has arrived at a similar conclusion to Woodcock's. Hill correctly argues that 'by 1652, Winstanley too had realized that his ideal society would need defending against the rudeness of the people'.[61] However, Hill goes too far by suggesting, as he has done elsewhere, that Winstanley's disillusion with an anarchic form of communism is symptomatic of the dissipation of his optimism and confidence.[62] Certainly Winstanley developed a somewhat deprecatory view of existing human nature, and thereby turned to more draconian means of realizing its amendment, but he remained fundamentally optimistic in his conviction that mankind could still be spiritually restored.

3

In *The Law of Freedom* Winstanley for the first time provides a reasonably comprehensive analysis of the commonwealth, along with detailed proposals for the structure of government. In keeping with his revised position Winstanley contends that the primary concerns of government are the regulation of the economy and of men's conduct:

> Government is a wise and free ordering of the Earth, and the Manners of Mankind by observing of particular Laws or Rules, so that all the Inhabitants may live peaceably in plenty and freedom in the Land where thay are born and bred.[63]

Winstanley's account of the origins of civil society and the foundations of political authority constitutes a valuable insight into his conception of 'true magistracy'. According to Winstanley, the general principle of 'true magistracy' is the recognition that political authority is necessary for 'common preservation'. Thus, authority is legitimate only in so far as it is exercised in the interest of common preservation. This condition enables Winstanley to introduce an element of consent into his theory of the commonwealth. He argues that the legitimacy of government could be determined by the people's willing subjection to it, as they perceive its actions as conducive to the common good.

Winstanley frames these ideas in a manner that is clearly intended to confute theories which countenance the prerogative rights of kingship. Hence his concern with the *origins* of political authority. He contends that 'the Original Root of Magistracy is common Preservation, and it rose up first in a private Family'.[64] Thus Winstanley's assumption that Adam was responsible for the control of his children because they were physically weak and too inexperienced to provide for their own subsistence.

Winstanley goes on to argue that the principle of common preservation legitimized the authority of the original ruler and stimulated the consent of the ruled:

> the Law of Necessity, that the Earth should be planted for the common preservation and peace of his household, was the righteous Rule and Law to Adam, and the Law was so clearly written in the hearts of his people, that they all consented quietly to any counsel he gave them for that end.[65]

From this position, Winstanley advances the view that the observation of the law of necessity (by both rulers and ruled) constitutes the only possible basis for political obligation, 'as the necessity for common preservation moves the people to frame a Law, and to chuse Officers to see the Law Obeyed, that they may live in peace'.[66] So whereas Winstanley observes that the promotion of particular interests effectively results in the bondage of the people (kingly power) he deduces that only the promotion of the common good would advance equity and justice and result in the establishment of a true commonwealth.

4

Winstanley's description of the legislative body in his true commonwealth is clearly an implicit criticism of its contemporary equivalent, the Rump Parliament.[67] In Winstanley's scheme, Parliament, 'the highest Court of Equity in the Land',[68] is to be responsible for supervising the cultivation of the land, for the restoration to the common treasury of all land which had previously been the subject of commercial transactions, and for the raising and maintenance of the armed forces. The utopian medium enables Winstanley to envisage the removal of all remaining vestiges of 'kingly power'. In his account of the legislative process, Winstanley expresses his concern to eliminate political corruption and intrigue, to accommodate the consent of the people, and to promote the public interest. Thus he stipulates that all legislative proposals must be declared publicly, and should be enacted only after a lapse of one month, during which time objections and amendments might be lodged.[69]

In his utopian scheme Winstanley also maintains that the election of officials such as 'overseers' (who are to be particularly concerned with the regulation of the economy) and 'ministers' should occur annually.[70] Winstanley specifies that all men of twenty years or over should be entitled to vote, and all those over forty years are to be considered eligible to be elected to public office, although none could campaign on his own behalf.[71] Winstanley apparently makes these provisions with two ends in mind. First, he evidently shares More's suspicion that a long period in office might result in the degeneration of the incumbant's moral character.[72] Winstanley assumes that exercising power might induce corruption from an attitude of humility to one of pride and covetousness. Winstanley's second reason for limiting the duration of office-holding is prescient of the overall purpose of

The Law of Freedom. He regards office-holding as a good to be bestowed upon all eligible individuals in turn. So he contends:

> It is good to remove Officers every year, that whereas many have their portions to obey, so many have their turns to rule, and this will encourage all men to advance Righteousness and good Manners in hopes of Honor.[73]

In Winstanley's utopia the responsibilities of office-holding confirm the successful accomplishment of the spiritual restoration of the individual; officers remain constrained by a system of mutual accountability.

5

It has already been established that ultimately Winstanley became convinced of the view that institutional circumstances determine the prospects of Man's moral regeneration. This conclusion is definitively expressed in the legalism of *The Law of Freedom*, and in Winstanley's discussion of the coercive facet of the state. All this casts considerable doubt upon the contention that Winstanley regarded coercion as an essential bolster to an 'interim holy commonwealth' in which the unregenerate were to be restrained until the occurance of the millenium.[74] Such an interpretation obviously requires revision given that, by this stage, Winstanley was concerned with the actual institutional means of effecting the restoration of Man, and not with awaiting the millenium. Any coercive interim, therefore, applied only to those individuals who had not, as yet, attained the age of reason. J.C. Davis has come nearer to the point in arguing that 'in Winstanley's last and utopian work are shifts of fundamental importance which arise from Winstanley's original confrontation with the problem of guaranteeing social justice in a world where men cannot be changed overnight'.[75] However, Davis had earlier contended that education and social discipline in Winstanley's utopia were both designed to confine the innate and original sin that manifested itself as men pursued their own self interest.[76] On reflection this evaluation seems more appropriate to More's position than to Winstanley's. If we recall Winstanley's account of the 'Fall of Man', and particularly the individuated version of this theory, then it follows that he did not believe in the prevalence of innate and original sin. In any case, Davis's interpretation fails to accommodate Winstanley's admission that citizens in his utopian society might be differentiated into the reasonable and the unreasonable, the regenerate and the unregenerate. An extreme version of the view that Winstanley's conception of human nature became disparaging is forwarded by Murphy, who argues that 'it is hard to imagine a better example of a primitive police state than the True Commonwealth'.[77] Such an abrupt and unconditional conclusion misses the sophistication of Winstanley's purposes.

In the final analysis, Winstanley concluded that the moral recovery of the individual would be a protracted procedure. It became obvious to him that in the meantime men would be susceptible to moral transgressions.[78] So in introducing *The Law of Freedom* he explains that 'because offences may arise from the spirit of unreasonable ignorance, therefore was the Law added'.[79] Such was the manner in which Winstanley tempered his confidence in human potential that he was now prepared to confess that 'there must be suitable Laws for every occasion and almost for every action that men do'.[80] As a facet of Winstanley's extended distrust of human nature he insisted that in a system of true magistracy, the rule of law should prevail to the exclusion of the discretion and prerogative of the individual legislator or executive.[81]

Winstanley's concluding pronouncement on the human predicament is pervaded by the fear that unless the state guards against the infringements perpetrated by the very individuals that civil society is designed to restore, the institutional achievements of the utopia might be disrupted. So Winstanley recognizes that in general men were not of the moral calibre characteristic of the Diggers, and indeed that some might even be prone to the excesses of Ranterism. Therefore, in his utopia, he provides for the enforcement of the law by a soldiery, the members of which were responsible to the superior officers of the commonwealth. Furthermore, the army was to be a citizen militia, to be raised either to protect the commonwealth from invasion, or alternatively, 'to beat down the turbulency of any foolish or self-ended spirit that endeavours to break their Common Peace'.[82]

Winstanley maintains that in a system of true magistracy those unreasonable and unrighteous persons who commit crimes should be offered the opportunity to repent and accept mercy prior to the full force of the punitive system being brought to bear.[83] However, for those malcontents who fail to take advantage of such leniency, Winstanley stipulates that the treatment meted out should be appropriately harsh. Thus he states that

> if they prove desperate, wanton, or idle, and will not quietly submit to the Law, the Task-master is to feed them with short dyet, and to whip them, for a rod is prepared for the fools back, till such a time as their proud hearts do bend to the Law.[84]

Winstanley insists that a process of retributive justice and punishment should apply to serious crimes. Hence he asserts that all individuals entering any arrangement involving the hiring of labour should forfeit their freedom. Further, he regards the death penalty as an appropriate sentence for those who seek to reintroduce private property into the commonwealth, and particularly for individuals who deal in the sale of 'the Earth or fruits therof'.[85] Significantly, Winstanley regards work as a corrective for the ill-diposed or unreasonable spirit. So he contends that, in an ideal commonwealth, bondage should imply hard labour rather than imprisonment, and that the criminal should be aware that his freedom might be restored should his character be adequately reformed.[86] In essence, in *The Law of Freedom* the stated purpose of 'Laws of moderate diligence, and purity of Manners' is not only to 'punish such ignorant and unrational practices'[87] but also to protect more reasonable citizens from the unrighteous disposition of their less enlightened fellows. Hence Winstanley stresses the utility of punitive measures in asserting that 'the Commonwealth Laws are to preserve a mans peace in his person, and in his private dwelling, against the rudeness and ignorance that may arise in Mankind'.[88]

While Winstanley holds that governmental institutions should be ever vigilant in their concern to preserve law and order, he clearly regards this facet of life as the somewhat negative achievement of his ideal commonwealth. Yet he is prepared to acknowledge that legal restraints are necessary because certain individuals are likely to be too unreasonable to conduct themselves in a satisfactory and uprighteous manner. It has already been intimated that Winstanley's recognition of the flawed character of many men derives from the development of his thought on Man's restoration. Initially Winstanley had supposed that the restoration of an individual would be a cataclysmic occurance. However, particularly as a consequence of the failure of the Digger experiment, Winstanley resolved that the spiritual restoration of an individual and that person's commensurate acquisition of reason would be a gradual and cumulative process. Winstanley realized that during the course of this restorative period an individual might be prone to occasional lapses of conduct, which could be dealt with by the legal system. In the meantime, however, he intended other institutions and social arrangements to contribute towards the restoration of the individual. One of these is patriarchalism.

6

Hill's claim that 'everything Winstanley touched he radicalized'[89] is clearly untenable when applied to Winstanley's treatment of patriarchalism. Indeed, as G.J. Schochet observes, Winstanley's conservatism with respect to the family might well typify the attitude of sectarians in general.[90] Schochet contends that 'Fatherhood for Winstanley had not been altered since the time of Adam; the responsibilities of the office continued to outweigh its powers by far'.[91] Elsewhere, in a discussion not directly related to Winstanley, Hill argues to greater effect that 'the theology of Protestantism was patriarchal'.[92] Walzer maintains a similar position, confirming that Protestants 'saw the family as a voluntary community dominated by the godly father'.[93] Clearly, the position assumed by Winstanley in *The Law of Freedom* encapsulates this predisposition. So, as Schochet establishes, 'Winstanley certainly did not derive his arguments from Filmer. Rather, his theories exemplify the genetic preoccupations of Stuart political thinkers and demonstrate the presence of partriarchal assumptions in populist doctrines'.[94]

The emphasis placed by Winstanley upon patriarchalism in *The Law of Freedom* is much greater than that observed by More in *Utopia*. There are two reasons for this. First, the family carries greater responsibility as a vehicle of social control in Winstanley's utopian commonwealth, particularly as his ideal state is devoid of many of the communal spheres of activity so evident in *Utopia*. Second, Winstanley utilizes the status associated with becoming a patriarchal householder as a standard to indicate that particular individuals have attained the degree of reasonableness necessary to their spiritual restoration. Thus Winstanley integrates his views on moral regeneration, eligibility for office-holding, and the principle of common preservation, arguing that 'a Father is a Commonwealths Officer, because the Necessity of the young children choose him by joynt consent, and not otherwise'.[95] Winstanley realizes that it would be both possible, and in some cases necessary, for younger men who had not reached the age of forty to display an advanced maturity and reasonableness by assuming the responsibilities associated with the patriarchal control of a family. So he includes a provision by which such individuals, who have presumably proved themselves to be adequately regenerate, might become officers of the commonwealth. With regard to technicalities such as this, Winstanley's position on the issue of the qualifying age for moral regeneracy is often undeveloped.

Winstanley's conception of the family involves certain important 'moral' considerations—for example, his insistence upon monogamous marriage. In this sense the family is attributed with a supervisory and restraining function. Winstanley's deference to the concepts of age and authority will be fully elucidated in due course, but at this stage it is worth noting that within the context of patriarchalism he renders this principle in its ultimate form. Winstanley holds that in a true commonwealth the 'ancients' should become 'general overseers' for the simple reason that they qualify as 'men of the highest experience in the Laws, for the keeping of Peace in the Commonwealth'.[96] So Winstanley insists that old men should be revered by all citizens as father-figures, with all that such a provision implies for the structure of authority.

By ensuring that all children whose families had been, for whatever reason, dissolved would immediately be placed in the care of another family,[97] Winstanley affirms his esteem for the family as an essential environment in which all members of society ought to be included. Obviously, by such means the dangers of poverty and vagrancy could be averted. Further, all children would be assured of the guiding influence of a father, 'to command them their work and see they do it, and not suffer them to live idle'.[98] In this manner children were to be set on the road to their spiritual regeneration.

In his design for a true commonwealth Winstanley retains the contemporary norm of the seven-year apprenticeship for the instruction of youth in a trade. Yet apprenticeship also constitutes an important element in Winstanley's outline of the restorative process. Thus he anticipates 'that by the experience of the Elders, the young people may learn the inward knowledge of the things which are, and find out the secrets of Nature'.[99] Not only does Winstanley believe that a strictly supervised apprenticeship would curb the inclinations of mischievous youth, but he also regards such training as necessary if the individual is to be equipped with sufficient reason to become one day the master of servants. Hence Winstanley's anxiety to ensure 'that every Family may be governed by stayd and experienced Masters, and not by wanton youth'.[100] What Winstanley means in his reference to servants is unclear. It is possible that he includes male apprentices in this category. However, given that Winstanley differentiates education (to be discussed shortly) according to sex, it is probable that he might also have intended the term 'servant' to apply to female domestics incorporated into the patriarchal household. That Winstanley envisages the retention of household servants seems to confirm that he upholds an essentially conservative stance on patriarchalism.

Winstanley's evaluation of the place of women in his utopian scheme presents something of a problem. Despite his generally favourable apprehension of the human condition Winstanley's utopian efforts to secure the emancipation of women are considerably less progressive than More's had been. Although Winstanley was undoubtedly radical in his religious opinions his theologically conservative attitude towards women is slightly disconcerting. For instance, at one point, Winstanley had argued that women were objects that enticed men to their Fall.[101] Even so, it would be a mistake to assume that this distrust is the sole reason for the role assigned by Winstanley to women in the true commonwealth. It is interesting to call to mind Keith Thomas's suggestion that, although separatists regularly emphasized the spiritual equality of women, and that although the claims made by sectarian women for liberty of conscience contributed to a momentary degree of emancipation from patriarchal command, 'it was completely in accordance with their stated principles that as soon as they took an institutional form even the most radical sects became conservative as regards the organisation and discipline of the family'.[102] We have already noted the extent of Winstanley's commitment to patriarchalism. With respect to Thomas's case, it seems significant that by the time he wrote *The Law of Freedom* Winstanley's thought had taken a perceptibly institutional turn. Clearly, this might explain his philosophical attitude towards women. However, one ameliorative consequence of Winstanley's position is his articulation of the Puritan attack upon the double standard of sexual morality.[103] Winstanley's patriarchalism and his indignant reaction to the loose-living Ranters both contributed to his sensitive appreciation of marital fidelity.

7

With the exception of his depracatory attitude to the place of women in society, which applies especially to the sphere of education, learning is as significant to Winstanley in *The Law of Freedom* as it had been to More in *Utopia*. There are both similarities and differences between More's and Winstanley's treatment of education and these are indicative of the different purposes each utopia was intended to fulfil. In general, Winstanley's education scheme is not only instructive in a utilitarian sense but also, because he conceived of the possibility of education bestowing rationality upon men,[104] it relates to his optimism concerning the spiritual reformation of human nature. In More's *Utopia* the priesthood is held responsible for education; in Winstanley's utopian commonwealth the 'ministers' are charged with the same function. Winstanley obviously wishes to emphasize the considerable distance separating the ministry in his utopian commonwealth from the contemporary clergy, whom he accused of unashamedly perpetuating and cultivating the ignorance of the common people.[105] By implication, Winstanley assumes that men are educable to improved standards of experience and reasonableness. So as a significant aspect of his appreciation of the potential of education he intends these ministers to imbue the young with a sound knowledge of the laws of the commonwealth. As has been noted, by the time he wrote *The Law of Freedom* Winstanley had settled on a largely disparaging opinion of youth:

> Mankinde in the days of his youth, is like a young Colt, wanton and foolish, till he be broke by Education and correction, and the neglect of this care, or the want of wisdom in the performance of it hath been, and is, the cause of much division and trouble in the world.[106]

Nevertheless, whereas Thomas More ultimately intended education to reform by contributing to the subjugation of ineradicably fallen human nature, Gerrard Winstanley believed that education possessed certain additional regenerative properties.

The educational provisions for women in Winstanley's ideal commonwealth are by no means as extensive as those recommended by More in *Utopia*. Thus Hill is quite mistaken in claiming with regard to education in *The Law of Freedom* that 'quite exceptionally for the seventeenth century, it was to be universal [for both sexes] and equal'.[107] Such a conclusion does not appear to accord with Winstanley's stipulation that 'as boyes are trained up in Learning and in Trades, so all Maides shall be trained up in reading, sewing, knitting, spining of Lynnen and Woollen, Musique, and all other easie neat works'.[108] Winstanley appears to have commissioned quite an explicit differentiation of educational curricula, according to sex. Such a position, especially when compared to More's insistence that women ought to received a humanist education, seems to confirm Lawrence Stone's contention that the spread of Protestantism coincided with a decline in the educational advancement of women, even among the elite.[109] According to Stone, this reversal set in after the brief interlude of humanist influence upon learning. So without this ideal to aspire to, Winstanley's utopian women appear to correspond to the daughters of the contemporary yeomanry, who possessed only such bare literacy as was deemed necessary for religious use, and who were instructed primarily in the management of domestic affairs.[110] In his authoritative analysis of various proposals for educational reform advanced during the Interregnum, Charles Webster concludes that 'very little reference was made to the education of women'.[111] To this extent Winstanley is unexceptional.

8

In the chronology of an individual lifespan, it is usually assumed that the period devoted to education will be succeeded by a commitment to some form of work. Within this context, apprenticeship might be regarded as a transition incorporating the twin facets of education and work, and it certainly seems that Winstanley conceived of the instruction of youth in a trade in just such a manner. These considerations form important aspects of Winstanley's scheme for the restoration of the individual. He maintains that, as education could facilitate the spiritual regeneration of the individual, so too could work and labour.

In his earlier writings Winstanley had expressed the conviction that by creating the 'common treasury' communal labour and cultivation of the land would be morally regenerative. For instance, in *An Appeale to all Englishmen* Winstanley contested more orthodox accounts of the 'Fall of Man',[112] arguing that the cultivation of the earth was not symptomatic of Man's fallen condition, but had been undertaken before the Fall, albeit in circumstances conducive to liberty. Similarly, in *An Humble Request* Winstanley asserted that, providing the universal obligation to work prevailed, strenous labour conducted in conditions of liberty should not be associated with the curse.[113] Concomitantly, in *A Vindication* Winstanley suggested that because the Ranters were idle, they were necessarily irrational.[114] It appears, therefore, perfectly admissible to deduce that Winstanley conceived of labour as a righteous action, and that since he associated labour with the acquisition of reason, he regarded it as an aspect of the moral and spiritual restoration of Man.

Winstanley appears to have amended the rationale informing the Protestant work ethic. By stipulating that work (which according to this ethic is a manifestation of election) should be obligatory, Winstanley extends the work ethic to accommodate the notion of universal regeneration. In *The Law of Freedom* Winstanley finally brings to fruition his thoughts on the relationship of labour to Man's spiritual condition. In particular, the form of land ownership postulated in this tract is clearly intended to afford the widest possible scope for *communal labour*. Similarly, goods produced by individual households are to be delivered to *communal* storehouses. Thus, by such means, two phenomena regarded by Winstanley as spiritually and morally corrupting—the hiring out of labour and commercial exchange—are rendered eradicable. So, too, might the 'alienating' sensations identified by Winstanley as facets of the contemporary circumstances under which labour was performed.

In a fairly comprehensive statement of his attitude to labour, Winstanley says:

> the reason why every young man shall be trained up in some work or other, is to prevent pride and contention; it is for the health of their bodies, it is a pleasure to the minde, to be free in labors one with another; it provides plenty of food and all necessaries for the Common-wealth.[115]

Not only does Winstanley regard labour as essential for the maintenance of his utopian communist economy, but he also believes it to possess certain morally significant attributes. Although Winstanley conceives of labour in general as a virtuous activity, he discerns that *communal labour* might be particularly conducive to the spiritual well-being of participants. He seems to be especially concerned with the inculcation of those other-regarding faculties required for individuals to undertake communal enterprises. By this means Winstanley supposes that self-interest, which is instrumental to the 'Fall of Man' as he perceives it, might be neutralized. Unfortunately, Winstanley fails to provide a detailed discussion of the manner in which he expects the cultivation of the land to be organized. Nevertheless, it is significant that he insists that all families, including those who might ordinarily be occupied in a trade, should participate in the *communal* tasks of tilling and planting the land (digging), and subsequently, of gathering the harvest.[116]

Engaging in the communal cultivation of the land is obviously regarded by Winstanley as essential to the moral well-being of the individual. There are a number of interrelated reasons for Winstanley's adherence to this view. The first of these is the benefits to individual character of participating in a communal venture. The second is the experimental, spiritual and aesthetic facet of working the land. An important aspect of Winstanley's design to ensure that individuals should have access to the 'common treasury' is his belief in the spiritually uplifting effect of physical communion with nature. The third reason is the opportunity to exercise an inclusive natural right, a facility which Winstanley appreciates as both the means to the attainment of the sensation of being fully human, and the consummation of that attribute.

We shall shortly turn to a more detailed discussion of Winstanley's concern with experimental knowledge. At this stage it is important to note an interesting corollary between his thought on this matter and his conception of labour. Winstanley equates experimental knowledge with labour, and thereby argues that the professional classes, such as the clergy and lawyers, profit by retailing received ideas obtained from the experimental knowledge and labour of other men. Consequently, 'to prevent the dangerous events of idleness in Scholars',[117] Winstanley incorporates the learning of a trade into the sphere of education. Thus he argues that labour might enable an individual to defy his fallen nature by furthering his accumulation of specifically experimental knowledge. It has been noted that individuals in Winstanley's utopia, on reaching the age of forty, are absolved from the *obligation* to labour. Hence, in *The Law of Freedom* a condition which contemporaries might conventionally have regarded as a facet of the curse incurred at the Fall is lifted. This 'redemption' is achieved, in part, by individuals undertaking the type of labour Winstanley regards as necessary to the acquisition of experimental knowledge and, eventually, to the restoration of Man to reasonableness.

Winstanley's assumptions concerning the relationship of labour to Man's spiritual restoration are particularly exemplified by the purpose he expected apprenticeship to fulfil. This, in turn, is inspired by his attitude to 'youth'. It is revealing that his arguments are framed in the following terms: 'all the work of the Earth, or in Trades, is to be managed by youth, and by such as have lost their Freedoms'.[118] Obviously, Winstanley does not ascribe young men of under forty to a condition of bondage, but he appears to suggest that the younger and less rational members of society should not be regarded as free and morally responsible agents in anything like a full sense. Hence, Winstanley's insistence that young people are to be especially closely supervised by their partriarchal masters, so that even as children they might 'live in Peace, like rational men, experienced in yielding obedience to the Laws and Officers of the Commonwealth, every one doing to another as he would another do to him'.[119]

The coherence of Winstanley's utopian institutionalism

1

The full significance of Winstanley's preoccupation with the ages of Man may be highlighted with reference to Keith Thomas's discussion of attitudes to age and authority in the early modern period. Thomas cites Winstanley, 'whose distrust of the young went unusually deep',[120] as a vehement exponent of certain well-subscribed beliefs. These include the apprehension that youth constitutes a morally dangerous period of life, and the conception of apprenticeship as an essential preliminary to the acquisition of a sufficient degree of reason eventually to enable an individual to become the master of a family.[121] According to Thomas, the age profile of the contemporary ruling group displayed a preponderance of quadragenarians and quinquagenerians. However, due to a more limited life expectancy,[122] the over-forties represented a far smaller proportion of the total population in the early modern period than they do today. What is more, persons who were over sixty years of age were so scarce as to be regarded as the custodians of experimental knowledge, of wisdom, and indeed of history.[123] As has been noted, this group of ancients was commensurately revered by Winstanley. Nevertheless, Winstanley seems to have been at odds with contemporary norms[124] in proposing the concept of retirement for men who might remain physically capable of performing manual labour. This, as we have suggested, is possibly because Winstanley wished to show that, in his ideal commonwealth, once an individual attained spiritual restoration he would have the burden of manual labour lifted from him. Yet in *The Law of Freedom*, such a person could continue to perform socially useful 'work', but do so in the capacity of an office-holder. It is evident that the age structure of Winstanley's ruling group reproduced the existing situation.

The prevalent institutions of apprenticeship and patriarchalism, and the almost neurotic contemporary concern for the preservation of good order, all prompt Thomas to conclude that 'the sixteenth and seventeenth centuries were conspicuous for a sustained drive to subordinate persons in their teens and early twenties and to delay their equal participation in the adult world'.[125] Thomas also points out that justification for this attitude to youth 'was found in the law of nature, in the fifth commandment, and in the proverbial wisdom of ages'.[126] Given all this, it becomes clear that, by the time he wrote *The Law of Freedom* Winstanley did not approach the question of age and authority from a radical standpoint. His conservatism in this area is entirely in keeping with his ultimate conclusion that the spiritual restoration of the individual would be a gradual process to be accomplished by institutional means. It appears that Winstanley might even have felt sympathetic toward the prevalent belief that the soul grew with the body.[127]

2

From the various institutional elements of *The Law of Freedom* it is possible to discern those factors identified by Winstanley as contributory to the process of restoring the individual to spiritual well-being. Winstanley's disavowal of anarchism is indicative of the developmental nature of his social theory. He ultimately recognized in the commonwealth the epitome of that institutionalism basic to early modern utopian proposals for the reformation of men's characters. Thus, in *The Law of Freedom* Winstanley outlines his views on authority and coercion. The provision of an element of coercion, a comprehensive legal system, and the codification of law, are intended not only as sanctions upon the conduct of recalcitrant and malevolent individuals, but also as a guide to the actions of all members of society. Such jurisprudence constitutes the minimum and rudimentary provision in Winstanley's scheme for the restoration of Man.

Winstanley's discussion of education is a more ambitious and positive aspect of his utopianism. This sphere also confirms the integrated and self-sustaining nature of Winstanley's utopian society. Education in *The Law of Freedom* manifests two basic aspects. The first is utilitarianism; there are obvious propitious implications for the maintenance of a stable and efficient economy, and for the successful operation of institutions in general, if citizens are well educated. But second, as we shall shortly note, Winstanley believed that by facilitating the acquisition of reason education would have a far more direct effect upon the process of moral regeneration. This he regarded as a prerequisite condition for the redemption of Man. Further, he was convinced of the importance of an experimentally-orientated scheme. Thus Winstanley's philosophy of education reflects his theological convictions; experimentalism is also an essential factor in Winstanley's conception of Man's spiritual restoration.

The next 'stage' in the maturing and restorative process adumbrated in *The Law of Freedom*, apprenticeship, is a similarly elaborate notion. In part, apprenticeship is intended by Winstanley to continue the educative role of social upbringing, but it also introduces the individual to work and to the obligation to labour. Clearly, this ensures an adequate provision of labour to sustain the economy, with all that communism in turn entails. However, Winstanley also postulates that labour possesses restorative potential, particularly when undertaken as a communal activity, or if it resulted in a contribution towards the prosperity of the community. Hence, all men are to work until they are at least forty years of age.

As we have noted, labour, private property and political authority were conventionally associated with the curse which had overcome fallen Man. Yet in *The Law of Freedom*, although fallen men are obliged to labour, this is to good effect, because it contributes to their restoration, Winstanley asserted that, ultimately,

No man shall be suffered to keep house, and have servants under him till he hath served seven years under Command to a Master himself; the reason is this, that a man may be of age, and of rational carriage, before he be a Governor of a family, that the Peace of the Commonwealth may be preserved.[128]

The more advanced stages of the restorative process outlined in *The Law of Freedom*, namely patriarchal authority and officialdom, also appear to serve a dual purpose. On the one hand, for an individual to become a patriarchal householder and an officer of the commonwealth is confirmation of the fact that the process of moral regeneration is well under way. On the other hand, because these two spheres exert so much influence upon life in Winstanley's utopian society, and because the fundamental purpose of that society is to effect the restoration of its citizens, the morally regenerate are in a position to assume responsibility for the supervision of the spiritual recovery of others. Thus, according to Winstanley's ideal, patriarchalism fulfils several functions. As we have seen, Winstanley regarded the family as an essential medium for the control of the conduct and the morality of all members of the true commonwealth. The family is also the basic unit for economic production in which the relationship between an apprentice and his master embodied both these aspects of family life. In Winstanley's view, to become a patriarchal householder is to attain a prestigious position. The correlation between this office and the restored condition means that ambition is necessarily directed towards spiritual as well as towards worldly accomplishment. Because the sphere of private property included by Winstanley in his essentially communist utopia is based upon the family, the responsibility for its management falls to the patriarchal householder. Thus, in contrast to what Winstanley believed of his own society, only the worthiest of citizens in the true commonwealth are allowed to control private property. It appears that Winstanley assumed that, because householders would be morally capable, they could be entrusted with the ownership of the property of the household without becoming corrupted by its influence.

Retirement from manual labour marks the consummation of the restorative process. At this point, an individual is absolved from the burdens associated with labour. As he acquires the potential to become a member of the officer class, he faces the prospect of undertaking a different form of work. Within the rigidly hierarchical structure of age and authority that pervades the utopian commonwealth, officers (again the morally regenerate sector of society), become responsible for exercising power, to the effect that younger members of society might be directed towards their own restoration.

3

Winstanley maintains that once a man has been educated, has served an apprenticeship, has worked for a number of years, and has in all probability become a patriarchal householder, he will be approaching the age of forty, by which time he should become eligible to retire from labour and to assume public office. During the course of *The Law of Freedom* Winstanley advances a detailed description of the responsibilities and functions of the officers of the commonwealth.[129] Together such officers constitute a hierarchical chain of authority justified by Winstanley in terms of the need to preserve good order throughout society. Hence Winstanley's advocacy of an ideal of mutual surveillance not all that dissimilar to the system proposed by More in *Utopia*. So he holds that, should 'many eyes be watchful, the Laws may be obeyed, for to preserve Peace'.[130] Winstanley entrusts the officers of his commonwealth with the task of guarding vigilantly against the development of covetousness and pride in the inhabitants, lest the commonwealth should decline from true magistracy into satanic tyranny. To this end Winstanley includes the crucially significant age qualification of forty years, to be attained before a man could become an officer.

It may not be merely coincidental that Winstanley had recently attained this age of maturity. At the age of forty he claimed to have experienced a spiritual restoration, and to have acquired the peace of mind which prompted him to inaugurate the Digger colony. The officers of Winstanley's utopian commonwealth are similarly enlightened, 'for these are most likely to be experienced men; and all these are likely to be men of courage, dealing truly, and hating Covetousness'.[131] Winstanley conceives of maturity as one criterion of restored human nature. Significantly, he stipulates that Royalists, and persons who have dealt in the buying and selling of land (all of whom he may have regarded as irretrievably fallen) are to be permanently exluded from holding office.

4

Winstanley's social theory is characterized by his retention of an essentially radical appreciation of Man's potential. Nevertheless, as time progressed he certainly developed a number of discernibly conservative ideas and dispositions. As we have shown, labour, private property and political authority were all conventionally justified as necessary constraints upon the actions of fallen men. This is obviously a position likely to recommend itself to the propertied classes who were not constrained to perform manual labour, but instead assumed in various guises the government of society. It is clear that both More and Winstanley recognized that this intensely conservative theory had degenerated as a consequence of the self-interested actions of various social groups. As a consequence More proposed the total abolition of private property, restraint in the exercising of political authority, and the equitable distribution of work, goods and pleasure. By contrast, Winstanley, although he initially refused to admit the necessity for maintaining either private property or political authority, finally acknowledged that both these institutions, properly constituted, could contribute towards the moral regeneration of Man—as indeed could work and labour. Although his utopian institutionalism involves the provision of political authority, the existence of a sphere of private property, and the obligation to labour, Winstanley ensures that none of these institutions could be used corruptly. By asserting that only those individuals who had been restored would be made responsible for power and property the dangers of fallen men abusing authority and appropriating labour are seemingly averted. In our concluding chapter we explore in greater depth some of the reasons informing the marked differences of intellectual disposition towards the question of Man's potential discernible in the stances adopted by More and Winstanley. For the moment it is appropriate to press the observation that whereas More proposed a series of extraordinarily radical institutional measures while maintaining an essentially conservative and pessimistic appreciation of human potential, Winstanley was by comparison a less radical institutionalist but more confident in his appraisal of human capabilities. Both More and Winstanley perceived social well-being as the corollary of a compound involving, on the one hand, the institutional fabric and, on the other, Man's moral capacity. Where they vary is in their evalution of the relative balance to be struck between these factors.

5

The primary end of Winstanley's utopia is to identify and to recommend the institutional requirements for the spiritual restoration of Man. It is appropriate that our analysis of Winstanley's thought concludes with a consideration of several further aspects of the social life and intellectual disposition detailed in *The Law of Freedom*. These aspects might be regarded as corollaries to Winstanley's fundamental purpose and include his proposals for law reform, his assessment of the proper role of religion in society, the relationship of science to education, and the nature of pleasure.

The theme of law reform was particularly close to Winstanley's heart and the construction of a utopia enabled him, theoretically at least, to correct the incongruities and anomalies that he saw and experienced in the contemporary legal system of fallen 'kingly government'. In his analysis of law[132] Winstanley argues that there are essentially two forms—'natural law', and 'written law' (by which we may assume him to mean positive law). He contends that because men may be either rational or unreasonable the calibre of written law will be determined largely by the prevailing disposition of human nature. Hence Winstanley's plea for rational men to formulate a written law incorporating the principles of natural law represents a clear indictment of the abuse of prerogative rights within common law. So in the light of his conception of equity, and in the hope of complementing the capacities of the reasonable and regenerate individuals who were to inhabit the utopian commonwealth, Winstanley designed the legal system of *The Law of Freedom*. Thus he defines as an ideal of law 'a Rule, whereby Man and other creatures are governed in their actions, for the preservation of the common peace'.[133] It is typical of Winstanley that he regarded a rational life, conducted in accordance with principles of reason, as a means towards the acquisition of peace of mind and the recovery of the 'light'. Postulating that whatever form of law is subscribed to by the most substantial numerical following will effectively constitute the rule according to which a particular society is governed, Winstanley contends that 'if the experienced, wise, and strong man bears rule, then he writes down his minde to curb the unreasonable law of covetousness and pride in unexperienced men, to preserve peace in the Commonwealth'.[134] Consequently, in his utopia, Winstanley attributes the responsibility for providing legislative guidance for the unregenerate elements of society to the regenerate elite.

It is perhaps paradoxical that despite his earlier appeals to ancient custom, Winstanley ultimately advocates the written codification of law. It can only be assumed that, given his emphasis upon reason and equity as bases for jurisprudence, Winstanley must have conceived of his own proposals as, to some extent, an embodiment of the common law as it existed before being corrupted by the Normans. This shift in emphasis was no doubt occasioned by Winstanley's revised view of human potential. Because he was no longer so confident of the prospect of Man's intuitive and self-imposed rectitude, Winstanley saw the need for a legal code as 'a bridle to unreasonableness'.[135] Thus, presumably, one reason for Winstanley's insistence that the people should be inculcated with a working knowledge of the law[136] is his conviction that they must be made fully aware of the manner in which they are expected to conduct themselves. Winstanley also required this principle to apply to magistrates.

One aspect of Winstanley's concern to provide his utopia with a legal system antithetical to the version employed in 'kingly government' is his omission of the practice of judicial interpretation. He insists that 'no single man ought to Judge or interpret the Law'.[137] Clearly, Winstanley perceives judicial interpretation as a derivation from the prerogative discernible in 'kingly government'. Hence, in an attempt to avoid any corruption in the purity of enactment Winstanley asserts that it would be 'the Law, who indeed is the true Judge'.[138] Further, Winstanley contends that in a true commonwealth there should be no lawyers; each individual would be permitted to argue his own case, just as Winstanley himself would have preferred to do during his days as a Digger. Through the institution of local 'peace makers', and the quarterly circulation of the 'judges court',[139] Winstanley aimed to achieve a somewhat more decentralized and efficient judicial system than that prevailing in contemporary society. To avoid the privations of unnecessary imprisonment, and to provide the opportunity for repentance, Winstanley proposes that bail should be readily available. All this is facilitated by a preference for short and pithy laws[140] to be annotated in the native tongue, and propagated regularly upon the sabbath.[141]

6

The impact of organized religion is less evident in Winstanley's portrayal of the true commonwealth[142] than it is in *Utopia*. The reason for this lies partly in the fact that for Thomas More the salvation of the Utopian was to be dependent upon the adherence to at least a degree of religious conformity. For Winstanley, however, the restoration of the individual depended upon men coming to an understanding of God's purpose through individual experience, an eventuality that did not depend upon any resort to the doctrines of organized religion. In *The Law of Freedom*, Winstanley expresses the hope that his utopian citizens would be provided with the type of experience of God that he had insisted upon in his earlier pamphlets. In his last piece Winstanley's anti-intellectualism and his anticlericalism achieve full expression.

Religion in the true commonwealth would be sustained by the conviction that God is the spirit of the whole creation.[143] Winstanley insists upon experimental perception because he regards the creation as the only possible source of certainty about God. Thus he contends that as knowledge of the secrets of nature will yield up knowledge of God, so, too, might the experimentalism involved in ascertaining such insights advance the individual's knowledge of the self. Winstanley contends that by this means men will realize certain truths about their spiritual condition. Thus he proclaims his own understanding of the fallacies of contemporary belief and psychology as

> a Doctrine of a sickly and weak spirit, who hath lost his understanding of the knowledge of the Creation, and of the temper of his own Heart and Nature, and so runs into fancies, either of joy or sorrow.
>
> And if the passion of joy predominate, then he fancies to himself a personal God, personal Angels, and a local place of glory which he saith, he, and all who believe what he saith, shall go to after they are dead.
>
> And if sorrow predominate, then he fancies to himself a personal Devil, and a local place of torment, that he shall go to after he is dead, and this he speaks with great confidence.
>
> . . . this Divining doctrine, which you call spiritual and heavenly things, torments people always when they are weak, sickly and under any distemper; therefore it cannot be the Doctrine of Christ the Saviour.[144]

Winstanley's emphasis upon experimentalism as the source of true spiritual awareness obviously entails the proviso that his utopian society should ensure a substantial degree of toleration and freedom of speech. To this end Winstanley rejects all notions of clerical authority and somewhat dramatically stipulates that 'he who professes the services of a righteous God by preaching and prayer, and makes a Trade to get the possessions of the Earth, shall be put to death for a Witch and a Cheater'.[145] Consequently, the 'ministry' in the true commonwealth is to be assigned a purely educative and propagandist function. Even so, Winstanley's notion of the sabbath approximates to the Puritan conception of sabbatarianism. Thus Winstanley recognizes the regenerative and social utility of a regular day of rest within the rhythm of labour.[146] In order to foster a sense of community Winstanley believes it essential that every parish should be afforded a regular opportunity to socialize. Obviously this represents a vital consideration in such an intensely patriarchal society which lacks the communal activities so evident in the daily life designated in *Utopia*. Hence Winstanley stipulates that on occasions when the parish is gathered together, the ministry should perform its educative work, and the people should be kept aware of the affairs of the commonwealth. Ironically, this means of disseminating information reflects an essential function of the contemporary clergy, which was arraigned so steadfastly by Winstanley. However, the sabbath in *The Law of Freedom* is envisaged as an occasion for making speeches on the arts and sciences, and on the nature of Man. In terms of Winstanley's religious outlook, this might almost be regarded as an opportunity for 'lay preaching'. Thus Winstanley's conception of civil religion defers both to considerations of social utility and to a conception of an experiential and rational understanding of the universe.

7

It would be inappropriate to leave this detailed consideration of *The Law of Freedom* without some reference to science, particularly as one of the most startling aspects of Winstanley's thought is the integration of his views on the spiritual facet of experimentalism within his appreciation of natural philosophy. Winstanley maintains an essentially utilitarian conception of science. He asserts that physics, surgery, astrology, astronomy, navigation, and husbandry are all sciences. He also contends that by studying these subjects 'men will come to know the secrets of Nature and Creation, within which all true knowledge is wrapped up'.[147] The inclusion of astrology in this list might appear somewhat anomolous. However, this provision indicates that Winstanley placed far greater emphasis upon the prospects of progress within the human condition than had Thomas More. The practice of astrology incidentally contributed to the discovery of the new cosmology which in turn stimulated scientific advance and reinforced a more optimistic conception of progress. So Winstanley's reference to astrology, far from constituting an antiquarian reminder, reflects the development of a new and aggressive attitude towards nature and ambitious proposals for the improvement of mankind's predicament. These themes are discussed below.

Winstanley's more optimistic worldview is also expressed in his advocacy of the experimental method which, partly as a consequence of his anti-intellectualism, again brings together his views on education and science. Thus Winstanley asserts that in a system of true magistracy, 'one sort of Children shall not be trained up solely to book learning, and no other imployment, called Schollars, as they are in the Government of Monarchy'.[148] One reason for this is Winstanley's association of manual labour with experimental knowledge as prerequisite to the spiritual regeneration of Man. So, conversely, he insists that 'Traditional Knowledge, which is attained by reading, or by the instruction of others, and not practical, but leads to an idle life; . . . is not good'.[149] Winstanley defines the experimental method as 'nothing by imagination, but what he hath found out by his own industry and observation in tryal'.[150] By providing an understanding of Nature, Winstanley expected this process to bring men closer to God. This casts doubt upon a claim made by one scholar to the effect that 'one striking aspect of Winstanley's programme of education was its total exclusion of religion'.[151] This understanding fails to render appropriate weight to the impression made by Winstanley's spirituality on the institutions advocated in *The Law of Freedom*.

8

In comparison to More's detailed evaluation of the philosophy of pleasure, Winstanley has little to say on the matter except so far as to assert that the citizens of his true commonwealth could expect to enjoy 'pleasure plentiful'.[152] One possible reason for this omission is Winstanley's somewhat greater emphasis upon ensuring material prosperity. Winstanley might well have expected labourers in his utopia to work longer hours. This is not a commitment anticipated by More, who in *Utopia* insisted that the provision of leisure time was to be paramount. Furthermore, Winstanley found himself obliged to compensate for those members of his utopian society who would retire from manual labour completely. However, although it might be assumed that this elite would effectively constitute a leisured class, Winstanley's efforts to charge the retired and the regenerate with the administration of the commonwealth tells against such an assumption.

It is significant that, unlike More, Winstanley is reluctant to discuss education as a form of pleasure. Instead he reiterates the theme of spiritual restoration and asserts that he will

> suffer no children in any Parish to live in idleness, and youthful pleasure, all their days, as many have been; but that they be brought up like men, and not like beasts: That so the Common-wealth may be planted with laborious and wise experienced men, and not with idle fools.[153]

It seems that Winstanley anticipated a society in which such 'wise and experienced men' would be too preoccupied with the supervision of the institutional process by which others could be restored to enjoy the luxury of free time.

The Law of Freedom is Winstanley's most systematic and considered piece. Although Winstanley's economic theory is undoubtedly often unsophisticated in the extreme, he compensates for this with an acute appreciation of the integrated nature of societal institutions. In *The Law of Freedom* Winstanley finally resolves, to his own apparent satisfaction, the basic problem that had pervaded his writings. The medium of utopianism proved useful, at least on the theoretical level, in enabling Winstanley to advance his proposals for the moral regeneration and spiritual restoration of man. In his final publication Winstanley's social theory is brought to an appropriate conclusion.

Part IV

7
Conclusion

In this final chapter an attempt is made to provide an account not only of the manner in which More's utopian communism and Winstanley's differ, but also of why this should be the case. Two major lines of enquiry are pursued—the first relating to developments within property theory, and the second to the wider perspective of the changing worldview and the emergence of a commitment to some notion of social progress. I refrain, however, from analysing those aspects of individualism which might be regarded as providing a link between the respective spheres of property theory and social progress.[1]

Property theory and utopian communism

The analysis of the development of property theory in the early modern period reveals that the emergence of an understanding of 'natural rights' as the basis of this aspects of social thought proved crucial in providing Winstanley with the theoretical wherewithal to structure his thinking on property in a manner which enabled him to recommend what he saw as the appropriate institutional arrangement for the amelioration of man's predicament. To appreciate fully the significance of this development it is necessary to look initially at some general aspects of property theory.

1

In keeping with the methodological predispositions informing this study, that is to say the utilization of analytical techniques to explore the implications of thought recovered through textual analysis, recourse is made to the growing literature on property theory[2] to illuminate a somewhat ill-considered aspect of early modern political thought. While a great deal has been written on the ideas of early modern proponents of private ownership, relatively little has been said of contemporary critics of this idea. The analysis offered in foregoing chapters and that sustained in this conclusion is informed by reference to eight essential aspects of property theory. Briefly, these are as follows.

Technical considerations and the nature of ownership. The history of property theory could be written as that of the exploration of that nature of ownership. Even the most general concern with the relationship between individuals and their interests in objects opens the way to discussion on the one hand, of systems of ownership and, on the other, of often technical issues such as rights of access, use, leashold, copyright, patent, and so on. In conjunction with the sophistication of legal theory, an enhanced technical appreciation of what might constitute rules of ownership has been sponsored through the centuries by the need to differentiate the manner and objects of ownership in various social situations. Crucially, it is generally agreed that recommendations as to systems of ownership, which may in turn be derived from broader moral principles, must, if they are to appear justifiable, accord with what Grunebaum terms 'the logical structure of ownership rules'.[3] Furthermore, it is important to appreciate that awareness of this type of requirement gained momentum during the early modern period, particularly in conjunction with developments within rights theory on the issue of titles as pertaining to persons and as delineating interests in ownable objects. For example, attempts to justify the private ownership of land often went hand in hand with the concern to elaborate upon the relative exclusivety of such rights. The question of landownership was of obvious significance to seventeenth-century political theorists, and the increased sensitivity to the concept of ownership thus promoted also sustained an interest in extending such understandings to other forms of property, an inclination which ultimately served to demonstrate the difficulties entailed in the attempt.[4] Even so, the philosophical, economic and jurisprudential sophistication of conceptions of ownership is of significance to our own analysis not least because whereas More's consideration of the precise nature of ownership is, to say the least, cursory, Winstanley's is somewhat more detailed.

Historical development. As is intimated above, through time conceptions of ownership have changed to the effect that what is known of the state of contemporary thought on the concept becomes relevant to the understanding of the writings of specific theorists. In tracing this aspect of the intellectual context it becomes necessary to acquire an awareness of attendant theoretical developments. In evaluating, with a mind to differentiating, the respective communist utopias of More and Winstanley, the crucial development of this kind is the manner in which the medieval synthesis of classical and patristic thought relating property theory to the doctrine of the Fall eventually generated, only to be superseded by, a more specifically rights-based appreciation of property.

Historical accounts employed within property theory. As a corollary of the previous aspect, analysis must uncover, with a view to discerning its theoretical significance and status, the role played at various times by explanatory theories which were often perceived as historical accounts of the origins and sources of systems of ownership. Most obviously, this present study has looked at the idea of the Fall of Man in this light. Doubts as to the facility of more conventional versions of this idea to provide an explanation of the origins of private property, and to justify the continuation of private ownership, clearly informed the thinking of both More and Winstanley. Our concern has been to understand why, in each case, this should be so.

Origins. Establishing the origins of a form of ownership, which may often entail attempting to demonstrate the consistency of a historical account with a set of moral principles, has long been a major preoccupation within property theory. Thus the question of origins is pivotal because, in relation to a conception of ownership, the justification or critique of that conception is inextricably linked to the identification of the derivation of the system. To use a well-known instance: in attempting to justify particular conceptions of the private ownership of land, seventeenth-century property theorists were engaged in a debate[5] as to the original status of the earth and of God's intentions for His creation—whether for communal ownership, usufruct, or private appropriation. A key concern of various accounts was to maintain the internal logical consistency of the attempt to relate an appreciation of the original status of the earth to the justification of a preferred understanding of how land should appropriately be owned. In this study it is contended that medieval versions of the origins of property influenced by an essentially 'Augustinian' account of the Fall utilized the understanding of the origin of private property posited by that account not so much to justify private ownership as to explain its existence. Thus, the work of the thirteenth-century natural law theorists marks a crucial departure in that their treatment of the origins and justification of private property as natural rather than conventional set in motion an intellectual tradition of justification which, with qualification, can be traced to the work of twentieth-century philosophers such as Robert Nozick.[6] However, the justification of private ownership in terms of a theory of natural rights also introduced, first, the possibility of the critique of private ownership from within that theory, a process to which Winstanley made an important and early contribution; and second, doubts as to whether an understanding of natural rights could indeed sustain the moral justification of private ownership. Here, classical Utilitarianism appears as the obvious example.

Property and labour. In discerning labour as a means by which certain objects constituting 'property' are created, or rendered 'useful', or imputed with value in exchange, property theory is concerned with the manner in which structures of ownership and forms of labour may be mutually reinforcing. In particular, thinkers such as Locke, Smith and J.S. Mill have provided different answers to the central question of what, if any, property rights are actually established via labour, a consideration which relates back in turn to the conceptual refinement of 'ownership'. Considering labour in relation to ownership is also liable to introduce issues such as the question of access to the labour market, related rights such as welfare rights, and the notion of the obligation to labour. The consideration of labour plays an important part in the thinking of both More and Winstanley largely because both thinkers view labour in conjunction with their appreciation of the nature and significance of the Fall. Both assert the obligation to labour alongside the stipulation that such exertion should secure an appropriate material reward. Both have things to say about the moral implications of the form and circumstances of labour.

Property and character. In approaching this complex facet of property theory it becomes immediately apparent that isolating the causal nexus linking forms of ownership and character has often been an important consideration within social thought. Views on the question have varied. Whereas some thinkers have seen a particular property system as an entailment of character, others have regarded character as itself in some way determined by the prevalent system of ownership. Similarly, within various approaches, opinion has differed as to whether and how amending the property system might effect changes of character or conduct. This aspect of property theory also relates to issues concerning forms of labour and to more general questions of moral justification.

Let us take the example of Aristotle's disagreement with Plato on the problem of what form of ownership would be most likely to promote the virtue of the citizen, a debate that persists to this day. Advocates of private ownership have differed as to how this form relates to considerations of character. Augustine provides an account in which character is regarded as immutable and requires restraint through rules of private ownership. Machiavelli and Hume, however, represent the view that private ownership, particularly of land, develops the virtuous personality and an attachment to the *patria*. More recently, a particular conception of private ownership has often been defended by proponents of late twentieth-century market liberalism on the grounds of what is perceived as its facility to satisfy a notion of individual wants informed by a version of Preference Utilitarianism. However, objections to private ownership have also been founded upon considerations of human nature and character. Here, the views of Marx on alienation and exploitation are the obvious example. In seeing character as contingent and determined by prevailing capitalist relations of ownership, Marx asserts that only the replacement of such relations could achieve what Elster terms the 'self-actualization of Man'.[7] In terms of our own study, it is important to stress that the issue of character changed from being quite possibly the predominant concern of property theory to being one of many, and did so quite markedly during the period separating More and Winstanley. For More, the issue of character is absolutely fundamental to his apprehension of property relations; for Winstanley character remains an important consideration but only within a somewhat more substantial conceptual appreciation of ownership.

Property and economics. A distinctly 'modern' facet of property theory is the concern to evaluate systems of ownership in terms of economic efficiency, a propensity traceable to the work of Petty and Locke in the seventeenth century, through thinkers of the Scottish Enlightenment, to the 'political economists'.[8] In this light, the writings of both More and Winstanley appear decidedly pre-modern in that, although they are aware of the need to demonstrate the economic advantages of their utopian schemes, they lack the language and the techniques to enable them to do so as systematically as might later have been the case.

Justification. The foregoing analysis posits the interrelatedness of various considerations within property theory. In particular, it is argued that the justification of a system of ownership must be informed by a coherent conception of ownership rules and that such rules are likely to be derived in conjunction with a conception of the origins of that system of ownership. Thus, historically, the basis of justification has changed. In this respect the political thought of the seventeenth century marks a watershed with regard to the development of theories aimed at justifying various conceptions of ownership. Three particular justificatory arguments—first occupancy, the labour theory of acquisition, and understandings of utility[9]—were developed and sharpened during the course of seventeenth-century debates on the original status of property, the derivation of forms of ownership, and the constitutional implications of such forms. The emergence of this type of discourse, particularly in the train of the development of natural rights theories, effectively distinguishes the mode of justification employed by Winstanley from that formerly utilized by More. More's justification of communal ownership is implicit. In effect, he offers in *Utopia* a critique of the still prevalent assumption that only private ownership might mitigate against the social disharmony likely to be occasioned by fallen Man. Contrastingly, by the mid-seventeenth century, the concern to approach matters in the light of a more acute and detailed understanding of origins and justification had been assimilated to the extent that thinkers of various persuasions structured their arguments accordingly.[10]

2

In that More and Winstanley are utopian communists they are property theorists. The interpretation of their writings is in this respect aided by understanding the developments in property theory that occurred through the early modern period. In essence, such developments shifted the emphasis within property theory from a concern with property in relation to character and virtue to an emphasis upon promoting more coherent and thereby justifiable theories of ownership.

Two related preoccupations link classical treatments of property to those of the medieval period: the concern to distinguish that form of ownership conducive to the moral development of the individual citizen; and the concern to identify that system of ownership capable of minimizing public strife and contention. These considerations throw considerable light upon the interpretation of More's *Utopia*. In that one scholar, Grunebaum, groups together Plato, Aristotle and Aquinas as 'Natural Perfectionists . . .

whose moral justification of ownership is grounded on the idea of virtuous perfection of human nature',[11] More may be understood as a thinker who relates property to character and who advocates communism in order to reduce the effects of what he sees as human imperfection. More is party to the ambivalence, discussed above,[12] as to whether the precepts of the natural law distinguish clearly between natural and conventional social institutions. In More's case, this ambivalence, as belied in the pages of *Utopia*, also extends to the issue of whether any institutional regime, even one founded upon communism, is capable of affording the possibility of the citizen leading the good life.

3

A characteristic of the development and refinement, during the early modern period, of natural rights theories is the failure to achieve a consensus on that theory of ownership best suited to the preservation and promotion of 'natural rights'.[13] In part, this debate at least reflects problems that came to light within medieval treatments of 'ownership rights' and 'rights of ownership'[14] such as that of providing a legitimate account of private ownership, one consistent with obligations to the needy, if that system is postulate as deriving from an original condition characterized by communal ownership. In the view of Richard Tuck, the radicals in this respect were the proponents of private ownership. Thus he contends that 'the fourteenth century saw a curious anticipation of what was to happen three hundred years later, when natural rights theories were developed by conservative thinkers as a defence of property, competition and other related values'.[15]

As is well appreciated, natural rights theories of ownership derived much of their contemporary political significance from debate within contractarian approaches as to the identity and form of 'natural liberty'. Hobbes regards property rights as conventional because, given his understanding of the state of nature, he believes such rights to be both illogical and indefensible. Locke, in following thinkers such as Grotius who treat liberty as commensurate with property, asserts the pre-political nature of property rights as an argument for limiting of the powers of governments. However, in taking this line Locke is committed to providing a conception of just acquisition consistent with his understanding of the circumstances of the original condition and with his conception of private ownership. To borrow James Tully's terminology, Locke is committed to providing an account of the manner in which 'exclusive rights' may be derived from 'inclusive rights'.[16] Two very obvious points have been made about arguments such as Locke's. The first is that the notion of an inclusive natural right to the use of the commons appears to be as consistent with the notion of usufruct as with that of private and exclusive ownership, if not more so. Locke is aware that in order to avoid a position according to which exclusive rights of private ownership are based upon what a thinker such as Winstanley would have termed 'conquest' or 'usurpation', some principle of just acquisition is necessary, and it remains open to question as to whether Locke's notion of the 'sufficiency limitation' is such a principle.[17] The second point is a corollary of the first and relates to the question of the private ownership of land. If it is accepted both that natural rights are universal and that land is a scarce resource, then it appears that, with regard to the 'intergenerational' implications of natural rights theories, 'latecomers' are at a possible disadvantage if previous generations have apportioned all available land according to a strong and exclusive conception of private ownership.[18] Thus it is evident that the natural rights approach to the justification of private ownership is susceptible to a critique whereby the precepts upon which such arguments are based are liable to be used by thinkers not enamoured of private ownership to attack that idea. Winstanley was such a thinker.

It is important to have it understood that the claim being advanced here is not that Winstanley emerges as a natural rights thinker of the calibre of Grotius, Pufendorf, or Locke. Rather, it is being suggested that the contemporary development of natural rights theories as a mode of discourse influenced Winstanley to the extent that he was able to use this way of thinking to hone his ideas into the utopian communism of *The Law of Freedom*.

Winstanley's views on the origins of property and of 'creation rights' are stringent and preclude lines of argument utilized by advocates of the natural rights basis of private ownership. His notion of the 'common treasury' is strictly applied; God's intention is that land and resources are to be communally owned. Furthermore, and commensurate with this principle, Winstanley's conception of the individual's birthright entails not only inalienable natural liberty but also the supposition that to exercise such right the individual must have access to the use and enjoyment of the 'common treasury'. Thus, Winstanley must be read as assuming that the ideal of communal ownership rendered operational via some principle of usufruct would successfully negotiate conflicts of rights to the extent that successive generations might continue to exercise inalienable natural rights.

Winstanley's understanding of the inalienability of natural rights accords with his belief that the loss of such rights, or their contravention to the effect that they cannot be exercised, is morally and spiritually damaging to the person. Hence his declamation of the hiring of labour in exchange, an activity apprehended by Winstanley as a manifestation of coercive social relationships.

These views sustain Winstanley's beliefs in the manner in which forms of ownership might or might not be justified. In Winstanley's opinion, there could be no justification for the private ownership of productive resources. The only explanation, therefore, of the existence of such ownership is that such property is both acquired and sustained illegitimately, by 'conquest'. The theory of labour entitlement cannot establish exclusive property rights for the individual. On the occasions when Winstanley draws upon the notion of labour entitlement he does so to assert the collective claims of the Digger commune. Nor, according to Winstanley, is any principle of rectification available to legitimize existing private ownership. Although he employs a rights-based theory of necessity, Winstanley treats with great suspicion the notion that propertied individuals should behave charitably towards the needy. Instead, such individuals should, according to Winstanley, relinquish their claims to private holdings.

The enhanced conceptual sensitivity to the idea of ownership achieved during the early modern period influenced Winstanley to the effect that he provides in the depiction of his utopian commonwealth a more refined apprehension of forms of ownership than that offered by More in *Utopia*. It is demonstrated above that Winstanley's differentiation of a sphere of communal ownership, pertaining to productive resources, from a sphere of private ownership, pertaining to the habits of consumption practised by the household, sustains what he sees as the broader moral justification of his proposals for the spiritual recovery of Man.

Winstanley's use of natural rights arguments to cast doubt upon the legitimacy of the private ownership of land and resources not only exposes weaknesses in the natural rights basis of private ownership that had been implicitly acknowledged for three centuries, but also foreshadows some of the ideas of a range of thinkers, including Thomas Paine, the 'Ricardian socialists', Herbert Spencer, and Henry George, on the general issue of the 'land problem'.[19]

Changing intellectual perspectives

Thomas More's utopia is a design for a largely static society dedicated to the promotion of moral rectitude. Gerrard Winstanley's utopia envisages not only the spiritual regeneration of the individual but also the progressive amelioration of the human condition through scientific and technological innovation. The respective worldview of More and Winstanley differ markedly in terms of the facility to improve upon the circumstances of life each considered Man to possess. An explanation so far as is possible, of this difference of perception is to be sought not in any fundamental societal transformation that occurred between 1516 and 1652, but in the intellectual changes that had begun to inform the world of ideas by the mid-seventeenth century. While it is possible to identify certain philosophical landmarks which indicate that a profound change of perspective was under way, it is far more difficult to trace and account for the popularization of a changing worldview and the general shift of intellectual atmosphere that had evidently taken place by the late seventeenth century.

1

The temptation exists simply to regard Winstanley as a thinker who possessed that commitment to the notion of 'progress' so evidently lacking in More's social philosophy. This inclination should be withstood until clarification is attained as to which, if any, of the various understandings of the term 'progress' it is appropriate to regard More as denying and

Winstanley as supporting.[20] Disagreement occurs, for example, as to whether progress entails chronological change and improvement of an indefinite kind or whether progress through time is towards some identifiable goal and objective.[21] The concept of progress is problematical not least because it may be invoked to denote both the (irreconcilable) conditions of constant change and movement towards a predetermined end.[22]

The attempt to attribute to the concept of progress specific criteria, such as the attainment of material prosperity, is as fraught with difficulty as the endeavour to be similarly precise about utopianism. Even seeking to define progress in terms of its association with a linear conception of history calls for caution because the converse assumption does not necessarily hold; belief in a linear history does not necessarily entail a commitment to the idea of progress. It is argued that the Greeks lacked an appreciation of progress because they maintained a cyclical theory of history which in turn sustained the belief that human circumstances were intermittently susceptible to improvement and deterioration.[23] Although this view was superseded by the Judaeo-Christian linear understanding of history, confidence in human progress did not arise as a consequence. Particularly under the influence of Augustine, Christianity posited the notion that, until the Apocalypse, time would elapse without any improvement in Man's conditions and indeed with the prospect of some degeneration.[24]

Neither the conviction that human well-being is susceptible to arbitrary fortune nor the belief that human history is informed by divine providence is conducive to the understanding that Man possesses a capacity to determine his destiny and thereby to achieve an improvement in his circumstances. This is because the basic criterion of the notion of progress apprehended by thinkers such as Winstanley is confidence in and anticipation of the resolution of the human predicament even when the precise means whereby that improvement will be attained cannot necessarily be specified. Thus, the respective positions of More and Winstanley on the issue of Man's competence to progress confirm Keith Thomas's view that 'the difference between the eighteenth and sixteenth centuries lies not in achievement but in aspiration'.[25]

2

The intellectual transformation characteristic of the early modern period and the revision of the worldview occasioned in large part by the 'scientific revolution'[26] is, in terms both of its nature and its causes, a vastly complex phenomenon to evaluate. However, it is clear that, for whatever reasons, contemporary observers such as Winstanley were aware that the revised understanding of the physical universe carried implications which meant that a change of outlook would not be confined to natural philosophy. The breakdown of the Aristotelian-Ptolemaic conception of the universe ultimately threatened the synthesis relating this view to established Christian doctrines such as those informing conventional appreciations of the Fall of Man and Man's place in the universe. The corollaries of these developments for social philosophy were bound to be profound.

The amended perception of the human domain promoted revised evaluations of Man's predicament and of his capacity to alleviate that situation. To some minds the development and prosecution of the experimental method entailed the supposition that by achieving a more comprehensive and credible understanding of nature, Man's facility to control the natural environment might be enhanced. The replacement of a geocentric conception of the cosmos with a heliocentric and ultimately an acentric and infinite perception of the universe invalidated belief in the immutability of the heavens, and in the natural and spiritual ordering of the world in terms of a 'great chain of being'. The evidence uncovered by the new scientific method undermined the physical basis of the belief that Man inhabited a region of sublunar degeneracy, yet the impact of this discovery cut both ways. While the revised cosmology could be taken as a complement to human dignity it also served to remind men that they inhabited just one planet in a vast universe, a view which threatened to challenge the Christian account of Man's uniqueness. Thus, speculation on the existence of God and the revised conceptions of God sponsored in conjunction with the new cosmology might have produced a substantial crisis of confidence had not these avenues of enquiry brought to light a considerable consolation. The discovery of what was apprehended as a mechanical universe, an order regulated by natural laws applying equally to celestial and terrestrial phenomena, certainly appeared to leave Man to his own devices by diminishing belief in the immanent intervention in his life of God and other supernatural forces, and by encouraging a tendency to delineate the natural and supernatural spheres; but the scientific disclosures which inspired such secularism appeared to provide Man with the means of determining his own affairs and future. It is a theme of the work of Herschel Baker that, during the course of the seventeenth century, the long-established balance of reason and revelation was disturbed to such an extent that the complexion of God's sovereignty was radically amended as new grounds for confidence in the powers of Man emerged.[27]

The relationship between the social theory of the mid- to late-seventeenth century and the concomitant restructuring of natural philosophy is a complex and often elusive one. What is evident is that the impact of this revised worldview entailed the questioning of certain assumptions previously regarded as axiomatic to social thought. For instance, the new cosmology as discerned via natural laws revealed what appeared as a harmonious universe whereas previously it had been assumed that this arrangement had been disrupted by the Fall of Man. Increasingly, investigations of the physical universe rendered questionable the political and social theory informed by the established appreciation of the doctrine of the Fall. By the end of the seventeenth century a reasonably substantial body of opinion existed to support the view that God—the God, for instance, of 'Newtonian Deism'—should be conceived as first cause, the *primum mobile* of a mechanistic universe, evident as effect in creation yet no longer providential. Baker captures the essence of this outlook in remarking that 'causality is seen to lie in the inherent mathematical harmony of the universe, a harmony that both describes the way things are and the reason that they are that way'.[28] Thus evil and misfortune need no longer be explained with reference to religion or to magic but could instead by accepted as explicable in terms of the natural laws regulating the entire universe. In certain quarters this rationale encouraged a spirit not only of optimism concerning the future but of confidence in Man's capacity to determine a future that would be an improvement upon the present.

3

The new understanding of the regularity of the laws governing the universe encouraged greater confidence in the belief that human activity could be similarly comprehended. The notion that, just as scientific knowledge could benefit Man by affording the means of controlling and ultimately exploiting the physical environment, by similarly discerning the 'laws' of human interaction perceived societal shortcomings might also be remedied, is one which gathered adherents during the course of the eighteenth century.[29] The intellectual atmosphere informing Enlightenment social theory represents a development of some of the then incipient assumptions which influenced Winstanley's utopianism.

As a means of gaining an insight into the influences bearing upon Winstanley and of understanding more precisely quite how and why the ideals promoted by Winstanley's social thought differ from those supported by More, it is opportune to consider briefly the work of Francis Bacon and, more especially, the impact of his writings. As quite possibly the work of the most eager early modern advocate of Man's potential for scientific and social progress, Bacon's writings illuminate our understanding of the changing worldview, not least because his aspirations were formulated in anticipation, and often without any precise awareness, of the scientific and technological means to their attainment. The popularization of 'Baconianism' substantially affected Winstanley's view of the world.

Bacon announces as his purpose the intention to 'lay more firmly the foundations, and extend more widely the limits, of the power and greatness of man'.[30] Clearly, a project of this kind presupposes the advocacy of a linear conception of human progress, one which brings into question established tendencies to regard the thought of 'the Ancients' as authoritative.[31] For Bacon, modernity implies wisdom; 'rightly', he argues, 'is truth called the daughter of time, not of authority'.[32] In this manner Bacon insists upon the eschewance of the cyclical view of scientific advance and recession and instead commends a radically revised appreciation of human potential. Bacon advances as a proposition crucial to his promotion of an amended worldview the following type of claim: 'by far the greatest obstacle to the progress of science and to the undertaking of new tasks and provinces therein, is found in this—that men despair and think things impossible'.[33] The requisite counter to the pessimism encouraged by resignation in the face of capricious fortune or of providence, argues Bacon, must be the installation of a far more positive attitude to the problems confronting Man; 'the mould of man's fortune', he writes, 'is in his own hands'.[34] It is, then, hardly surprising to discover Bacon proposing a stricter delineation of philosophy and theology than had previously been the norm.[35] In evaluating mankind's overall predicament Bacon concludes that

> man by the fall fell at the same time from his state of innocency and from his dominion over creation. Both of these losses however can even in this life be in some part repaired; the former by religion and faith, and the latter by arts and sciences.[36]

In discussing the wherewithal of effecting the second part of this design, the improvement of Man's more immediate circumstances, Bacon dwells especially on three major themes. First, Bacon believes that much of the adversity evident in the human condition persists not directly as an ineradicable consequence of the Fall but in good part as the result of Man's own folly, which could in principle be rectified. According to Bacon, the most pronounced instances of Man's erroneous judgement are discernible in existing scientific method. In claiming to reject the established syllogistic method which, he argues, mistakenly deduces general axioms from particular instances and merely encourages an over-reliance upon authority and received opinion, Bacon supports an inductive method founded upon experiment, according to which general axioms are to be ascertained via a gradual derivation from particular instances and 'middle axioms'.[37] It is questionable whether Bacon's proposed new method represents as dramatic a departure from the syllogism as he appears to have believed.[38] Nevertheless, given his commitment to a conception of progress characterized by aspiration, it was imperative for Bacon's purpose that he should regard the experimental method as a means of offsetting certain consequences of the Fall. Scientific advance is thus postulated as a remedy for the shortcomings of men through affirmations to the effect that 'it is a false assertion that the sense of man is the measure of all things'.[39] In advocating the quantitative measurement as opposed to the qualitative evaluation of nature, Bacon expected matter rather than substance to become the object of scientific enquiry. Indeed, according to Bacon, the scientific method could itself counter human fallibility if experiments were devised in such a way as to constrain men to proceed as required. Crucially, Bacon insists that experimental enquiry should attempt only to discern efficient causes. This, rather than the search for first causes, should define the limits of scientific investigation.

Second, Bacon is not unaware of the controversy likely to be occasioned by the advocacy of a rigorous approach to the investigation of nature and to the pursuit of knowledge. His reaction is to assign to natural philosophy the investigation of efficient causes only, while reserving for theology the revelation of first causes. Through this delineation Bacon attempts to repudiate the association of the search for scientific knowledge with that form of curiosity which led Adam and Eve to precipitate the Fall. The investigation of nature, he maintains, is a legitimate province of human enquiry which should not be confused with the desire to emulate God, by seeking to attain moral knowledge of good and evil.[40] 'Knowledge now being discharged of that venom which the serpent infused into it',[41] Bacon proceeds to establish the proper purpose of knowledge acquired through the experimental investigation of nature. Accordingly, he consistently adheres to certain basic propositions. He maintains that 'human knowledge and human power meet in one',[42] and that 'truth . . . and utility are . . . the very same'.[43] Thus, the utilitarian application of scientific knowledge is a pervading principle of Bacon's thought. The extent to which Bacon aspired to use science for the improvement of human life is evident in his description, in *New Atalantis*, of the scientific institution 'Salomon's House'. Here Bacon envisages the ultimate 'knowledge of the Causes and secret motions of things; and the enlarging of the bounds of Human Empire, to be effecting of all things possible',[44]

Third, Bacon addresses the widely held assumption that, as a consequence of the Fall, Man's domain over nature was forfeit. His belief is that, by the means already specified, human power would be so increased as to recover the dominion over nature. Bacon also surmises that the contemplation of His Creation by Man would be pleasing to God. It is important to establish that although Thomas More would have accepted this view, the aggressive facet of Baconianism, by which the experimental knowledge of nature is conceived as a means of enhancing power and progress through the control of the environment, is irreconcilable with More's assessment of limited human potential. Clearly, Bacon is to be discovered articulating a revised worldview. Hence the following confident proposal: 'let the human race recover that right over nature which belongs to it by divine bequest, and let power be given it; the exercise thereof will be governed by sound reason and true religion'.[45] These are sentiments later to be applauded by Winstanley.

4

The restrained attitude to the issue of social progress evident in *Utopia* accords with More's disparaging assessment of human conduct as evinced by the mores and practices of his own society. This overall outlook is illustrated by More's treatment of two aspects of life later to become important constituents of the Baconian project—education and science.[46] For More, the primary purpose of education is moral; even when recommended as a pleasurable experience, the educational provisions of *Utopia* remain basic to More's design for the cultivation of virtue. Thus More's intention is that education he conceived as a guide to individual conduct rather that as a means of projecting Man as a whole towards the progressive amelioration of his predicament. The use ascribed by More to science and technology is imbued with a similar intent. We are told that the Utopians enjoy contemplating nature and prove receptive to technological innovation, but we are given no indication of any design for a scientific programme or of any activity in the direction of seeking to ascertain knowledge for utilitarian reasons. Hence, in distinguishing More's views on education, science and progress form Winstanley's, it is not inappropriate to cite Bacon, who in arguing for an ordered methodology comments that 'simple experience, . . . if taken as it comes, is called accident; if sought for experiment.'[47]

The textual evidence suggesting Winstanley's adherence to elements of Baconianism is supported by circumstantial evidence to the effect that Winstanley was in all likelihood acquainted with aspects of the new science. It is, therefore, reasonable to assume that Winstanley was influenced by the early stages of the process by which, as the seventeenth century progressed, the new scientific and philosophical ideas maintained by the intellectual elite percolated down through society.[48] This impression is confirmed by Charles Webster's painstaking investigation into the popularization of Baconian philosophy,[49] a movement that was especially pronounced during the Civil War when thinkers such as Samual Hartlib, John Dury and Jan Comenius actively promoted the dissemination of Baconian ideas. More particularly, Winstanley's works can be scrutinized for hints of his familiarity with the writings and ideas of individual members of the scientific community. It is, for example, suggested that at one point in *The Law of Freedom* Winstanley reveals an awareness of the work of William Harvey.[50]

The analysis of Winstanley's utopian commonwealth offered above supports the view that he was deeply influenced by popular Baconianism, and by the changing emphases of the general worldview. Winstanley's experimentalism and hostility to received ideas in any sphere of human activity, and most especially in religion, represents an extension of a principle supported by Bacon. Winstanley's evaluation of education is similarly sympathetic to the Baconian ideal. While certainly conceiving of education as possessing a moral aspect, Winstanley's educational programme espouses a pronounced utilitarian rationale. In associating education with experimentalism, Winstanley evidently believed that men should be taught how to investigate nature in order not only that the spiritual felicity of the individual might be secured but also that Mankind as a whole should benefit from the dissemination of experimental discoveries. Thus, Winstanley's arguments for education extend, through his emphasis upon the experimental method, to his advocacy of scientific research. Although these ideas are often crudely formulated, Winstanley again associates himself with the principles of Baconianism. For instance, he argues that the experimental method entails the restriction of enquiry to efficient rather than to final causes. Thus he asks 'what other knowledge have you of God, but what you have within the circle of Creation?'[51] Perhaps more importantly, and on this point he is very much at odds with More, Winstanley advances the following recommendation:

> If any through industry or ripeness of understanding have found out any secret in Nature, or new invention in any Art or Trade, or in the Tillage of the Earth, or such like, whereby the Commonwealth may more flourish in peace and plenty; for which Vertues those persons received honor in the places where they dwelt.
>
> When other parts of the Land hear of it, many thereby will be encouraged to employ their Reason and industry to do the like, that so in time there will not be any Secret in Nature which now lies hid . . . but by some or other will be brought to light, to the beauty of our Commonwealth.[52]

This proposal encapsulates several vital aspects of the changing worldview. It involves not only an emphasis upon the utilitarian application of scientific discovery and the insistence upon the organized communication of such knowledge, but also the understanding that Man could justifiably aspire to the radical improvement of his condition.

5

Leaving aside the question of precisely how successful as a philosophical project *Utopia* actually is, it remains evident that a guiding principle of Thomas More's social theory is the conviction that institutional reform ought to be sought in order that men be trained in virtue so that they may, if at all possible, attain their salvation. Nearly a century and a half after the publication of *Utopia*, Gerrard Winstanley advanced the view that institutional reform could facilitate not only a form of spiritual restoration on earth, but also the restitution of both socio-political liberties and the dominion over nature. Later still, certain social theorists of the Enlightenment would speculate upon the idea of the perfectibility of Man. Whereas Thomas More's writings pre-date the development of secular aspiration, the works of Gerrard Winstanley are those of a thinker who lived through a transitional phase of increasing optimism. In answer, therefore, to the question why Winstanley's ideas on Man's predicament and the amelioration of that situation differed so markedly from More's, it is necessary to establish the manner in which Winstanley's writings reflect intellectual developments which in turn stimulated a more optimistic appraisal of the human condition. However, more fundamental problems arise once an *explanation* of such progressivism is demanded. While it is possible to cite a plethora of 'causes' for the type of intellectual upsurge associated with the early modern period, such explanations often fail to convince completely. In the main this is because greater optimism and the 'idea of progress' arose before many of the assumptions which would appear prerequisite to such belief had in fact been validated.[53] So while it is possible to provide a plausible analysis of the thought of the two major utopian social philosophers of early modern England, and to relate their writings to contemporary developments in political thought and property theory, the question of why the intellectual context respectively informing *Utopia* and *The Law of Freedom* had changed so considerably is one to be approached with appreciable caution.

Notes

Notes to chapter 1

1. H. Arendt, *The Human Condition* (Chicago, 1958), p. 9.
2. M. Oakeshott, Introduction to T. Hobbes, *Leviathan* (Oxford, 1946), p. ix.
3. Ibid., p. xi.
4. Ibid., p. ix.
5. J.B. Plamenatz, 'The Use of Political Theory' in A. Quinton (ed.), *Political Philosophy* (Oxford, 1967), p. 29. See also the introduction to J.B. Plamenatz, *Man and Society* (London, 1963).
6. A.O. Lovejoy, *The Great Chain of Being* (Cambridge, MA, 1936, 1964 edn), p. 15 and *passim*.
7. I. Berlin, 'Does Political Theory Still Exist?' in P. Laslett and W.G. Runciman (eds), *Politics, Philosophy and Society*, 2nd series (Oxford, 1962), p. 28, see also pp. 16–19, 29–31.
8. J. Dunn, 'The Identity of the History of Ideas', *Phil.*, XLIII (1968), p. 96.
9. Ibid., pp. 98–9.
10. See B. Parekh and R.N. Berki, 'History of Political Ideas: A Critique of Q. Skinner's Methodology', *JHI*, XXIV (1973), p. 184.
11. T.S. Kuhn, *The Structure of Scientific Revolutions* (Chicago, 1962, 1970 edn), p. viii. The definition used here is the first, and standard, but not Kuhn's only definition of a paradigm.
12. Ibid., p. 12.
13. S. Wolin, 'Paradigms and Political Theories' in P. King and B.C. Parekh (eds), *Politics and Experience: Essays Presented to Michael Oakeshott* (Cambridge, 1968), esp. pp. 139, 148–51.
14. L. Wittgenstein, *Philosophical Investigations* (Oxford, 1953, 1958 edn), sect. 43.
15. J.L. Austin, *How To Do Things With Words*, ed. J.O. Urmson (Oxford, 1962, 1975 edn), p. 94.
16. Ibid., p. 121.
17. Ibid., pp. 115–17, 121ff.
18. P.F. Strawson, 'Intentions and Conventions in Speech Acts', *PR*, 78 (1969), pp. 443–5.
19. Ibid., p. 454; see also pp. 450–3.
20. See H.P. Grice, 'Meaning', *PR*, 66 (1957); and, more particularly, his revised account 'Utterer's Meanings and Intentions, *PR*, 78 (1969).

21. Ibid., p. 158.
22. J.G.A. Pocock, *Politics, Language and Time* (London, 1970), p. 15.
23. J.G.A. Pocock, 'The Only Politician: Machiavelli, Harrington, and Felix Raab', *Historical Studies: Australia and New Zealand*, 12 (1966), p. 268.
24. J.G.A. Pocock, 'Verbalizing a Political Act: Towards a Politics of Speech', *PT*, 1 (1973), p. 31.
25. Pocock, *Politics, Language and Time*, p. 25.
26. For a recent restatement of the analytical approach, see B. Williams, 'Political Philosphy and the Analytical Tradition', in M. Richter (ed.), *Political Theory and Political Education* (Princeton, NJ, 1980).
27. See, for example, J.G.A. Pocock, 'Political Ideas as Historical Events: Political Philosophers as Historical Actors', in Richter, op.cit.; Pocock, 'The Machiavellian Moment Revisited: A Study in History and Ideology', *JMH*, 53 (1981).
28. J.G.A. Pocock, 'The Concept of a Language and the *metier d'historien*: Some Considerations on Practice' in A. Pagden (ed.), *The Languages of Political Theory in Early-Modern Europe* (Cambridge, 1987), p. 20.
29. On methodology, see, for example, the following works by Q. Skinner: 'The Limits of Historical Explanations', *HJ*, 8 (1966); 'Meaning and Understanding in the History of Ideas', *H & T*, 8 (1969); 'Conventions and the Understanding of Speech Acts', *P. Qtly*, 20 (1970); 'On Performing and Explaining Linguistic Actions', *P. Qtly*, 21 (1971); ' "Social Meaning" and the Explanation of Social Action' in P. Laslett, W.G. Runciman and Q. Skinner (eds), *Politics, Philosophy and Society*, 4th series (Oxford, 1972); 'Motives, Intentions and the Interpretation of Texts', *New Literary History*, 3 (1972); 'Some Problems in the Analysis of Political Thought and Action', *PT*, 2 (1974); 'The Role of History', *Cambridge Review*, 95 (1974); 'Hermeneutics and the Role of History', *New Literary History*, 7 (1975–6); 'The Idea of a Cultural Lexicon', *Essays in Criticism*, XXIX (1979); and, with M. Hollis, 'Action and Context', *Proceedings of the Aristotelian Society*, Supp. Vol. LII (1978).
30. Skinner, 'Hermeneutics and the Role of History', p. 217.
31. Skinner, 'Meaning and Understanding in the History of Ideas', pp. 37–8, on Wittgenstein.
32. Ibid., pp. 43–9.
33. Ibid., p. 51; and Skinner, 'Conventions and the Understanding of Speech Acts', pp. 125–6.
34. Skinner, 'On Performing and Explaining Linguistic Actions', p. 13.
35. Ibid., p. 3.
36. See, for example, Skinner, 'Conventions and the Understanding of Speech Acts', p. 121.
37. Skinner, 'Hermeneutics and the Role of History', p. 212.
38. See, for example, Skinner, 'Some Problems in the Analysis of Political Thought and Action'.
39. Skinner's response to accusations that he neglects this issue is contained in ibid., *passim*.
40. Q. Skinner, *The Foundations of Modern Political Thought* (Cambridge, 1978), see, for example, Vol. I., p. xi.
41. D. Boucher, *Texts in Context: Revisionist Methods for Studying the History of Ideas* (Dordecht, 1985).
42. See, for example, R.E. Goodin, 'Laying Linguistic Traps', *PT*, 5 (1977), p. 491 and *passim*.
43. See, for example, A. Ryan, ' "Normal" Science or Political Ideology?' in *P.P.S.*, 4th series; Boucher, op. cit., p. 64; J.V. Femia, 'An Historical Critique of "Revisionist" Methods for Studying the History of Ideas', *H & T*, XX

(1979); *idem*, *Gramsci's Political Thought: Hegemony, Consciousness, and the Revolutionary Process* (Oxford, 1981), p. 16.

44. Parekh and Berki, op cit., p. 184; and J. Higham, 'Intellectual History and Its Neighbours', *JHI*, XV (1954).
45. L. Mulligan *et al.* 'Intentions and Conventions: a Critique of Quentin Skinner's Method for the Study of the History of Ideas', *PS*, XXVII (1979), pp. 85–8.
46. See, for example, G.J. Schochet, 'Quentin Skinner's Method', *PT*, 2 (1973), pp. 270–2.
47. C.D. Tarlton, 'Historicity, Meaning and Revisionism in the Study of Political Thought', *H & T*, 12 (1973), p. 323.
48. Ibid., p. 326; and Parekh and Berki, op. cit., p. 168.
49. Femia, *Gransei's Political Thought*: this line is also advanced by Boucher, op. cit.
50. See A. MacIntyre, 'The Essential Contestability of Some Social Concepts', *Ethics*, 84 (1974), pp. 1–2; W.E. Connolly, *The Terms of Political Discourse* (Lexington, MA, 1974), pp. 22–5.
51. W.B. Gallie, 'Essentially Contested Concepts', *Proceedings of the Aristotelian Society*, LVI (1956), pp. 167–8, 179.
52. Ibid., p. 169.
53. Ibid., p. 168.
54. Ibid., pp. 177, 188–91.
55. Connolly, op. cit., p. 20; see also E. Gellner, *Contemporary Thought and Politics* (London, 1974), p. 95.
56. Gallie, op. cit., p. 175.
57. Ibid., pp. 171–2, 180.
58. Ibid., p. 172.
59. Ibid., p. 180.
60. Ibid., p. 178.
61. J.N. Gray, 'On the Contestability of Social and Political concepts', *PT*, 5 (1977), p. 345.
62. Gallie, op. cit., pp. 168, 176; Connolly, op. cit., pp. 30–3; J. Kekes, 'Essentially Contested Concepts: A Reconsideration', *Philosophy and Rhetoric*, 10 (1977), pp. 72, 76; Gray, op. cit., pp. 333, 342.
63. Connolly, op. cit., p. 10; see also Kekes, op. cit., 80–1.
64. Compare this to the claims advanced on behalf of operationalism by Connolly, op. cit., p. 15.
65. See MacIntyre, op. cit., p. 8, and Kekes, op. cit., p. 73. I am indebted also to J.F. Lively's unpublished paper, 'Essentially Contested Concepts: A Re-appraisal'.
66. Cf. Skinner, *Foundations of Modern Political Thought*, Vol. I., and Gray, op. cit.; *idem*, 'On Liberty, Liberalism and Essential Contestability', *British Journal of Political Science*, 8 (1978).
67. Recent consideration of utopianism in political thought includes B. Goodwin, *Social Science and Utopia: Nineteenth-Century Models of Social Harmony* (Brighton, 1979); F.E. Manuel and F.P. Manuel, *Utopian Thought in the Western World* (Oxford, 1979); J.C. Davis, *Utopia and the Ideal Society: a Study of English Utopian Writing* (Cambridge, 1981).
68. As in Q. Skinner, 'Sir Thomas More's Utopia and the language of Renaissance humanism', in Pagden, op. cit.
69. See, for example, F.E. Manuel (ed.), *Utopias and Utopian Thought* (London, 1965), p. xiv; R. Nozick, *Anarchy, State and Utopia* (Oxford, 1974), p. 309.
70. B. de Jouvenal, 'Utopia for Practical Purposes', *Daedalus*, 94 (1965), pp. 437.
71. See L.S. Feuer, 'The Influence of American Communist Colonies of Engels and Marx', *The Western Political Quarterly*, XIX (1966).

72. K. Marx, 'The Débat Social of February 6 on the Democratic Association', *Works*, 6, p. 538.
73. K. Marx, 'The Poverty of Philosophy ', *Works*, 6, p. 138, cf. p. 210.
74. K. Marx and F. Engels, *The Manifesto of the Communist Party* in *Works*, 6, p. 517; see also F. Engels, *Socialism: Utopian and Scientific* (London, 1875).
75. Marx and Engels, *Manifesto*, p. 517.
76. Ibid., p. 516.
77. Ibid., pp. 515–16.
78. K. Mannheim, *Ideology and Utopia* (London, 1936, 1960 edn), p. 173; and see, in general, pp. 173–236.
79. Ibid., pp. 176–7.
80. Ibid., p. 185.
81. See, for example, J.K. Fuz, *Welfare Economics in English Utopias from Francis Bacon to Adam Smith*, (The Hague, 1952); W.E. Moore, 'The Utility of Utopias', *American Sociological Review*, 31 (1966).
82. On this propensity see J.C. Davis, 'Utopias and History', *Historical Studies*, XIII (1968), p. 168.
83. J.N. Shklar, 'The Political Theory of Utopia: From Melancholy to Nostalgia', *Daedalus*, 94 (1965), pp. 367–9.
84. J.N. Shklar, *After Utopia: The Decline of Political Faith* (Princeton, NJ 1957), *passim*.
85. Ibid., p. 19.
86. Davis, *Utopia and Ideal Society*, p. 31.
87. See, for example, P. Bloomfield, *Imaginary Worlds* (London, 1932); G. Kateb, *Utopia and Its Enemies* (London, 1963).
88. See, for example, Davis, *op. cit.*; G. Negley and J. Max Patrick, *The Quest for Utopia* (Baltimore, 1971).
89. See, for example, H. Child, 'Some English Utopias', *Transactions of the Royal Society of Literature*, XII (1933).
90. Spinoza, *Ethics*, Pt IV; see J. Passmore, *The Perfectibility of Man* (London, 1970), p. 23.
91. See, for example, E.L. Tuveson, *Millennium and Utopia* (New York, 1949), pp. 8–10, and index, 'Utopia, see millennium'.
92. T. Kenyon, 'Utopia in Reality: "Ideal" Societies in Social and Political Thought', *History of Political Thought*, III (1982), pp. 139–49.
93. See B.S. Capp, 'Extreme Millenarianism', in P. Toon (ed.), *Puritans, the Millennium and the Future of Israel* (Cambridge, 1970), p. 75; *idem*, *The Fifth Monarchy Men: A Study in Seventeenth-Century English Millenarianism*, chs 6 and 7.
94. Davis, 'Utopias and History', p. 172.
95. B.S. Capp, 'Godly Rule and English Millenarianism', *P & P*, 52 (1970), p. 107; *idem*, 'The Millenium and Eschatology in England', *P & P*, 57 (1971), p. 158.
96. Capp, 'Godly Rule', p. 107.
97. Davis, 'Utopias and History', p. 174; see also *idem*, *Utopia and Ideal Society*, p. 34.
98. See F. Bloch-Laine, 'The Utility of Utopias for Reformers', *Daedalus*, 94 (1965), p. 424.
99. W.H. Greenleaf, *Order, Empiricism and Politics: Two Traditions of English Political Thought 1500–1700* (London, 1964), p. 30.
100. C. Webster, *The Great Instauration: Science, Medicine and Reform 1626–1660* (London, 1975), p. 19.
101. C. Hill, 'The Norman Yoke' in *idem*, *Puritanism and Revolution* (London, 1958), p. 51.

102. For an analysis of such perceptions and of the resort to supernatural means of counteracting the situation, see K.V. Thomas, *Religion and the Decline of Magic* (London, 1971).
103. These concerns are considered in W.J. MacDonald, 'Communism in Eden', *The New Scholasticism*, XX (1946).
104. see A.J. Carlyle, *A History of Medieval Political Thought in the West*, Vol. I (Edinburgh, 1936), p. 110ff.
105. See, Passmore, op. cit., p. 86.
106. See R. Schlatter, *Property: The History of an Idea* (London, 1951), pp. 48–55.
107. See, for example, G.J. Schochet, *Patriarchalism in Political Thought* (Oxford, 1975), pp. 226–8, and *passim*.
108. Hobbes, *EW*, Vol III, ch. XXXVIII, esp. pp. 437–9.
109. B. Willey, *The Seventeenth-Century Background* (London, 1934, 1972 edn), p. 35.
110. See n. 99.
111. Webster, op. cit., ch. V.i.
112. Thomas, op. cit.; B.S. Capp, *Astrology and the Popular Press: English Almanacs 1500–1800* (London, 1979); and C. Webster, *From Paracelsus to Newton: Magic and the Making of Modern Science* (Cambridge, 1982).
113. K.V. Thomas, *Man and the Natural World; Changing Attitudes in England 1500–1800* (London, 1983), p. 20.
114. See Lovejoy, op. cit.
115. See Greenleaf, op. cit., ch. II, esp. pp. 26–7.
116. Ibid., p. 55.
117. See, for example, M. Walzer, *The Revolution of the Saints: A Study in the Origins of Radical Politics* (London, 1966), p. 268.
118. See, Carlyle, op. cit.; *idem*, 'The Theory of Property in Medieval Theology' in *Property: Its Duties and Rights*, with an introduction by the Bishop of Oxford (London, 1922); Schlatter, op. cit.; R. Tuck, *Natural Rights Theories: Their Origin and Development* (Cambridge, 1979); B. Tierney, 'Tuck on Rights: Some Medieval Problems', *History of Political Thought*, IV (1983); and pages 227–34.
119. Carlyle, 'The Theory of Property in Medieval Theology', p. 128.
120. Schlatter, op. cit., p. 35.
121. See ibid., chs 1–4; Tuck, op. cit., ch. I; and the qualifying critique advanced by Tierney, op. cit.
122. See Tuck, op. cit., pp. 18–9, in the light of Tierney, op. cit., pp. 431–5.
123. On Aquinas's position see pages 46–47.
124. Locke's view that the industrious kind of person should be justly rewarded is brought out in the interpretation offered by J. Dunn, *The Political Thought of John Locke: An Historical Account of the Argument of the 'Two Treatises of Government'* (Cambridge, 1969); and G. Parry, *John Locke* (London, 1978).
125. See Genesis, 3:19.
126. R. Hooker, 'A Learned Sermon on the Nature of Pride' (pub. 1612) in J. Keble (eds.) *The Works of Mr. Richard Hooker*, Vol, III (Oxford, 1888), p. 602.
127. For the ideas of Francis Bacon on these matters see pages 237–240.
128. J. Milton, *The Doctrine and Discipline of Divorce* (1643) in *Prose Works*, Vol. II, p. 228.
129. J. Milton, *Areopagitica* (1644) in *Prose Works*, Vol II, p. 527.
130. J. Milton, *An Apology Against a Pamphlet* (1642) in *Prose Works*, Vol. I, p. 909.
131. Milton, *Areopagitica*, p. 514.
132. J. Milton, *The Tenure of Kings and Magistrates* (1649) in *Prose Works*, Vol. III, pp. 198–9.
133. J. Milton, *Tetrachordon* (1645) in *Prose Works*, Vol. II, p. 587.

134. J. Locke, *An Essay Concerning Human Understanding* (1690) in *Works*, Vols I and II, Bk. I, 'Of Innate Notions'.
135. For a recent critical re-evaluation of this view of Locke, see W.M. Spellman, *John Locke and the Problem of Depravity* (Oxford, 1988).
136. J. Locke, *The Reasonableness of Christianity* (1695) in *Works*, Vol VII, p. 8; and see also *idem*, *Essays on the Law of Nature*, ed. W. von Leyden (Oxford, 1954), p. 139, n.2.
137. E.M. Tillyard, *The Elizabethan World Picture* (Harmondsworth, 1963), p. 62.

Notes to chapter 2

1. In recent years this appreciation of post-Enlightenment moral philosophy has been emphasized by A. MacIntyre, *After Virtue: A Study in Moral Theory* (London, 1981), and *idem*, *Whose Justice? Which Rationality?* (London, 1988).
2. I have found the following particularly useful; A.H. Armstrong (ed.), *The Cambridge History of Later Greek and Early Medieval Philosophy* (Cambridge, 1967); N. Kretzmann *et al.* (eds.), *The Cambridge History of Later Medieval Philosophy* (Cambridge, 1982); C.B. Schmitt, *Aristotle and the Renaissance* (Cambridge, MA, 1983); J.Marenbon, *Later Medieval Philosophy: An Introduction* (London, 1987); C.B.Schmitt *et al.*, *The Cambridge History of Renaissance Philosophy* (Cambridge, 1988); J.H. Burns (ed.), *The Cambridge History of Medieval Political Thought* (Cambridge, 1988).
3. Aristotle, *Ethics* p. 111–7, 205–7 (1110–1, 1139).
4. Ibid., p. 122.
5. A point emphasized by G. Wieland, 'Happiness: The Perfection of Man' in Kretzmann *et al.*, op. cit., p. 674.
6. Augustine, *City*, XIII.
7. Ibid., p. 523.
8. See, for example, P.O. Kristeller. 'Augustine and the Early Renaissance', *Review of Religion*, VIII (1944).
9. For a standard if somewhat unrefined account, see H. Baker, *The Image of Man* (Gloucester, MA, 1975 edn), chs XI and XII.
10. See J.G.A. Pocock, *The Machiavellian Moment* (Princeton, NJ, 1975), p. 67.
11. This is expanded upon in MacIntyre, *Whose Justice? Which Rationality?* ch. IX.
12. See J.B. Korolec, 'Free Will and Free Choice', and D.E. Luscombe, 'Natural Morality and Natural Law', both in Kretzmann *et al.*, op. cit.
13. Augustine, *On Free Will*, reproduced in A. Hyman and J.J. Walsh (eds), *Philosophy in the Middle Ages* (Indianapolis, 1973); and Augustine, *City*, V, 7–11.
14. Augustine, *City*, p. 477.
15. Ibid., pp. 591–2.
16. Aquinas, *ST*, Prima Pars: 19, 22, 82.
17. Korolec, op. cit., pp. 640–1.
18. This analysis draws upon: J.N. Figgis, *The Political Aspects of St Augustine's City of God* (London, 1921); T.E. Mommsen, 'St Augustine and the Christian Idea of Progress', *JHI*, XII (1951); H.A. Deane, *The Political and Social Ideas of St. Augustine* (New York, 1963); R.A. Markus, *Saeculum: History and Society in the Theology of St. Augustine* (Cambridge, 1970); H. Chadwick, *Augustine* (Oxford, 1986).
19. Augustine, *City*, p. 568.
20. Deane, op. cit., p. 117.
21. Augustine, *City*, 9. 877.

22. Ibid., XIX: 24.
23. MacIntyre, op. cit., p. 205.
24. Aquinas, *ST*, Prima Secunda: 2–5.
25. Ibid., Prima Pars: 1.
26. Ibid., Prima Secunda: 92.
27. For an account of 'law' see ibid., Prima Secunda: 94–5.
28. Ibid., Prima Secunda: 94.
29. Ibid., Secunda Secundae: 66.
30. Ibid., Prima Secunda: 94.
31. MacIntyre, op. cit.
32. C.H. Lohr, 'The Medieval Interpretation of Aristotle' in Kretzmann *et al.*, op. cit.
33. See G. Wieland, 'The Reception and Interpretation of Aristotle's "Ethics" ', in Kretzmann *et al.*, op. cit., pp. 671ff.
34. Of the form developed in A.S. McGrade, 'Rights, Natural Rights, and the Philosophy of Law', in Kretzmann *et al.*, op. cit., p. 739.
35. For the circumstances informing the composition of Henry VIII's *Assertio Septem Sacramentorum* and for the details of More's confrontation with Luther, see J.H. Headley, introduction to More, *CW5*; R. Pineas, *Thomas More and Tudor Polemics* (Bloomington, 1968), *passim*; J.J. Scarisbrick, *Henry VIII* (London, 1968), *passim*, esp. p. 153; A. Fox, *Thomas More: History and Providence* (Oxford, 1982), chs 4–5; R. Marius, *Thomas More* (London, 1985), chs 17–18. On More's reputation as theologian, see G. Kernan, 'St. Thomas More Theologian', *Thought*, XVII (1942).
36. See Pineas, op. cit., *passim*; and L.A. Schuster, 'Reformation Polemic and Renaissance Values', *Moreana*, XI (1974), pp. 50–2.
37. See A.I. Taft (ed.), *The Apologye of Syr Thomas More, Knyght*, EETS, original series, 180 (London, 1930), pp. liii–lxiii; and J.B. Trapp, introduction to *CW9*, p. lxxxviii. For More's response to contemporary criticism of his methods, see *CW5*, pp. 5–10.
38. For More's most detailed discussions of ecclesiology see *CW6*.
39. Headley, op. cit, pp. 736–40.
40. More, *CW8*, pp. 119–33.
41. More, *A Dialogue Concerning Heresies* in *EW*, II, p. 122.
42. More, *CW8*, pp. 338–89.
43. More, *Dialogue Concerning Heresies* in *EW*, II, p. 97.
44. Ibid., pp. 143–4; and More, *CW5*, pp. 173, 623–5.
45. More, *CW8*, pp. 419–20, 428, 448, 452–3, 565, 777.
46. More, *Utopia*, pp. 67, 83–5.
47. More's changing position is discussed at length in J.H. Headley, 'Thomas Murner, Thomas More, and the First Expression of More's Ecclesiology', *Studies in the Renaissance*, XIV (1967), pp. 81–9; and *idem*, introduction to More, *CW5*, argues for More's developing support for Papal primacy. This is contested by R. Marius, introduction to More, *CW8*, pp. 1294–1315, who claims that More's English polemical works point towards an alternative thesis indicating More's support for the restraint of Papal authority through some consensually-orientated form of conciliarism. See also D. Hay, 'A Note on More and the General Council', *Moreana*, 15 (1967); D.B. Fenlon, 'England and Europe: Utopia and Its Aftermath', *Transactions of the Royal Historical Society*, 25 (1975), p. 134.
48. More, *CW5*, pp. 133–5.
49. *To Thomas Cromwell* in E.F. Rogers (ed.), *St. Thomas More: Selected Letters* (New Haven, CT, 1961).

50. Cf. R. Mandrou, *From Humanism to Science: 1480–1700* (Harmondsworth 1973) chs 1–3.
51. More, *CW8*, p. 179.
52. Ibid., pp. 956–61.
53. Ibid., pp. 97–101.
54. More, *CW13*, p. 193.
55. More, *Utopia*, p. 233.
56. See R. Marius, 'Thomas More and the Early Church Fathers', *Traditio*, 24 (1968).
57. More, *CW8*, pp. 151–7, 397, 647; and *idem*, *CW12*, pp. 18–28.
58. More, *Dialogue Concerning Heresies* in *EW*, II, pp. 76–7; *idem*, *CW8*, pp. 63, 255–74; and *idem*, *CW12*, p. 32.
59. More, *CW8*, p. 13.
60. More, *Dialogue Concerning Heresies* in *EW*, II, pp. 230–2, 234, 243, 252–3.
61. Ibid., pp. 79–83.
62. More, *The Four Last things* in *EW*, I, p. 467.
63. More, *CW14*, p. 213.
64. More, *A Dialogue Concerning Heresies* in *EW*, II, pp. 42–3.
65. For this theme see More's translation of 'A Prayer of Picus Mirandula, Unto God', *EW*, I, p. 395.
66. More, *CW13*, pp. 6, 18.
67. More, *CW8*, p. 839.
68. More, *CW13*, p. 41.
69. More, *CW8*, pp. 433, 487–9.
70. Ibid., p. 40.
71. More, *Four Last Things* in *EW*, I, p. 462.
72. More, *CW13*, p. 29.
73. Ibid., p. 40.
74. Aquinas, *ST*, Prima Secunda: 71–89.
75. More, *CW13*, p. 63.
76. More, *Four Last Things* in *EW*, I, p. 481, and *passim* for More's most detailed analysis of sin.
77. Ibid., p. 488.
78. More, *CW13*, p. 66.
79. More, *Four Last Things* in *EW*, I, p. 493.
80. A persistent theme of More, *CW14*.
81. Even in his earliest writings More warns against trusting in fortune because of its facility to nourish men's pride prior to inflicting a sudden reversal; see his *Meters for the Boke of Fortune* in *EW*, I.
82. More, *Utopia*, pp. 243–5.
83. More, *CW13*, p. 9; see also ibid., p. 7.
84. For More's impressions on the forms that pride might assume, see his *Four Last Things* in *EW*, I, p. 476–80.
85. More, *CW13*, p. 7.
86. More, *CW12*, p. 158.
87. See H. Oberman, *The Harvest of Medieval Philosophy* (Cambridge, MA, 1963), p. 222.
88. Cf. the general thesis of J.H. Hexter. See, for example, his introduction to *Utopia*; and his *More's Utopia: The Biography of an Idea* (Princeton, NJ, 1952).
89. More, *CW14*, pp. 169–71.
90. Ibid., p. 641.
91. More, *CW12*, p. 253.
92. More, *CW8*, pp. 427–35.

93. More, *CW8*, pp. 229ff.
94. See H. Hopfl, *The Christian Polity of John Calvin* (Cambridge, 1982).
95. See Marius, *Thomas More and the Early Church Fathers*, p. 384, and J.H. Headley, 'More Against Luther', *Moreana*, 15 (1967), *passim*.
96. More, *Dialogue Concerning Heresies* in *EW*, II, p. 277; see also ibid., pp. 279–80.
97. More, *CW8*, p. 799.
98. This notwithstanding, by the mid-1520s Luther was advancing an essentially authoritarian account of political obligation: see, for example, his 'Temporal Authority: To What Extent it Should be Obeyed' (1523), trans. J.J. Shindal, in W.I. Brandt (ed.), *Luther's Works*, 45 (Philadelphia, 1962). This and later works such as Tyndale's 'The Obedience of a Christian Man', in H. Walter (ed.), *Tyndale's Doctrinal Treatises &c.*, 32 (Cambridge, 1832), failed to dissuade More from the opinion that Protestant doctrine was potentially subversive.
99. More, *CW8*, p. 513.
100. Ibid., p. 495.
101. More, *CW13*, p. 115.
102. See B. Byron, *Loyalty in the Spirituality of St. Thomas More* (Nieuwkoop, 1972), p. 83.
103. More, *CW8*, p. 502.
104. Ibid., pp. 507–12.
105. More, *CW9*, p. 33; see also ibid., p. 37.
106. More, *CW8*, p. 547.
107. More, *CW12*, pp. 12–13.
108. More, *CW13*, p. 36.
109. More, *CW8*, p. 513.
110. More, *CW13*, pp. 37–8.
111. Ibid., p. 12.
112. Ibid., p. 13.
113. Cf. More's translation of Giafrancesco Pico's *The Life of Pico* in More, *EW*, I, p. 377.
114. More, *Dialogue Concerning Heresies* in *EW*, II, pp. 92–3.
115. Ibid., p. 86.
116. More, *CW8*, p. 457.
117. Ibid., p. 526.
118. Ibid., p. 458; see also More, *CW12*, pp. 24–5.
119. More, *CW8*, p. 526.
120. Ibid., p. 839–40.
121. More, *CW14*, p. 199–200.
122. More, *CW8*, p. 509.
123. R. Marius, introduction to *CW8*, p. 1329.
124. JJ. Rousseau, *The Social Concract and Discourses*, ed. G.D.H. Cole (London, 1913, 1973 edn), pp. 177, 250.
125. For More, see pages 63–67; for Rousseau, see 'Discourse on the Origins of Inequality in G.D.H. Cole (ed) *Jean Jacques Rousseau: The Social Contract and Discourses* (1973).
126. Aquinas, *ST*, Prima Secundae: 109.
127. See the commentary to More, *CW8*, pp. 203–8 at pp. 1540–1.
128. Ibid., pp. 205–6.
129. See ibid., p. 1750.
130. Ibid., pp. 508–12.
131. Ibid., p. 505.
132. Ibid., p. 511.
133. Ibid., p. 206; see also ibid., p. 783.

134. Ibid., pp. 527–8.
135. Ibid., p. 423.
136. Ibid., pp. 503–5.
137. Ibid., pp. 786–7.
138. More, *CW12*, p. 247; *idem*, *CW14*, pp. 463–5; and the intercessionary prayers included in *idem*, *CW13*.
139. Aquinas, *ST*, Prima Secundae: 109.
140. More, *CW8*, pp. 456, 524–5.
141. More, *CW14*, p. 447.
142. More, *CW12*, p. 165.
143. More, *CW8*, p. 429.
144. See, for example, ibid., pp. 77–8, 99, 105–6; *idem*, *CW12*, pp. 45, 58–9, 247.
145. See, for example, More, *CW8*, p. 958.
146. More, *Four Last Things* in *EW*, I, pp. 465, 493.
147. More, *Dialogue Concerning Heresies* in *EW*, II, p. 283; and *idem*, *CW12*, p. 39.
148. More, *CW13*, p. 198.
149. Ibid., pp. 116–17.
150. More, *Dialogue Concerning Heresies* in *EW*, II, p. 282.
151. For a particularly interesting exploration of this issue see H. Arendt, *The Human Condition* (Chicago, 1957), pp. 73–8.
152. More, *CW8*, pp. 442–3.
153. Ibid., p. 402; see also ibid., pp. 581, 849–51.
154. See A.W. Reed, introduction to More, *EW*, I., pp. 21–3.
155. More, 'A Ruful Lamentacion' in *EW*, I.
156. More, *Four Last Things* in *EW*, I, p. 474.
157. Ibid., pp. 469, 480.
158. More, *CW13*, p. 67.
159. More, *Four Last Things* in *EW*, I, p. 479.
160. More, *CW12*, pp. 303–6.
161. See, for example, More, *CW8*, p. 557.
162. Ibid., p. 957.
163. More, *CW12*, p. 169.
164. More, *CW8*, pp. 445–53, 673.
165. This particularly in response to the attack upon the notion launched by Simon Fish, *A suppliicacyon for the beggars* (1529), ed. F.J. Furnivall, EETS, extra series, 13 (London, 1871).
166. This is obviously the major theme of More, *Dialogue of Comfort Against Tribulation*.
167. More, *The Supplication of Souls* in E.M. Nugent (ed.), *The Thought and Culture of the English Renaissance* (Cambridge, 1956), pp. 232–3.
168. Ibid., p. 225.
169. Ibid., p. 233.
170. More, *To Martin Dorp* in *Selected Letters*, p. 36.
171. More, *Four Last Things* in *EW*, pp. 470–1.
172. More, *CW12*, pp. 59–60.
173. More, *CW8*, p. 755.
174. More, *CW13*, pp. 13, 39.
175. Ibid., p. 12.
176. More, *Answer to a Poisoned Book* in P.S. Allen (eds), *Selections from the English Works* (Oxford, 1934), p. 11.
177. More, *CW13*, p. 4.
178. Ibid., p. 5.
179. More, *CW14*, p. 371.

180. More, *CW13*, p. 14.
181. Ibid., pp. 16, 21.
182. Ibid., p. 17.
183. Ibid., p. 40.
184. Ibid., p. 22.
185. Ibid., pp. 25–6.
186. Ibid., p. 31; and *idem*, *CW14*, p. 341.
187. More, *CW13*, p. 120.
188. Ibid., p. 54.
189. Ibid., P. 26.
190. Ibid., pp. 45, 48.
191. Ibid., p. 19.
192. Ibid., p. 18.
193. Ibid.
194. More, *Utopia*, p. 159, on the involvement of women in education.
195. More, *CW13*, p. 17; see also ibid., p. 22.
196. Ibid., p. 24.
197. A view widely accepted in the early modern period; see, for example, C. Webster, *The Great Instauration: Science, Medicine and Reform, 1626–1660* (London, 1975), sect. IV.
198. More, *Utopia*, pp. 139–41.
199. More, *CW13*, pp. 18, 24.
200. More, *Utopia*, pp. 223–5.
201. More, *CW14*, p. 367.
202. More, *CW13*, p. 24; see also ibid., pp. 53–4.
203. More, *CW14*, p. 369.
204. More, *Utopia*, p. 101.
205. Ibid.
206. Informed by the work of J.H. Hexter; see introduction to *Utopia*.
207. More, *Utopia*, p. 63.
208. Ibid.
209. Ibid., p. 241.
210. Ibid., pp. 239–43; Winstanley, *The New Law of Righteousness* in *Works*, p. 200.
211. More, *Utopia*, p. 243.
212. Ibid., pp. 239–41.
213. Ibid., p. 241.
214. Ibid., pp. 61–3, 239.
215. Ibid., p. 67.
216. Ibid., p. 199.
217. Ibid., pp. 65, 91.
218. Ibid., pp. 91–3.
219. More, *CW9*, p. 48, and *passim*. Cf. More's defence of the clerical prosecution of heretics in his *Dialogue Concerning Heresies* in *EW*, II, Bk III.
220. More, *To a Monk* in *Selected Letters*, p. 129.
221. More, *To Martin Dorp* in *Selected Letters*, pp. 28–31.
222. More, *To a Monk* in *Selected Letters*, p. 121.
223. More, *Utopia*, p. 67.
224. Ibid., pp. 83–5.
225. See L. Stone, *The Crisis of the Aristocracy* (London, 1965), p. 240; Hexter, *Utopia*, pp. xxv–xxxvii, argues that More's entry into royal service was prompted in part by his disillusion with the legal world.
226. More, *Utopia*, p. 195.
227. An impression conveyed by J. Thirsk, 'Tudor Enclosures', *Historical Association*

Pamphlet, G. 41 (1959).
228. More, *Utopia*, pp. 65–7.
229. Ibid., p. 69.
230. Ibid.
231. Ibid., p. 61.
232. Ibid., p. 71.
233. Ibid., p. 61.
234. More, *Four Last Things* in *EW*, I, p. 484.
235. For an interesting account of More's view that although a Christian commonwealth should undoubtedly manifest charity, the poor should nevertheless be required to labour, see *CW9*, p. 105.
236. More, *Utopia*, pp. 75–9.
237. Ibid., pp. 73–5.
238. More, *CW13*, p. 7.
239. More, *Utopia*, p. 69.
240. See J.H. Hexter, 'Thomas More—On the Margins of Modernity', *Journal of British Studies*, I (1961), pp. 29–36.
241. More, *CW5*, pp. 276–80.
242. More, *Utopia*, p. 197.
243. More, *Four Last Things* in *EW*, I, p. 490.
244. More, *CW14*, p. 173, the 'one benefit' at issue presumably being salvation.
245. More, *Utopia*, p. 103.
246. Ibid., p. 105.
247. Ibid., p. 243.
248. Ibid., p. 105.

Notes to chapter 3

1. See, for example, E.L. Surtz, 'Thomas More and Communism', *Publications of the Modern Language Association of America*, 64 (1949); P.A. Duhamel, 'Medievalism in More's Utopia', *Studies in Philology*, LII (1955).
2. More, *CW5*, p. 277.
3. More, *Utopia*, p. 247.
4. See M. Fleisher, *Radical Reform and Political Persuasion: The Life and Writings of Thomas More* (Geneva, 1973), p. 63, and *passim*.
5. Cf. J.H. Hexter, 'Thomas More: On the Margins of Modernity', *Journal of British Studies*, I (1961), p. 33.
6. Cf., J.H. Hexter, introduction to More, Utopia, pp. lxxxvii–cxxiii.
7. Ibid., pp. lxxv–lxxvi.
8. Q. Skinner, 'More's Utopia', *P & P*, 38 (1967), pp. 158.
9. K. Kautsky, *Thomas More and His Utopia*, trans. H.J. Stenning (New York, 1959 edn).
10. More, *Utopia*, p. 107.
11. More, *The Four Last things* in *EW*, I, p. 488.
12. *Utopia*, p. 113.
13. Ibid., p. 179.
14. Ibid., pp. 125–7.
15. Ibid., p. 141.
16. Ibid., p. 117.
17. Ibid., pp. 129–31.
18. Cf. F. Seebohm, *The Oxford Reformers* (London, 1867), who calculates that the application of this stipulation to the contemporary situation would have

effected a reduction of working hours for the average labourer.
19. More, *Utopia*, pp. 127, 135.
20. Ibid., p. 127.
21. Ibid., p. 135.
22. Ibid., p. 127.
23. Ibid., p. 147.
24. More, *Four Last Things* in *EW*, I, p. 498.
25. More, *Utopia*, pp. 179–81.
26. Cf. Hexter, Intro. More, *Utopia*, p. ciii.
27. See More *Nyne Pageauntes: Age* in *EW*, I, p. 333, in which government is cited as a form of labour befitting mature men.
28. Cf. Fleisher, op. cit., pp. 49–50.
29. Ibid., p. 131.
30. Ibid., pp. 153–5.
31. F. Baumann, 'Sir Thomas More', *JMH*, IV (1932), p. 607.
32. A.L. Morton, *The English Utopia* (London, 1952), p. 46.
33. Marx's references in *Capital*, I (London, 1954), pp. 578, 673, 687, cite More as a reasonably acute observer of economic change and dislocation rather than as an advocate of a systematic critique and response.
34. More, *Utopia*, p. 239.
35. Ibid., pp. 117, 149.
36. Ibid., p. 135.
37. Ibid., p. 179.
38. Ibid., p. 123.
39. Ibid., p. 139.
40. Ibid., p. 165.
41. Ibid., p. 139.
42. My understanding of these issue has been enhanced through reading a number of as yet unpublished papers by Raymond Plant.
43. More, *Utopia*, p. 117.
44. Ibid., p. 137.
45. Ibid., p. 121.
46. As exemplified in J.G.A. Pocock, *The Machiavellian Moment: Florentine Political Thought and the Atlantic Republican Tradition* (Princeton, 1975), and particularly in Q. Skinner, 'Sir Thomas More's "Utopia" and the language of Renaissance Humanism', in A. Pagden (ed.), *The Languages of Political Theory in Early-Modern Europe* (Cambridge, 1987).
47. H. Hopfl, *The Christian Polity of John Calvin* (Cambridge, 1982), esp. p. 50.
48. More, *CW5*, p. 277.
49. See J.H. Headley, intro. More, *CW5*; and *idem*, 'More Against Luther', *Moreana*, 15 (1967).
50. These themes are discussed at length in B. Byron, *Loyalty in the Spirituality of St. Thomas More* (Nieuwkoop, 1972).
51. More, *CW5*, p. 197.
52. More, *Utopia*, p. 123.
53. Ibid., pp. 113, 147.
54. Ibid., p. 123.
55. Ibid., pp. 193–5.
56. Ibid., pp. 123–5.
57. Ibid., p. 125.
58. Ibid., pp. 131–3.
59. Hexter, introduction to More, *Utopia*, pp. ciii ff.
60. More, *Utopia*, p. 195.

61. See T.M. Parker, 'Sir Thomas More's Utopia' in G.V. Bennett and J.D. Walsh (eds), *Essays in Modern English Church History* (London, 1966), p. 13.
62. More, *Utopia*, p. 193.
63. More, *Utopia*, p. 457.
64. More, *Utopia*, p. 195.
65. For an analysis of More's position with regard to equity, see S.E. Prall, 'The Development of Equity in Tudor England', *American Journal of Legal History*, 8 (1964), pp. 7–8.
66. More, *Utopia*, p. 191.
67. Ibid., p. 229.
68. More, *CW13*, pp. 13, 18.
69. Hexter, introduction to More, *Utopia*, p. xlii.
70. Plato, *The Republic*, trans. H.P.D. Lee (Harmondsworth, 1974), BK V, pp. 225–59.
71. See W. Roper, *The Lyfe and Death of Sir Thomas Moore, Knighte*, ed. E.V. Hitchcock, EETS, original series, 197 (London, 1935), p. 8.
72. More, *Utopia*, p. 135ff.
73. Ibid., p. 115.
74. Ibid., p. 137.
75. Ibid., p. 127.
76. Ibid.
77. For Utopia, see ibid., p. 123.
78. Ibid., p. 233.
79. Roper, op. cit., p. 17.
80. More, *Utopia*, p. 187.
81. Ibid., p. 143.
82. See P. Aries, *Centuries of Childhood* (London, 1961, 1973 edn), pp. 150–99.
83. More, *Utopia*, pp. 187–9. An even more pragmatic explanation of this practice is offered by J.S. Cummins, 'Pox and Paranoia in Renaissance Europe', *History Today*, 38 (August 1988), p. 29.
84. D.B. Fenlon, 'England and Europe: Utopia and its Aftermath', *Transactions of the Royal Historical Society*, 25 (1975), p. 121.
85. More, *Utopia*, p. 225.
86. Ibid., p. 121.
87. Ibid., pp. 139–41.
88. Ibid., p. 143.
89. Ibid., p. 145.
90. Ibid., pp. 139–43.
91. Ibid., p. 121.
92. Ibid., p. 133.
93. More, *CW13*, p. 8 ('pardie' = indeed).
94. More, *Utopia*, p. 133.
95. Ibid.,p. 135.
96. See, for example, James Harrington, 'The Model of the Commonwealth of Oceana' (1656), in J.G.A. Pocock (ed.), *The Political Works of James Harrington* (Cambridge, 1977), p. 213. 'The third order distributeth the citizens into horse and foot by the sense or valuation of their estates; they who have above one hundred pounds a year in lands, goods or monies, being obliged to be of horse, and they who have under to be of foot.'
97. More, *Utopia*, p. 115.
98. Ibid., p. 147.
99. Ibid.
100. Ibid., pp. 151–3.

101. More, *CW13*, p. 8.
102. More, *Utopia*, p. 153.
103. Ibid., p. 151.
104. Ibid., p. 155.
105. Ibid., p. 139.
106. Ibid., pp. 145–7.
107. Ibid., p. 127.
108. Ibid., p. 187.
109. Cf. W.E. Campbell, *More's Utopia and His Social Teaching* (London, 1930), ch. 3.
110. E.L. Surtz, introduction to More, *Utopia*, p. cxxvi.
111. More, *Dialogue Concerning Heresies* in *EW*, II, pp. 886–7.
112. F. Caspari, *Humanism and the Social Order in England* (New York, 1954, 1968 edn), p. 123.
113. See Hexter, introduction to More, *Utopia*, E.F. Rogers (ed.), p. lxiii.
114. More, *To the University of Oxford* in E.F.Rogers (ed.), *Sir Thomas More: Selected Letters* (New Haven, CT, 1961), p. 98.
115. More, *Utopia*, pp. 127–9.
116. Ibid., p. 159.
117. Ibid., p. 229.
118. More, *To William Gonell* in *Selected Letters*, p. 105.
119. Ibid., p. 106.
120. See, for example, R.S Peters, 'Reason and Habit: the Paradox of Moral Education' in W.R. Niblett (ed.), *Moral Education in a Changing Society* (London, 1963); and A.C. Kazepides, 'What is the Paradox of Moral Education?', *Proceedings of the Philosophy of Education Society*, 3 (1969). I have received invaluable guidance in these matters from Mr P. Gardner.
121. More, *Utopia*, p. 163.
122. See Roper, op. cit., pp. 17–30.
123. For the clearest statement to this effect see E.L. Surtz, *The Praise of Wisdom: A Commentary on the Religious and Moral Problems and Backgrounds of St. Thomas More's Utopia* (Chicago, 1957).
124. More, *Utopia*, p. 161.
125. Ibid., p. 225. The place of magical belief within the contemporry mentality is explored in K.V. Thomas, *Religion and the Decline of Magic* (London, 1971). The compromise effected between Catholicism and superstition is discussed in ch.2, 'The Magic of the Medieval Church'.
126. More, *Utopia*, p. 163.
127. Ibid., p. 217.
128. Ibid., p. 161–3.
129. Ibid., p. 163.
130. Ibid., p. 217.
131. Ibid., p. 221.
132. Ibid., pp. 221–3.
133. See, for example, H. Oberman, *The Harvest of Medieval Theology* (Cambridge, MA, 1963), pp. 185–248.
134. More, *CW13*, p. 43.
135. More, *Utopia*, pp. 217–19.
136. A position also implied in More's translation of Giafrancesco Pico's *The Life of Pico* in *EW*, I, p. 359.
137. Cf. Hexter, introduction to More, *Utopia*, p. xlvi.
138. J.H. Hexter, *More's Utopia: the Biography of an Idea* (Princeton, NJ, 1952), pp. 48–56, goes so far as to argue that More's position cannot be reconstructed

from the evidence presented in *Utopia*.
139. More, *Utopia*, p. 227.
140. Ibid., pp. 227–31.
141. See Surtz, *Praise of Wisdom*, ch. IX.
142. More, *Utopia*, p. 235.
143. Ibid., pp. 231–7.
144. Ibid., p. 223.
145. Ibid., p. 237.
146. More, *CW14*, p. 631.
147. For the view that the renunciation of bodily pleasure in favour of the practice of mortification and spriritual examination would be conducive to a sound conscience and to the prospect of eternal reward, see More, *Four Last Things* in *EW*, I, pp. 463–4.
148. More, *Utopia*, p. 225.
149. Ibid., pp. 225–7.
150. Ibid., p. 227.
151. See, for example, More, *Answer to a Poisoned Book* in P.S. Allen and H.M. Allen (eds), *Selections from the English Works* (Oxford, 1934), pp. 112–13.
152. See Seebohm, op. cit.; and H. Taylor, 'Sir Thomas More on the Politics of Today', *Fortnightly Review*, XLIV (1870).
153. See, for example, E.L. Surtz, 'Epicurus in Utopia', *Journal of English Literary History*, XVI (1949); *idem*, 'The Defence of Pleasure in More's Utopia', *Studies in Philology*, XLVI (1949); and *idem*, *The Praise of Pleasure: Education and Communism in More's Utopia* (Cambridge, MA, 1957).
154. R.P. Adams, *The Better Part of Valour: More, Erasmus, Colet, and Vives, on Humanism, War, and Peace*, (Seattle, WA, 1962), p. 134.
155. See R.J. Schoeck, *The Achievement of Thomas More* (Victoria, BC, 1976), p. 49; R.P. Adams, 'The Philosophic Unity of More's Utopia', *Studies in Philology*, XXXVIII (1941), p. 63; and Fleisher, op. cit., p. 57.
156. See, for example, Adams, *The Better Part of Valour*, p. 140.
157. Surtz, 'Defence of Pleasure', pp. 105, 112.
158. Surtz, *Praise of Pleasure*, p. 152.
159. Surtz, 'Defence of Pleasure', pp. 108–9.
160. Fleisher, op. cit., p. 55.
161. More, *Utopia*, p. 167.
162. More, *Four Last Things* in *EW*, I, p. 462.
163. Ibid., pp. 461–2.
164. See T.I. White, 'Festivitas, Utilitas, et Opes: The Concluding Irony and Philosophical Purpose of Thomas More's Utopia' in M.J. Moore (ed.), *Quincentennial Essays on St. Thomas More* (Boone, N. Carolina, 1977), *passim*.
165. More, *Utopia*, p. 167.
166. Ibid., pp. 127–9.
167. Ibid., p. 145.
168. Ibid., p. 169.
169. Ibid., p. 161.
170. Ibid., p. 163.
171. More, *Four Last Things* in *EW*, I, p. 495.
172. More, *Utopia*, pp. 163–5.
173. Ibid.
174. Ibid., p. 175.
175. Ibid., p. 129.
176. Ibid., p. 167ff.
177. Ibid., p. 169.

178. Ibid., pp. 175–7.
179. Ibid., p. 175.
180. Ibid., p. 177.
181. Ibid., p. 161.
182. Ibid., p. 179.
183. See, for example, R. Knox, 'The Charge of Religious Intolerance' in R.W. Chambers (ed.), *The Fame of Blessed Thomas More* (London, 1929), p. 49.
184. See, for example, L. Miles, 'Persecution and the Dialogue of Comfort', *Journal of British Studies*, V (1965).
185. S. Avineri, 'War and Slavery in More's Utopia', *International Review of Social History*, VII (1962).
186. See, for example, P.A. Sawada, 'Laus Potentiae or the Praise of Realpolitik?: Hermann Oncken and More's Utopia', *Moreana*, 15 (1967).
187. Surtz, *Praise of Wisdom*, p. 268.
188. See, for example, D.B. Davis, *The Problem of Slavery in Western Culture* (New York, 1966), pp. 91–107.
189. See, for example, E.L. Surtz, 'Thomas More and the Great Books', *Philological Quarterly*, XXXII (1953). For More's advocacy of Greek see his *To Martin Dorp* and *To the University of Oxford* in *Selected Letters*.
190. More, *Utopià*, pp. 129–33.
191. Ibid., p. 183.
192. Ibid., p. 225.
193. Ibid., p. 183.
194. Ibid., p. 161.
195. More, 'A Ruful lamentacion' in *EW*, I, p. 337.
196. See Thomas, op. cit., chs 10–12; and B.S. Capp, *Astrology and the Popular Press* (London, 1979).
197. See, for example, T.S. Kuhn, *The Copernican Revolution: Planetary Astronomy and the Development of Western Thought* (Cambridge, MA, 1957, 1977 edn), pp. 93–4.
198. J.C. Davis, *Utopia and the Ideal Society* (Cambridge, 1981), p. 61.
199. See, for example, Hexter, *More's Utopia: the Biography of an Idea.*
200. J.C. Davis, op. cit., p. 54.
201. Aristotle, *Ethics*, BK III; I. Kant, *Fundamental Principles of the Metaphysic of Morals*, trans, T.K. Abbot (Indianapolis, 1948), third section; G.E. Moore, *Ethics* (London, 1912).
202. More, *CW14*, p. 99; cf. Aquinas, *ST*, Prima Secundae: 109, art 2.
203. More, *CW8*, p. 781.
204. Surtz, introduction to More, *Utopia*, p. clx.
205. I am grateful to Alistair Edwards for many valuable discussions on the issue of freedom of choice as an aspect of liberty.
206. More, *Utopia*, pp. 185, 191–3.
207. Ibid., p. 113.
208. Ibid., p. 121.
209. Ibid., p. 243.

Notes to Chapter 4

1. Winstanley, *An Humble Request to the Ministers of both Universities and to all Lawyers in every Inns-a-Court* in *Works*, p. 428.
2. Cf. as examples of the former position, G.H. Sabine, introduction to Winstanley, *Works*; W.S. Hudson, 'the Economic and Social Thought of Gerrard Winstanley:

Was He a Seventeenth-Century Marxist?, *JMH*, XVII (1946); P. Elmen, 'The Theological Basis of Digger Communism', *Church History*, 23 (1954); W.F. Murphy, 'The Political Philosophy of Gerrard Winstanley', *Review of Politics*, 19 (1957); L. Mulligan *et al.*, 'Winstanley: A Case for the Man as He Said He Was', *Journal of Ecclesiastical History*, 28 (1977); and as supporters of the latter view see, for example, D.W. Petegorsky, *Left Wing Democracy in the English Civil War* (New York, 1940); G.H. George, 'Gerrard Winstanley: A Critical Retrospect' in R.C. Cole and M.E. Moody (eds), *The Dissenting Tradition* (Ohio University Press, 1975); G. Juretic, 'Digger: No Millenarian', *JHI*, XXXVI (1975).

3. See the analysis recently developed by G.E. Aylmer, 'The Religion of Gerrard Winstanley' in J.F. McGregor and B. Reay (eds), *Radical Religion in the English Revolution* (Oxford, 1984).
4. Winstanley, *The Saints Paradice* in *Several Pieces*, pp. 48–9.
5. Winstanley, *The Breaking of the Day of God* in *Several Pieces*, p. 107.
6. Winstanley, *Saints Paradice*, p. A3.
7. Ibid., pp. 27, 64.
8. Ibid., pp. 55–6, cf. p. 63.
9. Winstanley, *Truth Lifting Up Its Head Above Scandals* in *Works*, p. 105.
10. Winstanley, *Saints Paradice*, p. 69; *idem*, *The New Law of Righteousnes* in *Works*, p. 168.
11. As implied in the 'left-wing' interpretations of George and Juretic. For a more tempered response see C. Hill, ' "Reason" and "Reasonableness" in Seventeenth-Century England', *British Journal of Sociology*, 20 (1969); and *idem*, 'Hobbes and Winstanley; Reason and Politics' in *idem*, *The World Turned Upside Down* (Harmondsworth, 1975), p. 389.
12. Winstanley, *Saints Paradice*, p. 79.
13. Winstanley, *The Law of Freedom* in *Works*, p. 579 (364).
14. Winstanley, *Truth Lifting*, p. 105.
15. Winstanley, *Saints Paradice*, p. 78.
16. Winstanley, *Truth Lifting*, p. 111.
17. See Elmen, op. cit., pp. 211–12.
18. Winstanley, *Truth Lifting*, p. 105.
19. Ibid., p. 109. This ideal is reiterated in Winstanley's later writings, see his *The True Levellers' Standard Advanced* in *Works*, p. 254 (80).
20. Winstanley, *Saints Paradice*, p. 77.
21. Winstanley, *Truth Lifting*, p. 101.
22. Winstanley, *Breaking of the Day*, p. 3.
23. Winstanley, *The Mysteries of God, Concerning the Whole Creation, Mankinde* in *Several Pieces*, p. 31.
24. Winstanley, *Saints Paradice*, p. 75.
25. Winstanley, *Truth Lifting*, pp. 112–17.
26. Winstanley, *Saints Paradice*, pp. 53–4; see also *idem*, *Truth Lifting*, p. 113.
27. Cf., for an interesting parallel, T.H. Green, *Lectures on the Principles of Political Obligation* with an introduction by A.D. Lindsay (London, 1941 edn), pp. 2–3.
28. Winstanley, *New Law of Righteousnes*, p. 166.
29. Winstanley, *Mysterie of God*, *passim*.
30. Winstanley, *Saints Paradice*, p. 56.
31. Winstanley, *Truth Lifting*, p. 135; and *idem*, *New Law of Righteousnes*, p. 158
32. Winstanley, *Saints Paradice*, pp. 65–6; see also pp. 29, 32–3.
33. Ibid., p. 19; see also pp. 68, 75.
34. Ibid., p. 38.
35. Ibid., p. 33.

36. Winstanley, *Breaking of the Day*, p. 119.
37. Winstanley, *New Law of Righteousnes*, p. 218.
38. Winstanley, *Mysterie of God*, pp. 51–2.
39. Winstanley, *New Law of Righteousnes*, p. 216.
40. Winstanley, *Law of Freedom in a Platform* in *Works*, pp. 565–7 (348–50).
41. Winstanley, *New Law of Righteousnes*, p. 219.
42. Winstanley, *Truth Lifting*, p. 101; see *idem*, *Breaking of the Day*, pp. 115–16.
43. Winstanley, *Truth Lifting*, pp. 122–4.
44. See, for example, C. Hill, introduction to L.D. Hamilton (ed.), *Gerrard Winstanley: Selections from His Works* (London, 1944), p. 5.
45. Winstanley, *Truth Lifting*, p. 128.
46. Winstanley, *Saints Paradice*, p. 8.
47. Winstanley, *Truth Lifting*, p. 122; and *idem*, *New Law of Righteousnes*, p. 165.
48. Winstanley, *Truth Lifting*, p. 126.
49. Winstanley, *Saints Paradice*, p. 10.
50. Winstanley, *New Law of Righteousnes*, p. 174; and *idem*, *Fire in the Bush*, *Works*, pp. 483–4 (256–7).
51. Winstanley, *Truth Lifting*, p. 118.
52. Winstanley, *A New-yeers Gift for the Parliament and Armie* in *Works*, p. 380 (192).
53. Winstanley, *Fire in the Bush*, pp. 468–9 (239).
54. See Timothy Kenyon, 'Labour—Natural, Property—Artificial: The Radical Insights of Gerrard Winstanley', *History of European Ideas*, 6 (1985).
55. Winstanley, *Truth Lifting*, p. 117.
56. Ibid., p. 120.
57. Winstanley, *New Law of Righteousnes*, p. 211.
58. Winstanley, *Truth Lifting*, p. 117.
59. Winstanley, *Saints Paradice*, p. 55.
60. Winstanley, *Truth Lifting*, pp. 112–13.
61. Winstanley, *New-yeers Gift*, p. 375 (186).
62. Winstanley, *New Law of Righteousnes*, p. 155.
63. Winstanley, *Mysterie of God*, p. 1.
64. Winstanley, *To the Lord Fairfax, Generall of the English Forces, and His Councell of War* in *Works*, p. 289.
65. Ibid., pp. 289–90.
66. Winstanley, *Humble Request*, p. 423.
67. Winstanley, *The Law of Freedom*, p. 564 (347–8).
68. Winstanley, *New-yeers Gift*, p. 376 (187).
69. Winstanley, *New Law of Righteousnes*, p. 182.
70. See 'The Dominion Over Nature' chap. V. pt. 1 of C. Webster, *The Great Instauration* (London, 1975).
71. Winstanley, *To the Lord Fairfax*, p. 289.
72. Winstanley, *True Levellers' Standard* in *Works*, p. 251 (77).
73. See, for example, Hill, *The World Turned Upside Down* p. 145; *idem*, *Winstanley: The Law of Freedom and other Writings*, pp. 54ff.; *idem*, *Milton and the English Revolution* (London 1977), pp. 341–4; *idem*, 'A Rejoinder', *P & P*, 89 (1980), p. 150.
74. Winstanley, *Fire in the Bush*, p. 452 (220) and, more generally, ch. I, 'What the Garden of Eden is'.
75. Winstanley, *Saints Paradice*, 77–8; *idem*, *Truth Lifting*, pp. 105, 109, 111; *idem*, *True Levellers' Standard*, p. 254. (79).
76. Winstanley, *Truth Lifting*, p. 134.
77. Ibid., p. 119.
78. Winstanley, *Mysterie of God*, pp. 1–9.

79. Ibid., p. 3.
80. Ibid., p. 45.
81. Winstanley, *New Law of Righteousnes*, p. 176; see also *idem*, *Fire in the Bush*, pp. 480–1 (254).
82. Ibid., p. 177.
83. Ibid., p. 212; cf. *idem*, *A New-yeers Gift*, p. 377 (188).
84. Winstanley, *Saints Paradice*, p. 45.
85. Winstanley, *Truth Lifting*, p. 135.
86. Winstanley, *New Law of Righteousnes*, p. 211.
87. Ibid., p. 177.
88. As detailed in Chapter 6, pages 199–202 Winstanley *Law of Freedom*. pp. 546–8 (326–8).
89. Winstanley, *Saints Paradice*, p. 38.
90. See Winstanley, *Fire in the Bush*, p. 489 (263–4).
91. Winstanley, *Truth Lifting*, p. 133.
92. T.W. Hayes, *Winstanley the Digger* (Cambridge, MA, 1979), p. 205; see also ibid., p. 203. Hayes' evaluation is applauded by Hill, *A Rejoinder*, p. 151, n. 37.
93. Hill, *Winstanley: The Law of Freedom*, p. 53.
94. C. Hill, 'The Religion of Gerrard Winstanley', *P & P* Supplement (Oxford, 1978), p. 33.
95. Hill, 'A Rejoinder', p. 150.
96. For Winstanley's view that private property was the curse see his *New Law of Righteousnes*, p. 156
97. Hill, 'A Rejoinder', pp. 150–1.
98. Winstanley, *New Law of Righteousnes*, p. 158.
99. Winstanley, *New-yeers Gift*, pp. 379 (191); see also *idem*, *Fire in the Bush*, pp. 460–1 (230) for the insidious role of 'imagination'—because men can imagine poverty, they fear it.
100. Winstanley, *New-yeers Gift*, pp. 379–80 (190–2); and *idem*, 'To the Lord Fairfax', p. 290.
101. Winstanley, *Saints Paradice*, p. 73; and Thomas Hobbes, *Leviathan*, ed. C.B. Macpherson (Harmondsworth, 1968) ch. XI.
102. Winstanley, *New Law of Righteousnes*, pp. 157–8.
103. Ibid., p. 158.
104. Winstanley, *Law of Freedom*, p. 532 (309).
105. Winstanley, *Fire in the Bush*, p. 459 (229).
106. Winstanley, *Saints Paradice*, pp. 29–30; *idem*, *New-yeers Gift*, p. 379 (191).
107. Winstanley, *Truth Lifting*, p. 114.
108. Ibid., p. 110.
109. C. Hill, 'The Norman Yoke' in *idem*, *Puritanism and Revolution* (London, 1958), p. 51.
110. Ibid., p. 67; see also ibid., p. 60.
111. J.G.A. Pocock, *The Ancient Constitution and the Feudal Law* (Cambridge, 1957, 1974 edn), p. 16.
112. Ibid., pp. 42, 53, 89, and *passim*.
113. Ibid., ch. V, esp. pp. 119–20.
114. Hill, 'The Norman Yoke', p. 63. Hill's position is contested by Pocock, op. cit., pp. 42–56, 125–6. More recently, however, Pocock's thesis has in turn been questioned by R. Tuck, *Natural Rights Theories* (Cambridge, 1979), pp. 83, 133–7, 149. For interesting positions also claiming critically to revise Pocock's view, see R.B. Seaberg, 'The Norman Conquest and the Common Law: the Levellers and the Argument from Continuity', *HJ*, 24 (1981); J.P. Sommerville, 'History and Theory: the Norman Conquest in Early Stuart Political Thought,

PS, XXXIV (1988).
115. Winstanley, *A Watch-Word to the City of London and the Armie*, *Works*, p. 322 (132).
116. See *Light Shining in Buckinghamshire*, reprinted in Winstanley, *Works*.
117. Hill, 'The Norman Yoke', p. 75; see also ibid., p. 78.
118. S.E. Prall, *The Agitation for Law Reform during the Puritan Revolution* (The Hague, 1966), p. 44.
119. Hill, 'The Norman Yoke', p. 84.
120. Ibid., p. 85; and *idem*, *The World Turned Upside Down*, pp. 133–4.
121. Pocock, op. cit., pp. 19, 126.
122. Winstanley, *A Watch-Word*, p. 324 (135).
123. An understanding made evident by A.W. Reeve, 'The Treatment of Property by Some English Economic, Legal and Social Writers Between 1600–1700', D. Phil. thesis, Oxford University, 1979, pp. 226–43.
124. Winstanley, *A New-yeers Gift*, p. 369 (180).
125. Ibid., p. 387 (199–200).
126. Winstanley, *New Law of Righteousnes*, p. 200; and *idem*, *True Levellers' Standard*, pp. 253, 258 (79–80, 85).
127. Winstanley, *A New-yeers Gift*, pp. 356–7 (164–5).
128. See Elmen, op. cit., pp. 209–12.
129. Winstanley, *Fire in the Bush*, p. 489 (264).
130. Ibid., p. 492 (267).
131. Ibid., p. 493 (268).
132. Winstanley, *New-yeers Gift*, p. 383 (195); see also ibid., p. 376 (187).
133. Winstanley, *True Levellers' Standard*, p. 259 (87).
134. Winstanley, *New-yeers Gift*, p. 354 (163).
135. Hill, 'The Norman Yoke', p. 43; see also *idem*, *The World Turned Upside Down*, p. 140. For a decidedly unsympathetic appraisal of Winstanley's anticlericalism, see F. Stripp, 'The Anticlericalism of Gerrard Winstanley', *The Historical Magazine of the Protestant Episcopelian Church* (1954).
136. J.F. Maclear, 'Popular Anticlericalism in the Puritan Revolution', *JHI*, XVII (1956), p. 443.
137. Ibid., pp. 453, 457.
138. Ibid., pp. 445, 450.
139. Ibid., pp. 447, 449.
140. Ibid., pp. 450–2.
141. Winstanley, *Truth Lifting*, p. 129.
142. Winstanley, *Saints Paradice*, p. 1; see also idem, *Mysterie of God*, pp. 33–4.
143. Winstanley, *Breaking of the Day*, p. 117.
144. Ibid., pp. 83–4.
145. Winstanley, *Truth Lifting*, p. 144.
146. Winstanley, *New Law of Righteousnes*, p. 242.
147. See M. James, 'The Political Importance of the Tithes Controversy in England', *History*, XXVI (1941), pp. 3–6.
148. Ibid., p. 11.
149. Winstanley, *A Watch-Word*, p. 333 (145); see also *idem*, *Fire in the Bush*, pp. 474–5 (246).
150. Winstanley, *New-yeers Gift*, p. 358 (166).
151. Winstanley, *New Law of Righteousnes*, p. 233.
152. Ibid., p. 187.
153. Winstanley, *Truth Lifting*, p. 143.
154. Winstanley, *New-yeers Gift*, pp. 357–8 (166); and *idem*, *Law of Freedom*, p. 522 (297–8).

155. Ibid., p. 523 (299).
156. R.L. Greaves, *The Puritan Revolution in Educational Thought* (New Brunswick, 1969), pp. 137–8.
157. Hill, *The World Turned Upside Down*, p. 153.
158. L.F. Solt, 'Anti-Intellectualism in the English Revolution', *Church History*, 25 (1956), p. 306.
159. Ibid., p. 308.
160. Ibid., p. 313.
161. Winstanley, *New Law of Righteousnes*, p. 238.
162. Winstanley, *A Declaration from the Poor Oppressed People of England* in *Works*, p. 271 (102); cf. *idem*, *Saints Paradice*, p. 10; and *idem*, *Fire in the Bush*, p. 463 (233).
163. Winstanley, *Fire in the Bush*, p. 463 (233).
164. Winstanley, *Saints Paradice*, p. 4.
165. Winstanley, *Fire in the Bush*, p. 474 (246).
166. Winstanley, *Law of Freedom*, pp. 565–6 (349).
167. Winstanley, *Truth Lifting*, p. 125.
168. Ibid., p. 137.
169. Winstanley, *New-yeers Gift*, p. 359 (168).
170. Ibid., p. 387 (199–200).
171. Ibid., p. 368.
172. Winstanley, *Declaration from the Poor*, p. 273 (103).
173. Winstanley, *Law of Freedom*, p. 558 (340).
174. Winstanley, *True Levellers' Standard*, p. 258 (85–6).
175. Winstanley, *Law of Freedom*, pp. 568–9 (352). See J. Thirsk, 'Younger Sons in the Seventeenth Century', *History*, LIV (1969).
176. Winstanley, *New-yeers Gift*, p. 361 (170).
177. Winstanley, *Fire in the Bush*, p. 491ff. (265ff.).
178. Winstanley, *New-yeers Gift*, p. 388 (201).
179. See, for example, Winstanley, *A Watch-Word*, p. 324 (135).
180. Winstanley, *To the Lord Fairfax*, p. 288.
181. Winstanley, *A Watch-Word*, p. 327 (138).
182. Winstanley, *Fire in the Bush*, p. 470 (241).
183. Winstanley, *Law of Freedom*, p. 587 (374).
184. Winstanley, *New-yeers Gift*, p. 361 (171).
185. Winstanley, *A Watch-Word*, p. 320 (130).
186. Winstanley, *Fire in the Bush*, p. 468 (239).
187. See, for example, W.G. Hoskins, *The Midland Peasant* (London, 1957), pp. 115–7, on land transactions involving 'the peasantry'. More recent work includes A. Macfarlane, *The Origins of English Individualism* (Oxford, 1978), esp. ch. 4. Evidence suggests that the position in the mid-seventeenth century differed markedly from that of the previous century; see J. Youings, *Sixteenth-Century England* (Harmondsworth, 1984), ch. 7.
188. C. Hill, 'Land in the English Revolution', *Science and Society*, 13 (1948); and, more recently, K. Wrightson, *English Society 1580–1680* (London, 1982), pp. 130–9; and J.A. Sharpe, *Early Modern England: A Social History 1550–1760* (London, 1987), ch. 6.
189. Winstanley, *Declaration from the Poor*, p. 271 (101).
190. Winstanley, *Mysterie of God*, pp. 6–8.
191. Winstanley, *Saints Paradice*, p. 60.
192. Winstanley, *New Law of Righteousnes*, pp. 157–8, 212.
193. Winstanley, *To the Lord Fairfax*, p. 290.
194. Winstanley, *New-yeers Gift*, p. 382 (194).

195. Winstanley, *Fire in the Bush*, p. 454 (223).
196. Winstanley, *Humble Request*, p. 428, see also ibid., p. 425.
197. Ibid., p. 426.

Notes to Chapter 5

1. This is especially true of those commentators who see Winstanley as something of an anticipatory socialist—see G.H. George, 'Gerrard Winstanley: A Critical Retrospect' in R.C. Cole and M.E. Moody (eds), *The Dissenting Tradition* (Ohio University Press, 1975); G. Juretic, 'Digger: No Millenarian', *JHI*, XXXVI (1975). Others, who support the view that Winstanley was essentially a millenarian thinker, experience difficulty in maintaining the consistency of this interpretation in applying it to all phases of his thought—see W.S. Hudson, 'The Economic and Social Thought of Gerrard Winstanley: Was He a Seventeenth-Century marxist?' *JHI*, XVII (1946); L. Mulligan *et al.*, 'Winstanley: A Case for the Man as He Said He Was', *Journal of Ecclesiastical History*, 28 (1977).
2. George, op. cit., p. 211.
3. Winstanley, '*The Mysterie of God Concerning the Whole Creation Mankinde* in *Several Pieces*, p. A2.
4. Ibid., pp. 10–11.
5. Ibid., pp. A2, 9–10.
6. Ibid., p. 16.
7. Ibid., p. 7.
8. Ibid., p. 9.
9. Ibid., p. 40.
10. Ibid., p. 45
11. Ibid., p. A3; see also, ibid., pp. 14–15, 23–4, 28, 41, 47–8.
12. Ibid., p. 7.
13. Ibid., p. 13.
14. Ibid., p. 7; see also ibid., pp. 23–6, 32–3.
15. See above, pp. 127–128, for Winstanley's views on the 'illegitimate' use of sin as a social sanction.
16. Winstanley, *Mysterie of God*, pp. 19–29, 26, 35–8, 42.
17. Ibid., p. 47; see also ibid., pp. 45–7, 50.
18. Ibid., p. 52.
19. Ibid., p. 59; see also ibid., pp. 35, 40–1.
20. Winstanley, *The Breaking of the Day of God*, *Several Pieces*, p. 71; see also ibid., p. 49.
21. Ibid., p. 70; see also ibid., pp. 53, 79.
22. Ibid., pp. 105, 123, 130.
23. Ibid., p. 62; see also ibid., pp. 61–3, 108. In ibid., pp. 63, 108, Winstanley applies the image of 'the Beast' to the Papacy and to Episcopacy.
24. Ibid., p. 28; see also ibid., pp. 16, 89.
25. Ibid., pp. 1, 10, 12, 34, 46.
26. Ibid., p. 26; see also ibid., pp. 29, 37.
27. Ibid., p. 72; see also ibid., p. 73.
28. Ibid., p. 96; see also ibid., pp. 47–69, 77, 109.
29. Ibid., pp. A4, 109, 126.
30. Ibid., pp. A3, 56.
31. Ibid., pp. 6–18.
32. Ibid., pp. 93–9.

33. Ibid., p. 88; see also ibid., pp. 99, 108.
34. Ibid., p. 133.
35. Ibid., p. A3.
36. Ibid., p. A4.
37. Ibid.
38. Ibid.
39. Ibid., p. 101.
40. Ibid., p. 64; see also ibid., pp. 14–15, 79, 116.
41. Ibid., p. 115.
42. Ibid., p. A4.
43. Ibid., p. 1, 11, 43, 68–9, 80–2, 120.
44. Ibid., pp. 94–5.
45. Ibid., p. 136.
46. Ibid., pp. A4, 40, 65.
47. Ibid., pp. 124; see also ibid., p. 125.
48. Ibid., p. 135.
49. Ibid., p. 131.
50. Ibid., p. 136.
51. For the debate on the dating of this pamphlet see G.H. Sabine, introduction to Winstanley, *Works*, p. 91.
52. Winstanley, *The Saints Paradice* in *Several Pieces*, p. A2.
53. Ibid., pp. 1, 6, 59.
54. Ibid., pp. 10–12, 20, 37.
55. Ibid., p. 39.
56. Ibid., pp. 20–4.
57. Ibid., p. A3.
58. Ibid., p. 4.
59. Ibid., pp. 3, 42.
60. Ibid., p. 47. On this occasion Winstanley uses these notions interchangeably.
61. Ibid., p. 30; see also ibid., pp. 17–18.
62. Ibid., p. 49.
63. Ibid., p. 77.
64. Ibid., p. 78.
65. See ibid., pp. 13, 26, 41, 64, 72.
66. Ibid., p. A3.
67. Ibid., p. 13; see also ibid., p. 27.
68. Ibid., p. 41.
69. Ibid., pp. 25, 28.
70. Ibid., p. 53.
71. Ibid., p. 56.
72. Ibid., pp. 25–7, 35–6.
73. Ibid., p. 48.
74. Winstanley, *Truth Lifting Up Its Head Above Scandals* in *Several Pieces*, p. 103.
75. Ibid., p. 105.
76. Ibid., pp. 111–12.
77. Ibid., p. 108.
78. Ibid., pp. 113–17.
79. Ibid., p. 115.
80. Ibid., p. 116.
81. Ibid., pp. 108, 115, 125–6, 139.
82. See, for example, ibid., p. 138.
83. Ibid., p. 121.
84. Winstanley, *The New Law of Righteousnes* in *Works*, p. 190.

85. *Light Shining in Buckinghamshire*, included in Winstanley, *Works*, was published on 5 December 1648 and has many themes in common with *The New Law of Righteousnes*: the sinfulness of human nature, problems stemming from the appropriation of private property from the commons, the illegitimacy of prevailing political authority, and most especially communalism as the solution to this situation; see *Works*, pp. 615–16.
86. Winstanley, *New Law of Righteousnes*, pp. 149, 163–4, 186, 205–7, 222, 230.
87. Ibid., pp. 204–5; see also ibid., p. 162.
88. Ibid., p. 228.
89. Ibid., p. 152.
90. Ibid., p. 166; see also ibid., p. 173.
91. Ibid., p. 150; see also ibid., p. 156.
92. Ibid., p. 165.
93. Ibid., p. 186; see also ibid., pp. 190, 194.
94. Ibid., p. 183.
95. Ibid., p. 170.
96. Ibid., p. 180.
97. Ibid., p. 188.
98. Ibid., p. 183.
99. Ibid., p. 196.
100. Ibid., p. 197; see also ibid., p. 195.
101. Ibid., p. 181; rather than emphasizing charity Winstanley advocates the right to labour as the appropriate solution to the problem of poverty.
102. Ibid., p. 179; see also ibid., p. 180.
103. Ibid., p. 184.
104. Ibid., pp. 185, 197–8.
105. Ibid., p. 184; cf. Winstanley, *The Law of Freedom* in *Works*, p. 532 (310): 'The Kingly Power is the old Heaven, and the old Earth, that must pass away, wherein unrighteousness, oppression and partiality dwels.'
106. A similar case was also advanced by Winstanley's fellow Digger Robert Coster; see Winstanley, *A Mite Cast Into the Common Treasury* in *Works*, pp. 655–8.
107. See, for example, D.W. Petegorsky, *Left-Wing Democracy in the English Civil War* (New York, 1940, 1972 edn), pp. 147, 200–1, although at p. 205 Petegorsky appears to retract; G. Juretic, 'The Mind of Gerrard Winstanley: from Millenarian to Socialist', doctoral dissertation, North Illinois University, 1972, p. 106.
108. A consideration recognized briefly and in passing by H.N. Brailsford, *The Levellers and the English Revolution* (London, 1961), p. 662; in considerably greater detail by J.C. Davis, 'Gerrard Winstanley and the Restoration of True Magistracy', *P & P*, 70 (1977), *passim*; and by C. Hill, 'The Religion of Gerrard Winstanley', *P & P* Supplement (Oxford, 1978), p. 26.
109. Winstanley, *New Law of Righteousnes*, pp. 158–9.
110. Ibid., p. 190.
111. Ibid., pp. 190–1.
112. Ibid., pp. 182–3.
113. Ibid., p. 190, see also ibid., pp. 194–5.
114. Ibid., pp. 195–6.
115. Ibid., p. 191.
116. Ibid., p. 200.
117. Ibid., p. 184.
118. Ibid., p. 191.
119. Ibid., p. 200, see also ibid., p. 205.
120. Ibid., p. 150.

121. Ibid., p. 157.
122. Ibid., p. 187.
123. Ibid., p. 200.
124. Ibid., p. 243; see also ibid., pp. 135, 178, 183.
125. Ibid., p. 185.
126. A view shared by Petegorsky, op. cit., pp. 146, 178.
127. For the details of Winstanley's exploits in the spring of 1649 see CSPD (1649–50), 16 April 1649, p. 95; and Bulstrode Whitelock, *Memorials of English Affairs* (1682) (Oxford, 1853), III, pp. 17–18.
128. See Sabine, op. cit., p. 18.
129. See, for example, M.E. James, *Social Problems and Policy During the Puritan Revolution* (London, 1930, 1966 edn), pp. 99–102; Brailsford, op. cit., ch. XXXIV; B. Moore, *Social Origins of Dictatorship and Democracy* (London, 1966), p. 500; C. Hill, *The World Turned Upside Down* (Harmondsworth, 1972, 1975 edn), p. 130; *idem* (ed.), *Winstanley: The Law of Freedom* (Harmondsworth, 1973), pp. 21–2; F. Brockway, *Britain's First Socialists* (London, 1980), pp. 125–6.
130. K.V. Thomas, 'Another Digger Broadside', *P & P*, 42 (1969), p. 58.
131. See *below* pages 182–185.
132. Sabine, op. cit., p. 55; K.V. Thomas, 'The Date of Gerrard Winstanley's "Fire in the Bush" ', *P & P*, 42 (1969), p. 162; Hill, *op. cit.*, p. 27.
133. Cf. Davis, op. cit., pp. 82–3.
134. Hudson, op. cit., p. 11.
135. Mulligan et al., op. cit., p. 69.
136. P. Zagorin, *A History of Political Thought in the English Revolution* (London, 1954), pp. 47–50.
137. Sabine, op. cit., p. 39.
138. P. Elmen, *The Theological Basis of Digger Communism*, p. 215.
139. Winstanley, *The True Levellers' Standard Advanced* in *Works*, p. 251 (77); and see above, pages 163–166.
140. Winstanley, *The True Levellers' Standard*, p. 253 (79).
141. Ibid., p. 254 (80); see also *idem*, *Truth Lifting*, p. 109.
142. Winstanley, *True Levellers' Standard*, pp. 255–6, (82).
143. Ibid., p. 261 (89), in terms similar to those employed in *idem*, *New Law of Righteousnes*, p. 196.
144. Winstanley, *True Levellers' Standard*. No. 1, p. 260 (87).
145. Ibid., No. 4, pp. 261–2 (89–90).
146. Ibid., No. 2, p. 260 (87–8).
147. Ibid., No. 3, pp. 260–1 (88).
148. Ibid., p. 257 (83).
149. Ibid., No. 5, pp. 262–3, (90–1).
150. Ibid., No. 6, pp. 263–4 (91–2).
151. Sabine, op. cit., p. 267, suggests that others besides Winstanley may have contributed to the writing of this pamphlet.
152. Winstanley, *A Declaration from the Poor Oppressed People of England* in *Works*, p. 269 (99).
153. Ibid., pp. 271–2 (102).
154. Ibid., pp. 269, 272–3 (99, 103).
155. Ibid., p. 269; see also ibid., p. 272 (100, 102).
156. Ibid., p. 276 (107).
157. Ibid., p. 274 (104–5.
158. Ibid., pp. 272–3, 274–5 (103, 105–6).
159. Ibid., p. 273 (104).

160. Winstanley, *To The Lord Fairfax, Generall of the English Forces, and His Councell of War* in *Works*, p. 281.
161. Ibid., p. 282.
162. See Winstanley, *A Declaration of the Bloudie and Unchristian Acting of Wiliam Star and John Taylor of Walton* in *Works.*
163. Winstanley, *To The Lord Fairfax*, pp. 282, 286–7.
164. Ibid., pp. 285–6, 291.
165. Ibid., p. 282.
166. Ibid.; see also ibid., pp. 286–91.
167. Ibid., p. 292.
168. Ibid., p. 282, by calling for patience. Either this was a retrograde move, which seems unlikely, or else Winstanley wished to renounce the subversive implications of anarchism.
169. Ibid., pp. 282–3.
170. Ibid., p. 284.
171. Cf. W. Schenk, *The Concern for Social Justice in the Puritan Revolution* (London, 1948), p. 104; and Davis, op. cit., pp. 91–2.
172. Winstanley, *An Appeal to the House of Commons*, *Works*, pp. 311–12 (123–4).
173. Ibid., p. 303 (113).
174. Ibid., p. 309 (120).
175. Ibid., p. 304 (114).
176. Ibid., p. 307 (119).
177. Ibid., p. 304 (115).
178. Ibid., p. 305 (116).
179. Ibid., p. 306 (116–17).
180. Ibid., p. 305 (115).
181. See above, pages 163–166.
182. Winstanley, *An Appeal*, p. 301 (111–2).
183. Winstanley, *A Watch-Word to the City of London and the Armie* in *Works*, p. 329 (141).
184. Ibid., pp. 328–9 (140).
185. Ibid., p. 322 (133).
186. Ibid., p. 366 (148).
187. Ibid., pp. 321–2 (132).
188. Ibid., pp. 319–20 (130).
189. Ibid., p. 327 (138).
190. Ibid., p. 324 (136).
191. Ibid.
192. Ibid., p. 325 (136).
193. Ibid., p. 326 (137).
194. Winstanley, *To His Excellency the Lord Fairfax and the Counsell of Warre the Brotherly Request of those that are Called Diggers Sheweth* in *Works*, pp. 343–5; and *idem*, *To My Lord Generall and His Councell of Warr* in *Works*, pp. 346–9.
195. In the preface to Winstanley, *Several Pieces Gathered Into One Volume*, p. A3, Winstanley speaks of his tireless exertions in the polemical defence of the Diggers' colony (Hill, op. cit., pp. 155–6). The very fact that Winstanley sanctioned at this time the reprinting of his five earliest and essentially theological tracts suggests that he continued to conceive of digging within the context of these initial premises.
196. Winstanley, *To My Lord Generall*, p. 347; see also ibid., 348.
197. Winstanley, *To His Excellency*, p. 344.
198. Winstanley, *To My Lord Generall*, p. 348.
199. Winstanley, *A New-yeers Gift for the Parliament and Armie* in *Works*, pp. 358–9 (167).

200. Ibid., pp. 356–7 (164–5).
201. Ibid., pp. 353–5 (162–3) for this differentiation.
202. Ibid., pp. 357–64, 380–1 (166–74, 192–3).
203. Ibid., p. 387 (199–200).
204. Ibid., pp. 369–71 (180–2).
205. Ibid., p. 353 (161).
206. Ibid., p. 353 (161–2).
207. Ibid., pp. 355, 357, 366, 372–3 (163, 166, 174, 183–4).
208. Ibid., p. 364 (174).
209. Ibid., p. 370 (181).
210. Ibid.
211. Ibid., p. 363 (173); see also ibid., p. 371 (182–3).
212. Ibid., p. 363 (172), at which point, however, Winstanley offers a unique insinuation to this effect.
213. Ibid., p. 384 (196).
214. John Locke, *Two Treatises of Civil Government*, with an introduction by P. Laslett (Cambridge, 1963), p. 330.
215. Winstanley, *New-yeers-Gift*, pp. 375–91 (186–204), 'The Curse and Blessing that is Mankinde'.
216. Ibid., p. 398 (203).
217. Ibid., p. 365 (175).
218. Ibid., pp. 381, 385–6 (193, 198).
219. Ibid., p. 361 (170).
220. Ibid., pp. 364–7 (174–7). For an account of the Ranters and their beliefs see A.L. Morton, *The World of the Ranters* (London, 1970); and various contributors to J.F. McGregor and B. Reay (eds), *Radical Religion in the English Revolution* (Oxford, 1984).
221. Winstanley, *New-yeers-Gift*, p. 367 (177).
222. Ibid., p. 366 (167).
223. Effectively from the domain of Mr Francis Drake, who owned the manor of Walton, to that of Parson John Platt, rector of West Horsely and, by marriage, owner of the manor of Cobham.
224. Winstanley, *A Vindication of those, whose Endeavor is only to make the Earth a Common Treasury, Called Diggers*; *idem*, *An Appeale to All Englishmen*; *idem*, *An Humble Request, to the Minsters of both Universities, and to all Lawyers in every Inns-a-court*.
225. Winstanley, *Fire in the Bush*; G.E. Aylmer, introduction to *England's Spirit Unfolded, or An Incouragement to Take the Engagement P & P*, 40 (1968).
226. Winstanley, *A Vindication*, p. 402; see also *idem*, *England's Spirit*, pp. 14–15.
227. Winstanley, *A Vindication*, p. 399.
228. Winstanley, *An Appeale to All*, p. 407.
229. Ibid., pp. 412–13, Winstanley also discusses the Engagement, again cf. '*England's Spirit*'.
230. Winstanley, *An Appeale to All*, p. 413.
231. Ibid., p. 409.
232. See Winstanley, *A Letter Taken at Wellingborough* in *Works*, p. 439.
233. Winstanley, *Humble Request*, p. 423.
234. Ibid., p. 425.
235. Ibid., pp. 430–1.
236. Ibid., p. 437.
237. Winstanley, *New-yeers-Gift*, p. 367 (177), see also *idem*, *True Levellers' Standard*, pp. 255, 262 (81, 90); *idem*, *Declaration from the Poor*, p. 269 (99); *idem*, *A Watch-Word*, pp. 328, 336, (139, 148).

238. Winstanley, *A Watch-Word*, p. 335 (147).
239. Ibid., p. 334 (146).
240. See, for example, Winstanley, *New-yeers-Gift*, 370 (181).
241. Thomas, op. cit., pp. 161–2.
242. See, for example, the subtitle of the tract, *The Spirit Burning, not Consuming, but Purging Mankind, OR, The great Battle of God Almightly, between Michael the Seed of Life, and the great red Dragon, the Curse, fought within the Spirit of Man.*
243. Winstanley, *Fire in the Bush*, p. 453 (221).
244. Ibid., p. 465 (235).
245. Ibid., p. 453 (222).
246. Ibid., pp. 451–5 (219–24).
247. Ibid., p. 455 (224).
248. Ibid., pp. 455–63 (224–33).
249. Ibid., pp. 462–3 (232–3).
250. Ibid., p. 458 (227).
251. Ibid., p. 461 (231).
252. Ibid., pp. 463–71 (233–42).
253. Ibid., p. 467 (237).
254. Ibid., pp. 471–6 (243–8).
255. Ibid., p. 472 (244).
256. Ibid., p. 473 (245).
257. Ibid., pp. 476–84 (248–57).
258. Ibid., pp. 477–8 (249–51).
259. Ibid., p. 479 (252).
260. Ibid., pp. 480–1 (254), see also ibid., pp. 484. 488–9, 493–4 (257, 261, 269).
261. Ibid., p. 478 (251).
262. Ibid., pp. 484–8 (257–63).
263. Ibid., p. 485 (259).
264. Ibid., pp. 489–97 (263–72).
265. Ibid., p. 493 (269).
266. Ibid., p. 494 (269).
267. Ibid., pp. 490–2 (265–6).
268. Ibid., p. 491 (265).
269. Ibid., p. 495 (270–1).
270. Aylmer, introduction to *England's Spirit*.
271. For the background to this debate, see J.M. Wallace, 'The Engagement Controversy 1649–52: An Annotated List of Pamphlets', *Bulletin of the New York Public library*, 68 (1964); and Q. Skinner, 'Conquest and Consent: Thomas Hobbes and the Engagement Controversy' in G.E. Aylmer (ed.), *The Interregnum: the Quest for a Settlement* (London, 1972).
272. Aylmer, introduction to *England's Spirit*, pp. 7–8.
273. *England's Spirit*, p. 13.
274. Winstanley, *The Law of Freedom in a Platform* in *Works*, p. 509 (285).
275. Sabine, op. cit., p. 58, suggests in this respect that Winstanley may have been anxious to dissociate his utopian proposals from the Digger disaster.
276. Winstanley, *Law of Freedom*, p. 510 (285).
277. Ibid., p. 510 (286): 'for under that you may see beauty. / It may be you will say . . .'.
278. Ibid., pp. 501–8 (275–83).
279. Ibid., p. 568 (352).

Notes to Chapter 6

1. For an instance of Cromwell's emotional excitement and confidence in the prospects for the Saints' Parliament see T.W. Carlyle (ed.), *Letters and Speeches of Oliver Cromwell*, II, speech 1, 4 July 1653, delivered at the opening of Barebone's Parliament.
2. See B.S. Capp, *The Fifth Monarchy Men* (London, 1972), pp. 62–3, for a discussion of the millenarian assumption that Cromwell was the 'Second Moses'.
3. G.H. Sabine, intro. to Winstanley, *Works*, p. 36.
4. Winstanley, *The Law of Freedom in a Platform or True Magistracy Restored* in *Works*, p. 509 (285).
5. Ibid., pp. 521–2, 529–32, 559 (297, 306–10, 343).
6. Although the bases of his various calculations differ it is worth comparing '*New Law of Righteousnes* in *Works*, p. 200, 'Divide England into three parts, scarce one part is manured'; *An Appeal to the House* in *Works*, p. 304 (115), 'one third part lies waste and barren'; *New-yeers Gift* in *Works*, p. 356 (165) 'seing there is Land enough, and more by half than is made use of', (3/5 ?); and *Law of Freedom*, p. 507 (282), 'there be Land enough in England, to maintain ten times as many people as are in it'.
7. Winstanley, *Law of Freedom*, p. 515 (291); cf. *idem*, *Fire in the Bush* in *Works*, p. 478 (251).
8. Winstanley, *Law of Freedom*, p. 526 (302–3.
9. Ibid., p. 526 (302).
10. Ibid.
11. C. Hill, introduction to *Winstanley: The Law of Freedom* (Harmondsworth, 1973), p. 53.
12. M. James, 'Contemporary Materialist Interpretations of the English Revolution' in C. Hill (ed.), *The English Revolution: Three Essays* (London, 1949), p. 96.
13. Winstanley, *Law of Freedom*, p. 511 (287).
14. Ibid., pp. 526–7 (303), see also ibid., p. 593 (381).
15. Ibid., p. 579 (365).
16. Cf. Winstanley, *Fire in the Bush* p. 493 (269). C. Hill, *Winstanley: The Law of Freedom*, p. 59, argues that 'Winstanley too saw childhood as innocence', and goes on to discuss his 'idealization of childhood as a state of innocence'. Although this impression correctly represents Winstanley's initial position, it must be applied with caution to Winstanley's stance in 'The Law of Freedom'.
17. Winstanley, *Law of Freedom*, pp. 548, 579 (329, 365).
18. Given that by today's standards relatively few men lived to the age of forty, Winstanley's provision would not appear to impose such a burden upon the utopian economy.
19. C. Webster, *The Great Instauration: Science, Medicine and Reform 1626–1660* (London, 1975), p. 362.
20. Winstanley, *Law of Freedom*, p. 592 (381).
21. Ibid., p. 550 (331).
22. Ibid., p. 579 (365).
23. Although this effectively constitutes a doubling of the holiday provisions detailed in Utopia, Winstanley may have compensated by envisaging a longer working day.
24. D.W. Petegorsky, *Left-Wing Democracy in the English Civil War* (New York, 1940, 1972 edn), p. 207.
25. See J.K. Fuz, *Welfare Economics in English Utopias from Francis Bacon to Adam Smith* (The Hague, 1952), p. 51.

26. Winstanley, *Law of Freedom*, p. 583 (369).
27. Ibid., p. 551 (332).
28. Ibid., p. 578 (364).
29. Ibid., pp. 582–3 (370).
30. Ibid., p. 583 (369–70).
31. Ibid., pp. 583–5 (370–2).
32. Ibid., pp. 526ff., 580 (302ff., 366).
33. Ibid., pp. 584–5 (371).
34. See, for example, Petegorsky, op. cit., p. 217.
35. W.F. Murphy, 'The Political Philosophy of Gerrard Winstanley, *Review of Politics*, 19 (1957), pp. 227–9.
36. Winstanley, *Law of Freedom*, p. 550 (330–1).
37. Ibid., p. 592 (380).
38. Ibid., p. 512 (288); see also ibid., p. 527 (304).
39. Ibid., p. 527 (303–4).
40. Ibid., pp. 546–7 (327).
41. Ibid., p. 583 (370).
42. Ibid., p. 527 (304); see also ibid., p. 547 (327).
43. Ibid., pp. 547–8 (328).
44. Ibid., p. 534 (313).
45. Ibid., p. 585 (371).
46. Ibid., p. 513 (289).
47. Ibid., p. 581 (367).
48. Petegorsky, op. cit., p. 203.
49. M. Walzer, 'Puritanism as a Revolutionary Ideology', *H & T*, III (1963–4), p. 67.
50. Winstanley, *Law of Freedom*, p. 587 (374).
51. Ibid., p. 533 (311).
52. Ibid., p. 585 (371).
53. Ibid., p. 534 (312).
54. Ibid., p. 576 (361).
55. Ibid., p. 577 (362).
56. Ibid.
57. Winstanley, *To the Lord Fairfax, Generall of the English Forces, and His Councell of War* in *Works*, pp. 282–4.
58. Winstanley, *Law of Freedom*, p. 552 (333).
59. Winstanley's utopian authoritarianism is particularly emphasized in the work of J.C. Davis, 'Gerrard Winstanley and the Restoration of True Magistracy', *P & P*, 70 (1977); *idem, Utopia and the Ideal Society: A Study of English Utopian Writing 1516–1700* (Cambridge, 1981), ch. 7.
60. G. Woodcock, *Anarchism* (Harmondsworth, 1963), pp. 42–6.
61. C. Hill, *Milton and the English Revolution* (London, 1977), p. 161.
62. C. Hill, introduction to *Winstanley: The Law of Freedom*, p. 41.
63. Winstanley, *Law of Freedom*, p. 528 (305).
64. Ibid., p. 536 (314).
65. Ibid., p. 536 (315).
66. Ibid., p. 540 (320).
67. See B. Worden, *The Rump Parliament* (Cambridge, 1974).
68. Winstanley, *Law of Freedom*, p. 556 (338).
69. Ibid., p. 559 (341).
70. Ibid., p. 540ff. (319ff.).
71. Ibid., p. 596 (385).
72. It must be assumed either that this provision is a loose end, or that Winstanley

believed that even the spiritually restored would not be immune from the corrupting influences of power exercised over a prolonged period.

73. Winstanley, *Law of Freedom*, 541 (321).
74. As argued by W.S. Hudson, 'The Economic and Social Thought of Gerrard Winstanley', *JMH*, 18 (1946), p. 19.
75. Davis, 'Gerrard Winstanley and the Restoration of True Magistracy', p. 90.
76. Ibid., pp. 84–5.
77. Murphy, op. cit., p. 237, see also p. 227.
78. Winstanley, *Law of Freedom*, pp. 535–6 (314); here Winstanley follows St Paul.
79. Ibid., p. 515 (292).
80. Ibid., p. 528 (305).
81. Ibid., pp. 528–9 (306).
82. Ibid., p. 539 (318); see also ibid., pp. 571–2 (356–7).
83. Ibid., p. 546 (326–7).
84. Ibid., p. 553 (335).
85. Ibid., pp. 594–5 (383).
86. Ibid., pp. 598–9 (387).
87. Ibid., p. 527 (304).
88. Ibid.
89. C. Hill, *Winstanley: The Law of Freedom*, p. 55.
90. G.J. Schochet, 'Patriarchalism, Politics and Mass Attitudes in Stuart England', *HJ*, XII (1969), p. 424.
91. G.J. Schochet, *Patriarchalism in Political Thought* (Oxford, 1975), p. 16.
92. C. Hill, *Society and Puritanism in Pre-Revolutionary England* (London, 1964), p. 436.
93. M. Walzer, *The Revolution of the Saints* (London, 1965), p. 307.
94. Schochet, *Patriarchalism in Political Thought*, pp. 162–3.
95. Winstanley, *Law of Freedom*, p. 538 (317).
96. Ibid., p. 552 (333).
97. Ibid., p. 549 (329).
98. Ibid., p. 545 (325).
99. Ibid., p. 548 (329).
100. Ibid., p. 550 (331).
101. Winstanley, *Fire in the Bush*, p. 494 (269).
102. K.V. Thomas, 'Women in the Civil War Sects', *P & P*, 13 (1958), 53.
103. K.V. Thomas, 'The Double Standard', *JHI*, XX (1959).
104. See G. Rosen, 'Left-Wing Puritanism and Science', *Bulletin of the Institute of the History of Medicine*, XV (1944), *passim*; W. Schenk, *The Concern for Social Justice in the Puritan Revolution* (London, 1948), p. 110; R.L. Greaves, 'Gerrard Winstanley and Education Reform in Puritan England', *British Journal of Educational Studies*, XVII (1969), pp. 169–76.
105. Winstanley, *Law of Freedom*, p. 544 (324).
106. Ibid., p. 576 (361).
107. C. Hill, *The World Turned Upside Down* (Harmondsworth, 1975), p. 137, see also *idem*, introduction to Winstanley, *Law of Freedom*, p. 47.
108. Winstanley, *Law of Freedom*, p. 579 (365).
109. L. Stone, *The Family, Sex and Marriage in England, 1500–1800* (London, 1977), p. 204.
110. Ibid., pp. 204–6.
111. Webster, op. cit., p. 219.
112. Winstanley, *An Appeale to All Englishmen* in *Works*, p. 409 and *passim*.
113. Winstanley, *An Humble Request*, *Works*, p. 423.
114. Winstanley, *A Vindication*, *Works*, p. 401.

115. Winstanley, *Law of Freedom*, p. 593 (381).
116. Ibid., pp. 592–3 (380–1).
117. Ibid., p. 577 (362).
118. Ibid.
119. Ibid., p. 545 (325).
120. K.V. Thomas, 'Age and Authority in Early-Modern England', *Proceedings of the British Academy*, LXII (1976), p. 26.
121. Ibid., p. 15.
122. See, for example, D.C. Coleman, 'Labour in the English Economy of the Seventeenth Century', *Econ. HR*, 2nd series, VIII (1956), p. 285: 'in seventeenth-century England, average expectation of life at birth was probably in the neighbourhood of 35 or less.
123. Thomas, *Age and Authority in Early-Modern England*, pp. 9–10, 31.
124. Ibid., pp. 34–5; however, although Winstanley would have citizens retire from manual labour, he assumed that they would continue to lead an active life.
125. Ibid., p. 12.
126. Ibid., p. 5.
127. See ibid., p. 8.
128. Winstanley, *Law of Freedom*, p. 600 (389).
129. Ibid., ch. IV, pp. 544–76 (324–61).
130. Ibid., p. 552 (333); see also ibid., p. 539 (318).
131. Ibid., p. 543 (323).
132. Ibid., pp. 587–9 (374–7).
133. Ibid., p. 587 (374).
134. Ibid., p. 588 (375).
135. Ibid., p. 588 (376).
136. Ibid., p. 590 (378).
137. Ibid., p. 554 (335).
138. Ibid., p. 554 (336).
139. Ibid., pp. 555–6 (337–8).
140. Ibid., pp. 552–3 (334).
141. Ibid., p. 563 (346).
142. For a comparison of Winstanley's position to that of Harrington, see M. Goldie, 'The Civil Religion of James Harrington' in A. Pagden (ed.), *The Languages of Political Theory in Early-Modern Europe* (Cambridge, 1987), p. 204ff.
143. Winstanley, *Law of Freedom*, p. 564 (347).
144. Ibid., pp. 567–8 (351–2).
145. Ibid., p. 597 (385).
146. Ibid., pp. 562–3 (345–6).
147. Ibid., p. 563 (346).
148. Ibid., p. 577 (362).
149. Ibid., p. 579 (364).
150. Ibid., p. 564 (347).
151. Greaves, op. cit., p. 172.
152. Winstanley, *Law of Freedom*, p. 585 (371).
153. Ibid., p. 576 (361).

Notes to Chapter 7

1. This theme is considered by A. Arblaster, *The Rise and Decline of Western Liberalism* (Oxford, 1984), esp. chs 5–7.

2. To which A. Reeve, *Property* (London, 1986), is a particularly insightful recent contribution. J. Waldron, *The Right to Private Property* (Oxford, 1988) appeared as this work was sent to press.
3. J.O. Grunebaum, *Private Ownership* (London, 1987), pp. 11–20 and *passim*. A seminal treatment of the nature and range of such rules is A.M. Honore, 'Ownership' in A.G. Guest (ed.), *Oxford Essays in Jurisprudence* (Oxford, 1961).
4. See, A. Reeve, 'The Treatment of Property by Some English Economic, Legal and Social Writers between 1600–1700', D.Phil. thesis, Oxford, 1979; and G.E. Aylmer, 'The Meaning and Definition of "Property" in Seventeenth-Century England', *P & P*, 86 (1980); A. Reeve, 'The Meaning and Definition of "Property" in Seventeenth-Century England', *P & P*, 89 (1980).
5. See J. Tully, *A Discourse on Property: John Locke and His Adversaries* (Cambridge, 1980).
6. R. Nozick, *Anarchy, State and Utopia* (Oxford, 1974).
7. J. Elster, *Making Sense of Marx*, pp. 82–92 (Cambridge, 1985).
8. See, K. Tribe, *Land, Labour and Economic Discourse* (London, 1978); M. Berg, *The Machinery Question and the Making of Political Economy 1815–1848* (Cambridge, 1980).
9. For an elaboration, see L.C. Becker, *Property Rights* (London, 1977), chs 3–5.
10. On this facet of Leveller social theory, see R. Tuck, *Natural Rights Theories: Their Origin and Development* (Cambridge, 1979), ch. 7.
11. Grunebaum, op. cit., p. 25. See also. A. Ryan, *Property* (Milton Keynes, 1987), ch. 1.
12. See above, page 28.
13. A consideration discussed in Ryan, op. cit., ch. 5.
14. See Tuck, op. cit., esp. ch. 1; B. Tierney, 'Tuck on Rights: some Medieval Problems', *History of Political Thought*, IV (1983); and also J. Coleman, 'Dominium in Thirteenth and Fourteenth-Century Political Thought and its Seventeenth-Century Heirs: John of Paris and Locke', *PS*, XXXIII (1985).
15. Tuck, op. cit., p. 22.
16. Tully, op. cit., chs 3 and 5.
17. There are, of course, many discussions of Locke's case. Among the most stimulating is J. Waldron, 'Two Worries About Mixing One's Labour', *P. Qtly*, 33 (1983).
18. A consideration not lost on Herbert Spencer; see his *Social Statics: or The Conditions Essential to Human Happiness* (1851 edn, reprinted New York, 1969), esp. ch. IX; and H. Steiner, 'Land, Liberty and the Early Herbert Spencer', *History of Political Thought*, III (1982).
19. See, for example, T. Paine on inheritance in 'Miscellaneous Chapter' in (1791–2, 1969 edn, Harmondsworth). On the notions of labour entitlement sponsored by the so-called 'Ricardian socialists', see, J.F. Bray, *Labour's Wrongs and Labour's Remedy* (Leeds, 1839); T. Hodgskin, *The Natural and Artificial Right of Property Contrasted* (London, 1832); W. Thompson, *Labour Rewarded: The Claims of Labour and Capital Conciliated* (London, 1827). On problems extending from the ineqitable distribution of land, see, H. George, *Poverty and Progress* (London, 1884). From the secondary literature, see, in particular, Ursula Vogel 'When the Earth Belonged to All: the Land Question in Eighteenth-Century Justifications of Private Property', *PS*, XXXVI (1988).
20. The conceptual difficulties entailed in employing the term 'progress' are discussed in T.A. Kenyon, 'Utopia in reality: "Ideal" Societies in Social and Political Theory', *History of Political Thought*, III (1982), pp. 149–52.
21. Cf. J.B. Bury, *The Idea of Progress* (New York, 1932), p. 2; and H. Butterfield, *The Origins of Modern Science* (London, 1949, 1980 edn), pp. 212–19.

22. See C. Becker, 'Progress' in *Encyclopaedia of the Social Sciences*, Vol. XII (New York, 1933), p. 498.
23. See, for example, Bury, op. cit., ch. I. i.
24. See T.E. Mommsen, 'St. Augustine and the Christian Idea of Progress', *JHI*, XII (1951).
25. K.V. Thomas, *Religion and the Decline of Magic* (London, 1971, 1973 edn), p. 788.
26. For a variety of widely differing accounts of the 'scientific revolution', see, for example, M. Boas, 'The Establishment of the Mechanical Philosophy', 'Osiris, X (1952); Butterfield, op. cit.; A. Koestler, *The Sleepwalkers: A History of Man's Changing Vision of the Universe* (London, 1959); T.S. Kuhn, *The Copernican Revolution: Planetary Astronomy in the Development of Western Thought* (Cambridge, MA, 1957); R.K. Merton, *Science, Technology and Change in Seventeenth-Century England* (1938) (New York, 1970); J.H. Randall, 'The Development of the Scientific Method in the School of Padua', *JHI*, I (1940).
27. H. Baker, *The Wars of Truth: Studies in the Decay of Christian Humanism in the Earlier Seventeenth Century* (Gloucester, MA, 1952, 1969 edn), p. 95 and *passim.*
28. Ibid., p. 314.
29. See, for example, C.L. Becker, *The Heavenly City of the Eighteenth-Century Philosophers* (New Haven, CT, 1932); R.O. Rockwood (ed.), *Carl Becker's Heavenly City Revisited* (Cornell, NY, 1958); E. Cassirer, *The Philosophy of the Enlightenment* (Princeton, NJ, 1951); C. Frankel, *The Faith of Reason* (New York, 1948); N. Hampson, *The Enlightenment* (Harmondsworth, 1968); P. Hazard, *The European Mind 1680–1715* trans J. Lewis (1935; Harmondsworth, 1973 edn); *idem, European Thought in the Eighteenth Century from Montesquieu to Lessing* (1946; Cleveland, 1963 edn); I.O. Wade, *The Intellectual Origins of the French Enlightenment* (Princeton, NJ, 1971).
30. F. Bacon, *Novum Organum* (1620) in *Works*, IV, Aphorism CXVI, p. 104.
31. F. Bacon, *The Great Instauration* (1620) in *Works*, IV, p. 13ff.
32. Bacon, *Novum Organum* (I), LXXXIV, p. 82.
33. Ibid. (I), XCII, p. 90.
34. F. Bacon, *Of Fortune* (1597; 1612 edn) in *Works*, VI, p. 472.
35. Bacon, *Novum Organum, passim.*
36. Ibid. (II), LII, pp. 247–8.
37. Ibid., *passim.*
38. For a recent evaluation along these lines see, A. Quinton, *Francis Bacon* (Oxford, 1980).
39. Bacon, *Novum Organum* (I), XLI, p. 54, and *passim.*
40. F. Bacon, *The Advancement of Learning* (1605) in *Works*, III, Bk I.
41. Bacon, *The Great Instauration*, p. 20.
42. Bacon, *Novum Organum* (I), III, p. 48; ibid., (II), IV, p. 120.
43. Ibid. (I), CXXIV, p. 110.
44. F. Bacon, *New Atlantis* (1627) in *Works*, III, p. 156.
45. Bacon, *Novum Organum* (I), CXXIX, p. 115.
46. For these aspects of Baconianism, see C. Webster, *The Great Instauration: Science, Medicine and Reform 1626–1660* (London, 1975), esp. ch. III.
47. Bacon, *Novum Organum* (I), LXXXII, p. 81.
48. See Thomas, op. cit., ch. 22, esp. pp.769–73; and B.S. Capp, *Astrology and the Popular Press* (London, 1979), ch. 9.
49. Webster, op. cit., *passim*, esp. p. 499.
50. C. Hill, 'William Harvey and the Idea of Monarchy', *P & P*, 27 (1964), n. 42, citing Winstanley, *The Law of Freedom* in *Works*, p. 565.
51. Winstanley, *The Law of Freedom* p. 565 (349).

52. Ibid., p. 571 (355–6).
53. See Thomas, op. cit., pp. 794–7.

Index

Acts, of the Apostles, 172
  apostolic communism, 72, 76, 99
Adams, R.P., 101n, 102n
Albert, The Great, 45
Allen, H.M., 64n, 101n
Allen, P.S., 64n, 101n
Ancient Constitution, 9
Aquinas, St. Thomas
  influence of Aristotle, 42, 43–44, 45, 46
  influence of Augustine, 42, 46
  on happiness, 45
  on law, 45–46
  on natural law, 46
  on property, 46–47
  on reason, 42, 45
  on the will and goodness, 58, 60n, 202n, 231
  private ownership as conventional, 32
  private ownership as natural, 33
Arblaster, Anthony, 227n
Arendt, Hannah, 5, 61n
Aries, Philippe, 89n
Aristotle, 28, 31, 46, 95
  on freedom of choice, 40, 111
  on the household, 40
  on natural justice, 40
  on the *polis*, 40
  on property, 230, 231
  on reason, 42
  private property as natural, 32
    see also Aristotelianism
Aristotelianism, 29, 88
  and Augustinianism, 40, 42
  and Christian thought, 39
  and medieval philosphy, 32, 40, 42
  cosmology, 235
  on civil institutions, 40
  teleology and natural justice, 40
    see also Aristotle
Armstrong, A.H., 40n
Augustine, of Hippo, St., 26, 30, 235
  character and ownership, 230
  on causation, 43
  on civil institutions, 45
  on the Fall, 41
  on history, 43
  on the will and freedom of choice, 42–43
  theory of history, 44
    *see also*Augustinianism
Augustinianism, conceptions of Fall, 26, 229
  and Aristotelianism, 40, 42
  and Christian tradition, 39
  and medieval philosophy, 40, 41
    see also Augustine
Austin, J.L., 8
autonomy of moral action, 110–113
  see also determinism
Avineri, Shlomo, 106n
Aylmer, G.E., 121n, 182n, 190n, 191, 228n

Bacon, Francis, 237–239
  and the dominion over nature, 239
  on the Fall, 238
  on history and progress, 237–238
  on philosophy and theology, 238
  scientific method, 238–239
Baconianism, 35
  see also Bacon
Baker, Herschel, 42n, 236
Barnes, Robert, 49
Baumann, F., 80n
Becker, Carl, L., 235n, 237n
Becker, Lawrence C., 231n
Bennett, G.V., 87n
Berg, Maxine, 231n
Berki, R.N., 6n, 11n, 12n
Berlin, Isaiah, 5
Bloch-Laine, F., 25n
Bloomfield, P., 21n
Boas, M., 235n
Boucher, David, 11n, 12n
Brailsford, H.N., 165n, 169n
Brandt, W.I., 55n
Bray, J.F. 'Ricardian socialist', 234n
Brockway, Fenner, 169n
Budé, Guillaume, 78
Burns, J.H., 40n
Bury, J.B., 235n
Butterfield, Herbert, 235n
Byron, B., 84n

Calvin, John, 26, 83
Campbell, W.E., 93n
Canon Law, 32
Capp, B.S., 23–24, 29n, 109n, 193n, 240n
Carlyle, A.J., 28n, 31
Carlyle, T.W., 193n
Cartesianism, 35
Caspari, F., 94n
Cassirer, Ernst, 237n
Chadwick, Henry, 44n
Chambers, R.W., 106n
Charles, I., 150, 178
  his execution, 171
  see also Winstanley
Child, H., 21n
Civil War, English, 123
Christian Humanism
  see humanism
classical republicanism, 9, 110
Coke, Edward, legal theorist, 142
Cole, G.D.H., 58n
Cole, R.C., 121n, 153n
Coleman, Janet, 232n
Colet, John, 109
Comenius, Jan, 240
common law, 142
communism and communal ownership, as natural, 32
Commonwealth, the
  see Interregnum
conceptual analysis, 12–16
Connolly, W.E., 12n, 13, 15
contact theory, 28, 232
  see also state of nature
Coster, Robert, Digger, 165n
Counter-Reformation, 49, 51
Cromwell, Oliver, 190, 192, 193
Cromwell, Thomas, 50
Cummins, J., 90n

Davis, J.C., 17n, 20, 21n, 23–24, 110. 165n, 169n, 174n, 205n
Davis, D.B., 188n
Deane, H.A., 44n, 45n
de Jouvenal, Bertrand, 17
Descartes, René
  see Cartesianism
determinism, informing meaning of texts, 12
  informing action, 110
  see also autonomy
Diggers
  see Winstanley
Dominicans, their philosophy, 42
dominium
  see private property
Dorp, Martin, 63n, 69n, 108n
Drake, Mr. Francis, landowner, adversary of Diggers, 169, 182n
Duhamel, P., 75n
Dunn, John, 6, 33n
Dury, John, 240

Edwards, Alistair, 114n
Elect Nation, 9
  see also Winstanley
Elizabeth of York, wife of Henry VII, 61
Elmen, P., 121n, 123n, 144n, 170
Elster, Jon, 230
Engagement', 'The. 1650, and controversy, 191
Engels, Friedrich, 18–19
Enlightenment, 20
  response to doctrine of the Fall, 27
  Scottish, 231, 237, 241
Epicureanism, 101–102
  see also Epicurus
Epicurus, 96
  see also Epicureanism
epistemology, sensationalism, 35
Erasmus, Desiderius, 50, 68, 78, 94, 99, 109
'essentially contested concepts', 13
eschatology, 9
  variety of beliefs, 23–24
Everard, William, Digger, collaborator and associate of Winstanley, 161, 168, 173

Fairfax, Sir Thomas, Lord, 131, 133n, 139n, 150n, 151, 168, 173–174, 178, 190, 192, 205
Fall of Man
  and cosmology, 235
  and dominion over nature, 29
  and obligation to labour, 29,33
  and origins of private property, 31
  and property theory 31, 228
  and social institutions, 30, 31
  as informing medieval and early–modern worldviews, 26, 235
  as an intellectual paradigm, 7, 9, 16
  explanatory force, 26
  forbidden knowledge, 29
  problem of causation, 27
Femia, J.V., 11n
  on methodological revisionism, 12
Fenlon, D.B., 50n, 90n
Feuer, L.S., 18n
Fifth Monarchists, 24
Figgis, J.N., 44n
Filmer, Sir Robert, 210
Fish, Simon, 49, 62n
Fisher, John, Bishop of Rochester, 75
Fleisher, M., 76n, 79n, 102n, 103n
Fourier, Charles, 18
Fox, A., 48n
Frankel, C., 237n
Fransiscans, their philosophy, 42
French Revolution, 20
Frith, John, 49
Furnivall, F.J., 62n
Fuz, J.K., 20n, 198n

Gallie, W.B., 12–14
Gardner, P., 95n
Genesis, Book of, 33n, 65
George, G.H., 121n, 122n, 153n
George, Henry, 234
Goldie, Mark, 221n
Gonell, William, 94
Goodin, R.E., 11n
Goodwin, B., 17n
Gratian, decretalist, 32
Gray, John, 14, 16n
Greaves, R.L., 147n, 212n, 224n
Green, T.H., 125n
great chain of being, 30
Greenleaf, W.H., 25, 30
Grice, H.P., 8
Grotius, Hugo, 232, 233
Grunebaum, James O., 228, 231
Guest, A.B., 228n

Hamilton, L.D., 127n
Hampson, Norman, 237n
Harrington, James, *Oceana* 21, 91n
Hartlib, Samuel, 240
Harvey, William, 240
Hay, D., 50n
Hayes, T.W., 138
Hazard, Paul, 237n
Headley, J.H., 48n, 49n, 50n, 55n, 84n
Henry VII, 61
Henry VIII, 48
Hexter, J.H., 54n, 67n, 69n, 71n, 76n, 79n, 86n, 88n, 94n, 99n, 110n

Hill, Christopher, 27, 122n, 127n, 133n, 138–139, 141–142, 143, 145n, 147, 151n, 165n, 169n, 195, 196n, 206, 210, 213, 240n
Hobbes, Thomas, 28, 83, 139, 145
  on property rights, 232
Hodgskin, Thomas, 234n
Honoré, A.M., 228n
Hooker, Richard, on the Fall, 34, 35
Höpfl, Harro, 55n, 83n
Hoskins, W.G., 151n
Hudson, W.S., 121n, 153n, 169n, 208n
human condition
  as described by the Fall, 26
  as facet of utopianism, 17, 19, 21
  as a predicament, 4–5
Humanism, 49, 87, 102
  christian humanism, 79, 86, 108
Hume, David, 230
Huxley, Aldous, 18
Hyman, A., 42n

idealism, 20
  as a facet of utopianism, 22
Interregnum, the, 153
ius naturale
  see natural law
Isidore, St., of Seville, 32

James, M.E., 146n, 169n, 195
John, of Paris, 232n
Juretic, G., 121n, 122n, 153n, 165n

Kant Immanuel, on moral choice, 111
Kateb, G., 21n
Kautsky, Karl, 76, 80
Kazepides, A.C., 95n
Kekes, J., 14n, 15n
Kenyon, Timothy, 23n, 129n, 235n
Kernan, G., 48n
Knox, R., 106n
Koestler, Arthur, 235n
Korolec, J.B., 42n, 44
Kretzmann, N., 40n
Kristellar, P.O., 42n
Kuhn, T.S., 6–7, 8, 109n, 235n

Lancashire, 154
Laslett, Peter, 180n
law
  see Canon Law, common law, equity, natural law, Roman Law
Laud, William, Archbishop of Canterbury, 147
Levellers, 123
  on the Norman Yoke, 142
  'True Levellers', 162, 231n
Lewis, J., 237n
Lindsay, A.D., 125n
Lively, Jack, 15n
Locke, John, on basis of private ownership, 33, 136, 180, 229
  on the Fall, 34
  on the nature of property rights, 230, 232, 233
Lohr, C.H., 47n
Lovejoy, A.O., 5, 30n
Luscombe, D.E., 42n
Luther, Martin, 47, 49, 55, 84, 116, *see also* Lutheranism
Lutheranism, 39
  see also Luther

MacDonald, W.J., 28n
Macfarlane, Alan, 151n
Machiavelli, Niccolo, 230
MacIntyre, Alasdair, 12n, 15n, 39n, 42n, 45n, 47n
magic, 29
Mandrou, Robert, 50n
Mannheim, Karl, 19–20
Manifesto of the Communist Party, 18
Manuel, F.E., 17n
Manuel, F.P., 17n
Marenbon, John, 40n
Marius, R., 48n, 50n, 51n, 55n, 58n
market liberalism, 230
Markus, R.A., 44n
Marx, Karl
  on alienation, 230
  on utopianism, 18–19, 80n
Marxism, approach to utopianism, 18–19
McClear, J.F., 145
McGrade, A.S., 47
McGregor, J.F., 121n, 181n
Melanchthon, Philip, 47

Merton, R.K., 235n
Miles, L., 106n
Mill, John Stuart, 229
millenarianism, 23
  in relation to utopianism, 23–24
  variety of forms, 24
    see also Winstanley
Milton, John, on the Fall, 34–35
Mirandula, Picus, 52n
Mommsen, T.E., 44n, 235n
monasticism, 88, 201
Moody, M.E., 121n, 153
Moore, Jnr, Barrington, 169n
Moore, G.E., on moral choice, 111
Moore, M.J., 103n
Moore, W.E., 20n
More, Thomas, 3, 9, 14, 16
  and natural law tradition, 28, 56, 87
  asceticism, 97, 100
  compared to Rousseau, 58
  conception of liberty, 112–115, 149, 193, 195, 198, 200, 201, 203, 204, 207, 210, 212, 213, 219, 222, 223, 224, 228, 230, 231, 234, 241
  conception of the person, 112
  conception of progress, 108
  his constitutionalism, 84
  influence of Aquinas, 44, 47, 53, 84, 113, 116
  influence of Aristotle, 47, 76, 88
  influence of Augustine, 42, 55, 65, 113, 115–116
  influence of Epicurus, 101–102
  influence of monasticism, 90, 201
  influence of Plato, 88
  influence of Stoics, 101–102
  on astrology, 109
  on categories of grace, 59, 111, 112–113, 115
  on celibacy, 106
  on Christ's Passion, 64–65
  on the Church, 49–50, 69
  on citizenship and freedom, 16, 113–114
  on communism and the utopian economy, 65, 74–82, 107
  on community, 90–93, 104
  on conditions for moral action, 59–60, 110–117
  on contemporary morality, 67
  on cremation, 106
  on crime and punishment, 70
  on death, 61, 66, 100
  on divorce, 106
  on education, 69, 89, 93–95, 108
  on enclosures, 70
  on equity, 87
  on euthenasia, 106
  on faith, 55–56, 57
  on faith and reason, 96–97
  on Fall of Man, 26, 47, 56–57, 63–67, 108, 109, 111
  on the family and patriarchalism, 88–90
  on forms and philosophy of pleasure, 68, 79–80, 100–107
  on freedom of choice, 111, 113–114
  on free will, 55–56, 57–58, 97, 111, 115
  on heaven and hell, 62
  on the just war, 106
  on labour, 64, 65, 76–78
  on land use, 60–70
  on law, 69, 87
  on marriage, 89–90
  on miracles, 97
  on natural and conventional forms of ownership, 33
  on nature of God, 52
  on the nature of happiness, 104
  on the nobility, 68, 105
  on the original condition, 63–64
  on political obligation, 110, 113
  on power and authority, 85
  on pride, 54, 61, 94
  on principles of distribution, 79–82
  on private property, 71–73
  on purgatory, 62
  on reason, 56–57, 93
  on revelation, 96, 99, 105
  on the role of the state and government, 83–87
  on sacramental worship, 51
  on salvation, 51, 62–63, 74, 94, 100, 101, 103, 107, 111

More, Thomas – *cont.*
  on science, 108, 239
  on scripture, 51–52
  on sin and original sin, 53–54, 66
  on slavery, 78, 93, 106
  on the treatment of heretics, 106
  on utopianism as political thought, 17, 23, 24, 30, 31, 54, 95, 116
  on vagrancy, 70, 93
  on virtue, 104
  on war, 68
  on women in society, 65–66, 77
  on works, 61
  periodization of writings, 48
  polemical response to Protestantism, 48, 60, 84
  the religious practices of Utopia, 97–99
  religious toleration, 98, 106
  the virtuous heathen, 98
Morton, A.L., 80, 181n
Mulligan, L., 11n, 121n, 153n, 169n
Murphy, W.F., 121n, 200, 208

natural philosophy, early–modern conceptions, 109
natural law, 28
  and origins of private property, 31
  and social institutions, 232
  and cosmology, 236
natural rights, 28, 227, 228, 229, 231, 232–234
Negley, G., 21n
nemesis, 44
Neo–Platonism *see* Plato
Newton, Isaac, and deism, 236
Niblett, W.R., 95n
Norman Yoke, myth, 141–142
Nozick, 17n, 229
Nugent, E.M., 62n

Oakeshott, Michael, 5
Oberman, H., 54n, 98n
Ockham, William of, 42
original sin
  see Fall of Man
Owen, Robert, 18
Ownership, of horses in early–modern England, 91, 229
  see also private property
Orwell, George, 18

Paine, Thomas, 234
Pagden, A., 221n
paradigms, as intellectual and linguistic, 6–7, 16
Parry, Geraint, 33n
Parekh, B., 6n, 11n, 12n
Parker, T.M., 87n
Parliament, Barebone's, 193n
  Rump, 207
Passmore, J., 22n, 28n
patriarchalism, 88
  see also More, Winstanley
Patrick, J. Max, 21n
Paul, St., 26
  influence on Augustine, 45
  on More, 98
  on Winstanley, 208n
Petegorsky, D.W., 121n, 165n, 168n, 197, 203
Peters, R.S., 95n
Petty, William, 230
Pico, Giafransesco, 57n, 99n
Pineas, 48n, 49n
Plamenatz, John, 5
Plant, Raymond, 81n
Plato
  The Republic, 21, 88
  on reason, 42
  on communism, 230–231
Platonism, 32, 88
  neo-Platonism, 40
  see also Plato
Platt, Parson John, adversary of Diggers, 169, 182, 184, 185
Pocock, J.G.A., 7, 9, 11, 42n, 83n, 91n, 142, 143
political economy, 231
Prall, S.E., 87n, 142
private property, in relation to the Fall, 27
  and restraint of sin, 30
  and natural law, 32
  and *dominium*, 32

property theory, in relation to Fall, 31, 227–231
progress, as facet of utopianism, 17, 20
  the concept, 234–235
Protestantism, 51
Pufendorf, Samuel, 233

Quinton, Anthony, 238n

Randall, J.H., 235n
Ranters, the
  see Winstanley on the Ranters
Reay, B., 121n, 181n
Reed, A.W., 61n
Reeve, Andrew, 144n, 227n, 228n
Reformation, 35, 49
republicanism, classical republicanism, 9
Ricardo, David, 'ricardian socialism', 234
Rockwood, R.O., 237
Rogers, E.F., 50n, 94n
Roman Law, 32
romanticism, 20
Roper, William More's son-in-law, 88n, 89n, 97n
Rosen, G., 212n
Rousseau, Jean-Jacques, 58
Ryan, Alan, 11n, 232n

Sabine, G.H., 121n, 159n, 169n, 170, 172n, 192n, 193n
Saint-German, Christopher, 49
Saint-Simon, Claud-Henri de, 18
Sawada, P.A., 106n
Scarisbrick, J.J., 48n
Schenk, W., 174n, 212n
Schlatter, Richard, 28n, 31, 32n
Schmitt, C.B., 40n
Schochet, G.J., 11n, 28n, 210
Schoeck, R.J., 102n
Schuster, L.A., 49n
'scientific revolution', of early modern period, 235–237
scientific socialism, 18–19
Scotus, Johannes Duns, 33, 42
Seaberg, R.B., 142n
Second Coming, 23
Seebohm, F., 78n, 101n
Sharpe, J.A., 151n
Shindal, J.J., 55n
Shklar, Judith, 20
Skinner, Quentin, 9–11, 16, 17n, 76n, 83n, 191n
Smith, Adam, 229
Solemn League and Covenant 1643, 172
Solt, L.F., 148
Sommerville, J.P., 142n
Spellman, W.M., 35n
Spencer, Herbert, on landownership, 233, 234
Spinoza, Benedict de, 22
Star, William, adversary of Diggers, 173n
state of nature, 28
  see also contract theory
state, the, and restraint of sin, 30
Steiner, Hillel, 233n
Stoicism, 32, 101–102
  influence on Augustine, 42, 43, 44
Stone, Lawrence, 69n, 213
Strawson, P.F., 8, 16
Stripp, F., 145n
Surtz, E.L., 75n, 93n, 97n, 99n, 101n, 102, 106n, 108n

Taft, A.I., 49n
Tarlton, C.D., 11n
Taylor, H., 101n
Taylor, John, adversary of Diggers, 173n
Thomas, Keith, 27n, 29, 97n, 109n, 169, 186, 212, 216–217, 235, 240n, 241n
Thomism, 43, 84
  see also Aquinas
Thompson, William, 'Ricardian socialist', 234n
Thirsk, J., 70n, 149n
Tierney, Brian, 31n, 32n
Tillyard, E.M.W., 35
Trapp, J.B., 49n
Tribe, Keith, 231n
Tuck, Richards, 31n, 32n, 142n, 231n, 232
Tully, James, 229n, 232
Tunstal, Cuthbert, 48

Tuveson, E.L., 23n
Tynedale, William, 49, 55

usufruct, 32, 229, 232
 see also Winstanley
utilitarianism, 71, 96, 101, 229, 230
utopian communism, 18
utopianism
 as a concept, 17
 historical perspectives, 18–20
 criteria of, 21–23
 as a 'jeu d'esprit', 21–22
 coincidence with ideas of progress and optimism, 23
 operational definition, 23, 24–25
 in relation to millenarianism, 23–24

value pluralism, 15
virtu, 9
vita active, *vita contemplativa*, 88, 107
Vogel, Ursula, 234n
von Leyden, W., 35n

Wade, I.O., 237n
Waldron, Jeremy, 227n, 233n
Wallace, J.M., 191n
Walsh, J.D., 87n
Walsh, J.J., 42n
Walter, H., 55n
Walzer, Michael, 30n, 203, 210
Weber, Max, 203
Webster, Charles, on Fall of Man, 27, 29n, 66n, 133n, 196n, 213, 239n, 240
White, T.I., 103n
Whitelock, Bulstrode, 168n
Wieland, G., 41n, 47n
Williams, Bernard, 9n
Willey, Basil, 29
William, I, 'the Conqueror', 147
 see also Winstanley, under Norman Yoke
Winstanley, Gerrard, 3, 9
 anti-Papalism and Antichrist, 147, 157
 calculations on land improvements, 167, 194n
 citation of Decalogue and Mosaic Law, 179, 190
 citation of Judas, 189
 clergy and anti-clericalism, the, 126, 145–147, 161, 183, 196, 213, 222
 conception of progress, 125, 234
 Digger commune, the, 160, 168–185
 experimental religion and knowledge, 121, 122, 146, 148, 154, 159, 161, 215, 222
 his anti-intellectualism, 124, 127, 146,147, 222
 influence of Augustine, 128
 influence of Baconianism, 237, 239, 240, 241
 influence of Calvin, 155
 influence of Edward Coke, 142
 influence of Leveller writings, 142, 162
 influence of Protestant work ethic and sabbatarianism, 195, 214, 222
 natural law tradition and natural rights, 28, 32, 134, 164–165, 215, 227, 232–234
 nature of Adam, 129, 135, 154
 nature of his millenarianism, 23, 143, 148, 153, 156–158, 162, 163, 171, 184, 187–191, 203, 208, 127–128, 129–130, 130–141, 142, 154, 163, 170, 174, 184, 186–188
 on the abolition of the monarchy and establishment of the commonwealth, 179
 on anarchism, 174, 181, 191, 217
 on Apostolic communism, 172
 on the Army, 179, 184, 190
 on the Book of Job, 161
 on civil religion, 221–222
 on civil society and political authority, 'true magistracy', 195, 205–210
 on the Civil War, 160, 173, 179, 183
 on commerce, 150–151, 165, 173
 on communal ownership and 'common treasury', 123–124, 126, 132–133, 137, 143, 144, 162, 163, 165, 172, 181, 183, 185, 189, 197, 198–199, 202–203, 214, 233
 on the dominion over nature, 133, 198
 on the four elements, 162
 on education, 212–213, 217
 on elect nation, 155, 160, 181
 on the Engagement controversy, 191

Winstanley, Gerrard – *cont.*
  on the eradication of poverty, 197–198
  on exclusive and private ownership, and landownership, 33, 123,128, 131, 135–136, 137, 150, 165–168, 175
  on execution Charles I, 150, 171, 204
  on Fall of Man, 26, 121, 123, 125
  on 'the flesh', 125
  on heaven and hell, 125–126
  on the idea of 'birthright', 128, 132, 171, 172, 173, 233
  on labour and right to labour, 123, 131–132, 101n, 165–166, 172, 176–177, 183, 194–197, 202, 211, 214–217
  on law and legal institutions, 144, 147, 149–150, 164, 175, 177, 220–221
  on the life cycle of the individual, 196, 204–205, 213, 216–219
  on 'National Covenant', covenants and contract, 172, 175–176, 178, 179, 180
  on nature of Christ, 124
  on nature of God, 122
  on nature of sin, 125, 127–128
  on the Norman Conquest and idea of the 'Norman Yoke', kingly power, 133, 141–145, 149, 161, 164, 165n, 171, 173–174, 175, 177, 179–180, 183, 185, 187, 188, 207, 221
  on origins of private ownership, 128–129, 136–138, 139, 144, 164–165
  on ownership of woodland, 172–173
  on Parliament, 175–176, 184, 190
  on patriarchalism, 89, 196–197, 201, 210–212, 218
  on perpetuation of evil, 140
   and idea of *usufruct*, 140, 200–201, 233
  on property in original condition, 132, 233
  on the Ranters, 181, 182, 186, 195, 214
  on reason, 122, 123, 160, 161, 199
  on science, 223–224, 228, 229, 230, 231, 239–240
  on scripture and the gospel, 125–127
  on servants, 88, 211–212
  on sphere of private property within system of communal ownership, 82, 200–202
  on the spirit, 124–125
  on spiritual and moral regeneration of mankind, 130, 133, 143, 151–152, 158, 159, 163, 167, 172, 174, 181, 184, 185, 189, 194, 196, 199, 203–215, 220
  on spiritual election of individual, 155
  on tithes, 146–147
  on utopianism as political thought and institutional reform, 16, 17, 23, 24, 30, 31, 64, 69, 125, 143, 152, 153, 157, 158–159, 160, 164, 174, 180, 190–191, 193, 203, 206
  on war, 139
  on women in society, 212, 213
  rejection of belief in original sin and congenital inheritance, 128, 129, 135, 208
  resurrection of Christ, 162
Wittgenstein, Ludwig, 7–8
Wolin, Sheldon, 7
Woodcock, G., 205, 206
Worden, B., 207n
worldviews, as paradigmatic, 7
Wrightson, K., 151n

Youings, Joyce, 151n

Zagorin, Perez, 170

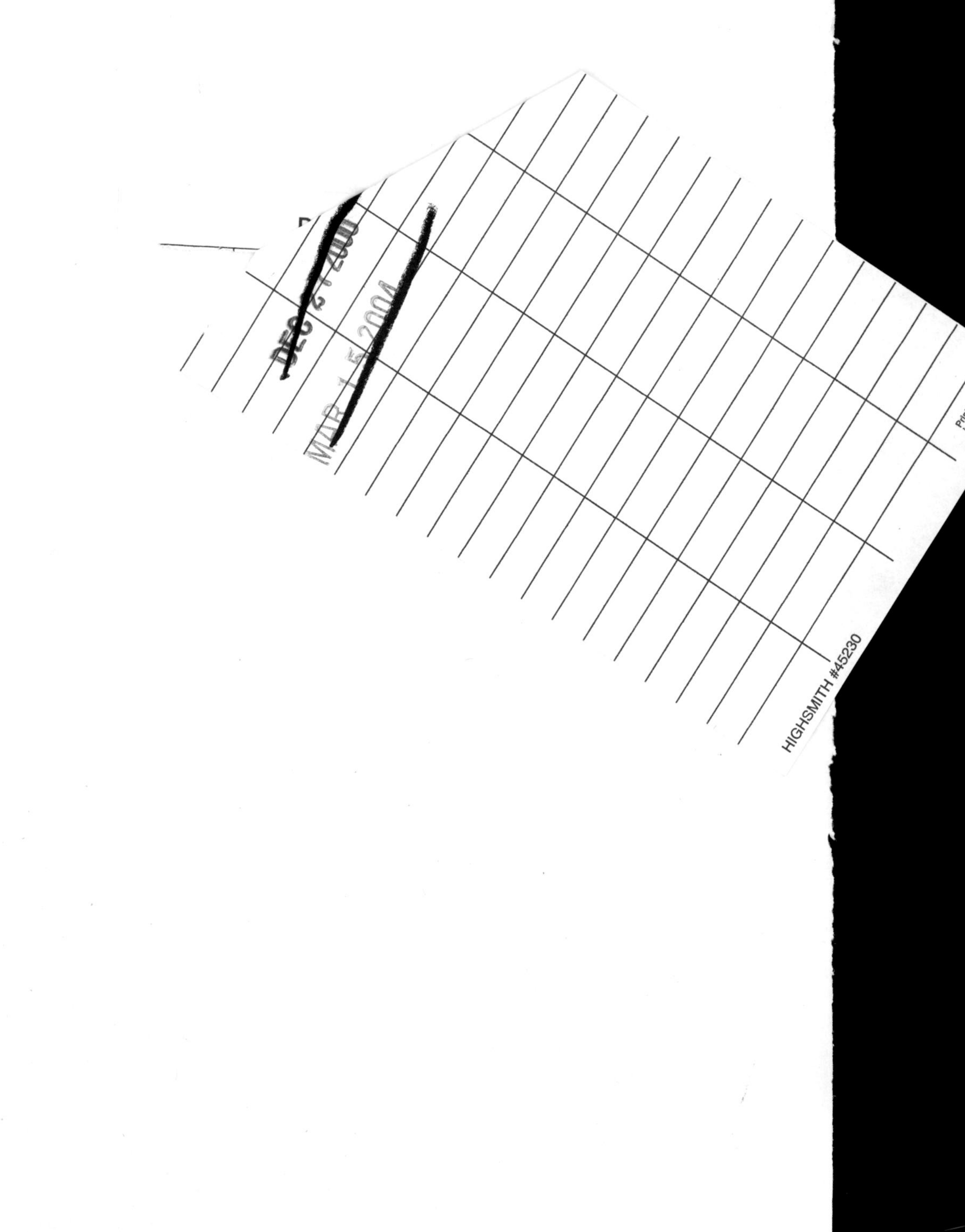